# Mathematical and Statistical Methods and Their Applications, 2nd Edition

# Mathematical and Statistical Methods and Their Applications, 2nd Edition

Guest Editor

**Jiujun Zhang**

MDPI

Basel • Beijing • Wuhan • Barcelona • Belgrade • Novi Sad • Cluj • Manchester

*Guest Editor*
Jiujun Zhang
School of Mathematics and
Statistics
Liaoning University
Shenyang
China

*Editorial Office*
MDPI AG
Grosspeteranlage 5
4052 Basel, Switzerland

This is a reprint of the Special Issue, published open access by the journal *Axioms* (ISSN 2075-1680), freely accessible at: https://www.mdpi.com/journal/axioms/special_issues/QY94OI6J88.

For citation purposes, cite each article independently as indicated on the article page online and as indicated below:

| Lastname, A.A.; Lastname, B.B. Article Title. *Journal Name* **Year**, *Volume Number*, Page Range. |
|---|

**ISBN 978-3-7258-6888-9 (Hbk)**
**ISBN 978-3-7258-6889-6 (PDF)**
**https://doi.org/10.3390/books978-3-7258-6889-6**

# Contents

# About the Editor

**Jiujun Zhang**

Jiujun Zhang is a professor at the School of Mathematics and Statistics, Liaoning University, where he serves as a doctoral supervisor and Head of the Department of Statistics and Data Science. He has been a visiting scholar at the University of Minnesota, USA, and currently acts as the Party Branch Secretary of the "Dual-Leader" faculty group at Liaoning University. His research interests focus on statistical theory, data science, survival analysis, and applied statistics. He has been selected for the 13th Liaoning Provincial Hundred-Thousand-Ten Thousand Talents Project (Hundred-Level tier) and recognized as a Leading High-Level Talent in Shenyang. His academic achievements include multiple teaching and professional honors at both university and provincial levels. He serves as a council member of the Multivariate Statistical Analysis Branch and the Survival Analysis Branch of the Chinese Society of Applied Statistics, as well as a council member of the Liaoning Mathematical Society. He has led and participated in more than ten projects funded by the National Natural Science Foundation of China and the Natural Science Foundation of Liaoning Province, and has published over 70 research papers.

*axioms*

MDPI

*Article*

# Analysis of Bulk Queueing Model with Load Balancing and Vacation

**Subramani Palani Niranjan [1], Suthanthiraraj Devi Latha [1,2,*], Sorin Vlase [3,4,*] and Maria Luminita Scutaru [3]**

1 Department of Mathematics, Vel Tech Rangarajan Dr. Sagunthala R&D Institute of Science and Technology, Chennai 600062, India; drniranjansp@veltech.edu.in
2 Department of Mathematics, Vel Tech Ranga Sanku Arts College, Chennai 600062, India
3 Department of Mechanical Engineering, Transilvania University of Brasov, Romania, B-dul Eroilor, 29, 500036 Brașov, Romania; lscutaru@unitbv.ro
4 Romanian Acad, Inst Solid Mech, Str C-tin Mille 15, 010141 Bucharest, Romania
* Correspondence: devilatha451@velsrscollege.com (S.D.L.); svlase@unitbv.ro (S.V.); Tel.: +40-722-643020 (S.V.)

**Abstract:** Data center architecture plays an important role in effective server management network systems. Load balancing is one such data architecture used to efficiently distribute network traffic to the server. In this paper, we incorporated the load-balancing technique used in cloud computing with power business intelligence (BI) and cloud load based on the queueing theoretic approach. This model examines a bulk arrival and batch service queueing system, incorporating server overloading and underloading based on the queue length. In a batch service system, customers are served in groups following a general bulk service rule with the server operating between the minimum value *'a'* and the maximum value *'b'*. But in certain situations, maintaining the same extreme values of the server is difficult, and it needs to be changed according to the service request. In this paper, server load balancing is introduced for a batch service queueing model, which is the capacity of the server that can be adjusted, either increased or decreased, based upon the service request by the customer. On service completion, if the service request is not enough to start any of the services, the server will be assigned to perform a secondary job (vacation). After vacation completion based upon the service request, the server will start regular service, overload or underload. Cloud computing using power BI can be analyzed based on server load balancing. The function that determines the probability of the queue size at any given time is derived for the specified queueing model using the supplementary variable technique with the remaining time as the supplementary variable. Additionally, various system characteristics are calculated and illustrated with suitable numerical examples.

**Keywords:** overloading; underloading; load balancing; batch service; supplementary variable technique

**MSC:** 60K30; 68M20

## 1. Introduction

The efficient management of servers in network systems is one of the challenging issues for improving service quality. Many mathematical techniques are implemented to study these issues and provide possible solutions. Server load balancing is an effective technique for efficiently managing system traffic. The modeling and analysis of symmetric bulk arrival queueing systems has attracted a lot of scientific attention. Takagi [1] gave a detailed explanation of symmetric bulk queueing systems both with and without server vacations. Numerous writers have also examined various combinations of queueing schemes and server vacations. Doshi [2] first carried out an extensive analysis of queueing systems with vacations, highlighting load balancing as one of their applications. Using the supplemental variable technique, Lee et al. [3] examined a $M^X/G/1$ queueing system with $N$ policy and multiple vacations. A queueing model with batch arrivals and a threshold was covered by Lee et al. [4]. Numerous academics have examined the steady-state analysis of a queueing system with non-Markovian symmetric bulk arrivals, batch service, vacation periods, and certain extensions. The paper by Krishna Reddy et al. [5] explores the operational dynamics of a queueing system characterized by symmetric bulk arrivals, an $N$-policy for managing queue length, multiple vacation periods for servers, and setup times between tasks. Using the supplementary variable technique, the authors analyze various aspects of system performance, including queue length distributions, server utilization rates, and overall system efficiency. Their approach not only contributes to theoretical advances in queueing theory but also provides practical insights into optimizing system parameters to enhance operational efficiency and minimize delays. A cost model for a symmetric bulk arrival and batch service queueing system without service interruption was also looked into by Jeyakumar and Senthilnathan [6]. In order to incorporate closedown times into their investigation, the author deduced the probability-generating function for the service process in their model. Arumuganathan and Jeyakumar [7] extended the above work with closedown times. The optimal cost analysis and certain performance characteristics of the $M^X/G(a,b)/1$ queueing system with interrupted vacation have been derived by Haridass and Arumuganathan [8]. Siddiqui et al. [9] present the QPSL queuing model as a notable advancement in load balancing within cloud computing. This approach improves the efficacy and efficiency of resource allocation in cloud environments by utilizing queuing theory, most especially the M/M/k queue with a FIFO discipline. The study highlights the model's potential to optimize performance, reduce latency, and improve overall system reliability through sophisticated load-balancing mechanisms. The analysis of queueing systems with breakdown is essential to deal with many real-time systems. Using a recursive technique, Praveen Kumar Agarwal et al. [10] investigated the best N-policy for a finite queue with server failures and state-dependent service rates.

A queueing system with batch services and symmetric bulk arrivals was presented by Niranjan et al. [11], adding queue size-dependent vacations for an unreliable server. An analysis of a symmetric bulk arrival queueing system with extra services and numerous vacation periods was conducted by Ayappan and Deepika [12]. Stochastic Petri nets should be used to evaluate the queuing models' performance, especially in distributed and multiprocessor systems, according to Siddiqui et al. [13]. By leveraging the strengths of SPNs, such as their visual and expressive power combined with stochastic modeling capabilities, the authors provide a compelling case for their adoption in performance evaluation studies.

Banerjee et al. [14] analyze rank-based routing policies in queuing systems, introducing MSBLB and MJSQ policies that reduce communication costs while ensuring effective load balancing supported by rigorous proof. Otten [15] examines the supply chain system with inventory-dependent routing, offering the explicit solutions and algorithms developed to optimize the production and inventory management, advancing supply chain efficiency. Van der Boor et al. [16] propose a hyper-scalable scheme with universal throughput bounds, optimizing distributed systems with limited communication. Liu and Ying [17] study load balancing in systems with constrained local queues, focusing on performance under heavy traffic in data centers. Ahmed et al. [18] introduce QLLB, a queue-length-based load-balancing scheme for data centers, addressing congestion and network asymmetries. Hellemans et al. [19] examine load-balancing policies for distributed systems with variable job sizes, highlighting latency reduction. Van der Boor et al. [20] review scalable adaptations of the JSQ policy, balancing delay performance with reduced communication overhead. Delasay and Akan [21] analyze a two-phase queuing model to optimize delay costs for tasks with different priority classes. Santos et al. [22] discuss the importance of pre-emptive evaluation and the optimization of IoT-based monitoring systems in smart buildings. The research offers a solid foundation for evaluating and enhancing system performance by using a queuing network-based message exchange architecture and carrying out an extensive sensitivity analysis using Design of Experiments (DoE). The findings can significantly aid in designing efficient, reliable, and responsive smart building infrastructures, ensuring better QoS and minimizing risks associated with system failures.

Rodrigues et al. [23] use an M/M/c/K queuing model to optimize IoP-based ambient assisted living systems, improving aged care with reliable and cost-effective health monitoring solutions. Katayama and Tachibana [24] propose a task allocation strategy for MEC and cloud servers, reducing latency and optimizing resource use in 5G and future network environments. Zhan et al. [25] explore how service environments and omni-channel sales affect customer behavior, helping merchants optimize service capacity and profits. Alnowibet et al. [26] introduce a stochastic inventory model considering lead times and impatient customers, improving real-world inventory management under random demand.

Existing queuing models overlook dynamically adjusting server capacity based on queue length, motivating the development of a batch-service queuing system with load balancing and server vacations to address real-time network congestion. Jin et al. [27] analyzed the nonlinear dynamics of TCP/AQM networks, identifying critical delay values for Hopf bifurcation and stability, using $\tau$-decomposition and central manifold theory. Numerical examples validate the framework for delay-stable intervals and bifurcation stability. Yen et al. [28] study an N-policy M/G/1 queue with working breakdowns, deriving steady-state results and optimizing thresholds and service rates for system stability. Numerical results and sensitivity analysis validate its practical application. Kothandaraman and Kandaiyan [29] examined a Markovian queue with heterogeneous, intermittently available servers under a hybrid vacation policy, using the matrix geometric method to derive stability conditions and performance indicators. Numerical examples highlight parameter impacts. Kempa and Paprocka [30] present a discrete-time queue model for a bottleneck production system with energy-saving features, analyzing performance and optimizing throughput using the Drum–Buffer–Rope concept. Simulations show its effectiveness in aligning arrival rates with capacity. Chydzinski and Adamczyk [31] investigated response time in queues with active/passive management and complex arrivals, deriving distributions and key properties using integral equations. Numerical results reveal insights into response time behavior across scenarios. Many authors have extensively researched bulk arrivals and batch services, exploring various parameters and their implications [32–35]. Niranjan and Devi Latha presented a novel two-phase bulk service queueing model incorporating active Bernoulli feedback, server vacations, breakdowns, and setup time. The model explores the queue size's probability-generating function and analyzes performance metrics with numerical examples [36]. Gautam et al. [37] explore optimizing power saving and QoS in LTE-A networks through a new DRX mechanism that switches between power-active and power-saving states based on user traffic. It uses an $M^{[X]}/G/1$ vacation queue model with N-policy to analyze performance and energy metrics. Numerical results identify optimal N values and DRX cycles to minimize power use. The study provides practical guidelines for balancing energy efficiency and network performance.

The main contributions of this study include the following:

1. Overloading and underloading of the server are addressed to reduce customer waiting time and minimize the system's total average cost.
2. An application in cloud computing using power BI is provided to demonstrate the effectiveness of the load-balancing approach.

The paper is organized as follows: Section 1 introduces the topic and provides a review of the relevant literature and discusses the application of the proposed model. Section 2 outlines the model description and methodology for the queuing system under consideration and defines the notations of the stochastic model, governing equations, and queue size distribution. Section 3 evaluates various performance measures and examines special cases. Section 4 develops the cost model for the system and includes numerical illustrations. Finally, Section 5 concludes the paper with suggestions for future research.

Cloud computing is the process of using and gaining access to a variety of online services, including apps, computer power, and data storage. Organizations and individuals can purchase and utilize hardware and software as needed from cloud service providers, eliminating the need to own and maintain physical assets.

Cloud computing is used predominately nowadays, as each and every process depends more on power BI. The application starts with the transfer of data files from the client to the server with a virtual prediction range of 500–900 GB scheduled as regular service. And if the service is 100–400 GB, it starts its process as an underloading service to access customer software in power BI, as it is used to prevent damage to the files given by the clients. When there are various needs to implement security and DAX (Double Application Extension) expressions that are more than 1000 GB, this is qualified as overloading, because there is a sudden spike in traffic and it consumes more power comparatively; however, the quality of service is not affected by this. The next process consists of cloud load where the expected data are marked with the expected time and space consumption in the burst of cloud load, which creates space, prevents the data from being formed as layers, and corrects errors using the Losant principle. In addition, there is a responsibility assigned to the class that has the necessary information to fulfill it. Thus, the process has been completed successfully. If the data are less than 100 GB, they are classified as vacation data and can be affected due to processes like input/output errors or file errors. To rectify the missed data, the software finds the relevant and required data and fixes the missing data, but there is a time sequence delay. Hence, the application for the cloud computing using power BI and cloud load can be modeled as a bulk arrival and batch service queueing model with load balancing and vacation.

## 2. Methods and Models

### 2.1. Model Description

Customers are demanding service in batches afforded to the Poisson process with rate $\xi$. In a bulk service system, customers are served in groups based on a general bulk service rule [38] with a lower bound of '$a$' and upper bound '$b$' of the server. Maintaining the constant threshold values of the server is not always possible in real-time systems; it has to be changed according to the number of service request. So, in this paper, the server threshold values for batch service may be increased or decreased (overloading or underloading) according to the number of service request. A regular batch service will be initiated only if at least '$\boldsymbol{a}$' customers are waiting for service. Upon service completion or vacation completion, if the queue length denoted by $\varepsilon$ satifies $\boldsymbol{a} \leq \varepsilon \leq \boldsymbol{b}$, then the service will be provided for $\boldsymbol{min}(\varepsilon, b)$ customers. Conversely, if the server finds more than 'N' ($N > b$) customers waiting, it selects 'N' customers for service by increasing the server's maximum capacity to 'N'. Sometimes, the queue length will be less than the minimum server capacity '$a$'; during that time, the minimum threshold value of the server may be reduced to '$c$'($c < a$) and take all '$c$' customers waiting for service. The primary benefit of the offered system is that the server capacity may be increased or decreased dynamically based on the queue size. The server goes on vacation if the queue length falls below '$c$'. After vacation completion, depending upon the queue length, the server will provide a regular symmetric bulk service or batch service with overloading or batch service with underloading. The above systematic procedure can be implemented in cloud computing (power BI) to solve congestion problems. To estimate various performance metrics of the server, which tends to minimize the overall cost of the cloud system, a diagram demonstration of the offered system is depicted below.

Notations

Let $Z$ be the random variable representing the group size of the arrival and $Z(Y)$ be the probability generating function (PGF) of Z (Table 1).

$\xi$—Poisson arrival rate.
$g_k$—The probability that a batch arrives '$k$' customers.
$C_q(t)$—At time $t$, the number of customers awaiting service.
$C_s(t)$—The number of customers currently receiving service at time $t$.

**Table 1.** Notations.

| | Cumulative Distribution Function | Probability Density Function | Laplace–StieltjesTransform | Remaining Service Time |
|---|---|---|---|---|
| Regular batch service | $B(z)$ | $b(z)$ | $\tilde{B}(\alpha)$ | $B^0(z)$ |
| Batch service with overloading | $B_1(z)$ | $b_1(z)$ | $\tilde{B}_1(\alpha)$ | ${B_1}^0(z)$ |
| Batch service with underloading | $B_2(z)$ | $b_2(z)$ | $\tilde{B}_2(\alpha)$ | ${B_2}^0(z)$ |
| Vacation | $V(z)$ | $v(z)$ | $\tilde{V}(\alpha)$ | $V^0(z)$ |

$$\psi(t) = \begin{cases} 0, \textit{ when the server is busy with regular batch service} \\ 1, \textit{ when the server is busy and doing batch service with overloading} \\ 2, \textit{ when the server is busy and doing service with underloading} \\ 3, \textit{ when the server is on vacation} \end{cases}$$

$$A_{ij}(z,t)\mathrm{d}t = P\left\{ C_s(t) = i, C_q(t) = j, \quad z \le B^0(t) \le z + dt, \psi(t) = 0 \right\} \mathrm{a} \le \mathrm{i} \le \mathrm{b};\ \mathrm{j} \ge 1;$$

is the probability that at time $t$, the server is busy with i customers under regular batch service and $j$ customers in the queue, and the remaining service time of a customer under service is between z and $z + dt$.

$$A^1_{Nj}(z,t)\mathrm{d}t = P\left\{ C_s(t) = N,\ \ C_q(t) = j, z \le {B_1}^0(t) \le z + dt, \psi(t) = 1 \right\} \mathrm{j} \ge 1; N > b,$$

is the probability that at time $t$, the server is busy with '$N$' customers under batch service with overloading and $j$ customers in the queue, and the remaining service time of a customer under service is between $z$ and $z + dt$.

$$A_{cj}^{2}(z,t)\mathrm{dt} = P\left\{C_s(t) = c,\ C_q(t) = j\ z \leq {B_2}^0(t) \leq z + dt,\ \psi(t) = 2\right\};\ j \geq 1;$$

is the probability that at time $t$, the server is busy with '$c$' customers under batch service with underloading and j customers in the queue, and the remaining service time of a customer under service is between z and $z + dt$.

$$S_n(z,t)dt = P\left\{\ C_q(t) = n,\ z \leq V^0(t) \leq z + dt,\ \psi(t) = 3\right\};\ \ 0 \leq n \leq c-1;$$

is the probability that at time $t$, the server is on vacation, the queue length is $n$ and the remaining vacation time of a customer at an arbitrary time is between z and $z + dt$.

*2.2. Steady-State Queue Size Distribution*

The supplementary variable technique is used to derive the steady-state system equations [39].

$$\begin{aligned} -\tfrac{d}{dz}A_{i0}(z) = -\xi A_{i0}\,(z) + \textstyle\sum_{m=a}^{b} A_{mi}(0)b(z) + A_{Ni}^{1}(0)b(z) \\ +A_{ci}^{2}(0)b(z) + S_i(0)b(z);\ c \ \leq\ i\ \leq\ \ b. \end{aligned} \tag{1}$$

Equation (1) denotes the different probabilities for the server in a regular batch service with 'i' customers in service and '0' customer in the queue in the remaining service time $z - \Delta t$ at time $t + \Delta t$. In the RHS, the first term indicates that there is no arrival at that time, and the second term indicates that when regular batch service is completed, if 'i' customers are in the queue, then 'i' customers go for regular batch service and '0' customers are waiting in the queue. The next term indicates that when overloading batch service is completed, if '$i$' customers are in the queue, then '$i$' customers go for a regular batch service, and '0' customers will be waiting in the queue. The fourth term indicates that when underloading batch service is completed, if '$i$' customers are in the queue, then '$i$' customers go for a regular batch service, and '0' customers will be waiting in the queue. The last term indicates after vacation completion, if '$i$' customers are in the queue, then 'i' customers go for regular batch service, and '0' customers will be waiting in the queue. Similarly, Equations (2)–(7) can be expressed with the help of a schematic representation of the queueing model shown in Figure 1.

$$-\frac{d}{dz}A_{ij}(z) = -\xi A_{ij}(z) + \textstyle\sum_{k=1}^{j} A_{i\,j-k}(z)\,\xi g_k;\ \ c\ \leq\ i\ \leq\ b-1;\ \ j\ \geq\ 1; \tag{2}$$

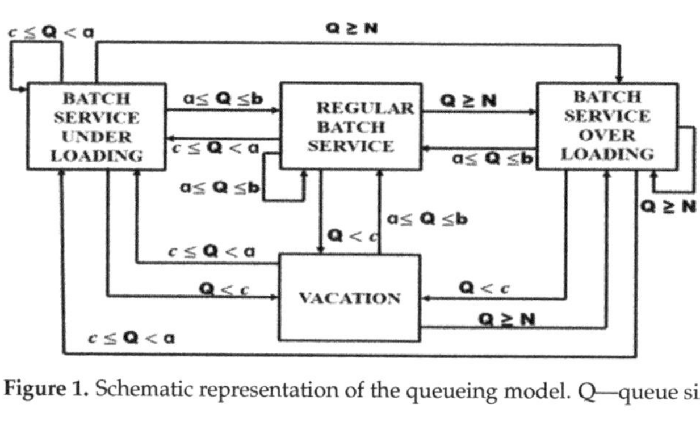


**Figure 1.** Schematic representation of the queueing model. Q—queue size.

$$-\frac{d}{dz}A_{bj}(z) = -\xi A_{bj}(z) + \sum_{k=1}^{j} A_{b\,j-k}(z)\,\xi g_k + A^1_{Nb+j}(0)\,b(z) + A^2_{cb+j}(0)\,b(z) + \sum_{m=c}^{b} A_{mb+j}(0)b(z) + S_{b+j}(0)b(z);\ j \geq 1; \tag{3}$$

$$-\frac{d}{dz}\boldsymbol{A^1_{Nj}(z)} = -\boldsymbol{\xi A^1_{Nj}(z)} + \sum_{\boldsymbol{k=1}}^{j} \boldsymbol{A^1_{Nj-k}(z)\xi g_k} + \boldsymbol{A^1_{NN+j}(0)b_1(z)} + \sum_{m=a}^{b} A_{mN+j}(0)b_1(z) + A^2_{c\ N+j}(0)b_1(z) + S_{N+j}(0)b_1(z);\ j \geq\ 0; \tag{4}$$

$$-\frac{d}{dz}\boldsymbol{A^2_{cj}(z)} = -\boldsymbol{\xi A^2_{cj}(z)} + \sum_{\boldsymbol{k=1}}^{j} \boldsymbol{A^2_{cj-k}(z)\xi g_k} + \boldsymbol{A^2_{cc+j}(0)b_2(z)} + \sum_{m=a}^{b} A_{m\ c+j}(0)b_2(z) + A^1_{N\ c+j}(0)b_2(z) + S_{c+j}(0)b_2(z); j \geq\ 0; \tag{5}$$

$$-\frac{d}{dz}\boldsymbol{S_0(z)} = -\boldsymbol{\xi S_0(z)} + \sum_{m=c}^{b} \boldsymbol{A_{m0}(0)V(z)} + \boldsymbol{A^1_{N0}v(z)} + \boldsymbol{A^2_{c0}v(z)} \tag{6}$$

$$-\frac{d}{dz}\boldsymbol{S_n(z)} = -\boldsymbol{\xi S_n(z)} + \sum_{m=c}^{b} \boldsymbol{A_{mn}(0)v(z)} + \boldsymbol{A^1_{Nn}(0)v(z)} + \boldsymbol{A^2_{cn}(0)v(z)} + \sum_{\boldsymbol{k=1}}^{n} S_{n-k}(z)\,\xi g_k\ ,\ \boldsymbol{1}\ \leq\ n\ \leq\ c-\boldsymbol{1}. \tag{7}$$

The Laplace–Stieltjes transforms of $\mathrm{A_{in}(y)}$, $\mathrm{S_n(y)}$, $\mathrm{A^1_{Nj}(y)}$ and $\mathrm{A^2_{cj}(y)}$ are defined as

$$\widetilde{A}_{in}(\alpha) = \int_0^\infty \mathrm{e}^{-\alpha z}\mathrm{A_{in}}(z)dz;\ \widetilde{S}_n(\alpha) = \int_0^\infty \mathrm{e}^{-\alpha z}\mathrm{S_n}(z)dz;$$

$$A^1_{Nj}(\alpha) = \int_0^\infty \mathrm{e}^{-\alpha z}A^1_{Nj}(z)dz;\ A^2_{cj}(\alpha) = \int_0^\infty \mathrm{e}^{-\alpha z}A^2_{cj}(z)dz.$$

Applying Laplace–Stieltjes transform to Equations (1)–(7),

$$\alpha\widetilde{A}_{i0}(\alpha) - A_{i0}(0) = \xi\widetilde{A}_{i0}(\alpha) + \sum_{m=a}^{b} A_{mi}(0)\widetilde{B}(\alpha) + A^1_{Ni}(0)\widetilde{B}(\alpha) + A^2_{ci}(0)\widetilde{B}(\alpha) + S_i(0)\widetilde{B}(\alpha)a \leq\ i\ \leq\ b \tag{8}$$

$$\alpha\widetilde{A}_{ij}(\alpha) - A_{ij}(0) = \xi\widetilde{A}_{ij}(\alpha) + \sum_{k=1}^{j} \widetilde{A}_{i\ j-k}(\alpha)\ \xi g_k; a \leq\ i\ \leq\ b-1; \tag{9}$$

$$\alpha\widetilde{A}_{bj}(\alpha) - A_{bj}(0) = \xi\widetilde{A}_{bj}(\alpha) + \sum_{k=1}^{j} \widetilde{A}_{b\ j-k}(\alpha)\ \xi g_k + A^1_{Nb+j}(0)\widetilde{B}(\alpha) + A^2_{cb+j}(0)\widetilde{\mathrm{B}}(\alpha) + \sum_{m=c}^{b} A_{mb+j}(0)\widetilde{\mathrm{B}}(\alpha) + S_{b+j}(0)\widetilde{\mathrm{B}}(\alpha);\ j \geq\ 1; \tag{10}$$

$$\alpha\overset{\sim 1}{A}_{Nj}(\alpha) - A^1_{Nj}(0) = \xi\overset{\sim 1}{A}_{Nj}(\alpha) + \sum_{k=1}^{j} \overset{\sim 1}{A}_{Nj-k}(\alpha)\ \xi g_k + A^1_{NN+j}(0)\widetilde{B}_1(\alpha) + \sum_{m=a}^{b} A_{mN+j}(0)\widetilde{B}_1(\alpha) + A^2_{c\ N+j}(0)\widetilde{B}_1(\alpha) + S_{N+j}(0)\widetilde{B}_1(\alpha);\ j \geq\ 0; \tag{11}$$

$$\alpha\overset{\sim 2}{A}_{cj}(\alpha) - A^2_{cj}(0) = \xi\overset{\sim 2}{A}_{cj}(\alpha) + \sum_{k=1}^{j} \overset{\sim 2}{A}_{c\ j-k}(\alpha)\ \xi g_k + A^2_{c\ c+j}(0)\widetilde{B}_3(\alpha) + \sum_{m=a}^{b} A_{m\ c+j}(0)\widetilde{B}_3(\alpha) + A^1_{N\ c+j}(0)\widetilde{B}_3(\alpha) + S_{c+j}(0)\widetilde{B}_3(\alpha);\ j \geq\ 0; \tag{12}$$

$$\alpha\widetilde{S}_0(\alpha) - S_0(0) = \xi\widetilde{S}_0(\alpha) + \sum_{m=c}^{b} A_{m0}(0)\widetilde{V}(\alpha) + A^1_{N0}\widetilde{V}(\alpha) + A^2_{c0}\widetilde{V}(\alpha); \tag{13}$$

$$\alpha\widetilde{S}_n(\alpha) - S_n(0) = \xi\widetilde{S}_n(\alpha)\sum_{m=c}^{b} A_{mn}(0)\widetilde{V}(\alpha) + A^1_{Nn}(0)\widetilde{V}(\alpha) + A^2_{cn}(0)\widetilde{V}(\alpha) + \sum_{k=1}^{n} \widetilde{S}_{n-k}(\alpha)\ \xi g_k;\ 1\ \leq\ n\ \leq\ a-1. \tag{14}$$

The following probability-generating functions are defined to obtain the PGF of the queue size at any given time.

$$\overset{\sim 2}{A}_c(y,\alpha) = \sum_{j=0}^{\infty} \overset{\sim 2}{A}_{cj}(\alpha)y^j;\ A_c^2(y,0) = \sum_{j=0}^{\infty} A_{cj}^2(0)y^j;$$

$$\widetilde{S}(y,\alpha) = \sum_{n=0}^{a-1} \widetilde{S}_n(\alpha)y^n;\ S(y,\ 0) = \sum_{n=0}^{a-1} S_n(0)y^n;$$

$$Let A_I = \sum_{i=a}^{b-1} \sum_{m=a}^{b} A_{mi}(0);\ A_N^1(0) = A_N^1\ ;\ A_c^2(0) = A_c^2\ ;$$

$$S_i(0) = S_i;\ \beta_i = A_c^2 + A_i + S_i + A_N^1.$$

By multiplying Equations (8)–(14) by suitable powers of $y^n$ and summing over $n$ then by using the PGF of queue size at an arbitrary time epoch, we obtain

$$(\alpha - \xi + \xi Z(y))\widetilde{A}_i(y,\alpha) = A_i(y,0) - \widetilde{B}(\alpha)\left(A_c^2 + A_i + S_i + A_N^1\right); \tag{15}$$

$$y^b(\alpha - \xi + \xi Z(y))\widetilde{A}_b(y,\alpha) = y^b A_b(y,0) - \widetilde{B}(\alpha)\sum_{j=b}^{N-1}\left(A_c^2 + A_i + S_i + A_N^1\right)y^j; \tag{16}$$

$$(\alpha - \xi + \xi Z(y))\overset{\sim 1}{A}_N(y,\alpha)y^N = A_N^1(y,0)y^N - \widetilde{B}_1(\alpha)h_1, \tag{17}$$

where $h_1 = \dfrac{\left(\sum_{m=a}^{b} A_m(y,0) - \sum_{j=b}^{N-1}(A_i y^j)\right) + \left(S(y,0) - \sum_{j=b}^{N-1}(S_i y^j)\right)}{\begin{matrix}\left(A_N^1(y,0) - \sum_{j=b}^{N-1}\left(A_j^1 y^j\right)\right) \\ \left(A_C^2(y,0) - \sum_{j=b}^{N-1}\left(A_j^2 y^j\right)\right)\end{matrix}}.$

$$(\alpha - \xi + \xi Z(y))\overset{\sim 2}{A}_c(y,\alpha)y^c = A_c^2(y,0)y^c - \widetilde{B}_2(\alpha)\sum_{n=0}^{c-1}\left(A_c^2 + A_i + A_N^1 + S_n\right)y^n; \tag{18}$$

$$(\alpha - \xi + \xi Z(y))\widetilde{S}(y,\alpha) = S(y,0) - \widetilde{S}(\alpha)\sum_{n=0}^{c-1}\left(A_c^2 + A_i + A_N^1 + S_n\right)y^n. \tag{19}$$

### 2.3. PGF of Queue Size at an Arbitrary Time

The function that generates the probability of queue size at an arbitrary time epoch can be obtained by using the below given equation

$$P(y) = \sum_{m=a}^{b-1} \widetilde{A}_m(y,0) + \widetilde{A}_b(y,0) + \overset{\sim 1}{A}_N(y,0) + \overset{\sim 2}{A}_c(y,0) + \widetilde{S}(y,0). \tag{20}$$

Substituting $\alpha = \xi - \xi Z(y)$ in Equations (15)–(19), after performing some algebraic manipulations, the PGF of queue size is defined below, and we obtain

$$P(y) = \frac{\begin{matrix}\left(\widetilde{B}(\xi - \xi Z(y)) - 1\right)\left(\sum_{j=0}^{N-1} \beta_j y^j + \sum_{i=a}^{b-1} \beta_i\right) \\ + \left(\widetilde{S}(\xi - \xi Z(y)) - 1\right) \sum_{j=0}^{C-1} \beta_j z^j \\ \left(\widetilde{B}_1(\xi - \xi Z(y)) - 1\right) f_1 + \left(\widetilde{B}_2(\xi - \xi Z(y)) - 1\right) \sum_{j=0}^{c} \beta_j y^j\end{matrix}}{\left(y^N - \widetilde{B}_1(\xi - \xi Z(y))\right)(-\xi + \xi Z(y))}, \tag{21}$$

$$\text{where } f_1 = \frac{\left(\sum_{m=a}^{b} A_m(y,0) - \sum_{j=b}^{N-1}(A_i y^j)\right) + \left(S(y,0) - \sum_{j=b}^{N-1}(S_i y^j)\right) - \sum_{j=b}^{N-1}\left(A_j^1 y^j\right)}{\left(A_C^2(y,0) - \sum_{j=b}^{N-1}\left(A_j^2 y^j\right)\right)}.$$

## 3. Results: Steady-State Condition

To ensure the existence of a steady state for the model under consideration, the condition $\rho < 1$ must be satisfied, where $\rho$ is defined as $\rho = N - \xi E(B_1)E(Z)$. The PGF P(y) must satisfy P(1) = 1. By applying L'Hospital's rule and evaluating $\lim_{y\to 1} P(y) = 1$, and equating the expression to 1, the condition $\xi E(Z)(N - \xi E(B_1)E(Z)) > 0$ is obtained (Algorithm 1).

**Algorithm 1. Algorithm to Find Unknown Probabilities**

Step 1: Use Equation (21) to initiate the procedure.
Step 2: Consider the unknowns $S_i$ and $\beta_j$ exists in P(Y).
Step 3: Apply Rouche's theorem of complex variables to find the vanishing points at $|Y| = 1$.
Step 4: 'N' equations and 'N' unknowns obtained in step 3 are solved using MATLAB 2020.

**Lemma 3.1.** *Let $\beta_i$ be the probability that 'i' customers arrive during the vacation. The probability generating function of $\beta_i$ is given by $\sum_{i=0}^{\infty} \beta_i y^i = \tilde{S}(\xi - \xi Z(y))$.*

**Proof:** Conditioning on the actual vacation length, number of arrivals and the group size, we obtain

$$\beta_i = \int_0^{\infty} \left(\sum_{m=0}^{i} \frac{(e^{-\xi t})(\xi t)^m g_i{}^m}{m!}\right) dv(t)$$

where $g_i{}^m$ is the m-fold convolution of $g_i$ with itself (i.e., the total of m arrivals make 'i' customers).

Multiplying the above equation by $z^i$ and taking the summation from $i = 0$ to $\infty$, we obtain

$$\begin{aligned}\sum_{i=0}^{\infty} \beta_i y^i &= \int_0^{\infty} e^{-\xi t} \left(\sum_{m=0}^{\infty} \frac{(\xi t)^m}{m!} \sum_{i=m}^{\infty} g_i{}^m y^i\right) dv(t)\\ &= \int_0^{\infty} e^{-\xi t} \left(\sum_{m=0}^{\infty} \frac{(\xi t)^m \quad (Z(y))^m}{m!}\right) dv(t)\\ &= \tilde{S}(\xi - \xi Z(y))\end{aligned}$$

Hence, the Lemma. □

**Theorem 3.1.** *The unknown constants $s_i$ are expressed in terms of $\beta_i$ as, $s_i = \sum_{i=0}^{n} \beta_{n-i}\omega_i$, $n = 0, 1, 2\ldots a-1$, where $\omega_i$ is the probability that 'i' customers arrive during the underloading or overloading service period.*

**Proof:** Substituting $\alpha = \xi - \xi Z(y)$ in Equation (19), we have

$$S(y,0) = \tilde{S}(\xi - \xi Z(y)) \sum_{n=0}^{c-1} \left(A_c^2 + A_i + A_N^1 + S_n\right) y^n$$

By using the above lemma

$$\sum_{n=0}^{a-1} s_n y^n = \left(\sum_{n=0}^{\infty} \omega_n y^n\right)\left(\sum_{n=0}^{a-1} \beta_n y^n\right)$$

$$\sum_{n=0}^{a-1} s_n y^n = \sum_{n=0}^{a-1} \left(\sum_{i=0}^{n} \beta_{n-i}\omega_i\right) y^n \tag{22}$$

Equating the coefficient of $y^n$; n = 0, 1, 2, 3 ... a − 1, on both sides of Equation (22), we obtain $s_i = \sum_{i=0}^{n} \beta_{n-i}\omega_i$. □

## 4. Discussion

### 4.1. *Efficiency Metrics of Cloud Resource Utilization*

In a queueing system, it is common practice to evaluate the average number of inputs to be processed in buffer and the average waiting time for inputs to be processed in buffer. This section derives efficiency metrics of cloud resource utilization from the steady-state probability distribution function, which are essential for determining the aggregate mean cost of the system.

#### 4.1.1. Average Number of Inputs to Be Processed in Buffer

The average number of inputs to be processed in buffer $L_{queue}$ at an arbitrary time epoch is obtained by differentiating $P(y)$ at $y = 1$ and is given by

$$L_{queue} = \lim_{y\to 1} P'(y)$$

#### 4.1.2. Average Waiting Time for Inputs to Be Processed in Buffer

The average waiting time for inputs to be processed in buffer $W_{queue}$ can be readily determined using Little's formula

$$W_{queue} = \frac{L_{queue}}{\varsigma E(Z)}$$

#### 4.1.3. Average Processing Period of the Cloud Server

$$L_{busy} = \frac{\sum_{i=a}^{N-1}\left(A_i^2 + A_i + A_i^1\right) + \left(1 - \sum_{i=a}^{N-1}\left(A_i^2 + A_i + A_i^1\right) + \left(1 - E(B_2)\right)\right)}{\sum_{i=0}^{a-1}\left(A_i^2 + A_i + A_i^1\right)}$$

$$L_{busy} = \frac{\mathrm{E(S)}}{\sum_{\mathrm{i}=0}^{\mathrm{a}-1}\left(\mathrm{P}^1{}_{\mathrm{i}} + \mathrm{R_i}\right)}.$$

#### 4.1.4. Average Sleep Time of the Cloud Server

The time interval between the start of the busy period and the vacation epoch is known as the cloud server's average sleep time.

Let I be the random variable for the 'idle period'.

$\alpha_j$, the probability that the system state visits '*j*' during an idle period is given by $j = 0, 1, 2 \ldots a - 1$.

$$\text{Let } I_j = \begin{cases} 1 \text{ if the state '}j\text{' during an idle period} \\ 0 \text{ otherwise} \end{cases}$$

Based on the size of the queue at the service completion epoch, we have $\alpha_0 = \pi_0$ :

$$\alpha_j = P(I_j = 1) = \pi_j + \sum_{k=0}^{c-1} \pi_k P\left(I_{j-k}{}^1 = 1\right); j = 1, 2, \ldots c-1.$$

Thus, the average sleep time of the cloud server is obtained:

$$L_{idle} = \frac{E(S)}{\sum_{n=0}^{a-1} \sum_{i=0}^{n} \alpha_i \left(A_{n-i}^2 + A_{n-i} + A_{n-i}^1\right)}.$$

4.2. *Special Case: Hyper-Exponential Regular Bulk Service Time*

When the regular service time follows hyper-exponential distribution with probability density function, then $b(z) = cde^{-dz} + (1-c)fe^{-fz}$ where $d$ and $f$ are parameters, and

$$\widetilde{B}(\xi - \xi Z(y)) = \frac{dc}{d + (\xi - \xi Z(y))} + \frac{f(1-c)}{f + (\xi - \xi Z(y))}.$$

The PGF of the queue size for hyper-exponential service time is derived by substituting the expression for $\widetilde{B}(\xi - \xi Z(y))$ in Equation (21).

4.3. *Cost Model*

Optimization techniques play a crucial role in minimizing the aggregate mean cost of a queueing system in many real-world situations. The rate investigation typically involves various constraints, such as switch-on cost, in-service cost, carrying cost and any potential remuneration costs. The primary objective in managing the system is to minimize the aggregate mean cost. The cost analysis of the proposed queueing system is presented in this section. Considering the following assumptions:

$$\gamma_h : \text{carrying cost per customer;}$$

$$\gamma_0 : \text{For each unit of time spent on service;}$$

$$\gamma_s : cost\ per\ cycle\ of\ switching\ on;$$

$$\gamma_r : \text{remuneration expense per cycle as aresult of vacation.}$$

Given that the cycle's duration is the product of the cloud server's average sleep time and processing period:

$$\text{Aggregate Mean Cost} = (\text{Average sleep time of the cloud server}) + (\text{Average processing period of the cloud server});$$

$$\text{Aggregate Mean Cost} = \frac{E(S)}{\sum_{n=0}^{a-1} \sum_{i=0}^{n} \alpha_i \left(A_{n-i}^2 + A_{n-i} + A_{n-i}^1\right)} + \frac{E(S)}{\sum_{I=0}^{a-1} (P^1{}_i + R_i)}.$$

$$\text{Aggregate Mean Cost} = [\gamma_s - \gamma_r E(I)] \frac{1}{E(T_c)} + \gamma_h E(Q) + \gamma_0 \rho;$$

where $\rho = \frac{(\xi E(B_1) E(Z))}{N}$.

Determining the optimal value c* that minimizes the aggregate mean cost is challenging to achieve through direct analytical methods. The definition of the optimal policy for a threshold $c^*$ to minimize the aggregate mean cost using the simple value direct search method is outlined below.

Stage 1: Determine the value of upper bound server capacity '$N$';
Stage 2: Select the value "c" that will fulfill the subsequent relation.

$$\text{AMC}(c^*) \leq \text{AMC}(c), \quad 1 \leq c \leq N;$$

Stage 3: The value $c^*$ is optimal, since it minimizes the aggregate mean cost.

The best value of $c^*$ that minimizes the aggregate mean cost function is obtained by following the preceding technique. In the following part, a numerical example will be provided to verify this solution.

### 4.4. Numerical Illustration

The theoretical findings derived for the proposed model are supported by numerical validation using the following assumptions and symbols (Table 2).

**Table 2.** Parameters and symbols.

| Parameter | Distribution | Symbols |
|---|---|---|
| Arrival rate | Poisson distribution | $\xi$ |
| Regular batch service time | 4-Erlang distribution | $\mu$ |
| Overloading batch service time | 3-Erlang distribution | $\mu_1$ |
| Underloading batch service time | 2-Erlang distribution | $\mu_2$ |
| Vacation time | Exponential distribution | $\varphi$ |

The group size distribution of the arrival is geometric with a mean of 3.

| | |
|---|---|
| Lower bound server capacity | $a$ |
| Upper bound server capacity | $b$ |
| Boundary value | $N$ |
| Switch-on cost | ₹6 |
| Carrying cost per customer | ₹3 |
| In service cost per unit time | ₹4 |
| Remuneration per unit time due to vacation | ₹2 |

### 4.5. Effects of Efficiency Metrics of Cloud Resource Utilization

The impacts of efficiency metrics of cloud resource utilization for fixed boundary values are presented. From Figure 2, it is clear that if the service rate increases, $L_{queue}$ and $L_{busy}$ decrease whereas $L_{idle}$ increases. From Table 3, it is evident that when the service rate is fixed for underloading and overloading but varies for regular batch service, as $\xi$ increases, $L_{queue}$ and $L_{busy}$ increase whereas $L_{idle}$ decreases. In Table 4 and Figure 3, it is evident that when the service rate is fixed for regular batch service and underloading but varies for the overloading service, as $\xi$ increases, $L_{queue}$ and $L_{busy}$ increase, whereas $L_{idle}$ decreases. From Table 5, it is evident that when the service rate is fixed for overloading and regular batch service but varies for underloading, as $\xi$ increases, $L_{queue}$ and $L_{busy}$ increase, whereas $L_{idle}$ decreases. Tables 3–5 present the impact of efficiency metrics on cloud resource utilization under varying arrival and service rates.

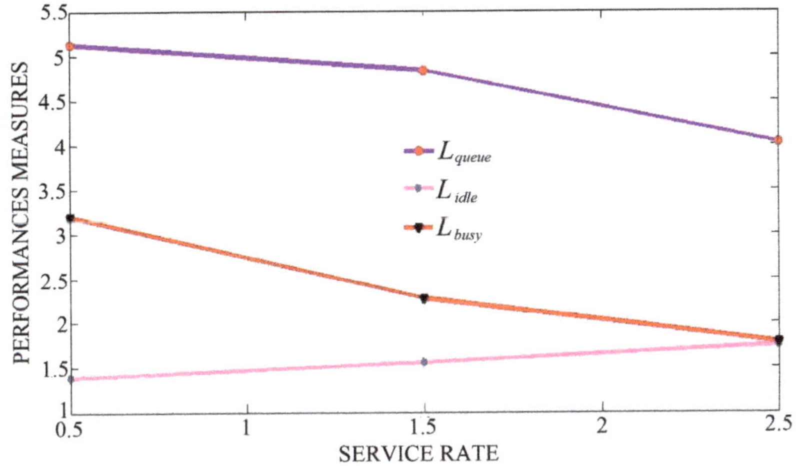


**Figure 2.** Service rate vs. efficiency metrics of cloud resource utilization.

**Table 3.** Arrival rate vs. efficiency metrics of cloud resource utilization ($\mu_1 = 3,\ \mu_2 = 4,\ \varphi = 5$).

| $\xi$ | $\mu = 0.5$ | | | $\mu = 1.5$ | | | $\mu = 2.5$ | | |
|---|---|---|---|---|---|---|---|---|---|
| | $L_{queue}$ | $L_{busy}$ | $L_{idle}$ | $L_{queue}$ | $L_{busy}$ | $L_{idle}$ | $L_{queue}$ | $L_{busy}$ | $L_{idle}$ |
| 1 | 5.0262 | 3.1932 | 1.9349 | 4.5935 | 2.5985 | 1.8412 | 4.1923 | 1.9134 | 1.7239 |
| 2 | 5.9271 | 3.9757 | 1.1352 | 5.0349 | 3.2431 | 1.4357 | 5.0921 | 2.5932 | 1.6128 |
| 3 | 6.8314 | 4.5932 | 0.9652 | 6.2145 | 4.9562 | 1.0932 | 6.3245 | 3.2398 | 1.3217 |
| 4 | 8.6783 | 5.3326 | 0.5923 | 7.3542 | 5.8235 | 0.7312 | 7.1256 | 4.4532 | 0.9234 |
| 5 | 9.1296 | 7.5561 | 0.1475 | 8.4563 | 6.9329 | 0.4956 | 8.3672 | 5.9431 | 0.5498 |

**Table 4.** Arrival rate vs. efficiency metrics of cloud resource utilization ($\mu = 4,\ \mu_2 = 5,\ \varphi = 6$).

| $\xi$ | $\mu_1 = 1.5$ | | | $\mu_1 = 2.5$ | | | $\mu_1 = 3.5$ | | |
|---|---|---|---|---|---|---|---|---|---|
| | $L_{queue}$ | $L_{busy}$ | $L_{idle}$ | $L_{queue}$ | $L_{busy}$ | $L_{idle}$ | $L_{queue}$ | $L_{busy}$ | $L_{idle}$ |
| 6 | 7.6212 | 4.3291 | 2.3229 | 5.5325 | 3.4574 | 2.7523 | 5.1259 | 2.5632 | 2.2423 |
| 6.2 | 8.7132 | 5.5785 | 1.9542 | 6.2382 | 4.5627 | 2.0286 | 5.9241 | 3.4574 | 1.3426 |
| 6.4 | 9.9823 | 7.7643 | 1.3326 | 7.4143 | 6.3387 | 1.5762 | 6.6229 | 4.9231 | 1.0572 |
| 6.8 | 10.7378 | 8.3265 | 0.9523 | 9.1732 | 7.6124 | 1.1421 | 7.2283 | 5.4213 | 0.8763 |
| 7 | 11.8126 | 9.2411 | 0.4875 | 10.3132 | 8.8332 | 0.7327 | 8.8621 | 6.1257 | 0.1287 |

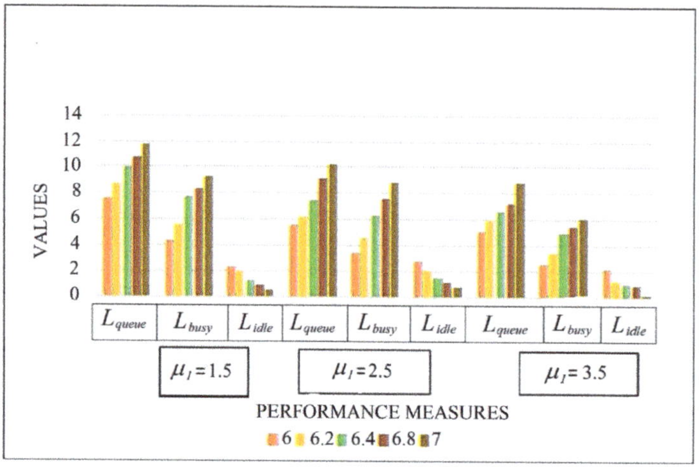


**Figure 3.** Arrival rate vs. efficiency metrics of cloud resource utilization.

**Table 5.** Arrival rate vs. efficiency metrics of cloud resource utilization ($\mu_1 = 3,\ \mu = 4,\ \varphi = 5$).

| $\xi$ | $\mu_2 = 2.5$ | | | $\mu_2 = 3.5$ | | | $\mu_2 = 4.5$ | | |
|---|---|---|---|---|---|---|---|---|---|
| | $L_{queue}$ | $L_{busy}$ | $L_{idle}$ | $L_{queue}$ | $L_{busy}$ | $L_{idle}$ | $L_{queue}$ | $L_{busy}$ | $L_{idle}$ |
| 9.1 | 4.6293 | 2.5932 | 2.5829 | 3.4328 | 2.3427 | 2.4523 | 5.6259 | 1.7752 | 2.1423 |
| 9.3 | 5.1247 | 3.6757 | 2.2542 | 4.5985 | 3.6727 | 1.9286 | 6.4241 | 2.4274 | 1.5426 |
| 9.5 | 6.4238 | 4.7932 | 1.8326 | 5.1253 | 4.5238 | 1.2762 | 7.1529 | 3.7423 | 1.0572 |
| 9.7 | 7.9378 | 5.2326 | 1.4523 | 6.9732 | 5.1763 | 0.8421 | 8.3283 | 4.5139 | 0.9763 |
| 9.9 | 9.8126 | 6.8561 | 0.9875 | 8.3547 | 6.8332 | 0.4327 | 9.0621 | 5.8237 | 0.0287 |

Consider a situation where the service times follow a hyper-exponential distribution under the following assumptions: $\mu = 5\ \mu_1 = 6,\ \mu_2 = 7,\ \varphi = 3$. From Table 6, it is clear that for regular batch service, underloading and overloading with hyper-exponentially distributed service times, as $\xi$ increases, both $L_{queue}$ and $L_{busy}$ grow, while $L_{idle}$ decreases.

**Table 6.** Hyper-exponential service time vs. efficiency metrics of cloud resource utilization. Service time follows hyper-exponential distribution $\mu = 5\ \mu_1 = 6,\ \mu_2 = 7,\ \varphi = 3$.

| $\xi$ | $L_{queue}$ | $L_{busy}$ | $L_{idle}$ |
|---|---|---|---|
| 2.1 | 5.3478 | 2.0749 | 1.4267 |
| 2.3 | 6.4523 | 2.9342 | 1.0542 |
| 3.5 | 7.9256 | 3.8432 | 0.9586 |
| 4.7 | 8.6431 | 4.5624 | 0.6752 |
| 5.9 | 9.2567 | 5.6572 | 0.4175 |

Table 7 and Figure 4 illustrates the impact of batch size 'c' on the aggregate mean cost for b = 15. To achieve the minimal aggregate mean cost, the lower bound server capacity should be set at c = 7. Furthermore, c should be optimized based on varying arrival, service, and vacation rates. For the best results, c = 7 and N == 20 should be maintained. Figure 5 demonstrates that increasing the threshold value '*a*' and $L_{queue}$ leads to a reduction in the aggregate mean cost. These results are essential for optimizing average system costs using power BI in cloud computing. The efficiency metrics for cloud resource utilization are presented below.

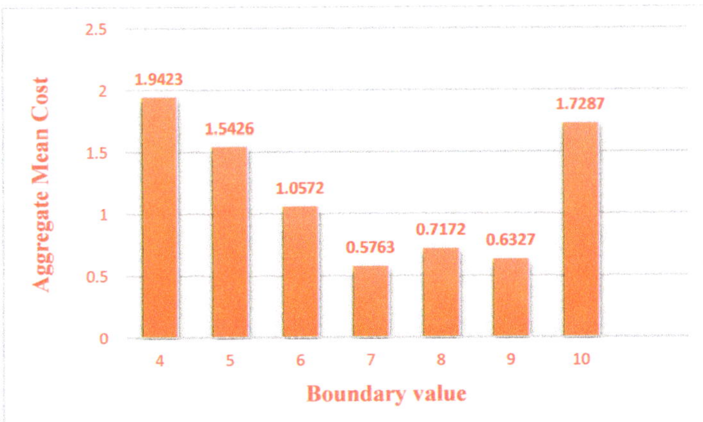


**Figure 4.** Boundary value '*c*' vs. aggregate mean cost.

**Table 7.** Boundary value '*c*' vs. aggregate mean cost, $\xi = 2$, $b = 15$, $\mathrm{N} = 20$, $\mu_1 = 7$, $\mu_2 = 6$, $\varphi = 5$, $a = 11$.

| $c$ | $L_{queue}$ | $L_{busy}$ | $L_{idle}$ | AMC |
|---|---|---|---|---|
| 4 | 4.6293 | 1.7752 | 2.5632 | 1.9423 |
| 5 | 5.1247 | 2.4274 | 3.4574 | 1.5426 |
| 6 | 6.4238 | 3.7423 | 4.9231 | 1.0572 |
| 7 | 7.9378 | 4.5139 | 5.4213 | 0.5763 * |
| 8 | 8.7132 | 7.7643 | 6.1257 | 0.7172 |
| 9 | 9.9823 | 8.3265 | 7.5392 | 0.6327 |
| 10 | 10.7378 | 9.2411 | 8.7982 | 1.7287 |

*—Denotes the lowest value of the aggregate mean cost.

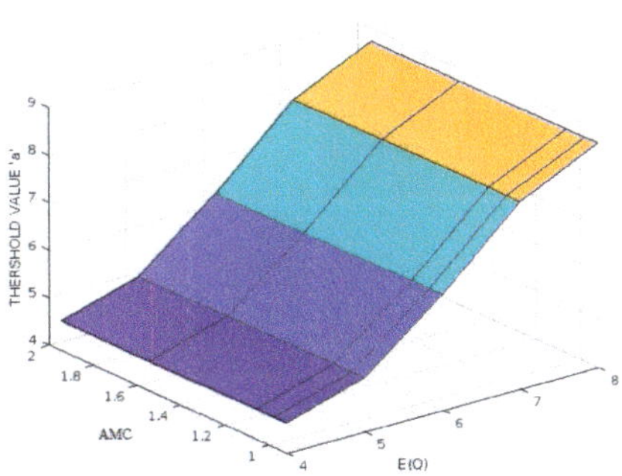


**Figure 5.** Boundary value '*a*' vs. aggregate mean cost, $\xi = 2$, $b = 5$, $N = 8$, $\mu_1 = 7$, $\mu_2 = 6$, $\varphi = 5$, $c = 3$.

### 4.6. Effects of Erlang Service Time and Hyper-Exponential Service Time over the Efficiency Metrics

Consider a situation where the service times follow a hyper-exponential distribution with $\mu = 5$, $\mu_1 = 6$, $\mu_2 = 7$, $\varphi = 3$. Table 6 shows that for regular batch service across underloading and overloading conditions, $L_{queue}$ and $L_{busy}$ increase as $\xi$ grows, while $L_{idle}$ decreases. In contrast, when service times follow an Erlang distribution, the efficiency metrics of cloud resource utilization are lower compared to those observed with the hyper-exponential distribution.

## 5. Conclusions

An approach to batch and bulk arrival service queuing that includes load balancing and vacation time is examined in this study. This queueing system differs from others in that it adds load balancing to a $M^X/G(a,b)/1$ queueing model that includes vacation. Through the use of supplementary variables, the PGF of the queue size at any given time is determined. Various efficiency metrics of cloud resource utilization are calculated, supplemented by appropriate numerical examples. The results obtained are highly useful for optimizing the total average system cost using power BI in the context of cloud computing.

**Author Contributions:** Conceptualization, S.P.N. and S.D.L.; methodology, S.P.N. and S.D.L.; software, S.P.N. and S.D.L.; validation, S.P.N., S.D.L., S.V. and M.L.S.; formal analysis, S.P.N., S.D.L., S.V. and M.L.S.; investigation, S.P.N. and S.D.L.; resources, S.P.N., S.D.L., S.V. and M.L.S.; data curation, S.P.N. and S.D.L.; writing—original draft preparation, S.P.N.; writing—review and editing, S.P.N., S.V. and M.L.S.; visualization, S.P.N., S.D.L., S.V. and M.L.S.; supervision, S.P.N., S.D.L., S.V. and M.L.S.; project administration, S.P.N. and S.D.L.; funding acquisition, S.P.N., S.D.L., S.V. and M.L.S. All authors have read and agreed to the published version of the manuscript.

**Funding:** The APC was funded by the Transilvania University of Brasov, HBS 2017/2024.

**Data Availability Statement:** The original contributions presented in the study are included in the article; further inquiries can be directed to the corresponding authors.

**Conflicts of Interest:** The authors declare no conflicts of interest.

## References


1. Takagi, H. *Queueing Analysis: A Foundation of Performance Evaluation*; Distributors for the U.S. and Canada, Elsevier Science Pub. Co.: Amsterdam, The Netherlands; New York, NY, USA, 1991.
2. Doshi, B.T. Queueing systems with vacations—A survey. *Queueing Syst.* **1986**, *1*, 29–66. [CrossRef]
3. Lee, H.W.; Lee, S.S.; Park, J.O.; Chae, K.C. Analysis of the Mx/G/1 queue by N-policy and multiple vacations. *J. Appl. Probab.* **1994**, *31*, 476–496. [CrossRef]
4. Lee, H.; Lee, S.; Chae, K. A fixed-size batch service queue with vacations. *J. Appl. Math. Stoch. Anal.* **1996**, *9*, 205–219. [CrossRef]
5. Krishna Reddy, G.V.; Nadarajan, R.; Arumuganathan, R. Analysis of a bulk queue with N-policy multiple vacations and setup times. *Comput. Oper. Res.* **1998**, *25*, 957–967. [CrossRef]
6. Jeyakumar, J.; Senthilnathan, B. A study on the behaviour of the server breakdown without interruption in a Mx/G(a, b)/1 queueing system with multiple vacations and closedown time. *Appl. Math. Comput.* **2012**, *219*, 2618–2633. [CrossRef]
7. Arumuganathan, R.; Jeyakumar, S. Steady state analysis of a bulk queue with multiple vacations, setup times with N-policy and closedown times. *Appl. Math. Model.* **2005**, *29*, 972–986. [CrossRef]
8. Haridass, M.; Arumuganathan, R. Analysis of a MX/G(a,b)/1 queueing system with vacation interruption. *RAIRO-Oper. Res.* **2012**, *46*, 305–334. [CrossRef]
9. Siddiqui, S.; Darbari, M.; Yagyasen, D. An QPSL Queuing Model for Load Balancing in Cloud Computing. *Int. J. E-Collab. (IJeC)* **2020**, *16*, 33–48. [CrossRef]
10. Agrawal, P.; Jain, M.; Singh, A. Optimal N-Policy for Finite Queue with Server Breakdown and State-Dependent Rate. 2017. Available online: https://www.semanticscholar.org/paper/Optimal-N-policy-for-Finite-Queue-with-Server-and-%22-Agrawal-Jain/784cd6d4343269915464c47eeb604ddc2ab4ff8c (accessed on 25 May 2024).
11. Niranjan, S.P.; Chandrasekaran, V.M.; Indhira, K. Two-Level Control Policy of an Unreliable Queueing System with Queue Size-Dependent Vacation and Vacation Disruption. In *Trends in Mathematics, Proceedings of the International Conference on Advances in Mathematical Sciences, Vellore, India, 1 December 2017*; Birkhäuser: Cham, Switzerland, 2018; Volume I, pp. 373–382. [CrossRef]
12. Govindan, A.; Deepa, T. Analysis of batch arrival bulk service queue with additional optional service multiple vacation and setup time. *Int. J. Math. Oper. Res.* **2019**, *15*, 1. [CrossRef]
13. Siddiqui, D.-S. Modelling and Simulation of Queuing Models Through the concept of Petri Nets ADCAIJ: Advances in Distributed Computing. *Adv. Distrib. Comput. Artif. Intell. J.* **2020**, *9*, 17–28.

14. Banerjee, S.; Budhiraja, A.; Estevez, B. Load Balancing in Parallel Queues and Rank-based Diffusions. *arXiv* **2024**, arXiv:2302.10317. [CrossRef]
15. Otten, S. Load balancing in a network of queueing-inventory systems. *Ann. Oper. Res.* **2023**, *331*, 807–837. [CrossRef]
16. van der Boor, M.; Borst, S.; van Leeuwaarden, J. Optimal hyper-scalable load balancing with a strict queue limit. *Perform. Eval.* **2021**, *149–150*, 102217. [CrossRef]
17. Liu, X.; Ying, L. Universal Scaling of Distributed Queues Under Load Balancing in the Super-Halfin-Whitt Regime. *IEEE/ACM Trans. Netw.* **2022**, *30*, 190–201. [CrossRef]
18. Ahmed, H.; Arshad, M.J.; Muhammad, S.; Ahmad, S.; Zahid, A.H. Queue length-based load balancing in data center networks. *Int. J. Commun. Syst.* **2020**, *33*, e4472. [CrossRef]
19. Hellemans, T.; Kielanski, G.; Van Houdt, B. Performance of Load Balancers with Bounded Maximum Queue Length in Case of Non-Exponential Job Sizes. *IEEE/ACM Trans. Netw.* **2023**, *31*, 1626–1641. [CrossRef]
20. der Boor, M.V.; Borst, S.C.; Van Leeuwaarden, J.S.H.; Mukherjee, D. Scalable Load Balancing in Networked Systems: A Survey of Recent Advances. *SIAM Rev.* **2022**, *64*, 554–622. [CrossRef]
21. Delasay, M.; Akan, M. Efficient Allocation of Load-Balancing and Differentiation Tasks in Tandem Queue Services; SSRN, 2024; p. 4830834. Available online: https://ssrn.com/abstract=4830834 (accessed on 13 December 2024).
22. Santos, B.; Soares, A.; Nguyen, T.-A.; Min, D.-K.; Lee, J.-W.; Silva, F.-A. IoT Sensor Networks in Smart Buildings: A Performance Assessment Using Queuing Models. *Sensors* **2021**, *21*, 5660. [CrossRef]
23. Rodrigues, L.; Rodrigues, J.J.P.C.; de Serra, S.B.; Silva, F.A. A Queueing-Based Model Performance Evaluation for Internet of People Supported by Fog Computing. *Future Internet* **2022**, *14*, 23. [CrossRef]
24. Katayama, Y.; Tachibana, T. Optimal Task Allocation Algorithm Based on Queueing Theory for Future Internet Application in Mobile Edge Computing Platform. *Sensors* **2022**, *22*, 4825. [CrossRef]
25. Zhan, W.; Jiang, M.; Wang, X. Optimal Capacity Decision-Making of Omnichannel Catering Merchants Considering the Service Environment Based on Queuing Theory. *Systems* **2022**, *10*, 144. [CrossRef]
26. Alnowibet, K.A.; Alrasheedi, A.F.; Alqahtani, F.S. Queuing Models for Analyzing the Steady-State Distribution of Stochastic Inventory Systems with Random Lead Time and Impatient Customers. *Processes* **2022**, *10*, 624. [CrossRef]
27. Jin, H.-L.; Di, T.-L.; Yu, H.; Zhang, R.R. On the τ Decomposition Method for the Stability and Bifurcation of the TCP/AQM Networks versus Time Delay. *Symmetry* **2022**, *14*, 463. [CrossRef]
28. Yen, T.-C.; Wang, K.-H.; Chen, J.-Y. Optimization Analysis of the N Policy M/G/1 Queue with Working Breakdowns. *Symmetry* **2020**, *12*, 583. [CrossRef]
29. Kothandaraman, D.; Kandaiyan, I. Analysis of a Heterogeneous Queuing Model with Intermittently Obtainable Servers under a Hybrid Vacation Schedule. *Symmetry* **2023**, *15*, 1304. [CrossRef]
30. Kempa, W.M.; Paprocka, I. A Discrete-Time Queueing Model of a Bottleneck with an Energy-Saving Mechanism Based on Setup and Shutdown Times. *Symmetry* **2024**, *16*, 63. [CrossRef]
31. Chydzinski, A.; Adamczyk, B. Response Time of Queueing Mechanisms. *Symmetry* **2024**, *16*, 271. [CrossRef]
32. Niranjan, S.P.; Devi Latha, S.; Mahdal, M.; Karthik, K. Multiple Control Policy in Unreliable Two-Phase Bulk Queueing System with Active Bernoulli Feedback and Vacation. *Mathematics* **2024**, *12*, 75. [CrossRef]
33. Cost Optimization in Sintering Process on the Basis of Bulk Queueing System with Diverse Services Modes and Vacation. Available online: https://www.mdpi.com/2227-7390/12/22/3535 (accessed on 13 December 2024).
34. Niranjan, S.P. Managerial decision analysis of bulk arrival queuing system with state dependent breakdown and vacation. *Int. J. Adv. Oper. Manag.* **2020**, *12*, 351–376. [CrossRef]
35. Niranjan, S.P.; Chandrasekaran, V.M.; Indhira, K. Queue size dependent service in bulk arrival queueing system with server loss and vacation break-off. *Int. J. Knowl. Manag. Tour. Hosp.* **2017**, *1*, 176–207. [CrossRef]
36. Niranjan, S.P.; Latha, S.D. Analyzing the Two-Phase Heterogeneous and Batch Service Queuing System with Breakdown in Two-Phases, Feedback, and Vacation. *Baghdad Sci. J.* **2024**, *21*, 2701. [CrossRef]
37. Gautam, A.; Choudhury, G.; Dharmaraja, S. Performance analysis of DRX mechanism using batch arrival vacation queueing system with N-policy in LTE-A networks. *Ann. Telecommun.* **2020**, *75*, 353–367. [CrossRef]
38. Neuts, M.F. A General Class of Bulk Queues with Poisson Input. *Ann. Math. Stat.* **1967**, *38*, 759–770. [CrossRef]
39. Cox, D.R. The analysis of non-Markovian stochastic processes by the inclusion of supplementary variables. *Math. Proc. Camb. Phil. Soc.* **1955**, *51*, 433–441. [CrossRef]

axioms

MDPI

Article

# A New Hybrid Class of Distributions: Model Characteristics and Stress–Strength Reliability Studies

Mustapha Muhammad [1], Jinsen Xiao [1,*], Badamasi Abba [2,*], Isyaku Muhammad [3] and Refka Ghodhbani [4]

[1] Department of Mathematics, Guangdong University of Petrochemical Technology, Maoming 525000, China; mmmahmoud12@sci.just.edu.jo or mmuhammad.mth@buk.edu.ng
[2] School of Mathematics and Statistics, Central South University, Changsha 410083, China
[3] College of Mechanical Engineering, Hubei University of Automotive Technology, Shiyan 442002, China; isyakuedu@yahoo.com
[4] Center for Scientific Research and Entrepreneurship, Northern Border University, Arar 73213, Saudi Arabia; refka.ghodhbani@nbu.edu.sa
* Correspondence: jinsenxiao@gdupt.edu.cn (J.X.); babba@yumsuk.edu.ng or badamasiabba@csu.edu.cn (B.A.)

**Abstract:** This study proposes a generalized family of distributions to enhance flexibility in modeling complex engineering and biomedical data. The framework unifies existing models and improves reliability analysis in both engineering and biomedical applications by capturing diverse system behaviors. We introduce a novel hybrid family of distributions that incorporates a flexible set of hybrid functions, enabling the extension of various existing distributions. Specifically, we present a three-parameter special member called the hybrid-Weibull–exponential (HWE) distribution. We derive several fundamental mathematical properties of this new family, including moments, random data generation processes, mean residual life (MRL) and its relationship with the failure rate function, and its related asymptotic behavior. Furthermore, we compute advanced information measures, such as extropy and cumulative residual entropy, and derive order statistics along with their asymptotic behaviors. Model identifiability is demonstrated numerically using the Kullback–Leibler divergence. Additionally, we perform a stress–strength (SS) reliability analysis of the HWE under two common scale parameters, supported by illustrative numerical evaluations. For parameter estimation, we adopt the maximum likelihood estimation (MLE) method in both density estimation and SS-parameter studies. The simulation results indicated that the MLE demonstrates consistency in both density and SS-parameter estimations, with the mean squared error of the MLEs decreasing as the sample size increases. Moreover, the average length of the confidence interval for the percentile and Student's t-bootstrap for the SS-parameter becomes smaller with larger sample sizes, and the coverage probability progressively aligns with the nominal confidence level of 95%. To demonstrate the practical effectiveness of the hybrid family, we provide three real-world data applications in which the HWE distribution outperforms many existing Weibull-based models, as measured by AIC, BIC, CAIC, KS, Anderson–Darling, and Cramer–von Mises criteria. Furthermore, the HLW exhibits strong performance in SS-parameter analysis. Consequently, this hybrid family holds immense potential for modeling lifetime data and advancing reliability and survival analysis.

**Keywords:** Weibull distribution; moments; mean residual life; maximum likelihood estimation; stress–strength reliability; bootstrap; simulation

**MSC:** 62E15; 60E05; 62F10

## 1. Introduction

With the advent of new technologies and innovative methods, the data they generate often exhibit characteristics that deviate from those described by traditional statistical models. These can include unusual patterns such as skewness, heavy tails, multimodal distributions, or atypical failure rates. Such discrepancies can make conventional models insufficient for accurate analysis and prediction, highlighting the need for more adaptable approaches. The creation of dynamic models that accurately encapsulate a variety of data types is a crucial challenge and opportunity within the realm of probability and applied statistics. This vital endeavor not only facilitates the integration of diverse aspects of real-world phenomena but also aids in the development of predictive insights. In this pursuit, statisticians have crafted numerous families of distributions using various methods, such as employing differential equations and manipulating parameters including location, scale, and shape, as well as incorporating confounding schemes and trigonometric and weighting techniques. These methodological advancements are similar to developing new data generation processes, which is comparable to creating fresh case studies. Such progress not only enhances our understanding of existing models but also improves our ability to tackle future challenges across various fields, including finance, engineering, biomedical sciences, and natural sciences. By extending these distributions, we develop more flexible and precise tools that contribute to both theoretical research and practical applications, particularly in analyzing complex and dynamic datasets. For instance, these advancements include various classes and extensions of distributions, see Table 1:

**Table 1.** G-classes of distributions.

| Model Name | Cumulative Distribution Function |
|---|---|
| Beta-G [1] | $F(x) = I_{G(x;\xi)}(a,b)$,<br>where, $I_y(a,b) = \frac{B_y(a,b)}{B(a,b)}$ is the incomplete beta function $a,b > 0, \xi \in \mathbb{R}$. |
| Generalized beta-G [2] | $F(x) = I_{G^c(x;\xi)}(a,b),\ a,b,c > 0, \xi \in \mathbb{R}$. |
| New Kumaraswamy-G [3] | $F(x) = 1 - \left(1 - \left(1 - \bar{G}(x;\eta)^{G(x;\eta)}\right)^a\right)^b, \quad a, b > 0, \eta \in \mathbb{R}$. |
| Kumaraswamy–Poisson-G [4] | $F(x) = 1 - \left(1 - \left(\frac{1-e^{-\lambda G(x;\eta)}}{1-e^{-\lambda}}\right)^a\right)^b, \lambda\, a, b > 0, \eta \in \mathbb{R}$. |
| Poisson-odd generalized exponential-G [5] | $F(x) = \frac{1-e^{-\lambda\left(1-e^{-\alpha\frac{G(x;\xi)}{\bar{G}(x;\xi)}}\right)^\beta}}{(1-e^{-\lambda})}, \quad \alpha,\beta,\lambda > 0, \xi \in \mathbb{R}$. |
| Extended Topp–Leone-G [6] | $F(x) = G^\alpha(x;\xi)(2 - G(x;\xi))^{\alpha\beta}, \quad \alpha > 0, \beta, \xi \in \mathbb{R}$ |
| Power Topp–Leone-G [7] | $F(x) = e^{\alpha\beta\left(1-\frac{1}{G(x;\xi)}\right)}\left(2 - e^{\beta\left(1-\frac{1}{G(x;\xi)}\right)}\right)^\alpha, \quad \alpha,\beta > 0, \xi \in \mathbb{R}$. |
| Weighted cosine-G [8] | $F(x) = \frac{e^{1-\cos(\frac{\pi G(x;\eta)}{1+G(x;\eta)})}-1}{e-1}, \quad \eta \in \mathbb{R}$. |
| Tan-G-loss family [9] | $F(x) = \tan\left(\frac{\pi}{4}\left(1 - \frac{\sigma\bar{G}(x;\xi)}{\sigma-\log\bar{G}(x;\xi)}\right)\right) \quad \sigma > 0, \xi \in \mathbb{R}$. |
| Exponent-G-exponential [10] | $F(x) = 1 - e^{-\lambda\left(\frac{1-e^{-G(x;\zeta)}}{e^{\bar{G}(x;\zeta)}-1}\right)}, \quad \lambda > 0, \zeta \in \mathbb{R}$. |

Furthermore, the field has seen the introduction of several Weibull-related distributions such as the exponentiated additive Weibull [11], improved Weibull–Weibull [12], modified exponential Weibull [13], discrete bivariate Frechet–Weibull [14], Dhillon-exponential power [15], and Mustapha–Badamasi modified Weibull [16], among others. The family of distributions given by (1) was introduced in [17].

$$F(x) = 1 - e^{-\alpha H(x;\zeta)}, \ \alpha > 0. \tag{1}$$

where $H(x;\zeta)$ is a non-negative monotonically increasing function, $x \in \mathbb{R}$, and $\zeta$ is a parameter vector. Different $H(x;\zeta)$ include some statistical models such as the following: $H(x) = x$ gives the exponential; $H(x) = x^2$, Rayleigh; $H(x) = \log(x/a)$, Pareto; $H(x) = a^{-1}(e^{ax} - 1)$, Gompertz; $H(x) = x^{\beta}$, Weibull; $H(x) = x^{\beta}e^{\lambda x}$, modified Weibull [18]; $H(x) = e^{\lambda x - \beta/x}$, flexible Weibull [19]; and $H(x) = (e^{(x/\alpha)^{\beta}} - 1)$, modified Weibull extension [20]. This innovation extends the classical Weibull model. However, this method has limitations due to the restricted set of suitable functions $H(x;\zeta)$ that are non-negative and monotonically increasing. Therefore, it is necessary to extend the method and provide alternative approaches.

*Objectives and Paper Organization*

Our target is to investigate the pivotal role of the function in (1), represented as $\alpha H(x;\zeta)$, to decompose it into two separate components: one exhibiting monotonic growth on $\mathbb{R}^+$ and the other confined within a unit interval to allow us to develop a novel hybrid-G class of models. This approach will pave the way for more adaptable models and offer fresh insights into data modeling and applied statistical research. Such innovation introduces novel statistical methods for data analysis, among other benefits. This development will exemplify the dynamic evolution of statistical distributions in adapting to complex data analysis needs and demonstrate the ongoing evolution and adaptation in statistical modeling to meet practical demands.

(i) We explored the key characteristics and practical illustrations of the proposed family, as well as various computational approaches and procedures for its implementation. This model not only facilitates the development of new probability models but also integrates with data simulation processes.
(ii) A special member called hybrid-Weibull–exponential is discussed extensively. Mathematical and statistical properties such as shape properties, moments, mean residual life, information measures, order statistics, model identifiability, and stress–strength (SS) reliability are explored.
(iii) The maximum likelihood estimation (MLE) method for parameter estimation is considered, and comprehensive simulation studies are conducted to rigorously assess the performance of the MLEs. We also employ nonparametric bootstrap techniques to construct confidence intervals and evaluate coverage probabilities associated with the SS-parameter.
(iv) To illustrate the practical effectiveness of the hybrid family, three real-world applications are explored for illustration.

The advantage of extended models is allowing for flexible modeling of data with a variety of shapes. The parameters controlled the skewness or heavy-tailed characteristics of the model, providing additional flexibility to accommodate highly skewed data and various failure rates. Different probability models serve different purposes and represent different data generation processes; as such, the proposed model can be a better alternative to various distributions.

The subsequent contents of the article are structured as follows: In Section 2, we propose the hybrid-W-G family of distributions and some useful properties. In Section 3, a special member called hybrid-Weibull–exponential is proposed and discussed. Properties such as moments, mean residual life, order statistics, information measure, and model identifiability are explored. In Section 4, the maximum likelihood estimation and simulation studies are presented. In Section 5, the stress–strength reliability parameter and its maximum likelihood estimation together with bootstrap confidence interval are studied, and a simulation analysis is performed. In Section 6, we present the applications of the hybrid-Weibull–exponential. Conclusions of the study are placed in Section 7.

## 2. The Proposed Hybrid Model

Let $G(x;\zeta) \in (0,1)$ preferably be any valid cumulative distribution function (CDF), where $\zeta$ is a parameter vector in $\mathbb{R}^n$. We proposed the use of an increasing function defined as $w(x;\xi) \in (c,\infty)$, where $c \geq 0$ and $\xi$ is a parameter vector in $\mathbb{R}^n$. The proposed hybrid family of distribution is defined as

$$F(x;\xi,\zeta) = 1 - e^{-w(x;\xi)G(x;\zeta)}. \tag{2}$$

The model should be called the hybrid-w-G family of distributions. For example, if $w(x;\xi) = \frac{1}{1-G(x)}$, we have an odd-G family, and $w(x;\xi)$ ranges from $c = 1$ to $\infty$. Hence, it is necessary to provide some possible $w(x;\xi)$ to facilitate the model generating process and naming, and also to provide the opportunity of introducing various $w(x;\xi)$. Table 2 gives some possible $w(x;\xi)$ with their names and ranges for $a, b, \alpha, \beta > 0$.

**Table 2.** Some possible $w(x_i;\xi)$ functions and ranges.

| Name | $w(x;\xi); x \in \mathbb{R}^+$ | Range |
|---|---|---|
| Exponential | $\alpha x$ | $(0,\infty)$ |
| Exponent | $e^{\alpha x}$ | $(1,\infty)$ |
| Weibull | $\alpha x^{\beta}$ | $(0,\infty)$ |
| Extended Power | $a x^{\beta} + bx,\ a,b > 0$ | $(0,\infty)$ |
| Hybrid-odd | $\frac{1}{1-G_2(x;\xi)}$ | $(1,\infty)$ |
| Sine | $\frac{1}{\sin(\frac{\pi}{2}(1-G(x;\xi)))}$ | $(1,\infty)$ |
| Cosine | $\frac{1}{\cos(\frac{\pi}{2}G(x;\xi))}$ | $(1,\infty)$ |
| Tangent | $\frac{1}{\tan(\frac{\pi}{4}(1-G(x;\xi)))}$ | $(1,\infty)$ |

**Note:** The hybrid-odd-w-G implies using different baseline CDF as $w(x;\xi)G(x;\zeta) = \frac{G_1(x;\zeta)}{1-G_2(x;\xi)}$—that is, $w(x;\xi) = \frac{1}{1-G_2(x;\xi)}$.

The corresponding probability density function (PDF), reliability function (RF), and failure rate function (FRF) of the hybrid-w-G are given, respectively, as

$$\begin{aligned} f(x) &= [w'(x;\xi)G(x;\zeta) + w(x;\xi)g(x;\zeta)]e^{-w(x;\xi)G(x;\zeta)}, \\ R(x) &= e^{-w(x;\xi)G(x;\zeta)}, \\ h(x) &= w'(x;\xi)G(x;\zeta) + w(x;\xi)g(x;\zeta). \end{aligned}$$

*Moments and Mean Residual Life*

Obtaining the mathematical characteristics of probability distributions holds significant importance for a numerous of reasons. Foremost among these is the capability to devise multiple statistical measures and to complexly regard the behaviors exhibited by the hybrid-w-G family. The moments of a probability distribution are essential tools in statistics for summarizing the shape and characteristics of distributions. The moments, including mean, variance, skewness, and kurtosis, provide insights into the central tendency, dispersion, asymmetry, and peakedness of the distribution. We can obtain the $r^{th}$ moments of $X$ having hybrid-w-G:

$$
\begin{aligned}
E[X^r] &= \int_{-\infty}^{\infty} x^r [w'(x;\xi)G(x;\zeta) + w(x;\xi)g(x;\zeta)]e^{-w(x;\xi)G(x;\zeta)}\,dx \\
&= \sum_{i=1}^{\infty} \frac{(-1)^i}{i!} \int_{-\infty}^{\infty} x^r w'(x;\xi) w^i(x;\xi) G^{i+1}(x;\zeta)\,dx \\
&+ \sum_{i=1}^{\infty} \frac{(-1)^i}{i!} \int_{-\infty}^{\infty} x^r w^{i+1}(x;\xi) G^i(x;\zeta) g(x;\zeta)\,dx.
\end{aligned}
$$

The mean residual life (MRL) at a given time $t$ is a statistical measure representing the expected remaining lifetime or duration until an event of interest, given survival up to time $t$. It is a crucial concept in survival analysis and reliability engineering, offering insights into the longevity or reliability of a component or system beyond a specified point in time. The MRL of hybrid-w-G is given by

$$
\mu_X(t) = \frac{1}{R(t)} \int_t^{\infty} e^{-w(x;\xi)G(x;\zeta)} dx = \frac{1}{R(t)} \sum_{i=1}^{\infty} \frac{(-1)^i}{i!} \int_t^{\infty} w^i(x;\xi) G^i(x;\zeta) dx.
$$

In the next section, we will discuss a special member of the hybrid-w-G and some of its important properties, namely, the hybrid-Weibull–exponential distributions.

## 3. The Hybrid-Weibull–Exponential (HWE)

The hybrid-Weibull–exponential is derived by taking $w(x_i;\alpha,\beta) = \alpha x^{\beta}$ and $G(x;\lambda) = 1 - e^{-\lambda x}$ as the exponential distribution CDF; hence, HWE has PDF, $R(x)$, and FRF as

$$
f(x) = \alpha\left[\beta x^{\beta-1}(1-e^{-\lambda x}) + \lambda x^{\beta} e^{-\lambda x}\right] e^{-\alpha x^{\beta}(1-e^{-\lambda x})}, \tag{3}
$$

$$
R(x) = e^{-\alpha x^{\beta}(1-e^{-\lambda x})}, \tag{4}
$$

and

$$
h(x) = \alpha\beta x^{\beta-1} - \alpha\beta x^{\beta-1} e^{-\lambda x} + \alpha\lambda x^{\beta} e^{-\lambda x}, \tag{5}
$$

respectively.

**Theorem 1.** *The FRF of the HWE in (5) can be unimodal with mode at* $x_0 = \frac{2\beta[2+(\beta-1)]}{\lambda[2-\beta(\beta-1)]}$, *for* $\beta \leq 1$.

**Proof.** This was proved by obtaining $h'(x)$. The derivative of $h(x)$ is obtained as

$$
h'(x) = \alpha x^{\beta-2} e^{-\lambda x}\left[\beta(\beta-1)e^{\lambda x} - \beta(\beta-1) + 2\beta\lambda x - \lambda^2 x^2\right].
$$

Some roots can be obtain by solving the following:

$$
\frac{\lambda^2}{\beta(\beta-1)}x^2 - \frac{2\lambda}{(\beta-1)}x - e^{\lambda x} + 1 = 0.
$$

Since it has many roots—and thus, to obtain at least one root—it can be expressed as

$$\frac{\lambda^2}{\beta(\beta-1)}x^2 - \frac{2\lambda}{(\beta-1)}x - \left[1 + \lambda x + \frac{\lambda^2 x^2}{2} + \sum_{i=3}^{\infty} \frac{\lambda^i x^i}{i!}\right] + 1 = 0.$$

For $i = 2$, we obtain

$$\frac{\lambda^2[2-\beta(\beta-1)]}{2\beta(\beta-1)}x^2 - \frac{\lambda[2+(\beta-1)]}{(\beta-1)}x - 0.$$

Hence,

$$x = \frac{2\beta[2+(\beta-1)]}{\lambda[2-\beta(\beta-1)]},$$

and $\beta \leq 1$. □

Figure 1 displays some possible shapes of the PDF and FRF of the HWE distribution for some parameter values.

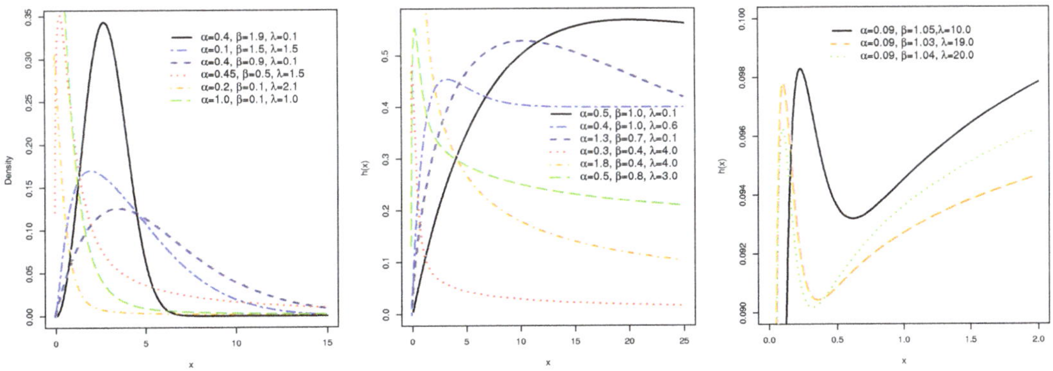


**Figure 1.** Graphical illustrations of PDF and FRF of HWE model for some selected parameters.

### *3.1. HWE Data Generating Process*

To generate a dataset that follows HWE, we need the following alternative process since HWE does not have a closed form quantile function. The quantile function $q(u)$ of the HWE is essential for random sampling and other statistical studies regarding HWE, and it is possible to use the Markov chain Monte Carlo (MCMC) method or employ an alternative specified technique to achieve this goal, as shown below. The CDF of the HWE is given as

$$F(x) = 1 - e^{-\alpha x^{\beta}(1-e^{-\lambda x})}. \tag{6}$$

The quantiles, $q(u) = X$ of HWE, are the exact solution of the following equation. The solution can be obtained using numerical root-finding methods like Newton–Raphson; an alternative function called `inverseCDF` in the package named `HDInterval` [21] in `R-software (version 4.3.2)` can be used to obtain the solution. The `inverseCDF` used a uniroot function, which provides an implementation of Newton–Raphson for finding the root of an equation in a given interval.

$$\log[1-u] = \alpha x^{\beta}(e^{-\lambda x} - 1). \tag{7}$$

To produce a random sample from the proposed HWE, we present some useful steps in Algorithm 1 as follows:

**Algorithm 1** HWE random sample procedure

1. Select $\alpha$, $\beta$, $\lambda$,
2. Generate $u_i \sim U(0,1), i = 1, 2, \ldots, n$,
3. Apply $u_i$ from 2 to evaluate $x_i$ by solving $\log[1-u_i] = \alpha x_i^{\beta}(e^{-\lambda x_i} - 1)$.

Under the quantile function, we subsequently discussed the skewness and kurtosis of the proposed HWE, which require the use of Algorithm 1. Bowley's skewness (Bo) and Moor's kurtosis (Mo) are quantile-based measures, respectively, defined as

$$Bo = \frac{q(\frac{3}{4}) - 2q(\frac{2}{4}) + q(\frac{1}{4})}{q(\frac{3}{4}) - q(\frac{1}{4})}, \quad and \quad Mo = \frac{q(\frac{7}{8}) - q(\frac{5}{8}) + q(\frac{3}{8}) - q(\frac{1}{8})}{q(\frac{6}{8}) - q(\frac{2}{8})}.$$

Figure 2 shows that for fixed $\alpha = 1$, the skewness is decreasing then increasing as both $\beta$ and $\lambda$ increase in the interval $[0.2, 5]$; meanwhile, the kurtosis is also decreasing then increasing as both $\beta$ and $\lambda$ increase in $[1, 6]$.

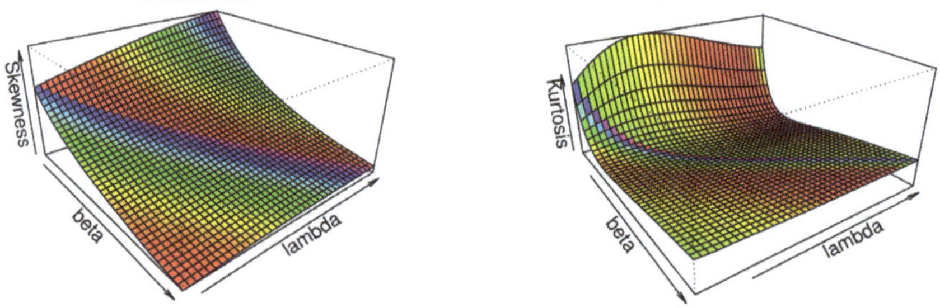


**Figure 2.** Plots of the Bo and Mo for the HWE model for fixed $\alpha = 1$

*3.2. Moments*

From the $r$th moments of HWE, we can obtain some characteristics including mean and variance, among others. The $r$th moment of HWE is derived as

$$\begin{aligned} E[X^r] &= \int_0^{\infty} x^r \alpha \left[\beta x^{\beta-1}(1-e^{-\lambda x}) + \lambda x^{\beta} e^{-\lambda x}\right] e^{-\alpha x^{\beta}(1-e^{-\lambda x})} dx \\ &= \sum_{i=0}^{\infty}\sum_{j=0}^{i+1} \frac{(-1)^{i+j}}{i!}\binom{i}{j}\alpha^{i+1}\beta \int_0^{\infty} x^{\beta(i+1)+r-1} e^{-\lambda j x}\, dx \\ &+ \sum_{i=0}^{\infty}\sum_{j=0}^{i} \frac{(-1)^{i+k}}{i!}\binom{i}{k}\alpha^{i+1}\lambda \int_0^{\infty} x^{\beta(i+1)+r-1} e^{-\lambda(k+1)x}\, dx \\ &= \sum_{i=0}^{\infty}\sum_{j=0}^{i+1} \rho_{i,j}^{(1)} \Gamma(\beta(i+1)+r) + \sum_{i=0}^{\infty}\sum_{j=0}^{i} \rho_{i,k}^{(2)} \Gamma(\beta(i+1)+r). \end{aligned} \tag{8}$$

where $\rho_{i,j}^{(1)} = \frac{(-1)^{i+j}\alpha^{i+1}\beta\binom{i}{j}}{i!\,[\lambda j]^{\beta(i+1)+r}}$ and $\rho_{i,k}^{(2)} = \frac{(-1)^{i+k}\alpha^{i+1}\lambda\binom{i}{k}}{i!\,[\lambda(k+1)]^{\beta(i+1)+r}}$. Also, $\Gamma(\cdot)$ is a gamma function. The mean $(E[X])$ and variance $Var = E[X^2] - (E[X])^2$ of the HWE can be obtained from (8) by setting $r = 1$ and $r = 2$. Figure 3 shows that for fixed $\alpha = 1$, the mean of the HWE is decreasing when both $\beta$ and $\lambda$ are increasing in the interval $[0.8, 20]$; also, the variance is decreasing when both $\beta$ and $\lambda$ are increasing in $[0.9, 5]$.

**Figure 3.** Plots of mean (left) and variance (right) for the HWE model for fixed $\alpha = 1$

### 3.3. Mean Residual Life and Asymptotic Behavior

In reliability engineering, statistical mechanics, and survival analysis, the mean residual life (MRL) is a key measure with broad applications. It represents the expected remaining lifetime of a system or entity at a given time, serving as an essential tool for evaluating the durability and performance of components, ranging from mechanical systems to software. The MRL for the HWE can be determined by solving the following integral:

$$\mu_X(t) = \frac{1}{R(t)} \int_t^\infty e^{-\alpha x^\beta (1-e^{-\lambda x})} \, dx = \frac{1}{R(t)} \sum_{i=0}^{\infty} \sum_{j=0}^{i} \frac{(-1)^{i+j} \alpha^i \binom{i}{j}}{i!} \int_t^\infty x^{\beta i} \, e^{-\lambda j x} \, dx$$

$$= \frac{1}{R(t)} \sum_{i=0}^{\infty} \sum_{j=0}^{i} \frac{(-1)^{i+j} \alpha^i \binom{i}{j}}{i! \, [\lambda j]^{\beta i + 1}} \Gamma(\beta i + 1, \, t\lambda j).$$

The MRL and FRF exhibit an inverse relationship, as they characterize different aspects of the same survival behavior. Mathematically, the MRL can be expressed using the FRF through the equation $s(t) = e^{\left[-\int_0^t h(x)dx\right]}$. Furthermore, there exists another mathematical relationship between the MRL and FRF $h(t)$, defined as $h(t) = [\mu_X'(t) + 1]/\mu_X(t)$. It is evident that $\mu_X'(t) \geq -1$. The MRL and FRF uniquely determine a probability distribution, as discussed in [22,23]. Additionally, ref. [24] established the following relationships: an increasing MRL implies a decreasing FRF, while a decreasing MRL implies an increasing FRF. Moreover, [25] demonstrated that an upside-down bathtub-shaped MRL corresponds to a bathtub-shaped FRF. In addition, [26] highlighted that the MRL and FRF have a reciprocal relationship expressed as $\lim_{t\to\infty} \mu_X(t) = \lim_{t\to\infty} \frac{1}{h(t)}$. Consequently, a bathtub-shaped MRL implies an upside-down bathtub-shaped FRF. Figure 4 provides a graphical illustration of several relationships between the MRL and FRF for the proposed model at possible $t$.

The asymptotic behavior of the MRL is a key tool for evaluating the long-term reliability of systems. It is particularly useful in complex engineering applications, providing insights into the evolution of system reliability over time, especially for aging or deteriorating components.

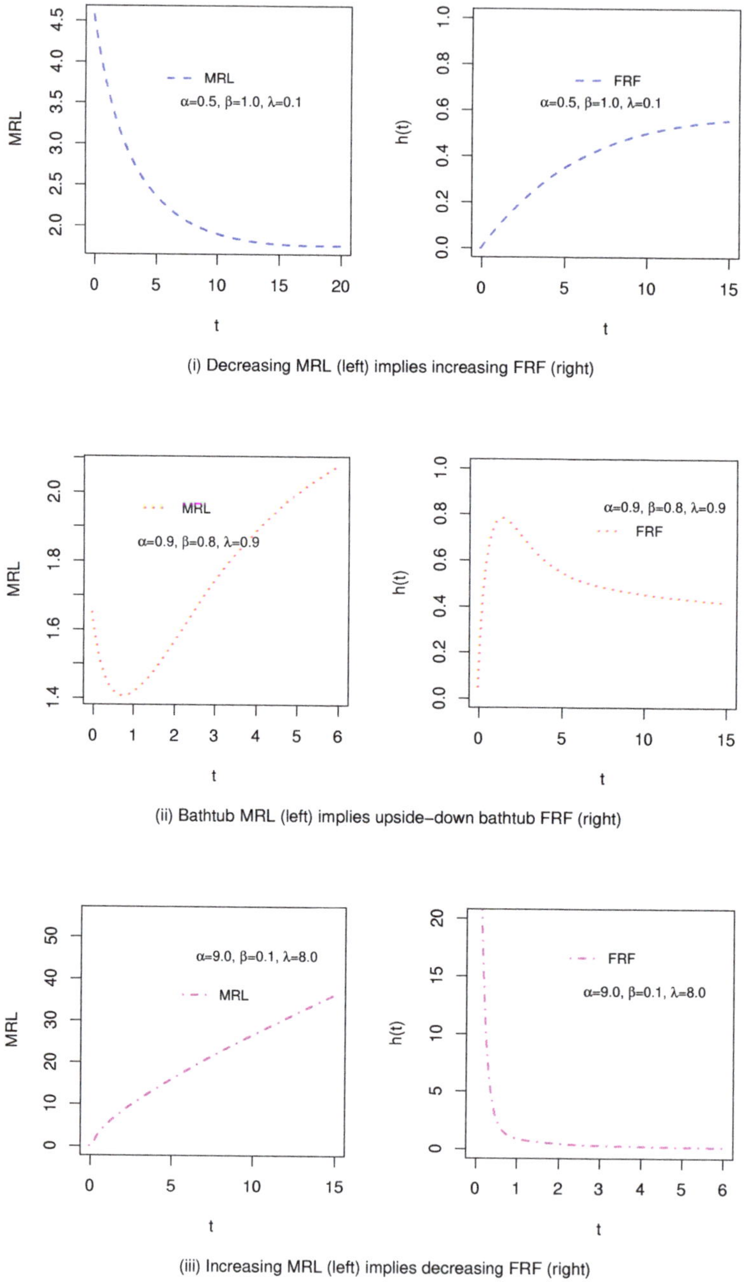


**Figure 4.** Graphical presentation demonstrating the reciprocal relationship between the MRL and FRF of the proposed model for some selected parameters shown in (**i–iii**).

**Theorem 2.** *The asymptote of the MRL of HWE as $t \to \infty$ is*

$$\mu_X(t) \sim \frac{e^{\alpha t^\beta}}{\alpha^{\frac{1}{\beta}}\beta}\Gamma(\frac{1}{\beta}, \alpha\, t^\beta). \tag{9}$$

**Proof.** Let us find the asymptote of $R(x)$ in (4),

$$\lim_{x\to\infty} R(x) \sim e^{-\alpha x^\beta}.$$

Therefore, as $t \to \infty$,

$$\mu_X(t) = E(X - t|X > t) = \int_0^\infty \frac{R(x+t)}{R(t)}dx \sim e^{\alpha t^\beta}\int_0^\infty e^{-\alpha(x+t)^\beta}dx.$$

Setting $u = \alpha(x+t)^\beta$, we obtain

$$\mu_X(t) \sim \frac{e^{\alpha t^\beta}}{\alpha^{\frac{1}{\beta}}\beta}\int_{\alpha t^\beta}^\infty u^{\frac{1}{\beta}-1}\, e^{-u}\, du = \frac{e^{\alpha t^\beta}}{\alpha^{\frac{1}{\beta}}\beta}\Gamma(\frac{1}{\beta}, \alpha\, t^\beta).$$

□

Figure 5 displays how good the asymptote of the MRL of HWE can be used to approximate the actual MRL of the HWE in some possible scenarios using some selected parameter values.

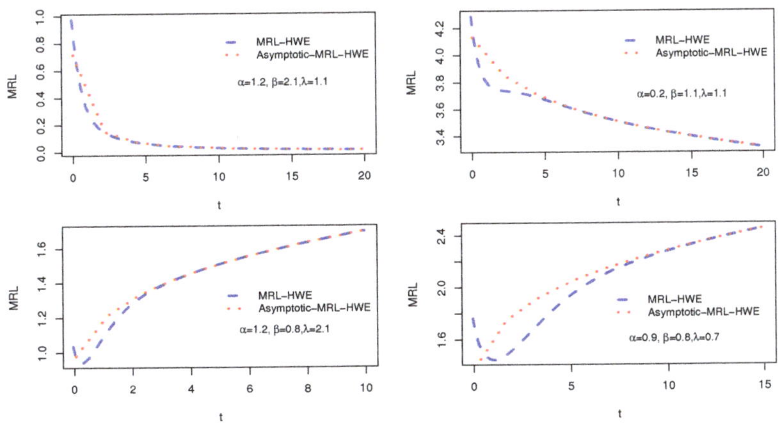


**Figure 5.** Plots of the MRL and asymptote of the MRL of the HWE model.

### 3.4. Order Statistics and Asymptotic Behavior

Let $X_1, X_2, \cdots, X_n$, $n \geq 1$ describe an ordered HWE sample; the $j$-th order statistics PDF is designated by $f_{j:n}(x)$:

$$f_{X_{j:n}}(x) = \sum_{m=0}^{n-j} \frac{n!\,(-1)^m f(x)F^{j+m-1}(x)}{(j-1)!(n-j-m)!\,m!}. \tag{10}$$

Therefore, for $F(x)$ in (6) and $f(x)$ in (3), we have

$$f_{X_{j:n}}(x) = \sum_{m=0}^{n-j} \frac{\alpha\, n!\, (-1)^m \left[\beta x^{\beta-1}(1-e^{-\lambda x}) + \lambda x^{\beta} e^{-\lambda x}\right]}{(j-1)!(n-j-m)!\, m!} \times e^{-\alpha x^{\beta}(1-e^{-\lambda x})} \left(1 - e^{-\alpha x^{\beta}(1-e^{-\lambda x})}\right)^{j+m-1}.$$

Thus, $f_{X_{j:n}}(x)$ can be written as a series of exponentiated-HWE with parameters $j+m-1,\ \alpha, \beta,$ and $\lambda$ as

$$f_{X_{j:n}}(x) = \sum_{m=0}^{n-j} \frac{n!\, (-1)^m\, f(x; j+m-1, \alpha, \beta, \lambda)}{(j+m-1)(j-1)!(n-j-m)!\, m!}.$$

The asymptotic distributions for the extreme order statistics, i.e., the minimum $X_{1:n}$ and maximum $X_{n:n}$ from $X_1, \ldots, X_n$ following HWE are built as follows. For more details and examples, one can see [27].

**Theorem 3.** *Let $X_1, \cdots, X_n$ be a random sample from HWE and let $B_n = (X_{n:n} - a_n)/b_n$; then, $B_n \xrightarrow{d} B$ implies that*

$$\lim_{n\to\infty} P(B_n \le x) = G(x) = e^{-e^{-x}},$$

*$\forall\, x \in \Re$ of $G(x)$ is continuous; $a_n = q(1-n^{-1})$ and $b_n = E[X - a_n | X > a_n]$ can be derived according to Theorem 8.3.4 of [27], where $q(\cdot)$ is the quantile function.*

**Proof.** To follow Theorem 8.3.2 of [27], we start by considering the limit of the MRL in (9) with some algebra, we have

$$\lim_{t\to\infty} E(X - t | X > t) \sim \lim_{t\to\infty} \frac{(\alpha t^{\beta})^{\frac{1}{\beta}-1}}{\alpha^{\frac{1}{\beta}} \beta} \lim_{t\to\infty} \frac{\Gamma(\frac{1}{\beta}, \alpha\, t^{\beta})}{e^{-\alpha t^{\beta}}\ (\alpha t^{\beta})^{\frac{1}{\beta}-1}} = \lim_{t\to\infty} \frac{t^{1-\beta}}{\alpha\beta}.$$

Thus, we can use the above result in Theorem 8.3.2 of [27] as

$$\lim_{t\to\infty} \frac{R(t + xE(X - t|X > t))}{R(t)} \sim \lim_{t\to\infty} \frac{e^{-\alpha\left(t + (\alpha\beta)^{-1} x t^{1-\beta}\right)^{\beta}}}{e^{-\alpha t^{\beta}}} \sim e^{-x}.$$

Clearly, if $\beta = 1$, the result holds; also, by binomial expansion with the power of $\beta \ge 2$ and a natural number, the result holds too. □

**Theorem 4.** *Let $X_1, \cdots, X_n$ be a random sample from HWE and let $B_n^* = (X_{1:n} - a_n^*)/b_n^*$; then, $B_n^* \xrightarrow{d} B^*$ is equivalent to saying*

$$\lim_{n\to\infty} P(B_n^* \le x) = G^*(x) = 1 - e^{-x^{\beta+1}},$$

*for every point $x \in \Re^+$ of $G^*(x)$ for which $G^*(x)$ is continuous. From Theorem 8.3.6 of [27], $a_n^* = 0$ and $b_n^* = q(\frac{1}{n})$, where $q(\cdot)$ is the quantile function.*

**Proof.** We start by

$$\lim_{x\to 0} F(x) \sim \alpha x^{\beta}(1 - e^{-\lambda x}) \sim \alpha\lambda x^{\beta+1}.$$

By Theorem 8.3.6 of [27], we can consider

$$\lim_{t\to 0} \frac{F(tx)}{F(t)} \sim \lim_{t\to 0} \frac{\alpha\lambda (tx)^{\beta+1}}{\alpha\lambda t^{\beta+1}} = x^{\beta+1}.$$

□

### 3.5. Extropy and Cumulative Residual Entropy

The concept of entropy, widely utilized in information theory and other scientific domains, serves as a measure of uncertainty associated with the occurrence of a specific event, given partial information about the event or system. Entropy plays a crucial role in a variety of studies. In this context, we introduce the notions of extropy and cumulative residual entropy. Recently, ref. [28] proposed a novel measure of randomness for a random variable, termed extropy (Ex), which is also regarded as the complement dual of Shannon entropy. For a recent application of Ex, see [29]. The Ex is defined as $Ex = -\frac{1}{2}\int_{-\infty}^{\infty} f^2(x)\,dx$, while the cumulative residual entropy (CRE) is given by $CRE = -\int_{-\infty}^{\infty} R(x)\log R(x)\,dx$, where $R(x)$ denotes the reliability function.

- The Ex for the HWE is calculated as

$$Ex = \sum_{k=0}^{2}\sum_{i=0}^{\infty}\sum_{j=0}^{k+i} \psi_{i,j,k}(\alpha,\beta,\lambda)\Gamma(\beta(i+2)-k+1).$$

where $\psi_{i,j,k}(\alpha,\beta,\lambda) = \binom{2}{k}\binom{k+i}{j}\frac{(-1)^{i+j+1}\alpha^{2+i}2^i\beta^k\lambda^{2-k}}{2\,i!\,[\lambda(j+2-k)]^{\beta(i+2)-k+1}}$.

- The CRE of the HWE model is derived as

$$CRE = \sum_{i=0}^{\infty}\sum_{j=0}^{i+1} \frac{\binom{i+1}{j}(-1)^{i+j}\alpha^{i+1}}{[\lambda j]^{\beta(i+1)+1}\,i!}\Gamma(\beta(i+1)+1).$$

Next, we discuss the nature of the above measures when the parameters values are growing. Figure 6 illustrated that for a fixed $\alpha = 1$, the Ex is decreasing when both $\beta$ and $\lambda$ are increasing in the interval $[0.001, 5]$; further, the CRE decreases as both $\beta$ and $\lambda$ increase within the interval $[0.8, 5]$.

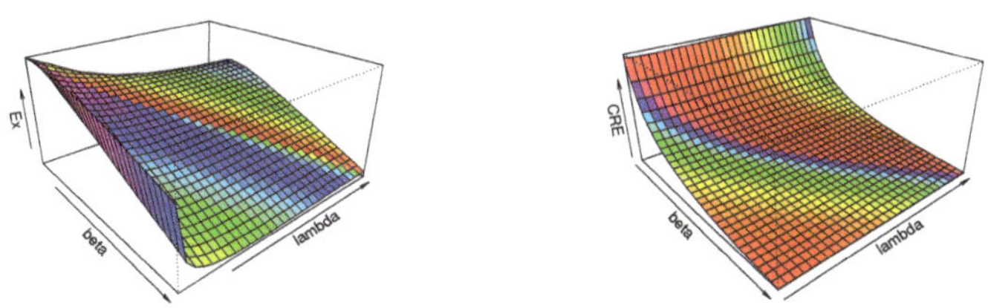


**Figure 6.** Plots of the Ex and CRE of the HWE for a fixed value of $\alpha = 1$.

### 3.6. Identifiability of the HWE

Assessing the identifiability of a distribution with respect to its parameters involves determining whether sufficient information exists to differentiate between distinct parameter values within the distribution. The Kullback–Leibler divergence (KLD) is a widely used method for examining parameter identifiability, as highlighted by [30]. In this study, we outline the standard criterion for evaluating identifiability in statistical distributions as follows:

Let $\Lambda(t,\gamma)$ be a statistical model. The parameter $\gamma \in \mathbf{R}^d$ is locally (globally) identifiable if and only if $\gamma$ is the unique solution of the equation $KLD(\gamma,\delta) = 0$ *in* $\mathbf{R}^d$ (an open neighborhood of $\gamma$), where

$$KLD(\gamma,\delta) = \mathbb{E}_\gamma\left(\log\frac{\Lambda(t,\gamma)}{\Lambda(t,\delta)}\right) = \int \Lambda(t,\gamma)\log\frac{\Lambda(t,\gamma)}{\Lambda(t,\delta)}\mathrm{d}t. \quad (11)$$

Note that $KLD(\gamma,\delta) \geq 0$ for all $\delta$. Furthermore, $KLD(\gamma,\delta) = 0 \Longleftrightarrow \Lambda(\boldsymbol{t},\gamma) = \Lambda(\boldsymbol{t},\delta)$ almost everywhere for $\boldsymbol{t} \in \mathbf{R}^d$. However, it is important to highlight that obtaining an analytical solution for (11) is often challenging due to the complexity of many density functions; see [30,31] for more details.

In this study, we define and compute the equation $KLD(\gamma,\delta)$ for our model numerically. Suppose we have two random variables, $X_1 \sim \text{HWE}(\gamma)$ and $X_2 \sim \text{HWE}(\delta)$, where $\gamma = (\alpha^\circ, \beta^\circ, \lambda^\circ)'$ and $\delta = (\alpha^*, \beta^*, \lambda^*)'$. Then, based on (11), we can express

$$\begin{aligned} KLD(\gamma,\delta) &= \mathbb{E}_\gamma\left(\log\frac{f_1(\boldsymbol{x}|\gamma)}{f_2(\boldsymbol{x}|\delta)}\right) \\ &= \int_0^\infty f_1(x|\gamma)\log[f_1(x|\gamma)]dx - \int_0^\infty f_1(x|\gamma)\log[f_2(x|\delta)]dx. \end{aligned} \tag{12}$$

By substituting the PDFs of $f_1$ and $f_2$ into (12), we obtain

$$\begin{aligned} KLD(\gamma,\delta) = &\int_0^\infty \alpha^\circ\left[\beta^\circ x^{\beta^\circ-1}(1-e^{-\lambda^\circ x}) + \lambda^\circ x^{\beta^\circ}e^{-\lambda^\circ x}\right]e^{-\alpha^\circ x^{\beta^\circ}(1-e^{-\lambda^\circ x})} \\ &\times \log\left[\alpha^\circ\left[\beta^\circ x^{\beta^\circ-1}(1-e^{-\lambda^\circ x}) + \lambda^\circ x^{\beta^\circ}e^{-\lambda^\circ x}\right]e^{-\alpha^\circ x^{\beta^\circ}(1-e^{-\lambda^\circ x})}\right]dx \\ &- \int_0^\infty \alpha^\circ\left[\beta^\circ x^{\beta^\circ-1}(1-e^{-\lambda^\circ x}) + \lambda^\circ x^{\beta^\circ}e^{-\lambda^\circ x}\right]e^{-\alpha^\circ x^{\beta^\circ}(1-e^{-\lambda^\circ x})} \\ &\times \log\left[\alpha^*\left[\beta^* x^{\beta^*-1}(1-e^{-\lambda^* x}) + \lambda^* x^{\beta^*}e^{-\lambda^* x}\right]e^{-\alpha^* x^{\beta^*}(1-e^{-\lambda^* x})}\right]dx. \end{aligned} \tag{13}$$

Here, $\gamma$ and $\delta$ represent vectors of real values derived from $(\alpha,\beta,\lambda)'$. Solving (13) analytically may be infeasible; therefore, we adopt a numerical approach using the one-dimensional integral function in `R`-software by selecting specific cases to examine identifiability. We consider three cases of $\gamma$:

- Case I: $\gamma = (\alpha^\circ = 1.5, \beta^\circ = 1.2, \lambda^\circ = 3.0)'$.
- Case II: $\gamma = (\alpha^\circ = 0.5, \beta^\circ = 0.9, \lambda^\circ = 0.8)'$.
- Case III: $\gamma = (\alpha^\circ = 5.0, \beta^\circ = 8.0, \lambda^\circ = 12.0)'$.

Also, we form eight different $\delta$ based on the cases I, II, and III, where $\gamma \neq \delta$ in the seventh cases and $\gamma = \delta$ in the eighth case. The computed results for all cases are presented in Table 3. The results indicate that $KLD(\gamma,\delta) > 0$ in the first seven cases, while it equals zero when $\gamma = \delta$. These findings substantiate the identifiability of the HWE. However, we acknowledge that these specific cases are not enough to generalize conclusions about the local or global identifiability of the HWE based on its parameters.

**Table 3.** Numerical evaluation of identifiability of the HWE model based on some parameters values (13).

| Case I | Hypothesis $\gamma \neq \delta$ and $\gamma = \delta$ | $KLD(\gamma,\delta)$ | Absolute Error |
|---|---|---|---|
| 1 | $\alpha^\circ \neq \alpha^*, \beta^\circ = \beta^*, \lambda^\circ = \lambda^*$ | $0.07213 > 0$ | $1.9 \times 10^{-05}$ |
| 2 | $\alpha^\circ = \alpha^*, \beta^\circ \neq \beta^*, \lambda^\circ = \lambda^*$ | $0.63184 > 0$ | $7.8 \times 10^{-05}$ |
| 3 | $\alpha^\circ = \alpha^*, \beta^\circ = \beta^*, \lambda^\circ \neq \lambda^*$ | $0.001113 > 0$ | $6.9 \times 10^{-05}$ |
| 4 | $\alpha^\circ \neq \alpha^*, \beta^\circ \neq \beta^*, \lambda^\circ = \lambda^*$ | $0.21883 > 0$ | $7.3 \times 10^{-05}$ |
| 5 | $\alpha^\circ \neq \alpha^*, \beta^\circ = \beta^*, \lambda^\circ \neq \lambda^*$ | $0.02205 > 0$ | $8.2 \times 10^{-05}$ |
| 6 | $\alpha^\circ = \alpha^*, \beta^\circ \neq \beta^*, \lambda^\circ \neq \lambda^*$ | $0.02658 > 0$ | $6.0 \times 10^{-05}$ |
| 7 | $\alpha^\circ \neq \alpha^*, \beta^\circ \neq \beta^*, \lambda^\circ \neq \lambda^*$ | $0.35663 > 0$ | $4.0 \times 10^{-05}$ |
| 8 | $\alpha^\circ = \alpha^*, \beta^\circ = \beta^*, \lambda^\circ = \lambda^*$ | 0 | 0 |

**Table 3.** *Cont.*

| | | | |
|---|---|---|---|
| **Case II** | | | |
| 1 | $\alpha^\circ \neq \alpha^*, \beta^\circ = \beta^*, \lambda^\circ = \lambda^*$ | $2.39056 > 0$ | 0.00011 |
| 2 | $\alpha^\circ = \alpha^*, \beta^\circ \neq \beta^*, \lambda^\circ = \lambda^*$ | $2.84839 > 0$ | $7.3 \times 10^{-05}$ |
| 3 | $\alpha^\circ = \alpha^*, \beta^\circ = \beta^*, \lambda^\circ \neq \lambda^*$ | $0.03128 > 0$ | $6.6 \times 10^{-05}$ |
| 4 | $\alpha^\circ \neq \alpha^*, \beta^\circ \neq \beta^*, \lambda^\circ = \lambda^*$ | $11.69699 > 0$ | 0.0014 |
| 5 | $\alpha^\circ \neq \alpha^*, \beta^\circ = \beta^*, \lambda^\circ \neq \lambda^*$ | $1.14845 > 0$ | 0.000011 |
| 6 | $\alpha^\circ = \alpha^*, \beta^\circ \neq \beta^*, \lambda^\circ \neq \lambda^*$ | $2.89721 > 0$ | $7.3 \times 10^{-05}$ |
| 7 | $\alpha^\circ \neq \alpha^*, \beta^\circ \neq \beta^*, \lambda^\circ \neq \lambda^*$ | $12.15810 > 0$ | 0.00120 |
| 8 | $\alpha^\circ = \alpha^*, \beta^\circ = \beta^*, \lambda^\circ = \lambda^*$ | 0 | 0 |
| **Case III** | | | |
| 1 | $\alpha^\circ \neq \alpha^*, \beta^\circ = \beta^*, \lambda^\circ = \lambda^*$ | $1.40259 > 0$ | $7.1 \times 10^{-06}$ |
| 2 | $\alpha^\circ = \alpha^*, \beta^\circ \neq \beta^*, \lambda^\circ = \lambda^*$ | $3.381249 > 0$ | $1.3 \times 10^{-05}$ |
| 3 | $\alpha^\circ = \alpha^*, \beta^\circ = \beta^*, \lambda^\circ \neq \lambda^*$ | $1.42533 > 0$ | $6.5 \times 10^{-06}$ |
| 4 | $\alpha^\circ \neq \alpha^*, \beta^\circ \neq \beta^*, \lambda^\circ = \lambda^*$ | $2.03998 > 0$ | $1.9 \times 10^{-05}$ |
| 5 | $\alpha^\circ \neq \alpha^*, \beta^\circ = \beta^*, \lambda^\circ \neq \lambda^*$ | $1.35215 > 0$ | $1.2 \times 10^{-05}$ |
| 6 | $\alpha^\circ = \alpha^*, \beta^\circ \neq \beta^*, \lambda^\circ \neq \lambda^*$ | $3.63908 > 0$ | $1.4 \times 10^{-05}$ |
| 7 | $\alpha^\circ \neq \alpha^*, \beta^\circ \neq \beta^*, \lambda^\circ \neq \lambda^*$ | $3.32781 > 0$ | $2.2 \times 10^{-05}$ |
| 8 | $\alpha^\circ = \alpha^*, \beta^\circ = \beta^*, \lambda^\circ = \lambda^*$ | 0 | 0 |

## 4. Estimation

In this section, MLE is used for parameter estimation and to aid in model comparison. Let $x_1, \cdots, x_n$ be observed values from a sample of size $n$ that follow the proposed hybrid-w-G. Let $\boldsymbol{\Theta} = (\xi, \zeta)^T$; then, the MLEs of $\boldsymbol{\Theta}$—that is, $\hat{\boldsymbol{\Theta}} = (\hat{\xi}, \hat{\zeta})^T$—can be obtained by the maximization of $L(\Theta)$ :

$$\log L = \sum_{i=1}^{n} \log[w'(x_i;\xi)G(x_i;\zeta) + w(x_i;\xi)g(x_i;\zeta)] - \sum_{i=1}^{n} w(x_i;\xi)G(x_i;\zeta). \quad (14)$$

Alternatively, maximizing the following equations can be accomplished using an iterative method such as Broyden–Fletcher–Goldfarb–Shanno (BFGS) algorithm through the `maxLik` package in R software [32].

$$\frac{\partial \log L}{\partial \xi} = \sum_{i=1}^{n} \frac{w'(x_i;\xi)^{\xi'} G(x_i;\zeta) + w(x_i;\xi)^{\xi'} g(x_i;\zeta)}{w'(x_i;\xi)G(x_i;\zeta) + w(x_i;\xi)g(x_i;\zeta)} - \sum_{i=1}^{n} w(x_i;\xi)^{\xi'} G(x_i;\zeta)$$

$$\frac{\partial \log L}{\partial \zeta} = \sum_{i=1}^{n} \frac{w'(x_i;\xi)G(x_i;\zeta)^{\zeta'} + w(x_i;\xi)g(x_i;\zeta)^{\zeta'}}{w'(x_i;\xi)G(x_i;\zeta) + w(x_i;\xi)g(x_i;\zeta)} - \sum_{i=1}^{n} w(x_i;\xi)G(x_i;\zeta)^{\zeta'}.$$

where $\frac{\partial}{\partial \xi}(\frac{\partial w}{\partial x}) = w'(x_i;\xi)^{\xi'}$. The asymptotic distribution of the estimator $\hat{\boldsymbol{\Theta}}$ can be approximated by $N_{p+q}(0, \hat{J}^{-1})$, a multivariate normal, provided the standard boundary conditions for the parameters are satisfied. Here, $p$ and $q$ represent the number of parameters associated with the components $\xi$ and $\zeta$, respectively. The matrix $J$ in this context is defined as the Hessian matrix of the $L(\boldsymbol{\Theta})$, with its elements given by the second-order partial derivatives:

$$J_{ij} = \frac{\partial^2 \log L(\boldsymbol{\Theta})}{\partial \boldsymbol{\Theta}_i \partial \boldsymbol{\Theta}_j}, \quad \text{for } i, j = 1, \ldots, p + q.$$

where $\boldsymbol{\Theta}_r$ and $r$ denote the $r^{\text{th}}$ parameter in the vector $\boldsymbol{\Theta}$, an asymptotic confidence interval (ACI) can be constructed. The confidence interval provides an estimate of the range within which the true value of $\boldsymbol{\Theta}_r$ is expected to lie with a specified level of confidence, denoted by $100(1-\epsilon)\%$. This interval is derived as

$$ACI_r = \left(\boldsymbol{\Theta}_r \pm \omega_{\epsilon/2}\sqrt{\hat{J}_{rr}}\right).$$

where $\hat{J}_{rr}$ is the $(r,r)$th diagonal element of the inverse Hessian matrix $\hat{J}^{-1}$, which represents the estimated variance of $\mathbf{\Theta}_r$. $\omega_{\epsilon/2}$ is the $(1-\epsilon/2)$ quantile of the standard normal distribution, providing the critical value for the specified confidence level.

This approach ensures that the confidence intervals are asymptotically valid, meaning that they are reliable when the sample size is sufficiently large. The use of the Hessian matrix, a critical component in the computation, reflects the curvature of the log-likelihood function, thereby encapsulating information about parameter variability. Such intervals are particularly useful in assessing the precision of parameter estimates in complex models where analytical solutions may not be feasible.

*Simulation Results I*

In this section, we assess the MLEs for the parameters of the HWE. Following the procedures outlined in Section 3.1, we generate some moderate random samples of sizes $n = 50, 100, 150, 200$ from the HWE using specific parameters and replicate this process $N = 1000$ times. The selected parameters allow us to explore a variety of distributional behaviors (shape), which we assumed to capture a broad range of possible scenarios relevant to various applications. For each sample, we compute the MLEs, and evaluate their biases and mean squared errors (MSEs). As evident from Tables 4 and 5, the bias tends to decrease as the sample size grows, often approaching zero. This trend suggests that the accuracy of the estimates increases with larger sample sizes. Additionally, the MSE consistently diminishes as the sample size expands, indicating an overall enhancement in the precision and reliability of the estimates with increasing sample sizes. Particularly, we observe that when $\alpha = 1.4, \beta = 0.6$, and $\lambda = 1.8$, the estimates converge well as $n$ increases, with a noticeable decrease in bias and MSE. For lower values of $\alpha$ and $\lambda$, such as $\alpha = 0.3, \beta = 0.5$, and $\lambda = 0.3$, estimates remain close to the true values even for smaller $n$ and exhibit low MSEs. For small sample sizes ($n = 50$), the estimates tend to have noticeable bias and higher MSE. Parameters such as $\lambda = 1.0$ and $\lambda = 0.6$ show instability at smaller $n$, but this improves significantly by $n = 100$ or more. The estimation of $\beta$ appears more stable across different values of $n$.

**Table 4.** Simulation results for HWE: the average estimate (AE), MSE, and Bias in parenthesis-I.

| n | | $\alpha = 1.1$ | $\beta = 0.5$ | $\lambda = 1.1$ | $\alpha = 1.4$ | $\beta = 0.6$ | $\lambda = 1.8$ |
|---|---|---|---|---|---|---|---|
| 50 | AE | 1.1647 | 0.5215 | 1.0525 | 1.9986 | 0.6703 | 1.5355 |
| | MSE | 0.7286 | 0.0421 | 0.6053 | 0.1876 | 0.0895 | 0.7451 |
| | Bias | (1.0647) | (0.0215) | (0.9525) | (3.5986) | (0.0703) | (0.7355) |
| 100 | | 1.2153 | 0.5234 | 1.4455 | 1.5015 | 0.6379 | 1.9396 |
| | | 0.6799 | 0.0217 | 0.5096 | 0.1236 | 0.0569 | 0.2240 |
| | | (0.1153) | (0.0234) | (0.3455) | (1.1015) | (0.0379) | (0.3996) |
| 150 | | 1.1779 | 0.5088 | 1.2756 | 1.8160 | 0.6488 | 1.6290 |
| | | 0.2454 | 0.0137 | 0.5017 | 0.1173 | 0.0452 | 0.1857 |
| | | (0.0779) | (0.0088) | (0.1756) | (0.4160) | (0.0488) | (0.3690) |
| 200 | | 1.1249 | 0.5155 | 1.2585 | 1.4845 | 0.6326 | 1.6060 |
| | | 0.0865 | 0.0097 | 0.3963 | 0.0861 | 0.0357 | 0.0780 |
| | | (0.0249) | (0.0155) | (0.1585) | (0.2845) | (0.0326) | (0.2660) |

**Table 4.** *Cont.*

| n | $\alpha = 0.4$ | $\beta = 0.6$ | $\lambda = 1.0$ | $\alpha = 0.5$ | $\beta = 0.5$ | $\lambda = 0.5$ |
|---|---|---|---|---|---|---|
| 50 | 0.4686 | 0.6129 | 1.1136 | 0.5993 | 0.5249 | 0.7617 |
| | 0.2696 | 0.0208 | 0.7570 | 0.7640 | 0.0217 | 1.4837 |
| | (0.0686) | (0.0129) | (2.4136) | (0.0993) | (0.0249) | (0.2617) |
| 100 | 0.4207 | 0.6112 | 1.0092 | 0.5410 | 0.5175 | 0.7202 |
| | 0.0324 | 0.0106 | 0.3579 | 0.6182 | 0.0102 | 1.3801 |
| | (0.0207) | (0.0112) | (0.3092) | (0.0410) | (0.0175) | (0.2202) |
| 150 | 0.4117 | 0.6082 | 0.9483 | 0.5087 | 0.5086 | 0.5573 |
| | 0.0310 | 0.0064 | 0.2896 | 0.0194 | 0.0055 | 0.0523 |
| | (0.0117) | (0.0082) | (0.2483) | (0.0087) | (0.0086) | (0.0573) |
| 200 | 0.4091 | 0.6059 | 0.7651 | 0.5045 | 0.5086 | 0.5580 |
| | 0.0093 | 0.0048 | 0.0877 | 0.0134 | 0.0046 | 0.0142 |
| | (0.0091) | (0.0059) | (0.0651) | (0.0045) | (0.0086) | (0.0580) |
| n | $\alpha = 0.6$ | $\beta = 0.5$ | $\lambda = 0.6$ | $\alpha = 0.3$ | $\beta = 0.5$ | $\lambda = 0.3$ |
| 50 | 0.6297 | 0.5232 | 0.9092 | 0.3227 | 0.5219 | 0.4598 |
| | 0.2717 | 0.0170 | 1.8623 | 0.0422 | 0.0128 | 0.7901 |
| | (0.1297) | (0.0232) | (0.3092) | (0.0227) | (0.0219) | (0.1598) |
| 100 | 0.5216 | 0.5139 | 0.7284 | 0.3114 | 0.5077 | 0.4754 |
| | 0.0917 | 0.0087 | 0.3203 | 0.0131 | 0.0057 | 0.6813 |
| | (0.0216) | (0.0139) | (0.1284) | (0.0114) | (0.0077) | (0.1754) |
| 150 | 0.5123 | 0.5078 | 0.6834 | 0.3032 | 0.5084 | 0.3400 |
| | 0.0222 | 0.0053 | 0.2814 | 0.0062 | 0.0040 | 0.0688 |
| | (0.0123) | (0.0078) | (0.0834) | (0.0032) | (0.0084) | (0.0400) |
| 200 | 0.5090 | 0.5040 | 0.6375 | 0.3036 | 0.5057 | 0.3211 |
| | 0.0111 | 0.0035 | 0.0435 | 0.0047 | 0.0029 | 0.0140 |
| | (0.0090) | (0.0040) | (0.0375) | (0.0036) | (0.0057) | (0.0211) |
| n | $\alpha = 0.8$ | $\beta = 0.8$ | $\lambda = 0.8$ | $\alpha = 0.4$ | $\beta = 0.6$ | $\lambda = 0.4$ |
| 50 | 0.7147 | 0.7650 | 1.0193 | 0.5665 | 0.6335 | 0.5399 |
| | 0.8917 | 0.0858 | 1.0267 | 1.7151 | 0.0321 | 0.4472 |
| | (2.9147) | (−0.0350) | (0.2193) | (0.1665) | (0.0335) | (0.5399) |
| 100 | 0.8418 | 0.7839 | 0.9830 | 0.4531 | 0.6103 | 0.5258 |
| | 0.5853 | 0.0592 | 0.6344 | 0.0893 | 0.0168 | 0.3194 |
| | (1.0418) | (−0.0161) | (0.1830) | (0.0531) | (0.0103) | (0.1258) |
| 150 | 1.3960 | 0.7783 | 0.9133 | 0.4310 | 0.6107 | 0.4760 |
| | 0.5329 | 0.0478 | 0.4175 | 0.0626 | 0.0115 | 0.0842 |
| | (0.5960) | (−0.0217) | (0.1133) | (0.0310) | (0.0107) | (0.0760) |
| 200 | 1.0949 | 0.7952 | 0.9480 | 0.4201 | 0.6079 | 0.4593 |
| | 0.4051 | 0.0371 | 0.4013 | 0.0464 | 0.0087 | 0.0655 |
| | (0.2949) | (−0.0048) | (0.1480) | (0.0201) | (0.0079) | (0.0593) |

**Table 5.** Simulation results for HWE: the average estimate (AE), MSE, and Bias in parenthesis-II.

| n | | $\alpha = 0.1$ | $\beta = 0.5$ | $\lambda = 0.1$ | $\alpha = 0.4$ | $\beta = 0.6$ | $\lambda = 0.7$ |
|---|---|---|---|---|---|---|---|
| 50 | AE | 0.1044 | 0.5232 | 0.2293 | 0.5777 | 0.6131 | 1.1722 |
| | MSE | 0.0068 | 0.0087 | 1.2860 | 0.7409 | 0.0218 | 1.5306 |
| | Bias | (0.0044) | (0.0232) | (0.3293) | (0.1777) | (0.0131) | (0.4722) |
| 100 | | 0.1023 | 0.5105 | 0.2808 | 0.4282 | 0.6058 | 0.9120 |
| | | 0.0016 | 0.0039 | 1.2025 | 0.0599 | 0.0103 | 1.0262 |
| | | (0.0023) | (0.0105) | (0.1808) | (0.0282) | (0.0058) | (0.2120) |
| 150 | | 0.1006 | 0.5077 | 0.1517 | 0.4102 | 0.6081 | 0.8076 |
| | | 0.0009 | 0.0026 | 0.0587 | 0.0174 | 0.0067 | 0.4280 |
| | | (0.0006) | (0.0077) | (0.0517) | (0.0102) | (0.0081) | (0.1076) |
| 200 | | 0.1019 | 0.5035 | 0.1203 | 0.4036 | 0.6091 | 0.7943 |
| | | 0.0007 | 0.0019 | 0.0146 | 0.0088 | 0.0048 | 0.1282 |
| | | (0.0019) | (0.0035) | (0.0203) | (0.0036) | (0.0091) | (0.0943) |

**Table 5.** *Cont.*

| n | $\alpha = 0.4$ | $\beta = 0.3$ | $\lambda = 0.5$ | $\alpha = 2.0$ | $\beta = 0.9$ | $\lambda = 0.9$ |
|---|---|---|---|---|---|---|
| 50 | 0.4072 | 0.3109 | 0.5049 | 2.3740 | 0.8766 | 1.1057 |
| | 0.0153 | 0.0031 | 0.9124 | 1.3627 | 0.0972 | 1.1911 |
| | (0.0072) | (0.0109) | (0.1049) | (3.4740) | (−0.0234) | (0.2057) |
| 100 | 0.4076 | 0.3031 | 0.4218 | 1.6541 | 0.8622 | 1.0649 |
| | 0.0077 | 0.0014 | 0.0190 | 0.7120 | 0.0777 | 0.8293 |
| | (0.0076) | (0.0031) | (0.0218) | (1.7541) | (−0.0378) | (0.1649) |
| 150 | 0.4017 | 0.3029 | 0.4200 | 1.7929 | 0.8673 | 1.0268 |
| | 0.0043 | 0.0008 | 0.0114 | 0.0845 | 0.0596 | 0.6346 |
| | (0.0017) | (0.0029) | (0.0200) | (0.8929) | (−0.0327) | (0.1268) |
| 200 | 0.4027 | 0.3025 | 0.4137 | 1.3375 | 0.8809 | 1.0378 |
| | 0.0036 | 0.0006 | 0.0096 | 0.0197 | 0.0471 | 0.5277 |
| | (0.0027) | (0.0025) | (0.0137) | (0.4375) | (−0.0191) | (0.1378) |
| n | $\alpha = 1.0$ | $\beta = 0.9$ | $\lambda = 0.3$ | $\alpha = 1.5$ | $\beta = 1.1$ | $\lambda = 1.1$ |
| 50 | 1.4472 | 0.8512 | 0.3481 | 1.5807 | 1.0737 | 1.2864 |
| | 0.6709 | 0.0949 | 0.1440 | 0.8743 | 0.1247 | 0.5345 |
| | (1.1472) | (−0.0488) | (0.0481) | (4.4807) | (−0.0263) | (0.1864) |
| 100 | 1.0783 | 0.8539 | 0.3353 | 1.4598 | 1.0450 | 1.2122 |
| | 0.4591 | 0.0722 | 0.0738 | 0.8636 | 0.0907 | 0.1647 |
| | (0.7783) | (−0.0461) | (0.0353) | (2.5598) | (−0.0550) | (0.1122) |
| 150 | 0.7613 | 0.8472 | 0.3092 | 1.5477 | 1.0681 | 1.2462 |
| | 0.5897 | 0.0540 | 0.0460 | 0.8000 | 0.0757 | 0.0507 |
| | (0.4613) | (−0.0528) | (0.0092) | (1.4477) | (−0.0319) | (0.1462) |
| 200 | 0.9864 | 0.8538 | 0.3067 | 1.7882 | 1.0840 | 1.2905 |
| | 0.3148 | 0.0465 | 0.0386 | 0.5194 | 0.0574 | 0.0201 |
| | (0.2864) | (−0.0462) | (0.0067) | (0.6882) | (−0.0160) | (0.1905) |
| n | $\alpha = 1.1$ | $\beta = 1.1$ | $\lambda = 1.1$ | $\alpha = 0.5$ | $\beta = 0.1$ | $\lambda = 0.5$ |
| 50 | 1.2415 | 1.1620 | 1.4288 | 0.5724 | 0.0504 | 0.6447 |
| | 0.0672 | 0.1382 | 0.9878 | 0.2326 | 0.0927 | 0.3110 |
| | (0.9415) | (−0.0380) | (0.1288) | (0.4724) | (−0.0496) | (0.5447) |
| 100 | 1.2692 | 1.1377 | 1.4034 | 0.5909 | 0.0472 | 0.6221 |
| | 0.0460 | 0.0992 | 0.5514 | 0.2018 | 0.0028 | 0.2776 |
| | (0.9692) | (−0.0623) | (0.1034) | (0.4909) | (−0.0528) | (0.5221) |
| 150 | 1.0112 | 1.1631 | 1.4532 | 0.5936 | 0.064 | 0.6122 |
| | 0.0379 | 0.0786 | 0.3995 | 0.1036 | 0.0020 | 0.2048 |
| | (0.7112) | (−0.0369) | (0.1532) | (0.4936) | (−0.0536) | (0.5122) |
| 200 | 1.0366 | 1.1696 | 1.4625 | 0.5032 | 0.0463 | 0.6060 |
| | 0.0148 | 0.0308 | 0.2053 | 0.0115 | 0.0002 | 0.1006 |
| | (0.2366) | (−0.0304) | (0.1625) | (0.4932) | (−0.0537) | (0.5060) |

## 5. Stress–Strength Reliability Parameter $R_s$

In mechanical reliability analysis, the stress–strength (SS) parameter, denoted as $R_s = P(X < Y)$, plays a vital role in evaluating system performance. This parameter represents the probability that the strength $Y$ of a component exceeds the applied stress $X$, with system failure occurring when the stress surpasses the strength. Beyond its primary application in reliability studies, $R_s$ is also a critical measure for comparing two distinct populations, making it applicable across various fields [33]. These fields include engineering, biomedical sciences, and economics, where the parameter's usage is well-documented. Research on the SS-parameter $R_s$, under the assumption that $X$ and $Y$ are independent random variables, spans multiple distribution models. Examples under various perspectives include the studies on the generalized-exponential distribution [34], inverse Pareto [35], Poisson half logistic [36], Weibull distribution [37,38], weighted exponential-Lindley [39], Weibull [40], two-parameter exponential [41], alpha power exponential [42], and bivariate iterated Farlie–Gumbel–Morgenstern [43], among others.

Next, we outline the formulation of a reliability parameter within the context of the HWE. Let $X$ be a random variable with a density function $f_1(x;\alpha,\beta_1,\lambda)$, and let $Y$ be another random variable with a cumulative distribution function $F_2(y;\alpha,\beta_2,\lambda)$, where $X$ and $Y$ are independent. The SS-reliability parameter is then obtained using the computations described in (8).

$$R_s = \int_0^\infty f_1(x)F_2(x)dx$$
$$= \alpha \int_0^\infty \left[\beta_1 x^{\beta_1-1}(1-e^{-\lambda x}) + \lambda x^{\beta_1} e^{-\lambda x}\right]\left(1 - e^{-\alpha x^{\beta_2}(1-e^{-\lambda x})}\right) e^{-\alpha x^{\beta_1}(1-e^{-\lambda x})}\, dx,$$

thus,

$$R_s = 1 - \left[\sum_{i,j,k=0}^{\infty} \rho^{(1)*}_{i,j,k}\,\Gamma(\beta_1(j+1)+\beta_2 i) + \sum_{i,j,l=0}^{\infty} \rho^{(2)*}_{i,j,l}\,\Gamma(\beta_1(j+1)+\beta_2 i+1)\right].$$

Here, $\rho^{(1)*}_{i,j,k} = \frac{\beta_1\,\alpha^{i+j+1}\,(-1)^{i+j+k}\binom{i+j+1}{k}}{i!\,j!\,[\lambda k]^{\beta_1(j+1)+\beta_2 i}}$ and $\rho^{(2)*}_{i,j,l} = \frac{\lambda\,\alpha^{i+j}\,(-1)^{i+j+l}\binom{i+j}{l}}{i!\,j!\,[\lambda l]^{\beta_1(j+1)+\beta_2 i+1}}$.

Consider the random variables $X_1, X_2, \ldots, X_n$, where $n \geq 1$, as a sample of independent observations drawn from the $HWE(\alpha,\beta_1,\lambda)$ distribution, and $Y_1, Y_2, \ldots, Y_m$, where $m \geq 1$, as a sample of independent observations drawn from the $HWE(\alpha,\beta_2,\lambda)$ distribution. The observed values of these samples are denoted by $x_1, x_2, \ldots, x_n$ and $y_1, y_2, \ldots, y_m$, respectively. Let $\theta = (\alpha,\beta_1,\beta_2,\lambda)^T$ represent the vector of parameters, and let $\hat{\theta} = (\hat{\alpha},\hat{\beta}_1,\hat{\beta}_2,\hat{\lambda})^T$ denote the MLE of $\theta$. Further, let $\hat{R}_s$ denote the estimator of $R_s$. The log-likelihood function is then expressed as

$$\log L_{R_s} = (n+m)\log\alpha + \sum_{i=1}^{n}\log\left[\beta_1 x_i^{\beta_1-1}(1-e^{-\lambda x_i}) + \lambda x_i^{\beta_1} e^{-\lambda x_i}\right] - \alpha\sum_{i=1}^{n} x_i^{\beta_1}(1-e^{-\lambda x_i})$$
$$+ \sum_{j=1}^{m}\log\left[\beta_2 y_j^{\beta_2-1}(1-e^{-\lambda y_j}) + \lambda y_j^{\beta_2} e^{-\lambda y_j}\right] - \alpha\sum_{j=1}^{m} y_j^{\beta_2}(1-e^{-\lambda y_j})$$

Similarly, this can be accomplished using an iterative approach, such as the Broyden–Fletcher–Goldfarb–Shanno (BFGS) algorithm, to solve the nonlinear equation provided below. This method is implemented through the `maxLik` package [32] in the R programming environment.

$$\frac{\partial \log L_{R_s}}{\partial \alpha} = \frac{n+m}{\alpha} - \sum_{i=1}^{n} x_i^{\beta_1}(1-e^{-\lambda x_i}) - \sum_{j=1}^{m} y_j^{\beta_2}(1-e^{-\lambda y_j})$$

$$\frac{\partial \log L_{R_s}}{\partial \beta_1} = \sum_{i=1}^{n} \frac{x_i^{\beta_1-1}(1-e^{-\lambda x_i}) + \beta_1 x_i^{\beta_1-1}(1-e^{-\lambda x_i})\log x_i + \lambda x_i^{\beta_1}(1-e^{-\lambda x_i})\log x_i}{\left[\beta_1 x_i^{\beta_1-1}(1-e^{-\lambda x_i}) + \lambda x_i^{\beta_1} e^{-\lambda x_i}\right]}$$
$$- \alpha\sum_{i=1}^{n} x_i^{\beta_1}(1-e^{-\lambda x_i})\log x_i$$

$$\frac{\partial \log L_{R_s}}{\partial \beta_2} = \sum_{j=1}^{m} \frac{y_j^{\beta_2-1}(1-e^{-\lambda y_j}) + \beta_2 y_j^{\beta_2-1}(1-e^{-\lambda y_j})\log y_j + \lambda y_j^{\beta_2}(1-e^{-\lambda y_j})\log y_j}{\left[\beta_2 y_j^{\beta_2-1}(1-e^{-\lambda y_j}) + \lambda y_j^{\beta_2} e^{-\lambda y_j}\right]} - \alpha \sum_{j=1}^{m} y_j^{\beta_2}(1-e^{-\lambda y_j})\log y_j$$

$$\frac{\partial \log L_{R_s}}{\partial \lambda} = \sum_{i=1}^{n} \frac{\beta_1 x_i^{\beta_1-1} x_i e^{-\lambda x_i} + x_i^{\beta_1} e^{-\lambda x_i} + \lambda x_i^{\beta_1+1} e^{-\lambda x_i}}{\left[\beta_1 x_i^{\beta_1-1}(1-e^{-\lambda x_i}) + \lambda x_i^{\beta_1} e^{-\lambda x_i}\right]} + \sum_{j=1}^{m} \frac{\beta_2 y_j^{\beta_2-1} y_j e^{-\lambda y_j} + y_j^{\beta_2} e^{-\lambda y_j} + \lambda y_j^{\beta_2+1} e^{-\lambda y_j}}{\left[\beta_2 y_j^{\beta_2-1}(1-e^{-\lambda y_j}) + \lambda y_j^{\beta_2} e^{-\lambda y_j}\right]} - \alpha \sum_{i=1}^{n} x_i^{\beta_1+1} e^{-\lambda x_i} - \alpha \sum_{j=1}^{m} y_j^{\beta_2+1} e^{-\lambda y_j}$$

### *5.1. Bootstrap Confidence Interval for $R_s$*

In this section, we propose the use of two non-parametric bootstrap confidence intervals: the percentile bootstrap confidence interval and the student's t bootstrap confidence interval, as described in [44]. Algorithm 2 outlines the steps required to compute the bootstrap confidence intervals. Additionally, a flowchart in Figure 7 is provided to facilitate a clearer understanding of the algorithm. Then, bootstrap CIs of $R_s$ can be obtained in the following:

**Algorithm 2** Bootstrap confidence interval for $R_s$

1. Simulate independent data $x_1, \ldots, x_n$ from the $HWE_1(\alpha, \beta_1, \lambda)$.
2. Simulate independent data $y_1, \ldots, y_m$ from the $HWE_2(\alpha, \beta_2, \lambda)$.
3. For $j = 1$.
4. Draw independent bootstrap samples: $x_1^*, x_2^*, \ldots, x_n^*$ and $y_1^*, y_2^*, \ldots, y_m^*$ by sampling with replacement from steps 1 and 2 in above.
5. Determine the MLEs of $\theta$ from the bootstrap sample in 4, say $\hat{\theta}^{*(j)} = (\hat{\alpha}^{*(j)}, \hat{\beta}_1^{*(j)}, \hat{\beta}_2^{*(j)}, \hat{\lambda}^{*(j)})^T$.
6. Calculate the MLE of $\hat{R_s}^{*(j)}(\hat{\theta}^{*(j)})$ using MLEs in 5.
7. Repeat step 4 to 6 B-times to get a set of bootstrap samples of $\hat{R_s}^{*(j)}$.
8. Set the samples in 7 in increasing order: $\hat{R_s}^{*(1)} \leq \hat{R_s}^{*(2)}, \ldots, \leq \hat{R_s}^{*(B)}. j = 1, \ldots, B$.
9 Obtain the bootstrap CI of $\hat{R}_s$.

#### 5.1.1. Percentile Bootstrap Confidence Interval (BpCI):

Let $\hat{R}_{s(\delta)}^*$ be the $\delta$ percentile of $\hat{R}_{sj}^*, j = 1, 2, 3, \ldots, B$—that is,

$$\frac{1}{B} \sum_{j=1}^{B} I_{\{\hat{R}_{sj}^* \leq \hat{R}_{s\delta}^*\}} = \delta, \quad 0 < \delta < 1$$

where $I_{\{.\}}$ is an indicator function. A $100(1-\epsilon)\%$ BpCI of $R_s$ is

$$\left(\hat{R}_{s(\epsilon/2)}^*, \hat{R}_{s(1-\epsilon/2)}^*\right).$$

#### 5.1.2. Student's t Bootstrap Confidence Interval (BtCI)

Let us set

$$\bar{\hat{R}}_s^* = \frac{1}{B}\sum_{j=1}^{B} \hat{R}_{sj}^*, \quad se(\hat{R}_s^*) = \sqrt{\frac{1}{B}\sum_{j=1}^{B}\left(\hat{R}_{sj}^* - \bar{\hat{R}}_s^*\right)^2},$$

and $\hat{t}_\delta^*$ be the $\delta$ percentile of $(\hat{R}_{sj}^* - \hat{R}_s)/se(\hat{R}_s^*), j = 1, 2, \ldots, 3$, such that

$$\frac{1}{B}\sum_{j=1}^{B} I_{(\hat{R}_{sj}^* - \hat{R}_s)/se(\hat{R}_s^*) \le \hat{t}_\delta^*} = \delta, \qquad 0 < \tau < 1,$$

with these, a $100(1-\epsilon)\%$ $BtCI$ of $R_s$ is given as

$$\left(\bar{\hat{R}}_s^* - \hat{t}_{(\epsilon/2)}^* se(\hat{R}_s^*), \bar{\hat{R}}_s^* + \hat{t}_{(\epsilon/2)}^* se(\hat{R}_s^*)\right).$$

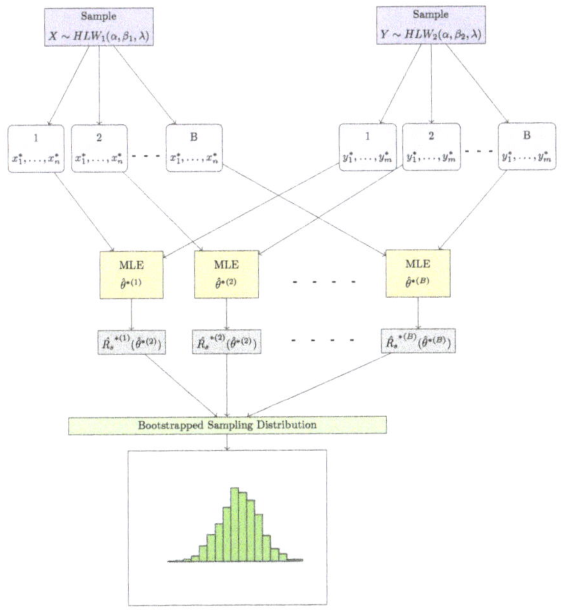


**Figure 7.** Flowchart demonstrating the bootstrap samples for the $\hat{R}_s$.

### 5.2. Simulation Results II

In this section, simulations are performed to evaluate the performance of the MLE for $R_s$ and the bootstrap confidence intervals (CIs) of $R_s$. Simulated samples of size 1000 were generated using Algorithm 1 for varied sample sizes and parameters from the distributions $HWE(\alpha, \beta_1, \lambda)$ and $HWE(\alpha, \beta_2, \lambda)$. Let $n$ and $m$ represent the sample sizes, respectively. The cases considered for $(n, m)$ are $(20, 20)$, $(20, 30)$, $(40, 50)$, and $(60, 60)$. The MLEs of $R_s$ were computed, and the standard deviation (SD), bias, and MSE of $R_s$ were analyzed. Additionally, a 95% CI for $R_s$ was constructed using the non-parametric BpCI and the BtCI. The bootstrap procedure was carried out with $B = 1000$ replications. The findings from the simulation study, summarized in Table 6, demonstrate notable trends as the sample sizes increase. Specifically, both the SD and the MSE of the estimates decrease, indicating improved precision and accuracy. Additionally, the estimated value of $R_s$ exhibits convergence towards its true value as the sample size grows, highlighting the consistency of the estimator. Moreover, the average length of the confidence interval (ALCI) for both bootstrap methods diminishes with larger sample sizes, reflecting tighter bounds around the estimates. This reduction in interval length is indicative of increased reliability in the parameter estimation. Importantly, the coverage probability (CP) progressively aligns with the nominal confidence level of 95%, demonstrating that the bootstrap methods maintain their validity under larger samples. These results collectively validate the robustness of the proposed methods in terms of both accuracy and reliability, especially as sample sizes grow. This behavior underscores the importance of larger datasets for achieving more precise and trustworthy statistical inferences.

**Table 6.** Parameter values, $R_s$, $\hat{R}_s$ with (SD) below, MSE of $\hat{R}_s$ with (bias) below, and ALCI with (CP) below in parenthesis.

| $(\alpha, \beta_1, \beta_2, \lambda)$ | $R_s$ | $(n, m)$ | $\hat{R}(SD)$ | $MSE(bias)$ | $ALBpCI(CP)$ | $ALBtCI(CP)$ |
|---|---|---|---|---|---|---|
| $(1.1, 2.1, 1.5, 1.1)$ | 0.4965 | (20,20) | 0.4966 | 0.00026 | 0.0807 | 0.0836 |
| | | | (0.0162) | (0.0012) | (0.98) | (0.99) |
| | | (20,30) | 0.4967 | 0.00021 | 0.0695 | 0.0719 |
| | | | (0.01436) | (0.00020) | (0.98) | (0.98) |
| | | (40,50) | 0.4966 | $8.015 \times 10^{-5}$ | 0.0422 | 0.0446 |
| | | | (0.0089) | (0.00011) | (0.98) | (0.96) |
| | | (60,60) | 0.4965 | $5.735 \times 10^{-5}$ | 0.0335 | 0.0355 |
| | | | (0.0075) | $(-3.165 \times 10^{-5})$ | (0.97) | (0.98) |
| $(2.0, 3.0, 1.0, 1.5)$ | 0.6356 | (20,20) | 0.6374 | 0.0021 | 0.1821 | 0.1689 |
| | | | (0.0459) | (0.0019) | (0.93) | (0.92) |
| | | (20,30) | 0.6342 | 0.0017 | 0.1606 | 0.1465 |
| | | | (0.0407) | (−0.0036) | (0.94) | (0.91) |
| | | (40,50) | 0.6358 | 0.0008 | 0.1178 | 0.1098 |
| | | | (0.0295) | (0.0003) | (0.95) | (0.93) |
| | | (60,60) | 0.6348 | 0.00067 | 0.1011 | 0.0956 |
| | | | (0.0259) | (−0.00073) | (0.95) | (0.93) |
| $(1.9, 0.9, 0.8, 0.8)$ | 0.5046 | (20,20) | 0.5050 | 0.00045 | 0.1008 | 0.0981 |
| | | | (0.0213) | (0.0003) | (0.98) | (0.96) |
| | | (20,30) | 0.5059 | 0.00037 | 0.0875 | 0.0813 |
| | | | (0.0192) | (0.0013) | (0.97) | (0.98) |
| | | (40,50) | 0.5056 | 0.00018 | 0.0562 | 0.0526 |
| | | | (0.01333) | (0.0009) | (0.96) | (0.97) |
| | | (60,60) | 0.5047 | 0.00012 | 0.0456 | 0.0434 |
| | | | (0.0108) | $(4.665 \times 10^{-5})$ | (0.96) | (0.98) |
| $(1.5, 1.5, 1.9, 1.5)$ | 0.4815 | (20,20) | 0.4817 | 0.00076 | 0.1232 | 0.1323 |
| | | | (0.0276) | (0.00018) | (0.95) | (0.96) |
| | | (20,30) | 0.4832 | 0.00065 | 0.1075 | 0.1117 |
| | | | (0.0254) | (0.0017) | (0.94) | (0.95) |
| | | (40,50) | 0.4818 | 0.00036 | 0.0734 | 0.0772 |
| | | | (0.0189) | (0.00034) | (0.93) | (0.94) |
| | | (60,60) | 0.4801 | 0.00023 | 0.06121 | 0.0656 |
| | | | (0.0152) | (−0.00095) | (0.95) | (0.96) |
| $(5.9, 3.9, 6.0, 2.8)$ | 0.3074 | (20,20) | 0.3067 | 0.0059 | 0.3015 | 0.2887 |
| | | | (0.0772) | (−0.00066) | (0.94) | (0.93) |
| | | (20,30) | 0.3069 | 0.0049 | 0.2732 | 0.2598 |
| | | | (0.0702) | (−0.00051) | (0.94) | (0.93) |
| | | (40,50) | 0.3052 | 0.0028 | 0.2006 | 0.1943 |
| | | | (0.0531) | (−0.0021) | (0.94) | (0.92) |
| | | (60,60) | 0.3087 | 0.0019 | 0.1735 | 0.1698 |
| | | | (0.0444) | (0.0014) | (0.94) | (0.94) |
| $(1.0, 1.0, 1.0, 1.0)$ | 0.500 | (20,20) | 0.4995 | 0.0028 | 0.0798 | 0.0806 |
| | | | (0.0168) | (−0.0044) | (0.98) | (0.98) |
| | | (20,30) | 0.4998 | 0.0017 | 0.0668 | 0.0702 |
| | | | (0.0134) | (−0.00018) | (0.98) | (0.96) |
| | | (40,50) | 0.4997 | $9.014 \times 10^{-5}$ | 0.0418 | 0.0429 |
| | | | (0.0095) | (−0.00029) | (0.97) | (0.98) |
| | | (60,60) | 0.4997 | $5.599 \times 10^{-5}$ | 0.0324 | 0.0326 |
| | | | (0.0075) | (−0.00025) | (0.96) | (0.97) |

Table 6. Cont.

| $(\alpha, \beta_1, \beta_2, \lambda)$ | $R_s$ | $(n, m)$ | $\hat{R}(SD)$ | $MSE(bias)$ | $ALBpCI(CP)$ | $ALBtCI(CP)$ |
|---|---|---|---|---|---|---|
| (0.5, 0.5, 0.5, 0.5) | 0.4999 | (20,20) | 0.4997 (0.4704) | 0.0022 (−0.0003) | 0.1881 (0.89) | 0.1906 (0.90) |
| | | (20,30) | 0.4948 (0.0409) | 0.0017 (−0.0052) | 0.1615 (0.91) | 0.1740 (0.93) |
| | | (40,50) | 0.5001 (0.0285) | 0.0008 (0.0001) | 0.1075 (0.92) | 0.1109 (0.94) |
| | | (60,60) | 0.5001 (0.0239) | 0.0006 (0.0006) | 0.0906 (0.92) | 0.0903 (0.93) |
| (5.0, 5.5, 3.5, 6.5) | 0.6993 | (20,20) | 0.7016 (0.0759) | 0.0058 (0.0023) | 0.2904 (0.93) | 0.3032 (0.94) |
| | | (20,30) | 0.7027 (0.0704) | 0.0049 (0.0034) | 0.2614 (0.93) | 0.2683 (0.93) |
| | | (40,50) | 0.6979 (0.0529) | 0.0028 (−0.0014) | 0.1961 (0.93) | 0.2009 (0.94) |
| | | (60,60) | 0.6999 (0.0130) | 0.0019 (0.0007) | 0.1683 (0.94) | 0.1720 (0.95) |

## 6. Application

In this section, we demonstrate the performance of the HWE distribution through three applications to real datasets by comparing the HWE with several other existing distributions and in SS-analysis. We estimated the parameters of all competing models using MLE and evaluated the fitted models using various information criteria such as the Akaike information criterion (AIC), Bayesian information criterion (BIC), and consistent Akaike information criterion (CAIC). Additionally, we considered goodness-of-fit statistics including the Kolmogorov–Smirnov (KS), Anderson–Darling (A), and Cramer–von Mises (W) tests. The goodness of fit comparison involves distributions with the reliability function given in Table 7.

Table 7. Reliability function of the competing distributions $x, \alpha, \beta, \lambda, \gamma > 0$.

| Distribution | R(x) |
|---|---|
| Modified Weibull (MW) [18] | $\exp(-\alpha x^{\beta} e^{\lambda x})$ |
| Exponentiated Weibull (EW) [45] | $1-(1-e^{-\alpha x^{\beta}})^{\lambda}$ |
| Exponentiated sine Weibull (ESW) [46] | $\sin^{\alpha}\left(\frac{\pi}{2}[1-e^{-\alpha x^{\beta}}]\right)$ |
| Additive Weibull (AddW) [47] | $e^{-\alpha x^{\beta}-\lambda x^{\gamma}}$ |
| Sarhan–Zaindin modified Weibull (SZW) [48] | $e^{-\alpha x-\lambda x^{\gamma}}$ |
| Modified Weibull extension (MWE) [20] | $\exp(\alpha\lambda(1-e^{(x/\alpha)^{\beta}}))$ |
| Extended cosine Weibull (ESW) [49] | $1-\left(1-\cos\left(\frac{\pi}{2}e^{-\alpha x^{\beta}}\right)\right)^{\lambda}$ |

### 6.1. Fitting HWE and Other Weibull Based Models

This subsection evaluates the performance of the HWE distribution by fitting it to two real-world datasets: remission times of bladder cancer patients and failure times of specific components. The assessment is carried out by comparing HWE against several Weibull-related distributions using the aforementioned model selection criteria and goodness-of-fit measures.

#### 6.1.1. First Dataset

The dataset consists of remission times from 128 bladder cancer patients, originally documented by [50]. We calculated the maximum likelihood estimates and detailed the numerical results for each model in Tables 8 and 9. The findings demonstrate that the HWE distribution provides a better fit than the competing models.

In Table 9, the HWE distribution is notable for its log-likelihood value of −409.80, the most favorable among the models compared, indicating its superior fit to the data. The HWE distribution also excels in other statistical criteria and goodness-of-fit measures, achieving a balanced and effective representation of the data. Notably, it records the lowest values for AIC, CAIC, BIC, A, W, and KS among all considered distributions, strongly advocating for its appropriateness for this dataset. Furthermore, Figure 8 illustrates an exemplary match with the empirical data through the fitted PDF and survival functions, while Figure 9 includes a box plot and quantile–quantile (QQ) plot, affirming the HWE's consistency with the observed data.

**Table 8.** MLEs for first datasets.

| Distribution | $\alpha$ | $\beta$ | $\lambda$ | $\gamma$ |
|---|---|---|---|---|
| HWE | 0.592 (0.6431) | 0.5103 (0.2616) | 0.0973 (0.08700) | - |
| W | 0.0939 (0.0190) | 1.0478 (0.0675) | - | - |
| MW | 0.0939 (0.0172) | $1.2\times10^{-7}$ (1.0035) | 1.0478 (0.0955) | - |
| EW | 0.4539 (0.2386) | 0.6542 (0.1338) | 2.7973 (1.2577) | - |
| AddW | 0.0120 (5.2031) | 1.0480 (0.1545) | 0.0818(7.8070) | 1.0477 (0.0415) |
| MWE | $1.5\times10^{5}$ (0.5461) | 1.0490 (0.8420) | 1.6740 (0.1306) | - |
| ESW | 2.7589 (1.0894) | 0.6208 (0.1138) | 0.2666 (0.1174) | - |
| ECSW | 0.3199 (0.0282) | 0.1749 (0.0001) | 1.0030 ($1.1\times10^{6}$) | - |

**Table 9.** L, AIC, BIC, CAIC, A, W, KS, and p-value for first data sets.

| Distribution | $L$ | $AIC$ | $BIC$ | CAIC | $A$ | $W$ | $KS(PV)$ |
|---|---|---|---|---|---|---|---|
| HWE | −409.80 | 825.61 | 834.17 | 825.80 | 0.1234 | 0.0174 | 0.0310 (0.9997) |
| W | −414.09 | 832.17 | 837.88 | 832.27 | 0.7817 | 0.1309 | 0.0701 (0.5552) |
| MW | −414.09 | 834.17 | 842.73 | 834.37 | 0.7815 | 0.1308 | 0.0704 (0.5507) |
| EW | −410.68 | 827.36 | 835.92 | 827.55 | 0.2885 | 0.0437 | 0.0450 (0.9578) |
| AddW | −414.09 | 836.17 | 847.58 | 836.49 | 0.1314 | 0.7863 | 0.0700 (0.5573) |
| MWE | −414.08 | 834.18 | 842.73 | 834.37 | 0.7831 | 0.1311 | 0.0710 (0.5388) |
| ESW | −410.48 | 826.95 | 835.51 | 827.15 | 0.2595 | 0.0394 | 0.0436 (0.9682) |
| ECSW | −413.44 | 832.88 | 841.44 | 833.07 | 0.6917 | 0.1154 | 0.0660 (0.6335) |

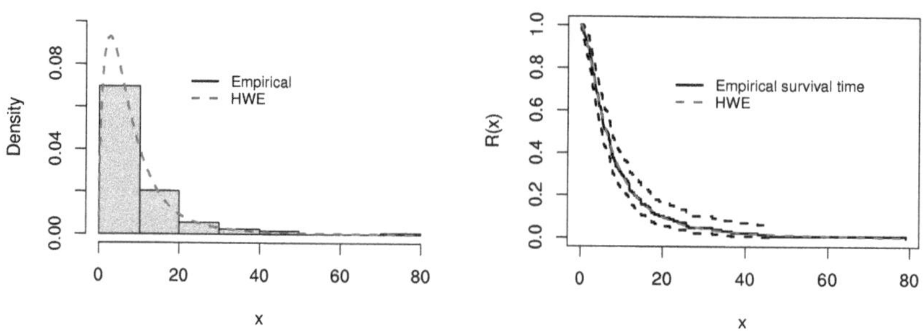


**Figure 8.** Plots of the histogram and fitted PDF (**left**), and empirical and fitted survival functions (**right**), for the first data.

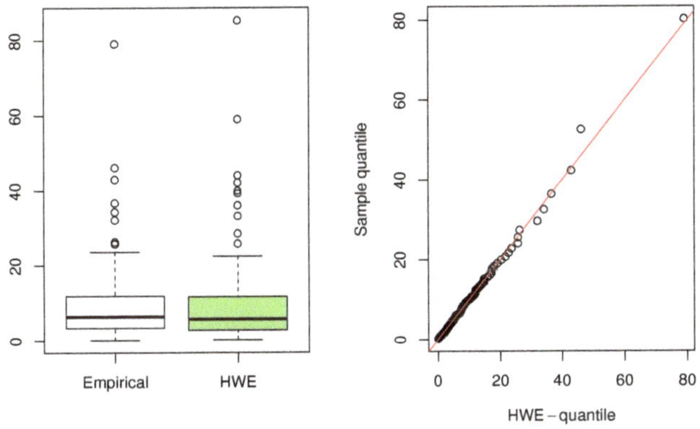


**Figure 9.** Box plot (**left**) and quantile–quantile plot (**right**) for the first data.

### 6.1.2. Second Dataset

This dataset, initially reported in [51], consists of failure times for fifty components over 1000 h. Table 10 presents the MLEs for each model, while Table 11 shows that the HWE distribution provides a superior fit compared to other models. The HWE distribution consistently achieves more of the smallest values in the evaluative criteria and goodness-of-fit measures, positioning it as the first ranked model. This indicates its excellent capability to accurately represent the data, suggesting that it is the most appropriate model for these data according to these metrics. Additionally, to support our findings, Figure 10 illustrates the HWE's excellent fit with the displayed fitted PDF and survival function. Furthermore, Figure 11 includes a box plot and a quantile–quantile (QQ) plot, demonstrating the HWE's alignment with the data.

**Table 10.** MLEs for second dataset.

| Distribution | $\alpha$ | $\beta$ | $\lambda$ | $\gamma$ |
|---|---|---|---|---|
| HWE | (0.6015) (0.1123) | 0.5989 (0.0785) | 13.5171 ( 6.2122 ) | - |
| W | 0.5412 (0.0995) | 0.6611 (0.0747) | - | - |
| MW | 0.4964 (0.0.0990) | 0.5615 (0.0975) | 0.0335 (0.0248) | - |
| EW | 0.3859 (1.1141) | 0.7698 (0.9441) | 0.7856 (1.4754) | - |
| AddW | 0.5289 (8.8612) | 0.6611 (0.0830 ) | 0.0124 (8.8614) | 0.6603 (1.5778) |
| SZMW | 0.4926 (0.1807) | 0.6197 (0.1544) | 0.0438 (0.1314) | - |
| MWE | 21.4159 (7.0007) | 0.5845 (0.0766) | 0.1319 (0.0264) | - |
| ESW | 0.4288 (0.7410) | 1.1379 (1.5183) | 0.0695 (0.3030) | - |
| ECSW | 6.3682 (7.0763) | 0.0528 (0.0582) | 0.6489 (0.0744) | - |

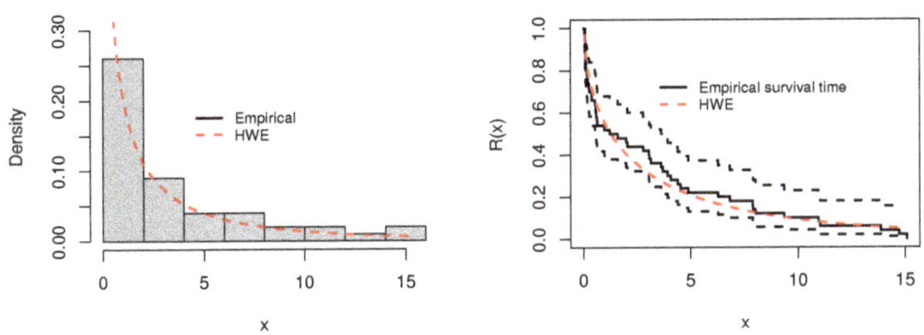


**Figure 10.** Plots of the histogram and fitted PDF (**left**), and empirical and fitted survival functions (**right**), for the second data.

**Table 11.** L, AIC, BIC, CAIC, A, W, KS, and p-value for second datasets.

| Distribution | $L$ | $AIC$ | $BIC$ | CAIC | $W$ | $A$ | $KS(PV)$ |
|---|---|---|---|---|---|---|---|
| HWE | −99.07 | 204.15 | 209.88 | 204.67 | 0.6765 | 0.1109 | 0.1122 (0.5186) |
| W | −102.36 | 208.73 | 212.55 | 208.98 | 0.9393 | 0.1507 | 0.1269 (0.3652) |
| MW | −101.36 | 208.73 | 214.46 | 209.25 | 0.8504 | 0.1300 | 0.1326 (0.3144) |
| EW | −102.37 | 210.71 | 216.45 | 211.23 | 0.9459 | 0.1499 | 0.1333 (0.3083) |
| AddW | −102.36 | 212.73 | 220.38 | 213.62 | 0.9393 | 0.1507 | 0.1270 (0.3642) |
| SZMW | −102.32 | 210.64 | 216.38 | 211.16 | 0.9304 | 0.1487 | 0.1278 (0.3563) |
| MWE | −101.94 | 209.88 | 215.62 | 210.40 | 0.8908 | 0.1402 | 0.1375 (0.2747) |
| ESW | −102.51 | 211.02 | 216.76 | 211.54 | 0.9417 | 0.1453 | 0.1504 (0.1877) |
| ECSW | −102.30 | 210.59 | 216.33 | 211.11 | 0.1489 | 0.9305 | 0.1289 (0.3471) |

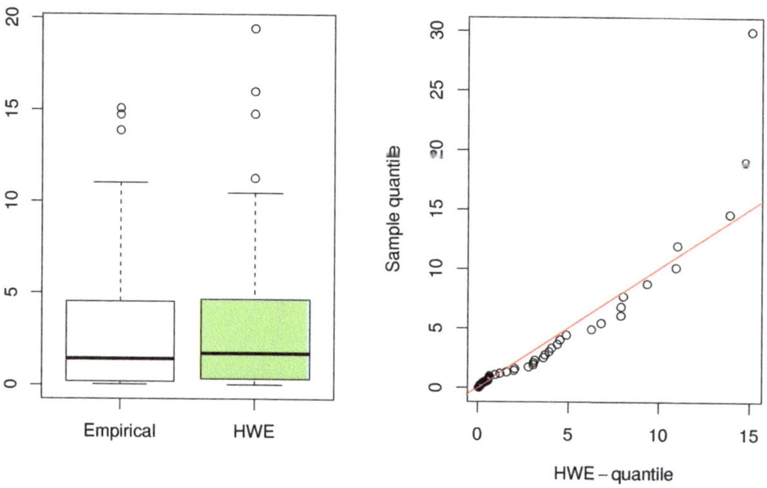


**Figure 11.** Box plot (**left**) and quantile–quantile plot (**right**) for the second data.

### 6.1.3. On the Performance of HWE on the Fitted Datasets

HWE performed well in comparison with the other models based on the presented datasets. HWE exhibits enhanced flexibility due to its three parameters: $\alpha$(scale), $\beta$ (shape), and $\lambda$ from the hybridization. This structure allows HWE to adapt to a wider range of shape behaviors, which are common in reliability and biomedical applications. Compared to classical models (e.g., Weibull, Exponential), the HWE model offers some key advantages: the term $(1 - e^{-\lambda x})$ introduces an additional degree of flexibility in shaping the distribution's tail. This helps to capture heavy-tailed or light-tailed behaviors, improving the fit for datasets exhibiting deviations from standard Weibull or Exponential assumptions. The hybrid structure can allows for a better trade-off between short-term and long-term failure risks, making it particularly suitable for lifetime and reliability data. In addition, the MLE adoption shows that HWE's parameter estimates align well with the underlying dataset's distributions by reducing model bias. Thus, based on the two datasets, we can say that the HWE can capture complex data structures better by balancing the flexibility of Weibull and exponential components while retaining interpretability in reliability and survival studies.

### 6.2. Third Dataset (Stress–Strength Reliability ($R_s$))

In this section, we illustrate the applicability of the HWE model in reliability analysis by applying it to two real-world datasets. This demonstration highlights the practical utility of the proposed estimation techniques. The reliability parameter $R_s$ is estimated using the MLE method. Additionally, 95% confidence intervals for $R_s$ are constructed using non-parametric bootstrap BpCI and BtCI, based on $B = 1000$ bootstrap replications. To evaluate the fit of the HWE model to the datasets, the KS test is employed, providing a rigorous assessment of the model's goodness-of-fit. The datasets, as described in [52], consist of two distinct types of measurements. The first dataset, denoted as $X$, corresponds to single fibers tested under tension at a gauge length of 10 mm, with a sample size of $n = 63$. The second dataset, denoted as $Y$, pertains to impregnated tows of 1000 fibers tested at a gauge length of 20 mm, with a sample size of $m = 69$.

This analysis not only validates the practical feasibility of the HWE model in handling real-world data but also demonstrates its capability in providing reliable estimates of $R_s$ and its associated confidence intervals. The application of the KS test further reinforces the suitability of the HWE model for these datasets, ensuring its robustness in SS-reliability studies.

The estimated values from the analysis are presented in Table 12. The results clearly demonstrate that the HWE model provides a good fit to both datasets, as indicated by the KS test for the $HWE_1(\alpha, \beta_1, \lambda)$ distribution for dataset ($X$) and the $HWE_2(\alpha, \beta_2, \lambda)$ distribution for dataset ($Y$). These findings suggest that the HWE model is a suitable candidate for reliability analysis. Figure 12 illustrates the empirical and fitted CDFs of the HWE model, along with the density of the estimated bootstrap values of $R_s$ for the datasets. Figure 13 displays the bootstrap estimates of $R_s$ and their density, which clearly approximate normality, demonstrating that the bootstrap CIs are reliable. Additionally, Figure 14 presents the profile log-likelihood of the estimated parameters, confirming the uniqueness of the maximum.

**Table 12.** MLEs, $L_{R_s}$, $R_s$, KS with p-value in parenthesis, and ALCI with 95% CI within parentheses for the stress–strength dataset.

| $\hat{\theta}$ | $L_{R_s}$ | $HWE_1 - KS$ | $HWE_2 - KS$ | $\hat{R}_s$ | $BpCI$ | $BtCI$ |
|---|---|---|---|---|---|---|
| $\hat{\alpha} = 0.00599$ | 111.4004 | 0.1057 | 0.0654 | 0.7299 | 0.1323 | 0.1284 |
| $\hat{\beta}_1 = 4.43233$ | | (0.45103) | (0.9107) | | (0.6657, 0.7979) | (0.6657, 0.7941) |
| $\hat{\beta}_2 = 5.43053$ | | | | | | |
| $\hat{\lambda} = 0.62129$ | | | | | | |

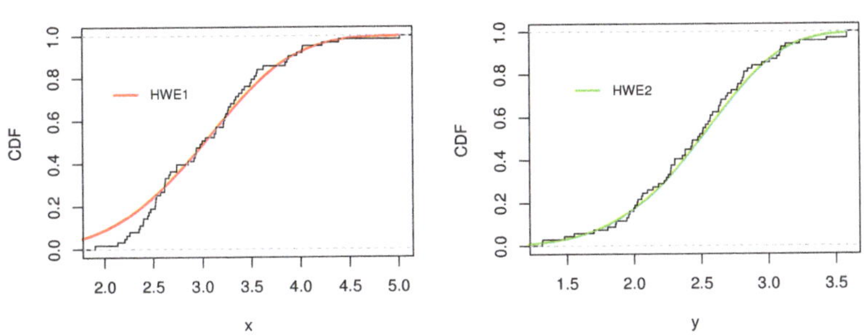


**Figure 12.** Plots of the empirical and fitted $HWE_1$ and $HWE_2$ models for the SS-datasets.

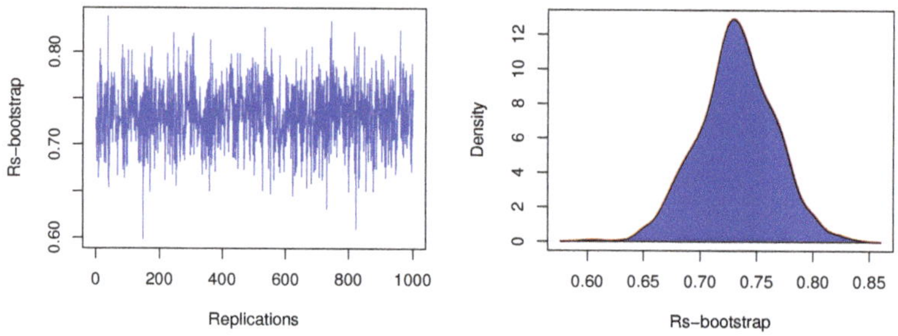


**Figure 13.** Plots illustrating the estimated bootstrap values of $R_s$ and their density for the SS-datasets.

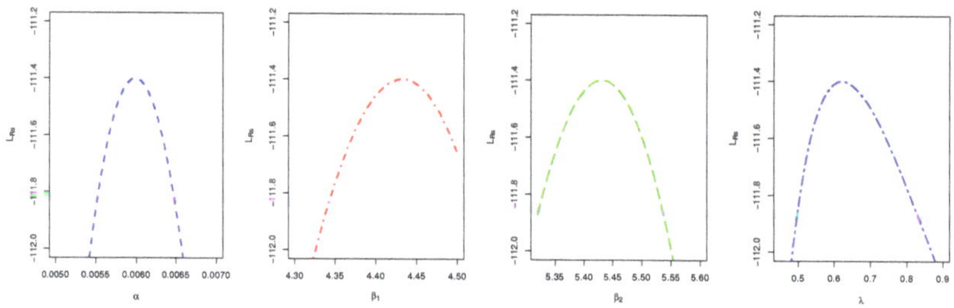

**Figure 14.** Plots of the profile log-likelihood of the parameters for the SS-data.

## 7. Conclusions

In this paper, we introduced a novel hybrid family of distributions that includes a flexible set of hybrid functions to extend a variety of existing distributions. Another key contribution of this family is the three-parameter hybrid-Weibull–exponential distribution, for which we thoroughly investigated several core mathematical properties, including moments, random data generation procedures, MRL analyses that involve the study of its reciprocal relationship with FRF, and relevant asymptotic of the MRL. Additionally, we computed advanced information metrics such as the extropy and cumulative residual entropy, and derived order statistics along with their asymptotic behaviors. The model's identifiability was further verified numerically using the Kullback–Leibler divergence; based on some selected parameters, the findings substantiate the identifiability of the HWE. Parameter estimation was performed via MLE, with extensive simulations assessing the performance of the MLEs in density estimation and SS-parameter studies. We also utilized nonparametric bootstrap techniques to construct confidence intervals and evaluate coverage probabilities for the SS-parameter. Notably, the MSE of the density estimates and the SS-parameter estimates decreased as sample size increased. Similarly, as sample size increases, the average width of nonparametric percentile and Student's t bootstrap confidence intervals narrowed, and the coverage probabilities converged to the nominal 95% level for the SS-parameter. We validated the practical effectiveness of this hybrid family using three real-world datasets. The HWE outperforms several prominent Weibull-based models in fitting the remission times of bladder cancer patients, and failure times for some components, as discussed based on AIC, BIC, CAIC, KS, A, and W metrics. Furthermore, HWE exhibited robust performance in the SS-parameter analysis of two sets of fiber data tested under tension at various gauge lengths, thus underscoring the potential of this hybrid family for advancing reliability and survival studies.

This research not only spotlights the versatility of the hybrid-w-G family in a broad range of statistical applications but also sets the stage for further theoretical and applied developments. Future work may focus on constructing additional hybrid-w-G distributions with different $w(x;\xi)$ and $G(x;\zeta)$ configurations, extending the inferential approaches (e.g., Bayesian methods), addressing censored data, and providing more analytical framework. In addition, several applied studies based on Weibull and other distributions (for instance, refs. [53–55]) can be advanced by considering members of the hybrid-w-G family as an alternative. The limitations of the hybrid-w-G family is that many members might have non-closed form quantile functions for random data generation, but this limitations was overcome using the package stated in Section 3.1.

**Author Contributions:** Conceptualization, M.M., B.A., I.M., and R.G.; methodology, M.M., J.X., B.A., I.M., and R.G.; software, M.M., B.A., and I.M.; validation, M.M., J.X., B.A., I.M., and R.G.; formal analysis, M.M., J.X., B.A., I.M., and R.G.; investigation, M.M., J.X., B.A., I.M., and R.G.; resources, M.M., J.X., B.A., I.M., and R.G.; data curation, M.M., J.X., B.A., I.M., and R.G.; writing—original draft preparation, M.M., B.A., and I.M.; writing—review and editing, M.M., J.X., B.A., I.M., and R.G.; visualization, M.M., J.X., B.A., I.M., and R.G.; supervision, M.M., J.X., B.A., I.M., and R.G.; project administration, M.M., J.X., B.A., I.M., and R.G.; funding acquisition, M.M., J.X., and R.G. All authors have read and agreed to the published version of the manuscript.

**Funding:** This work was funded by the Characteristic Innovation Project of Guangdong Province Ordinary University (2023KTSCX089), and Guangdong Provincial Education Science Planning Project (2024GXJK561). The authors extend their appreciation to Northern Border University, Saudi Arabia, for supporting this work through project number (NBU-CRP-2025-2461)

**Data Availability Statement:** Data are contained within the article.

**Conflicts of Interest:** The authors declare no conflicts of interest.

## References

1. Eugene, N.; Lee, C.; Famoye, F. Beta-normal distribution and its applications. *Commun.-Stat.-Theory Methods* **2002**, *31*, 497–512. [CrossRef]
2. Alexander, C.; Cordeiro, G.M.; Ortega, E.M.; Sarabia, J.M. Generalized beta-generated distributions. *Comput. Stat. Data Anal.* **2012**, *56*, 1880–1897. [CrossRef]
3. Tahir, M.H.; Hussain, M.A.; Cordeiro, G.M.; El-Morshedy, M.; Eliwa, M.S. A new Kumaraswamy generalized family of distributions with properties, applications, and bivariate extension. *Mathematics* **2020**, *8*, 1989. [CrossRef]
4. Chakraborty, S.; Handique, L.; Jamal, F. The Kumaraswamy Poisson-G family of distribution: Its properties and applications. *Ann. Data Sci.* **2022**, *9*, 229–247. [CrossRef]
5. Muhammad, M. Poisson-odd generalized exponential family of distributions: Theory and applications. *Hacet. J. Math. Stat.* **2016**, *47*, 1652–1670. [CrossRef]
6. Chesneau, C.; Sharma, V.K.; Bakouch, H.S. Extended Topp–Leone family of distributions as an alternative to beta and Kumaraswamy type distributions: Application to glycosaminoglycans concentration level in urine. *Int. J. Biomath.* **2021**, *14*, 2050088. [CrossRef]
7. Bantan, R.A.; Jamal, F.; Chesneau, C.; Elgarhy, M. A new power Topp–Leone generated family of distributions with applications. *Entropy* **2019**, *21*, 1177. [CrossRef]
8. Odhah, O.H.; Alshanbari, H.M.; Ahmad, Z.; Rao, G.S. A weighted cosine-G family of distributions: Properties and illustration using time-to-event data. *Axioms* **2023**, *12*, 849. [CrossRef]
9. Abonongo, J. Properties and applications of the Tan Weibull loss distribution. *Kuwait J. Sci.* **2025**, *52*, 100304. [CrossRef]
10. Muhammad, M.; Abba, B.; Muhammad, I.; Bakouch, H.S.; Xiao, J. A new versatile family of distributions: Log-linear regression model and applications to real data. *Kuwait J. Sci.* **2025**, *52*, 100385. [CrossRef]
11. Abd EL-Baset, A.A.; Ghazal, M. Exponentiated additive Weibull distribution. *Reliab. Eng. Syst. Saf.* **2020**, *193*, 106663.
12. Wang, H.; Abba, B.; Pan, J. Classical and Bayesian estimations of improved Weibull–Weibull distribution for complete and censored failure times data. *Appl. Stoch. Model. Bus. Ind.* **2022**, *38*, 997–1018. [CrossRef]

13. Al-Essa, L.A.; Muhammad, M.; Tahir, M.; Abba, B.; Xiao, J.; Jamal, F. A new flexible four parameter bathtub curve failure rate model, and its application to right-censored data. *IEEE Access* **2023**, *11*, 50130–50144. [CrossRef]
14. Das, D.; Alshammari, T.S.; Rashedi, K.A.; Das, B.; Jyoti Hazarika, P.; Eliwa, M.S. Discrete Joint Random Variables in Fréchet-Weibull Distribution: A Comprehensive Mathematical Framework with Simulations, Goodness-of-Fit Analysis, and Informed Decision-Making. *Mathematics* **2024**, *12*, 3401. [CrossRef]
15. Abba, B.; Muhammad, M.; Isa, M.S.; Jingbiao, W. A Bi-failure Mode Model for Competing Risk Modeling with HMC-Driven Bayesian Framework. *arXiv* **2025**, arXiv:2502.11507.
16. Muhammad, M.; Abba, B. A Bayesian inference with Hamiltonian Monte Carlo (HMC) framework for a three-parameter model with reliability applications. *Kuwait J. Sci.* **2025**, *52*, 100365. [CrossRef]
17. Gurvich, M.; Dibenedetto, A.; Ranade, S. A new statistical distribution for characterizing the random strength of brittle materials. *J. Mater. Sci.* **1997**, *32*, 2559–2564. [CrossRef]
18. Lai, C.; Xie, M.; Murthy, D. A modified Weibull distribution. *IEEE Trans. Reliab.* **2003**, *52*, 33–37. [CrossRef]
19. Bebbington, M.; Lai, C.D.; Zitikis, R. A flexible Weibull extension. *Reliab. Eng. Syst. Saf.* **2007**, *92*, 719–726. [CrossRef]
20. Xie, M.; Tang, Y.; Goh, T.N. A modified Weibull extension with bathtub-shaped failure rate function. *Reliab. Eng. Syst. Saf.* **2002**, *76*, 279–285. [CrossRef]
21. Meredith, M.; Kruschke, J. *HDInterval: Highest (Posterior) Density Intervals*; CRAN: Contributed Packages; R Foundation for Statistical Computing, Vienna, Austria, 2016.
22. Barlow, R. *Statistical Theory of Reliability and Life Testing*; Holt, Rinehart and Winston: New York, NY, USA, 1975.
23. Guess, F.; Proschan, F. 12 mean residual life: Theory and applications. *Handb. Stat.* **1988**, *7*, 215–224.
24. Xie, M.; Goh, T.N.; Tang, Y. On changing points of mean residual life and failure rate function for some generalized Weibull distributions. *Reliab. Eng. Syst. Saf.* **2004**, *84*, 293–299. [CrossRef]
25. H. Olcay, A. Mean residual life function for certain types of non-monotonic ageing. *Commun. Stat. Stoch. Model.* **1995**, *11*, 219–225. [CrossRef]
26. Calabria, R.; Pulcini, G. On the maximum likelihood and least-squares estimation in the inverse Weibull distribution. *Stat. Appl.* **1990**, *2*, 53–66.
27. Arnold, B.C.; Balakrishnan, N.; Nagaraja, H.N. *A First Course in Order Statistics*; SIAM: New York, NY, USA, 1992; Volume 54.
28. Lad, F.; Sanfilippo, G.; Agro, G. Extropy: Complementary dual of entropy. *Stat. Sci.* **2015**, *30*, 40–58. [CrossRef]
29. Shrahili, M.; Kayid, M. Excess lifetime extropy of order statistics. *Axioms* **2023**, *12*, 1024. [CrossRef]
30. Ran, Z.Y.; Hu, B.G. Determining parameter identifiability from the optimization theory framework: A Kullback–Leibler divergence approach. *Neurocomputing* **2014**, *142*, 307–317. [CrossRef]
31. Abba, B.; Wang, H.; Bakouch, H.S. A reliability and survival model for one and two failure modes system with applications to complete and censored datasets. *Reliab. Eng. Syst. Saf.* **2022**, *223*, 108460. [CrossRef]
32. Henningsen, A.; Toomet, O. maxLik: A package for maximum likelihood estimation in R. *Comput. Stat.* **2011**, *26*, 443–458. [CrossRef]
33. Kotz, S.; Lumelskii, Y.; Pensky, M. *The Stress–Strength Model and Its Generalizations: Theory and Applications*; World Scientific: Singapore, 2003.
34. Saber, M.M.; Mohie El-Din, M.M.; Yousof, H.M. Reliability Estimation for the Remained Stress-Strength Model under the Generalized Exponential Lifetime Distribution. *J. Probab. Stat.* **2021**, *2021*, 7363449. [CrossRef]
35. Garg, R.; Kumari, M.; Sahoo, R.K.; Kumari, A. Stress-strength reliability estimation of multicomponent system with non-identical strength components from inverse Pareto distribution. *Life Cycle Reliab. Saf. Eng.* **2024**, *13*, 351–363. [CrossRef]
36. Muhammad, I.; Wang, X.; Li, C.; Yan, M.; Chang, M. Estimation of the reliability of a stress–strength system from Poisson half logistic distribution. *Entropy* **2020**, *22*, 1307. [CrossRef] [PubMed]
37. Krishnamoorthy, K.; Lin, Y. Confidence limits for stress–strength reliability involving Weibull models. *JOurnal Stat. Plan. Inference* **2010**, *140*, 1754–1764. [CrossRef]
38. Kundu, D.; Gupta, R.D. Estimation of P [Y< X] for Weibull distributions. *IEEE Trans. Reliab.* **2006**, *55*, 270–280.
39. Sharma, S.; Kumar, V. Reliability estimation in multicomponent stress-strength model using weighted exponential-Lindley distribution. *J. Stat. Comput. Simul.* **2024**, *94*, 2385–2411. [CrossRef]
40. Sarhan, A.M.; Tolba, A.H. Stress-strength reliability under partially accelerated life testing using Weibull model. *Sci. Afr.* **2023**, *20*, e01733. [CrossRef]
41. Ahmadi, M.V. Estimating stress-strength reliability based on two-parameter exponential records in the presence of inter-record times. *Qual. Technol. Quant. Manag.* **2024**, *14*, 1–32. [CrossRef]
42. Nassar, M.; Alotaibi, R.; Zhang, C. Product of Spacing Estimation of Stress–Strength Reliability for Alpha Power Exponential Progressively Type-II Censored Data. *Axioms* **2023**, *12*, 752. [CrossRef]

43. Chandra, N.; James, A.; Domma, F.; Rehman, H. Bivariate iterated Farlie–Gumbel–Morgenstern stress–strength reliability model for Rayleigh margins: Properties and estimation. *Stat. Theory Relat. Fields* **2024**, *8*, 315–334. [CrossRef]
44. Tibshirani, R.J.; Efron, B. *An introduction to the Bootstrap. Monographs on Statistics and Applied Probability*; Chapman and Hall/CRC: New York, NY, USA, 1993; Volume 57, pp. 1–436.
45. Pal, M.; Ali, M.M.; Woo, J. Exponentiated weibull distribution. *Statistica* **2006**, *66*, 139–147.
46. Muhammad, M.; Alshanbari, H.M.; Alanzi, A.R.; Liu, L.; Sami, W.; Chesneau, C.; Jamal, F. A new generator of probability models: The exponentiated sine-G family for lifetime studies. *Entropy* **2021**, *23*, 1394. [CrossRef] [PubMed]
47. Xie, M.; Lai, C.D. Reliability analysis using an additive Weibull model with bathtub-shaped failure rate function. *Reliab. Eng. Syst. Saf.* **1996**, *52*, 87–93. [CrossRef]
48. Sarhan, A.M.; Zaindin, M. Modified Weibull distribution. *Appl. Sci.* **2009**, *11*, 123–136. [CrossRef]
49. Muhammad, M.; Bantan, R.A.; Liu, L.; Chesneau, C.; Tahir, M.H.; Jamal, F.; Elgarhy, M. A new extended cosine—G distributions for lifetime studies. *Mathematics* **2021**, *9*, 2758. [CrossRef]
50. Lee, E.T.; Wang, J. *Statistical Methods for Survival Data Analysis*; John Wiley & Sons.Inc.: Hoboken, NJ, USA, 2003; Volume 476.
51. Murthy, D.P.; Xie, M.; Jiang, R. *Weibull Models*; John Wiley & Sons: Hoboken, NJ, USA, 2004.
52. Bader, M.; Priest, A. Statistical aspects of fibre and bundle strength in hybrid composites. In *Progress in Science and Engineering of Composites, Proceedings of the forth International Conference on Coomposite Materials, ICCM-IV, Tokyo, Japan, 25–28 October 1982*; Japan Society for Composite Materials: Tokyo, Japan, 1982; pp. 1129–1136.
53. Ma, M.; Chen, X.; Wang, S.; Liu, Y.; Li, W. Bearing degradation assessment based on weibull distribution and deep belief network. In Proceedings of the 2016 International symposium on flexible automation (ISFA), Cleveland, OH, USA, 1–3 August 2016; IEEE: Piscataway, NJ, USA, 2016; pp. 382–385.
54. Xu, A.; Fang, G.; Zhuang, L.; Gu, C. A multivariate student-t process model for dependent tail-weighted degradation data. *IISE Trans.* **2024**, 1–17. [CrossRef]
55. Li, Y.; Zhao, L.; Gao, J.; Ru, Y.; Zhang, H. Evaluation of the fatigue performance of full-depth reclamation with portland cement material based on the weibull distribution model. *Coatings* **2024**, *14*, 437. [CrossRef]

*axioms*

MDPI

*Article*

# Analytical and Geometric Foundations and Modern Applications of Kinetic Equations and Optimal Transport

**Cécile Barbachoux † and Joseph Kouneiher *,†**

INSPE, Côte d'Azur University, 83300 Draguignan, France; cecile.barbachoux@univ-cotedazur.fr
* Correspondence: joseph.kouneiher@univ-cotedazur.fr
† These authors contributed equally to this work.

**Abstract:** We develop a unified analytical framework that systematically connects kinetic theory, optimal transport, and entropy dissipation through the novel integration of hypocoercivity methods with geometric structures. Building upon but distinctly extending classical hypocoercivity approaches, we demonstrate how geometric control, via commutators and curvature-like structures in probability spaces, resolves degeneracies inherent in kinetic operators. Centered around the Boltzmann and Fokker–Planck equations, we derive sharp exponential convergence estimates under minimal regularity assumptions, improving on prior methods by incorporating Wasserstein gradient flow techniques. Our framework is further applied to the study of hydrodynamic limits, collisional relaxation in magnetized plasmas, the Vlasov–Poisson system, and modern data-driven algorithms, highlighting the central role of entropy as both a physical and variational tool across disciplines. By bridging entropy dissipation, optimal transport, and geometric analysis, our work offers a new perspective on stability, convergence, and structure in high-dimensional kinetic models and applications.

**Keywords:** kinetic theory; Boltzmann equation; hypercoercivity; entropy dissipation; optimal transport; Wasserstein geometry; Ricci curvature; Vlasov–Poisson system; Fokker–Planck equation

**MSC:** 35Q84; 35Q20; 35B40; 35A23; 49Q22; 60H10; 82C40; 82C22; 83C10; 65C35; 53C21; 68T07

## 1. Introduction

The theory of kinetic equations provides a powerful analytical framework for describing the statistical evolution of large systems of interacting particles. Central to this framework is the Boltzmann equation, which captures the interplay between transport, collisions, and relaxation in thermodynamic equilibrium. The mathematical analysis of such equations presents profound challenges due to the nonlinearity, high dimensionality, and degeneracies present in the operators involved. Among the most significant achievements in this domain is the development of the hypocoercivity method, which rigorously quantifies the convergence to equilibrium despite the lack of uniform ellipticity. This method, introduced by Villani and further developed by Hérau, Mouhot, and others, couples entropy dissipation techniques with commutator structures and geometric control to recover coercivity in degenerate kinetic settings.

Optimal transport theory, originating in the work of Monge and Kantorovich, has recently emerged as a unifying geometric framework for understanding a wide class of dissipative and diffusive phenomena. The introduction of the Wasserstein space of probability measures as a metric space endowed with Riemannian-like structure enables the variational interpretation of many kinetic and diffusion equations. In particular, the Fokker–Planck equation can be viewed as a gradient flow of the relative entropy functional with respect to the Wasserstein metric. This geometric viewpoint reveals deep connections between curvature, functional inequalities (e.g., logarithmic Sobolev, HWI), and the rate of convergence to equilibrium.

The synthesis of hypocoercivity and optimal transport has led to significant advances in the rigorous analysis of both linear and nonlinear kinetic models. These include the derivation of exponential decay rates, propagation of regularity, stability of steady states, and quantitative hydrodynamic limits. Applications span a wide range of physical systems, from collisional relaxation in magnetized plasmas and compressible flows to the long-time behavior of self-gravitating systems modeled by the Vlasov–Poisson equation.

In recent years, the techniques developed in kinetic theory and optimal transport have also found profound applications beyond traditional physical systems. Notably, in the context of data science and machine learning, the geometry of the space of probability measures, the analysis of Wasserstein gradient flows, and the structure of entropy functionals have become central to modern generative models, variational inference, and sampling algorithms. A detailed study of Wasserstein gradient flows for kinetic equations is presented in [1]. Score-based diffusion models, underdamped Langevin dynamics, and entropic regularized optimal transport (e.g., Sinkhorn distances) are now widely employed in high-dimensional statistical learning. These methods reflect, at a computational level, the same mathematical structures—entropy decay, functional inequalities, convergence in metric measure spaces—that underlie kinetic relaxation.

This paper develops a unified and rigorous perspective on these interrelated themes. We begin by revisiting the foundational aspects of the Boltzmann equation, entropy dissipation, and the H-theorem. We then present the framework of hypocoercivity in both linear and nonlinear settings, highlighting its geometric and analytical underpinnings. The roles of functional inequalities, commutator estimates, and hypoellipticity are emphasized throughout. Building on this, we explore connections with optimal transport and the geometry of the Wasserstein space, with special attention to the Ricci curvature lower bounds and convexity of entropy.

The latter sections of the paper are devoted to applications: we study the relaxation behavior of plasmas under external magnetic fields, the derivation of fluid models from kinetic equations, the dynamics of self-gravitating astrophysical systems, and the implementation of kinetic-inspired algorithms in data science. Throughout, we stress the conceptual role of entropy as both a physical observable and a variational structure, linking microdynamics, macrodynamics, and probabilistic learning.

Although this study covers diverse models, including Boltzmann, Fokker–Planck, Vlasov–Poisson, and optimal transport in data science, these share common mechanisms such as entropy dissipation, geometric regularization, and variational structures. This unified viewpoint enables a coherent analytical treatment across seemingly disparate areas.

While the specific models studied range from plasma physics and fluid dynamics to astrophysics and machine learning, their underlying dynamics reveal a unifying structure: entropy-driven geometric regularization across high-dimensional kinetic systems. This highlights the broad interdisciplinary applicability of our framework.

While significant progress has been achieved separately in hypocoercivity theory and optimal transport geometry, integrated frameworks linking entropy dissipation, geometric control, and metric structures remain underdeveloped. Classical hypocoercivity techniques, although powerful, often treat the geometry implicitly and rely heavily on coercivity arguments localized in velocity space. In contrast, our approach explicitly incorporates the Wasserstein geometry of probability measures and the role of geometric commutators, allowing for the systematic transfer of regularity and dissipation across phase space. This perspective not only yields sharper convergence rates under weaker assumptions, but also extends the analytic reach of entropy methods to models traditionally outside the classical hypocoercivity setting, such as kinetic flows in machine learning and field-driven Vlasov dynamics.

### 1.1. Notation and Terminology

Throughout this paper, we use the following notations:

- $f(t, x, v)$: particle distribution function.
- $Q(f, f)$: Boltzmann collision operator.
- $F[f]$: self-consistent force field.
- $H(f)$: entropy functional.
- $W_2$: 2-Wasserstein distance.
- $B(|v - v_*|, \cos\theta)$: collision kernel.
- $\theta$: scattering angle.
- $\nabla_x, \nabla_v$: spatial and velocity gradients.

Since our approach bridges kinetic theory, entropy methods, and optimal transport geometry, the notations introduced here are chosen to emphasize structural parallels across these domains. In particular, we stress the dual role of entropy both as a functional on probability measures and as a dynamical quantity governing relaxation phenomena. Moreover, we adopt conventions that highlight the geometric control mechanisms fundamental to hypocoercivity and Wasserstein gradient flows. The reader is encouraged to refer back to this section throughout the manuscript as the interplay between analytic and geometric structures unfolds.

### 1.2. Historical and Modern Developments of Optimal Transport

The geometric structure plays a crucial role in overcoming degeneracies: through commutator relations, it ensures smoothing and control across position and velocity variables. In particular, Hörmander's hypoellipticity framework guarantees regularity even when direct diffusion is absent, providing a geometric route to hypocoercivity.

The history of optimal transport theory can be traced back to multiple independent discoveries, evolving through different mathematical frameworks over centuries. This text provides an overview of its foundational contributors and the subsequent evolution of the field.

The first formulation of the optimal transport problem was introduced by *Gaspard Monge* in 1781 in his *Mémoire sur la théorie des déblais et des remblais* [2]. Monge's problem involved minimizing transportation costs when moving materials from one place to another. His formulation sought a deterministic optimal coupling that would assign each unit of material to a specific destination, minimizing the total cost based on distance.

Monge's geometric intuition led to key mathematical insights, such as transport occurring along orthogonal straight lines to certain surfaces, leading to discoveries in differential geometries. However, his mathematical treatment lacked formal rigor by modern standards.

Monge's ideas resurfaced much later in the 1938 work of *Leonid Kantorovich*, a Soviet mathematician and economist, who reformulated the problem in the language of linear programming [3]. He introduced *Kantorovich relaxation*, allowing mass to be split and transported probabilistically rather than deterministically.

Kantorovich also developed duality theory, which became fundamental in solving transport problems. His work extended beyond mathematics into economics, leading to his Nobel Prize in Economics (1975) for contributions to the theory of resource allocation. A key contribution to optimal transport was the definition of the *Kantorovich–Rubinstein distance*, a metric that measures the cost of transporting one probability measure into another [4].

Throughout the mid-to-late 20th century, statisticians and probabilists expanded on Kantorovich's ideas, particularly in probability theory and functional analysis. In the 1970s, *Dobrushin* applied optimal transport distances to study interacting particle systems [5]. *Hiroshi Tanaka* used these techniques in kinetic theory, particularly in understanding variants of the Boltzmann equation [6].

By the 1980s, three independent research directions had emerged that reshaped the field: *John Mather* (Dynamical Systems) connected action-minimizing curves in Lagrangian mechanics with optimal transport problems [7]; *Yann Brenier* (fluid mechanics and PDEs) established links between OT and incompressible fluid mechanics, particularly via the Monge–Ampère equation and convex analysis [8]; and *Mike Cullen* (meteorology) showed that semi-geostrophic equations in meteorology could be reinterpreted using optimal transport principles [9].

A major turning point came in the early 2000s with the groundbreaking work of *Cédric Villani*, who systematically unified the field and extended its applications across geometry, analysis, and physics. His two monographs, *Topics in Optimal Transportation* (2003) and *Optimal Transport: Old and New* (2009) [4,10], became foundational texts, synthesizing decades of fragmented work and establishing a coherent theoretical framework.

Villani's work, often in collaboration with researchers such as Léonard, Ambrosio, McCann, Otto, and others, led to the geometrization of probability spaces using optimal transport. He helped formalize the *Wasserstein geometry* in the space of probability measures, enabling a differential structure akin to Riemannian geometry. This gave rise to gradient flows in the Wasserstein space (notably developed by Felix Otto and Ambrosio–Gigli–Savaré) [11,12]; new insights into Ricci curvature bounds in metric measure spaces via the Lott–Sturm–Villani theory [13]; and applications to entropy, diffusion, and functional inequalities (e.g., Talagrand, HWI inequalities) [10]. These developments had powerful implications in geometric analysis, particularly in understanding spaces with lower bounds on Ricci curvature and the analysis of heat flow in non-smooth settings. Generalizations of kinetic transport equations to metric measure spaces are studied in [14].

In the 21st century, optimal transport has become a highly interdisciplinary field, with diverse applications in machine learning and data science—particularly in generative models (e.g., Wasserstein GANs) [15], domain adaptation, clustering, and distributional learning; in image processing and computer vision, including color transfer, shape matching, and texture synthesis [16]; in economics, especially in matching theory and income inequality metrics; in statistics, for defining distances between distributions in high dimensions [17]; and in quantum physics, statistical mechanics, and density functional theory.

Recent advances have also explored unbalanced transport, where mass is allowed to be created or destroyed (e.g., Chizat, Peyré, Schmitzer) [18]; entropy-regularized OT, making computation feasible at large scales (e.g., Sinkhorn distances) [19]; discrete OT for graphs and networks; dynamic formulations (Benamou–Brenier), leading to efficient numerical methods [20]; and barycenters in Wasserstein space, with applications in image averaging and consensus learning [21].

The evolution of optimal transport theory showcases the power of mathematical abstraction to transcend disciplinary boundaries. From Monge's geometric intuition to Kantorovich's probabilistic reformulation, and culminating in the modern theory shaped by Villani and his collaborators, optimal transport has become a central tool in mathematics and beyond. Its current growth is fueled by its unifying nature, geometric depth, and computational versatility, with active research directions still unfolding across mathematics, computer science, physics, and the social sciences.

This paper explores the foundational issues underlying these theories, with an emphasis on stability, entropy methods, hypoellipticity, and geometric connections. We will systematically analyze the key principles and challenges associated with each domain, shedding light on their intersections and mathematical richness.

## 2. Boltzmann Breakthrough: Kinetic Theory, Optimal Transport, and Entropy

Mathematics plays a crucial role in describing the fundamental processes governing natural and physical phenomena. Among the various branches of applied mathematics, *kinetic theory* and *optimal transport* have emerged as essential tools in understanding how particles and probability distributions evolve over time. Kinetic equations describe the statistical behavior of particle systems, either with or without collisions, while optimal transport theory provides a powerful framework for studying the movement of mass in the most efficient manner. Both areas have profound implications, from plasma physics and fluid mechanics to geometry and functional analysis.

The mathematical study of kinetic equations dates back to Ludwig Boltzmann's pioneering work in the 19th century, leading to the well-known *Boltzmann equation*, which models gas dynamics:

$$\frac{\partial f}{\partial t} + v \cdot \nabla_x f = Q(f,f), \tag{1}$$

where $f(t,x,v)$ is the *distribution function*, describing the probability density of particles at time $t$, position $x \in \mathbb{R}^d$, and velocity $v \in \mathbb{R}^d$.

The term $Q(f,f)$ is the *collision operator*, which accounts for the change in velocity distribution due to interactions between particles. It encodes the fundamental mechanism by which a gas approaches thermal equilibrium. The Boltzmann equation provides a statistical description of a system with many interacting particles, bridging the microscopic laws of physics with macroscopic thermodynamic behavior. In its classical form for hard spheres, the collision operator $Q(f,f)$ takes the form

$$Q(f,f)(v) = \int_{\mathbb{R}^d} \int_{\mathbb{S}^{d-1}} B(|v - v_*|, \cos\theta) \left[ f(v')f(v'_*) - f(v)f(v_*) \right] d\sigma \, dv_*, \tag{2}$$

where

- $v, v_*$ denote the *pre-collision velocities*;
- $v', v'_*$ denote the *post-collision velocities* resulting from elastic scattering;
- $B(|v - v_*|, \cos\theta)$ is the *collision kernel*, depending on the *relative velocity* $|v - v_*|$ and the *scattering angle* $\theta$.

In Equation (2), we consider $f$ at a fixed time $t$ and position $x$, treating it as a function of the velocity variable $v$ only. This reflects the local action of the collision operator in velocity space.

The variables $v$ and $v_*$ represent the velocities of two particles before collision, while $v'$ and $v'_*$ denote the corresponding velocities after collision, determined by the conservation of momentum and energy during an elastic collision.

The collision rate depends on the *relative velocity* $|v - v_*|$ between the particles, and the collision kernel also depends on the *scattering angle* $\theta$ between the incoming and outgoing relative velocities.

This equation plays a central role in kinetic theory, as it models how particle collisions influence the macroscopic behavior of a gas. It encapsulates the transition from microscopic Newtonian interactions to emergent thermodynamic laws.

The Boltzmann equation marks a significant conceptual shift in the understanding of physical systems. Historically, classical mechanics provided deterministic descriptions of particle motion, governed by Newton's laws. In contrast, kinetic theory introduces a statistical perspective, acknowledging the impracticality of tracking every individual particle in a large system. This shift from a deterministic to a probabilistic framework highlights the deep epistemological divide between microscopic mechanics and macroscopic thermodynamics.

The function $f(t,x,v)$ encapsulates our knowledge of a system not in terms of precise trajectories but in terms of probability distributions. This probabilistic description aligns with the broader conceptual transition in physics from classical determinism to statistical and quantum interpretations. The use of distribution functions reflects an epistemological necessity: our inability to resolve individual particle positions and velocities necessitates a coarse-grained, statistical approach.

Furthermore, the introduction of the *collision operator* $Q(f,f)$ represents an abstraction of microscopic interactions, reducing complex many-body dynamics into an effective statistical mechanism. This reduction raises questions about the emergent nature of macroscopic laws: how do local, microscopic interactions give rise to global, thermodynamic behavior? The principle of *entropy increase*, embedded in Boltzmann's H-theorem, illustrates how irreversibility emerges from time-reversible microscopic laws. This paradox, deeply connected to Loschmidt's and Zermelo's objections to Boltzmann's theory, remains a foundational issue in the philosophy of physics.

A key insight is encoded in Boltzmann's celebrated *H-theorem*, which introduces the *entropy functional*

$$\mathcal{H}(f)(t) := \int_{\mathbb{R}^d} \int_{\mathbb{R}^d} f(t,x,v) \log f(t,x,v)\, dv dx, \tag{3}$$

and asserts that its time derivative satisfies

$$\frac{d}{dt}\mathcal{H}(f)(t) \leq 0, \tag{4}$$

with equality only at equilibrium (e.g., Maxwellian distribution). This inequality reflects the second law of thermodynamics: entropy does not decrease.

This result—despite being derived from time-reversible microscopic dynamics—predicts the irreversible trend toward equilibrium, generating tension with the reversibility of Newtonian mechanics (as noted in Loschmidt's paradox and Zermelo's recurrence objection). These philosophical challenges remain foundational in statistical physics [22,23].

Moreover, kinetic theory serves as a bridge between various mathematical and physical domains. It connects functional analysis, measure theory, and PDE theory with physical concepts such as equilibrium, fluctuations, and dissipation. The Boltzmann equation is a nonlinear integro-differential equation, and its study has led to significant advances in the theory of PDEs, particularly in hypoellipticity and hypocoercivity [24,25].

Finally, the Boltzmann equation and its generalizations continue to inform modern research in non-equilibrium statistical mechanics, stochastic processes, and even quantum kinetic theory. The conceptual and foundational challenges it poses, such as the justification of the molecular chaos hypothesis, the nature of entropy, and the emergence of macroscopic irreversibility, remain at the heart of ongoing discussions in both mathematical physics and the philosophy of science. Recent perspectives on the Boltzmann–Grad limit have been developed in [26].

More recently, the *Vlasov equation*

$$\frac{\partial f}{\partial t} + v \cdot \nabla_x f + F[f] \cdot \nabla_v f = 0 \tag{5}$$

has been used to describe large-scale astrophysical and plasma systems where collisions are negligible. Here, $F[f]$ denotes the *self-consistent force field*, typically obtained from $f$ via a field equation such as Poisson's or Maxwell's equation. In this collisionless regime, questions about Landau damping, plasma echo, and long-time stability dominate [27].

Parallel to kinetic theory, *optimal transport* has provided deep insights into the geometry of probability distributions and functional inequalities. Optimal transport theory now connects Ricci curvature [13], statistical mechanics and entropy [11], partial differential equations, and diffusion via Wasserstein geometry.

The Wasserstein distance $W_2$ between two probability densities, $\mu$ and $\nu$, is defined as

$$W_2^2(\mu,\nu) := \inf_{\gamma\in\Pi(\mu,\nu)} \int_{\mathbb{R}^d\times\mathbb{R}^d} |x-y|^2\, d\gamma(x,y), \tag{6}$$

where $\Pi(\mu,\nu)$ is the set of couplings with marginals $\mu$ and $\nu$. This defines a geodesic metric in the space of probability measures with finite second moments.

By bridging these fields, optimal transport offers novel perspectives on fundamental mathematical problems. Modern treatments of optimal transport in kinetic theory are presented in [28].

## 3. Entropy and the H-Theorem

A key feature of the Boltzmann equation is its deep connection to *entropy*. *Boltzmann entropy*, denoted by $H(f)$, is defined as

$$H(f) = \int_{\mathbb{R}^d}\int_{\mathbb{R}^d} f(x,v)\log f(x,v)\, dvdx. \tag{7}$$

This function measures the disorder in the system and plays a crucial role in thermodynamic laws. Ludwig Boltzmann introduced the celebrated *H-theorem*, which states that entropy increases over time:

$$\frac{dH}{dt} \le 0. \tag{8}$$

More precisely, the entropy dissipation rate $D(f)$ is defined by

$$D(f) := -\frac{d}{dt}H(f) = -\int Q(f,f)\log f\, dv, \tag{9}$$

which is non-negative, i.e., $D(f) \ge 0$. This provides a statistical explanation for the second law of thermodynamics: a closed system will evolve irreversibly toward a state of maximum entropy, corresponding to *thermal equilibrium*.

To understand the mechanism behind entropy production, we note that collisions in the Boltzmann equation drive the system towards a *Maxwellian equilibrium*:

$$f_\infty(v) = \frac{\rho}{(2\pi T)^{d/2}}\exp\left(-\frac{|v-u|^2}{2T}\right), \tag{10}$$

where $\rho$ is the density, $T$ the temperature, and $u$ the mean velocity of the gas. The entropy of this Maxwellian distribution is maximized, which explains why physical systems naturally evolve toward this state. Recent refinements of entropy methods for nonlocal kinetic equations can be found in [29].

### *Cercignani's Conjecture and Entropy Dissipation*

While the H-theorem establishes that entropy increases, it does not provide an explicit rate of convergence to equilibrium. *Cercignani's conjecture* [30] refines this understanding by proposing a quantitative relationship between entropy dissipation and deviation from equilibrium. The conjecture states the following:

$$D(f) \geq C(H(f) - H(f_\infty)), \tag{11}$$

where $C > 0$ is a constant depending on the collision kernel and physical parameters. This inequality suggests that the closer the system is to equilibrium, the slower the entropy dissipation, leading to explicit control of the convergence rate.

In a precise sense, $D(f)$ quantifies the rate at which entropy is produced in a system described by the Boltzmann equation. Conceptually, it measures how fast the system evolves towards equilibrium by accounting for the effects of collisions on the distribution function. It is a key quantity in proving stability and convergence results, with deep connections to *functional inequalities*, such as logarithmic Sobolev inequalities and the spectral gap.

Thus, the entropy dissipation rate $D(f)$ serves as a fundamental bridge between microscopic dynamics (collisions) and macroscopic thermodynamic behavior (irreversibility and equilibrium). In kinetic theory, collisions redistribute velocities, and $D(f)$ reflects the effectiveness of this redistribution. As per the H-theorem, we have

$$\frac{dH(f)}{dt} = -D(f) \leq 0. \tag{12}$$

Entropy production arises from the redistribution of particles in velocity space. The stronger the collisions (i.e., the more mixing occurs), the greater the entropy dissipation, meaning the system reaches equilibrium faster.

Cercignani's conjecture, restated as

$$D(f) \geq C(H(f) - H(f_\infty)), \tag{13}$$

connects entropy dissipation to the distance from equilibrium. It emphasizes the stabilizing role of collisions in driving the system toward maximum entropy.

The concept of entropy dissipation extends beyond the Boltzmann equation into broader thermodynamic contexts. It represents the rate at which a system loses free energy due to internal interactions. In fluid dynamics, for example, entropy dissipation is analogous to *viscous dissipation*, where kinetic energy is irreversibly converted into heat.

Cercignani's conjecture remained an open problem for many years and is known to be *not* universally true in its original form. However, significant progress was made by *Villani* and *Toscani* [22,31], who established modified versions of the conjecture. In particular, they proved that

$$D(f) \geq \lambda\, \Phi(H(f) - H(f_\infty)), \tag{14}$$

for some convex function $\Phi$, under suitable regularity and moment assumptions. These results provided a rigorous framework for quantifying entropy dissipation and convergence rates in kinetic theory.

## 4. Hypercoercivity: Resolving Degeneracy and Ensuring Convergence

The geometric structure plays a crucial role in overcoming degeneracies: through commutator relations, it ensures smoothing and control across position and velocity variables. In particular, Hörmander's hypoellipticity framework guarantees regularity even when direct diffusion is absent, providing a geometric route to hypocoercivity.

One of the central mathematical challenges in analyzing the long-time behavior of kinetic equations—such as the Boltzmann or linear Fokker–Planck equations—is the issue of *degeneracy* in the collision or diffusion operator. Specifically, in the Boltzmann equation,

$$\frac{\partial f}{\partial t} + v \cdot \nabla_x f = Q(f, f),$$

the *collision operator* $Q(f, f)$ acts only in the velocity variable $v$ and leaves the spatial variable $x$ untouched. This degeneracy obstructs the direct application of standard coercivity arguments (such as Poincaré or spectral gap inequalities) in the full phase space $(x, v)$.

In particular, the linearized Boltzmann equation around a Maxwellian equilibrium $f_\infty(v)$ is typically written as

$$\partial_t h + v \cdot \nabla_x h = \mathcal{L}h,$$

where $h := f - f_\infty$, and $\mathcal{L}$ is the linearized collision operator. While $\mathcal{L}$ is coercive in $v$ (modulo kernel), the transport term $v \cdot \nabla_x$ introduces oscillations and mixing that are not controlled directly by $\mathcal{L}$.

To overcome this, *Cédric Villani* introduced the method of *hypercoercivity* [24], a general framework designed to handle this type of degeneracy and establish quantitative exponential convergence rates toward equilibrium.

### 4.1. Functional Setting and Degeneracy

Degeneracy manifests as the lack of full coercivity of the generator of the kinetic semigroup. Consider a Hilbert space $\mathcal{H}$, such as $L^2(\mathbb{T}^d_x \times \mathbb{R}^d_v, \mu^{-1} dx dv)$, where $\mu(v) = e^{-|v|^2/2}$ is the Gaussian or Maxwellian weight. Define the evolution operator:

$$\mathcal{A} := -v \cdot \nabla_x + \mathcal{L}.$$

The operator $\mathcal{L}$ typically satisfies

$$\langle \mathcal{L}h, h \rangle \leq -\lambda \|h^\perp\|^2,$$

where $h^\perp$ is the projection of $h$ orthogonal to the kernel of $\mathcal{L}$ (i.e., macroscopic modes). However, $\mathcal{A}$ is not coercive in $\mathcal{H}$ due to the transport term, and in fact, it may not even be sectorial.

### 4.2. Villani's Hypercoercivity Method

Villani's key insight was to modify the energy functional to include cross-derivative terms that couple $x$ and $v$ regularities, in order to exploit *commutator structure* and transfer the velocity dissipation to spatial variables.

Let us define the modified energy functional:

$$\mathcal{E}(h) := \|h\|^2 + \alpha \langle \nabla_x h, \nabla_v h \rangle + \beta \|\nabla_x h\|^2,$$

with appropriately chosen $\alpha, \beta > 0$. Then, one shows that

$$\frac{d}{dt}\mathcal{E}(h(t)) \leq -\lambda \mathcal{E}(h(t)),$$

for some explicit $\lambda > 0$, leading to

$$\mathcal{E}(h(t)) \leq \mathcal{E}(h_0) e^{-\lambda t}.$$

This decay estimate implies that

$$\|h(t)\|_{L^2} \leq Ce^{-\lambda t}\|h(0)\|_{H^1}, \tag{15}$$

which demonstrates exponential convergence to equilibrium in a weighted $L^2$ norm.

### 4.3. Geometric and Analytical Structure

The success of the hypercoercivity method relies on three interconnected ingredients:

- *Entropy dissipation*: The collision operator provides dissipation in the $v$ variable, which controls the non-equilibrium modes.
- *Hypoellipticity and regularity transfer*: Inspired by Hörmander's theory [32], certain commutators between the transport operator and the collision operator generate smoothing effects in $x$.
- *Commutator estimates*: The key to propagating dissipation from velocity to spatial variables involves bounding expressions like $[\nabla_x, \mathcal{L}^{-1}v \cdot \nabla_x]$ or higher-order mixed derivatives.

The convergence result can be interpreted as a non-symmetric analog of coercivity: Although the generator is not coercive in the standard sense, the flow generated by it dissipates energy due to the interaction between the dissipative and conservative directions.

### 4.4. Abstract Hypocoercivity Theorem (Villani)

Let $A = B + C$ in a Hilbert space $\mathcal{H}$, with $B$ being symmetric and dissipative, and $C$ antisymmetric (e.g., $C = v \cdot \nabla_x$). Under certain bracket conditions,

$$\exists\, n \in \mathbb{N} \text{ such that } \mathrm{Lie}^n(B, C) \supset \mathrm{Id},$$

and assuming that $B$ has a spectral gap, $A$ generates a semigroup satisfying

$$\|e^{tA}f - f_\infty\| \leq Ce^{-\lambda t}\|f - f_\infty\|.$$

This gives exponential decay toward equilibrium with explicit control at the rate $\lambda$.

### 4.5. Applications and Extensions

This theory has been successfully applied to a wide class of kinetic models:

- Linearized Boltzmann and Landau equations with periodic or confining domains [27,33].
- Kinetic Fokker–Planck equations with external potentials [34,35].
- Quantum and semi-classical limits of collisional kinetic models.

Villani's hypercoercivity program provides a unified functional analytic framework for proving convergence to equilibrium in degenerate, non-symmetric PDEs where classical coercivity fails. It combines tools from semigroup theory, PDEs, microlocal analysis, and differential geometry.

$$\|f(t,x,v) - f_\infty\|_{L^2_\mu} \leq Ce^{-\lambda t}\|f(0,x,v) - f_\infty\|_{H^1_\mu}, \tag{16}$$

where $\mu(v) = e^{-|v|^2/2}$ is the Maxwellian weight.

## 5. Wasserstein Geometry and Villani's Contributions to Optimal Transport

Villani's work, often in collaboration with researchers such as Léonard, Ambrosio, McCann, Otto, and others, led to the geometrization of probability spaces using optimal transport. He helped formalize the *Wasserstein geometry* in the space of probability measures, enabling a differential structure akin to Riemannian geometry.

Let $\mathcal{P}_2(M)$ be the space of Borel probability measures on a Riemannian manifold $M$ with a finite second moment. The *2-Wasserstein distance* between $\mu, \nu \in \mathcal{P}_2(M)$ is defined as

$$W_2(\mu,\nu) := \left( \inf_{\pi \in \Pi(\mu,\nu)} \int_{M\times M} d(x,y)^2 \, d\pi(x,y) \right)^{1/2},$$

where $\Pi(\mu,\nu)$ is the set of transport plans, i.e., Borel probability measures on $M \times M$ with marginals $\mu$ and $\nu$.

This metric endows $\mathcal{P}_2(M)$ with a geodesic structure: there exists a constant-speed geodesic $(\mu_t)_{t\in[0,1]}$ between any two measures, $\mu_0$ and $\mu_1$. This structure is key to formulating *displacement convexity*, an idea introduced by McCann [36].

In the early 2000s, Felix Otto observed that the heat equation on $\mathbb{R}^n$,

$$\partial_t \rho = \Delta \rho,$$

can be viewed as the *gradient flow* of the entropy functional in the space $(\mathcal{P}_2(\mathbb{R}^n), W_2)$ [11]. That is, the dynamics of $\rho$ is the steepest descent of the Boltzmann entropy:

$$\mathcal{H}(\rho) := \int_{\mathbb{R}^n} \rho(x) \log \rho(x) \, dx.$$

This interpretation led to a formal Riemannian structure on $\mathcal{P}_2$, defined rigorously through the dynamic formulation of $W_2$ by Benamou and Brenier [20]:

$$W_2^2(\mu_0,\mu_1) = \inf_{\rho_t, v_t} \left\{ \int_0^1 \int_{\mathbb{R}^n} \rho_t(x) \|v_t(x)\|^2 dx\, dt \,\middle|\, \partial_t \rho_t + \nabla \cdot (\rho_t v_t) = 0 \right\}.$$

This geometrization was rigorously developed by Ambrosio, Gigli, and Savaré [12], who created a full theory of gradient flows in metric spaces. Their work introduced *evolution variational inequalities* (EVIs) and characterized $\lambda$-convex functionals in Wasserstein space.

Villani, together with Lott [13] and, independently, Sturm [37,38], extended this framework to general metric measure spaces $(X,d,m)$ via convexity of the entropy along Wasserstein geodesics. Let

$$\mathcal{H}_m(\mu) := \int \log\left(\frac{d\mu}{dm}\right) d\mu$$

be the relative entropy with respect to a reference measure $m$. The space satisfies a curvature-dimension condition $CD(K,\infty)$ if for any geodesic $(\mu_t)_{t\in[0,1]}$ in $\mathcal{P}_2(X)$,

$$\mathcal{H}_m(\mu_t) \leq (1-t)\mathcal{H}_m(\mu_0) + t\mathcal{H}_m(\mu_1) - \frac{K}{2} t(1-t) W_2^2(\mu_0,\mu_1).$$

This *Lott–Sturm–Villani theory* generalizes Ricci curvature lower bounds to singular spaces, and applies to heat flow, functional inequalities, and geometric analysis.

One of the celebrated applications of this geometric formalism is *Talagrand's inequality* [39], which asserts that for the standard Gaussian measure $\gamma$ and any measure $\mu$ that is absolutely continuous with respect to $\gamma$,

$$W_2^2(\mu,\gamma) \leq 2\, \mathrm{Ent}_\gamma(\mu).$$

Building on this, Otto and Villani derived the *HWI inequality* [40], interpolating between relative entropy $H$, Wasserstein distance $W$, and Fisher information $I$:

$$\mathrm{Ent}_\gamma(\mu) \leq W_2(\mu,\gamma)\sqrt{I(\mu|\gamma)} - \frac{K}{2} W_2^2(\mu,\gamma),$$

where

$$I(\mu|\gamma) := \int \left\| \nabla \log\left(\frac{d\mu}{d\gamma}\right) \right\|^2 d\mu.$$

These inequalities imply logarithmic Sobolev inequalities, hypercontractivity, and exponential convergence to equilibrium, and they demonstrate the profound unification of geometry, analysis, and probability enabled by optimal transport.

Thus, Villani's work and its extensions reshaped entire domains of geometric analysis, particularly the theory of metric measure spaces with curvature bounds, and offered a powerful, flexible framework to study heat diffusion, entropy dissipation, and nonlinear PDEs from a variational and geometric perspective.

### 5.1. Commutator Estimates and Propagation of Regularity

A critical aspect of the hypercoercivity framework developed by Villani [24] is the propagation of regularity from the velocity variable $v$ to the spatial variable $x$. This is achieved through a careful analysis of *commutator estimates*, which exploit the non-commutative algebra of the vector fields involved in the kinetic equation.

Consider the kinetic transport operator

$$T := \partial_t + v \cdot \nabla_x,$$

and the linearized kinetic equation

$$Tf = \mathcal{L}f,$$

where $\mathcal{L}$ is the linearized collision operator, which acts only on the velocity variable $v$. While $\mathcal{L}$ provides coercivity in $v$, it does not directly control $\nabla_x f$. To resolve this, Villani's insight was to consider the Lie algebra generated by the differential operators appearing in the system.

Define the first-order differential operators:

$$X_0 := \partial_t + v \cdot \nabla_x, \quad X_i := \partial_{v_i}, \quad i = 1, \dots, d.$$

Note that

$$[X_0, X_i] = \partial_{x_i}.$$

Thus, although $\partial_{x_i}$ is not in the original list of vector fields, it is obtained via a commutator. This aligns with the structure required by Hörmander's hypoellipticity theorem [32]: if the Lie algebra generated by a collection of vector fields spans the tangent space at each point, then the associated operator is hypoelliptic.

This commutator structure implies that regularity in the velocity variable, when combined with transport in $x$, induces regularity in $x$. This mechanism is formalized through estimates of the form

$$\|[X_i, X_j]f\|_{L^2} \le C\|\mathcal{L}f\|_{L^2}, \tag{17}$$

where $[X_i, X_j] := X_iX_j - X_jX_i$ denotes the commutator of two operators. Since $\mathcal{L}$ provides dissipation in $v$, and since $\nabla_x$ can be expressed as a commutator involving $\nabla_v$, we obtain indirect control over the spatial derivatives of $f$.

This transfer of regularity is crucial for constructing coercive energy functionals, as in the hypercoercive Lyapunov framework:

$$\mathcal{E}(f) := \|f\|^2 + \alpha\langle \nabla_x f, \nabla_v f\rangle + \beta\|\nabla_x f\|^2.$$

Differentiating $\mathcal{E}(f(t))$ along the solution and applying commutator bounds (such as (17)) yields:

$$\frac{d}{dt}\mathcal{E}(f(t)) \leq -\lambda\mathcal{E}(f(t)) + \text{lower-order terms},$$

which shows that the modified energy decays exponentially with time.

The resolution of degeneracy in kinetic equations hinges on a geometric mechanism: even when direct diffusion acts only in the velocity variables, the interplay between transport and collisions generates an indirect regularization in space. This is a manifestation of Hörmander's hypoellipticity principle, where the non-commutativity of vector fields creates effective diffusion across the entire phase space. Specifically, the transport operator couples position and velocity, and the commutators of transport with collision vector fields span the full tangent space. Geometrically, the system evolves along a sub-Riemannian structure, where accessibility through commutator paths replaces the need for isotropic diffusion. This insight allows us to systematically construct energy functionals that propagate velocity regularity into spatial smoothing, thus recovering global convergence even when classical coercivity fails. In our framework, this geometric control is not an incidental technicality but a structural principle: it underpins the flow of entropy across kinetic and macroscopic variables, bridging the microscopic and macroscopic descriptions naturally.

### 5.2. Explicit Convergence Rate

By combining entropy dissipation, hypoelliptic smoothing, and commutator estimates, the hypercoercivity method allows one to rigorously prove *explicit exponential convergence to equilibrium*. For a wide class of linear kinetic equations—including the linearized Boltzmann and Fokker–Planck equations—one obtains

$$\|f(t,x,v) - f_\infty(v)\|_{L^2_\mu} \leq Ce^{-\lambda t}\|f(0,x,v) - f_\infty(v)\|_{H^1_\mu}, \tag{18}$$

where $\mu(v) = e^{-|v|^2/2}$ is the Maxwellian weight, $f_\infty$ is the equilibrium state (often a global Maxwellian), and the constants $C, \lambda > 0$ depend on parameters such as the collisional cross-section, dimension $d$, and domain geometry [34,35].

This result rigorously confirms that any smooth solution to the linearized kinetic equation with a periodic or confined spatial domain converges toward equilibrium at an explicitly quantifiable rate. Quantitative hypocoercivity techniques based on optimal transport approaches are developed in [41].

In the nonlinear case, such as the full Boltzmann equation with hard spheres and periodic boundary conditions, similar exponential decay results have been obtained under close-to-equilibrium assumptions via nonlinear hypocoercivity methods [27,33].

These quantitative estimates validate Boltzmann's physical intuition about the *irreversible trend toward equilibrium* and connect probabilistic entropy arguments with sharp analytic inequalities.

## 6. Applications and Broader Implications

Beyond their mathematical interest, the techniques developed in this study have profound implications for the modeling of physical and computational systems. Many applications—ranging from plasma confinement to galactic evolution and high-dimensional generative models—exhibit inherent degeneracies, nonlinearity, and high-dimensionality, where classical coercivity-based analyses become ineffective. Our unified framework, grounded in geometric control and entropy dissipation, provides a versatile analytical tool to rigorously predict stability, relaxation rates, and convergence properties even in such challenging settings. In plasma physics, for instance, the geometric smoothing across position–velocity variables is critical for understanding collisional relaxation under magnetic fields. In fluid dynamics, entropy-based methods offer explicit control over hydrodynamic limits, including shock and boundary layers. In data science, Wasserstein-gradient flows and kinetic sampling algorithms directly benefit from geometric convergence properties, enhancing algorithmic stability and efficiency. Thus, by systematically bridging microscopic interactions, macroscopic behaviors, and probabilistic learning, our approach offers a conceptual and technical foundation for robust multiscale modeling across disciplines.

The study of entropy production, hypocoercivity, and stability in kinetic equations has far-reaching consequences across mathematical physics, applied mathematics, and geometry. These methods establish rigorous bridges between the microscopic particle description of systems and their macroscopic thermodynamic behavior, enabling multiscale modeling and convergence analysis in a variety of settings (see Figure 1).

$$MicroscopicDynamics \longrightarrow KineticEquations \longrightarrow EntropyDissipation \longrightarrow GeometricStructures \longrightarrow MacroscopicModels$$

**Figure 1.** Schematic representation of analytical connections between microscopic dynamics, kinetic equations, entropy dissipation, geometry, and macroscopic models.

The mathematical structures discussed in this study find natural applications in fields such as machine learning (sampling methods generative modeling), astrophysics (galactic equilibrium and evolution), plasma physics (collisional and collisionless regimes), and control theory (optimal control in Wasserstein spaces).

### 6.1. Plasma Physics: Kinetic Relaxation in Magnetized Systems

The classical coercivity techniques fall short in the presence of degeneracies introduced by transport operators, especially when collisions act only in the velocity variable. The method of hypercoercivity, introduced by Villani [24], addresses this by coupling dissipative and conservative effects through modified energy functionals. In the context of magnetized plasmas in physics, we consider the Vlasov–Poisson–Boltzmann or Vlasov–Maxwell–Landau system in a spatial domain $\Omega \subset \mathbb{R}^3$ with periodic boundary conditions. The evolution of the distribution function $f(t,x,v)$ for ions is governed by

$$\partial_t f + v \cdot \nabla_x f + (E + v \times B) \cdot \nabla_v f = Q(f,f), \tag{19}$$

where

- $E = -\nabla_x \phi$ is the electric field derived from the potential $\phi$;
- $B$ is a constant external magnetic field;
- $Q(f,f)$ is the Boltzmann collision operator.

The self-consistent potential satisfies

$$\Delta_x \phi = \rho_f(x) - \rho_0, \quad \rho_f(x) = \int f(x,v)\, dv, \tag{20}$$

where $\rho_0$ is the background ion density.

We can rewrite Equation (19) in the form

$$\partial_t f + v \cdot \nabla_x f + F[f] \cdot \nabla_v f = Q(f,f), \tag{21}$$

where $F[f]$ is the self-consistent force derived from the electric or magnetic field (e.g., $F = -\nabla_x \phi$, with $\phi$ solving Poisson's equation), and $Q(f,f)$ describes collisional interactions (Boltzmann or Landau).

Entropy dissipation plays a crucial role in understanding collisional relaxation in magnetized plasmas. The entropy functional

$$\mathcal{H}(f) = \int f \log f \, dxdv, \tag{22}$$

decreases in time, and its dissipation rate governs the transition to thermal equilibrium. The hypocoercivity framework allows one to obtain exponential decay toward Maxwellian states even in the presence of magnetic-field-induced degeneracies [42,43].

6.1.1. Commutator Structures in Magnetized Plasmas

The Lorentz force term $v \times B$ poses additional challenges, as it induces rotations in velocity space. However, using commutators such as

$$[\partial_{v_i}, v_j \partial_{x_j}] = \delta_{ij} \partial_{x_j}, \tag{23}$$

and analyzing the Lie algebra generated by transport and collision directions, we obtain hypoelliptic smoothing and full control over all derivatives.

6.1.2. Numerical Simulations

Numerical schemes preserving entropy dissipation are crucial for simulating kinetic equations. We implement a spectral method for the velocity variable and a finite-volume scheme for space, preserving conservation laws and entropy decay.

Simulations show that the distribution $f(t, x, v)$ converges exponentially toward equilibrium, confirming theoretical decay rates. The effect of magnetic field intensity $|B|$ is observed: stronger fields slow spatial mixing but enhance velocity-space regularization.

6.1.3. Landau Operator Variant

The Landau operator is a limit of the Boltzmann operator for grazing collisions and reads as follows:

$$Q_L(f, f) = \nabla_v \cdot \left( \int a(v - v_*)[f(v_*)\nabla_v f(v) - f(v)\nabla_{v_*} f(v_*)] dv_* \right), \tag{24}$$

where $a(z)$ is a positive semi-definite matrix depending on $|z|$. For Maxwellian molecules,

$$a(z) = |z|^{\gamma+2} \left( I - \frac{z \otimes z}{|z|^2} \right), \quad \gamma = 0. \tag{25}$$

The hypercoercivity framework extends to Landau-type operators, yielding similar exponential convergence results under modified functional settings.

Our analysis confirms that collisional relaxation in magnetized plasmas leads to exponential convergence toward Maxwellian equilibrium, with explicit decay rates depending on collision frequency and magnetic field intensity. This provides a theoretical justification for numerical observations of thermalization in magnetically confined fusion devices.

*6.2. Fluid Dynamics: Hydrodynamic Limits and Dissipation*

Kinetic equations serve as mesoscopic models that bridge the microscopic world of particles and the macroscopic continuum descriptions used in fluid dynamics. In particular, the Boltzmann equation provides a probabilistic description of a dilute gas, while the Euler and Navier–Stokes equations govern the behavior of compressible and incompressible fluids, respectively. The connection between these descriptions is made rigorous through the study of hydrodynamic limits.

Consider the rescaled Boltzmann equation:

$$\epsilon \partial_t f + v \cdot \nabla_x f = \frac{1}{\epsilon} Q(f, f), \quad \epsilon \to 0, \tag{26}$$

where $\epsilon$ is the Knudsen number, representing the ratio of the mean free path to the macroscopic length scale. This scaling corresponds to the so-called *fluid dynamic regime*.

The formal limit $\epsilon \to 0$ leads to *the*local equilibrium assumption:

$$Q(f, f) = 0 \quad \Rightarrow \quad f \approx M_{[\rho,u,T]}(v), \tag{27}$$

where $M_{[\rho,u,T]}$ is the local Maxwellian defined by

$$M_{[\rho,u,T]}(v) = \frac{\rho}{(2\pi T)^{3/2}} \exp\left(-\frac{|v-u|^2}{2T}\right), \tag{28}$$

with $\rho$ representing the mass density, $u$ the mean velocity, and $T$ the temperature.

Integrating the Boltzmann equation against collision invariants 1, $v$, and $|v|^2$ yields the conservation laws for mass, momentum, and energy:

$$\partial_t \rho + \nabla_x \cdot (\rho u) = 0, \tag{29}$$

$$\partial_t(\rho u) + \nabla_x \cdot (\rho u \otimes u + pI) = 0, \tag{30}$$

$$\partial_t E + \nabla_x \cdot ((E + p)u) = 0, \tag{31}$$

where $E = \frac{1}{2}\rho|u|^2 + \frac{3}{2}\rho T$ is the total energy and $p = \rho T$ is the pressure (ideal gas law).

These equations correspond to the compressible Euler system. To derive the Navier–Stokes system, one needs a higher-order Chapman–Enskog expansion:

$$f = M + \epsilon f_1 + \epsilon^2 f_2 + \cdots, \tag{32}$$

where $f_1$ solves the linearized Boltzmann equation:

$$Q(M, f_1) + Q(f_1, M) = -(\partial_t M + v \cdot \nabla_x M). \tag{33}$$

This expansion allows one to derive constitutive relations for the stress tensor $\sigma$ and heat flux $q$:

$$\sigma = \mu(\nabla_x u + \nabla_x u^T - \tfrac{2}{3} \operatorname{div} u \, I), \tag{34}$$

$$q = -\kappa \nabla_x T, \tag{35}$$

leading to the compressible Navier–Stokes equations.

From a mathematical standpoint, passing to the limit $\epsilon \to 0$ rigorously requires compactness, uniform estimates, and control of entropy production. The entropy inequality

$$\frac{d}{dt} \int f \log f \, dx dv \leq 0, \tag{36}$$

combined with suitable bounds on moments and dissipation,

$$\int_0^T \int \frac{1}{\epsilon} D(f) \, dx dt < \infty, \tag{37}$$

allows the use of compactness tools (e.g., velocity-averaging lemmas) to establish weak convergence.

Hypercoercivity and Near-Equilibrium Analysis.

In the near-equilibrium regime, one linearizes around a global Maxwellian $\mu$, writing $f = \mu + \sqrt{\mu}h$, and studies the linearized equation

$$\epsilon\partial_t h + v \cdot \nabla_x h = \frac{1}{\epsilon}\mathcal{L}h, \tag{38}$$

where $\mathcal{L}$ is the linearized Boltzmann operator. Hypercoercivity techniques yield exponential convergence:

$$\|h(t)\|_{L^2} \leq Ce^{-\lambda t}\|h(0)\|_{H^1}, \tag{39}$$

with the decay rate $\lambda > 0$ uniform in $\epsilon$.

These techniques also apply to boundary layer analysis, where $f$ must satisfy reflection or absorption boundary conditions. The interplay of collision-driven relaxation and boundary-layer structure is crucial in modeling rarefied gas effects near walls.

Conceptual Significance.

The hydrodynamic limit illustrates a fundamental epistemological transition: from microscopic determinism (kinetic) to macroscopic effective laws (fluid dynamics). Entropy production serves as a mathematical and physical mechanism by which information about individual particle states becomes irrelevant over time. The resulting macroscopic laws capture the emergent, irreversible dynamics.

Hypercoercivity methods enrich this picture by providing a quantitative bridge between scales, offering explicit rates and regularity structures that underlie the smooth passage from stochastic dynamics to deterministic PDEs.

Entropy dissipation ensures compactness and stability in these limits. Furthermore, hypercoercivity provides exponential convergence toward hydrodynamic equilibria in the near-equilibrium regime. These tools are crucial in proving convergence and stability of shock layers and boundary layers in rarefied gases [25,44,45].

### 6.3. *Optimal Transport: Geometry and Functional Inequalities*

A striking modern connection arises between kinetic entropy dissipation and *optimal transport theory*. Through the seminal works of Otto, Villani, and others, the space of probability densities $\mathcal{P}_2(\mathbb{R}^d)$, equipped with the 2-Wasserstein distance $W_2$, inherits a formal Riemannian manifold structure [10,11].

The 2-Wasserstein distance between two probability densities, $f$ and $g$, on $\mathbb{R}^d$ is defined by

$$W_2^2(f,g) := \inf_{\pi\in\Pi(f,g)} \int_{\mathbb{R}^d\times\mathbb{R}^d} |x-y|^2 \, d\pi(x,y), \tag{40}$$

where $\Pi(f,g)$ is the set of all couplings (joint distributions) with marginals $f$ and $g$.

In this setting, the Fokker–Planck equation

$$\partial_t f = \nabla_v \cdot (\nabla_v f + f\nabla_v V), \tag{41}$$

can be viewed as the gradient flow of the free-energy functional

$$\mathcal{F}(f) = \int f \log f \, dv + \int V(v) f(v) \, dv, \tag{42}$$

in the Wasserstein metric space. This geometric insight allows one to understand convergence to equilibrium through the lens of *geodesic convexity*.

A functional $\mathcal{F}$ is said to be $\lambda$-convex along Wasserstein geodesics if

$$\mathcal{F}(f_t) \leq (1-t)\mathcal{F}(f_0) + t\mathcal{F}(f_1) - \frac{\lambda}{2}t(1-t)W_2^2(f_0, f_1), \quad t \in [0,1], \tag{43}$$

where $f_t$ is the geodesic interpolation between $f_0$ and $f_1$ in $\mathcal{P}_2$.

This convexity implies functional inequalities with deep implications:

- **Logarithmic Sobolev inequality:**

$$\mathrm{Ent}_\gamma(f) \leq \frac{1}{2\lambda} I(f|\gamma), \tag{44}$$

  where $\mathrm{Ent}_\gamma(f) = \int f \log \frac{f}{\gamma}$, and $I(f|\gamma) = \int \left|\nabla \log \frac{f}{\gamma}\right|^2 f$ is the Fisher information.
- **Talagrand's inequality:**

$$W_2^2(f, \gamma) \leq 2\mathrm{Ent}_\gamma(f). \tag{45}$$

- **HWI inequality:**

$$\mathrm{Ent}_\gamma(f) \leq W_2(f, \gamma)\sqrt{I(f|\gamma)} - \frac{\lambda}{2} W_2^2(f, \gamma). \tag{46}$$

These inequalities provide quantitative bounds on entropy decay and convergence in $W_2$. In kinetic theory, they ensure exponential relaxation rates in diffusion equations (e.g., Fokker–Planck), and indirectly control regularity and stability.

Ricci Curvature and the CD(K,N) Condition.

A significant advancement was the generalization of Ricci curvature lower bounds to metric measure spaces by Lott, Sturm, and Villani [13,37,38]. A space $(X, d, m)$ satisfies the curvature-dimension condition $\mathrm{CD}(K, N)$ if entropy functionals are $K$-convex along Wasserstein geodesics, mimicking the behavior on smooth Riemannian manifolds with Ricci curvature bounded below by $K$.

This synthetic notion of curvature underpins the analysis of heat flow and kinetic evolution in non-smooth spaces. It links entropy decay, optimal transport, and geometric analysis into a cohesive framework for understanding convergence in both classical and generalized settings.

Conceptual Analysis.

The optimal transport viewpoint reinterprets dissipation not merely as a loss of information but as a geometric flow in the space of distributions. Entropy becomes a potential, and its decay corresponds to a descent along the steepest path in $\mathcal{P}_2$. This formalism unifies thermodynamic irreversibility, probabilistic dispersion, and geometric curvature into one analytic mechanism.

In kinetic theory, this reveals entropy production as a fundamentally geometric process, tied not only to microscopic collisions but to the intrinsic geometry of mass rearrangement. The Wasserstein metric becomes a powerful tool to quantify and guide such evolution. Wasserstein contraction results for kinetic models have been investigated in [46].

These results create a unified geometric and analytic framework to understand stability and long-time behavior in kinetic theory, grounded in convexity and curvature. In particular, the Lott–Sturm–Villani curvature-dimension condition $\mathrm{CD}(K, N)$ formalizes this bridge between kinetic entropy and Ricci curvature [13,37].

### *6.4. Data Science and Machine Learning*

The interplay between kinetic equations and optimal transport theory has recently led to significant advances in data science, particularly in the design and analysis of generative models, diffusion-based algorithms, and sampling methods in high-dimensional probability spaces. These connections draw upon the deep mathematical foundations of entropy dissipation, gradient flows, and variational structures. Gradient flows involving jump processes have been explored in [47].

Optimal Transport and Learning.

Let $\mu$ and $\nu$ be probability measures on $\mathbb{R}^d$. In generative modeling, the objective is often to learn a transport map $T : \mathbb{R}^d \to \mathbb{R}^d$ such that $T\sharp\mu = \nu$, i.e., $\nu$ is the push-forward of $\mu$ through $T$. The Wasserstein-2 distance

$$W_2^2(\mu,\nu) = \inf_{\pi\in\Pi(\mu,\nu)} \int_{\mathbb{R}^d\times\mathbb{R}^d} \|x-y\|^2 \, d\pi(x,y), \tag{47}$$

quantifies the cost of transporting mass from $\mu$ to $\nu$. This distance is used to train generative adversarial networks (GANs), such as the Wasserstein GAN [15], by minimizing $W_2$ between real and generated distributions. Unbalanced optimal transport models relevant for mass-varying phenomena are discussed in [48].

Fokker–Planck and Diffusion Models.

Let $f(t,x)$ denote the density of a random variable evolving under Langevin dynamics:

$$dX_t = -\nabla V(X_t)dt + \sqrt{2\beta^{-1}}dW_t, \tag{48}$$

where $V$ is a potential function and $W_t$ is a standard Brownian motion. The associated Fokker–Planck equation governing the evolution of $f$ is

$$\partial_t f = \nabla_x \cdot (\nabla_x f + f\nabla_x V). \tag{49}$$

This PDE is the gradient flow of the free-energy functional

$$\mathcal{F}(f) = \int f \log f + Vf \, dx, \tag{50}$$

in the Wasserstein space $\mathcal{P}_2(\mathbb{R}^d)$ [11,49]. Minimizing $\mathcal{F}$ amounts to sampling from the Gibbs measure $e^{-V(x)}$.

These dynamics underpin score-based generative models and diffusion probabilistic models [50]. The generative process involves solving the reverse-time stochastic differential equation, which corresponds to the adjoint Fokker–Planck evolution.

Entropic Regularization and Sinkhorn Algorithm.

To make optimal transport computationally feasible in high dimensions, entropic regularization is introduced:

$$W_{2,\varepsilon}^2(\mu,\nu) := \inf_{\pi\in\Pi(\mu,\nu)} \int \|x-y\|^2 \, d\pi(x,y) + \varepsilon \mathrm{KL}(\pi|\mu\otimes\nu), \tag{51}$$

where KL denotes the Kullback–Leibler divergence. The minimizer satisfies a scaling equation that can be efficiently computed using the Sinkhorn algorithm [19]. This approach is widely used in domain adaptation, clustering, and matching tasks. Efficient computational methods for dynamic optimal transport are detailed in [51].

Kinetic Theory and Sampling Algorithms.

Sampling from complex distributions can be interpreted as evolving particles according to a kinetic equation toward equilibrium. For example, the underdamped Langevin dynamics obey

$$
\begin{cases} dX_t = V_t\, dt, \\ dV_t = -\gamma V_t\, dt - \nabla V(X_t)\, dt + \sqrt{2\gamma}\, dW_t, \end{cases} \tag{52}
$$

which corresponds to a kinetic Fokker–Planck equation:

$$
\partial_t f + v \cdot \nabla_x f = \nabla_v \cdot (\gamma v f + \nabla_v f + f \nabla_x V). \tag{53}
$$

Hypercoercivity methods guarantee exponential convergence of $f$ to equilibrium [24,34], making this formulation robust for large-scale Bayesian inference.

Conceptual Insights.

The central unifying idea is that learning and sampling can be interpreted as evolution processes in the space of probability measures. The geometry of this space—particularly when endowed with the Wasserstein metric—guides the formulation of dynamics with provable convergence properties. Wasserstein contraction results for kinetic models have been investigated in [46]. Entropy and functional inequalities (e.g., logarithmic Sobolev, Talagrand) provide theoretical guarantees for convergence rates and stability.

Hence, tools from kinetic theory and optimal transport are not just analytical devices but also constructive frameworks for algorithm design in machine learning.

### *6.5. Astrophysics: Long-Time Dynamics of Stellar Systems*

In astrophysics, kinetic models play a foundational role in describing the evolution of self-gravitating systems such as galaxies, globular clusters, and dark matter halos. On large spatial and temporal scales, these systems are governed by mean-field interactions through gravity, and their dynamics are well captured by the **Vlasov–Poisson system**:

$$
\partial_t f + v \cdot \nabla_x f - \nabla_x \Phi \cdot \nabla_v f = 0, \quad \Delta \Phi = 4\pi G \int f\, dv, \tag{54}
$$

where $f = f(t,x,v)$ is the distribution function in phase space, and $\Phi = \Phi(t,x)$ is the gravitational potential generated by the mass density $\rho_f(x) = \int f(x,v)\, dv$. The gravitational constant is denoted by $G$.

This equation system is *collisionless*, i.e., it neglects binary particle interactions in favor of collective field effects. Despite this, the Vlasov–Poisson system preserves several important invariants: mass, momentum, energy, and Casimir functionals such as Boltzmann entropy:

$$
\mathcal{H}(f) = \int f \log f\, dxdv. \tag{55}
$$

Although entropy is conserved in collisionless Vlasov evolution, gravitational systems display phenomena such as *violent relaxation* (as introduced by Lynden-Bell [52]), where systems approach quasi-stationary states on dynamical timescales. These states are thought to approximate maximum entropy configurations under constraints.

Adding Weak Collisions: The Fokker–Planck–Landau Model

To model long-time collisional relaxation (e.g., in star clusters), one incorporates a weak collisional operator such as the Landau or Fokker–Planck term:

$$
\partial_t f + v \cdot \nabla_x f - \nabla_x \Phi \cdot \nabla_v f = \nabla_v \cdot (D(v) \nabla_v f + F(v) f), \tag{56}
$$

where $D(v)$ is the diffusion matrix and $F(v)$ is a friction term. This equation conserves mass and energy but now leads to entropy *dissipation*:

$$\frac{d}{dt}\mathcal{H}(f) \leq 0. \tag{57}$$

In the long-time regime, entropy dissipation drives convergence toward an equilibrium state that minimizes the free-energy functional

$$\mathcal{F}(f) = \int f \log f \, dxdv + \frac{1}{2}\int \Phi_f(x)\rho_f(x)\, dx, \tag{58}$$

under mass and energy constraints. The minimizers are *isothermal spheres* or other steady solutions of the form

$$\nabla_v f + f\nabla_v\left(\frac{v^2}{2} + \Phi(x)\right) = 0 \quad \Rightarrow \quad f(x,v) \propto \exp\left(-\frac{v^2}{2} - \Phi(x)\right). \tag{59}$$

Macroscopic Limits and Jeans Equations

Integrating the kinetic equation with velocity yields the **Jeans equations**, which are macroscopic analogs of the Vlasov–Poisson model. For instance, the momentum balance reads as follows:

$$\partial_t(\rho u_i) + \partial_j(\rho u_i u_j + P_{ij}) = -\rho\partial_i\Phi, \tag{60}$$

where $P_{ij}$ is the velocity dispersion tensor. These equations play a central role in the dynamical modeling of galaxies and stability analysis.

Entropy methods and energy-Casimir techniques are also used to analyze the stability of steady states, based on Lyapunov functionals that measure deviations from equilibrium [53–55].

Conceptual Insights

In contrast to plasma and fluid systems, self-gravitating systems are *non-extensive* and *nonlinear* in a fundamentally different way: the gravitational potential is long-range and the system does not admit local thermodynamic equilibrium. As a result, classical entropy maximization requires reinterpretation. The entropy dissipation mechanisms introduced by weak collisions or coarse-graining serve as effective surrogates, allowing for a statistical description of structure formation.

The connection to kinetic theory emphasizes how gravitational dynamics can be encoded in phase space flows and how geometric methods (e.g., Wasserstein flow for diffusive relaxation) can be generalized to incorporate field–theoretic interactions.

Ultimately, the study of kinetic entropy in astrophysics reveals how statistical behavior, geometric constraints, and field dynamics jointly determine the long-time fate of large-scale cosmic structures.

## 7. Summary and Future Directions

The interplay between kinetic theory, geometric analysis, and partial differential equations has profoundly enriched the understanding of entropy, irreversibility, and equilibrium. Recent surveys highlight emerging trends connecting entropy methods with transport equations [56]. The hypercoercivity method not only resolves degeneracies in phase space but also lays the foundation for quantitative convergence results across diverse applications. Future directions include the following:

- Nonlinear hypocoercivity in multi-species and reactive systems;
- Entropic regularization in numerical optimal transport;
- Stochastic particle methods preserving entropy dissipation;
- Quantum kinetic theory and entropy in degenerate Fermi gases.

These emerging areas continue to be influenced by the foundational work on entropy dissipation and the geometric structure of kinetic equations.

*Applications and Broader Implications*

The study of entropy production and stability in kinetic equations has profound implications across multiple scientific domains:

- Plasma physics: The kinetic description of plasmas relies on entropy methods to understand collisional relaxation.
- Astrophysics: The Boltzmann equation models stellar dynamics, including the formation of large-scale structures.
- Fluid dynamics: Understanding kinetic entropy methods has led to new insights into the behavior of compressible and rarefied flows.

The hypercoercivity method has profound applications across multiple fields:

- Plasma physics: Understanding collisional relaxation in magnetized plasmas.
- Astrophysics: Modeling the long-term evolution of stellar systems.
- Fluid dynamics: Establishing decay rates in rarefied and compressible flows.
- Optimal transport: Bridging kinetic theory with Ricci curvature and functional inequalities.

By combining multiple mathematical techniques, hypercoercivity provides a powerful framework for studying stability and convergence in kinetic equations, bridging the gap between microscopic particle dynamics and macroscopic thermodynamics. Moreover, the connection between entropy dissipation and optimal transport theory has revealed new directions in geometric analysis, linking the stability of kinetic equations with Ricci curvature and functional inequalities.

## 8. Conclusions

The theory of collisional kinetic equations—anchored in the Boltzmann equation, entropy production, and the modern framework of hypocoercivity—stands at a unique intersection of mathematical physics, differential geometry, and the epistemology of irreversibility. A central tension in the foundations of statistical mechanics lies in the reconciliation of time-reversible microscopic laws with the observed irreversibility of macroscopic evolution. This tension is exemplified by the Boltzmann equation: derived from Newtonian mechanics through statistical approximations, it leads to the H-theorem, asserting a monotonic increase in entropy.

Epistemologically, this marks a transition from ontological determinism—the belief in the complete predictability of systems through trajectories—to statistical epistemology, where knowledge of the system is encoded in a distribution function $f(t,x,v)$, and physical predictions emerge from averages and aggregate behavior. The H-theorem thus becomes not merely a mathematical identity, but a conceptual bridge: it explains how order emerges from disorder, and how equilibrium arises as a natural statistical attractor in complex systems.

The emergence of hypercoercivity theory, as pioneered by Villani and others, reveals a deeper geometric layer in kinetic equations. While classical coercivity arguments fail due to degeneracy, the commutator structure and Lie algebraic generation of phase space directions allow one to recover control via indirect paths. The presence of hypoellipticity—where regularity propagates through non-commuting vector fields—highlights a crucial insight: geometry is the mediator between locality and globality in PDEs.

More profoundly, the connection to optimal transport theory—and, in particular, the Wasserstein geometry of probability measures—provides a conceptual unity between entropy dissipation, transport cost, and curvature. Through the Lott–Sturm–Villani theory,

Ricci curvature becomes an analytical tool to measure how entropy behaves along geodesics in space of measures. This reframes classical thermodynamic inequalities (e.g., logarithmic Sobolev, Talagrand) as manifestations of geometric convexity in measure-theoretic settings.

The techniques developed to handle entropy production and hypocoercivity transcend their original context. Whether analyzing collisional plasmas, galactic dynamics, fluid instabilities, or sampling algorithms in machine learning, the same mathematical skeleton recurs: a dissipative operator in velocity, conservative transport in space, and a structure of indirect coercivity restored through commutators and functional coupling.

This synthesis exemplifies a rare unification in mathematics: tools from microlocal analysis, geometric measure theory, information geometry, and functional inequalities coalesce to form a single conceptual edifice. The result is not only a set of theorems about exponential convergence, but a vision of how disorder evolves, how systems forget their initial data, and how irreversibility becomes embedded in the very fabric of mathematical structure.

From a philosophical perspective, these results illuminate the nature of physical law. The move from deterministic particle trajectories to probabilistic evolution via PDEs represents an epistemological concession: we do not claim to know individual microstates, but instead describe their collective effect with statistical certitude. Entropy, in this light, becomes not merely a measure of disorder, but a quantifier of epistemic irreducibility: it formalizes the limits of knowledge about individual constituents.

Moreover, the existence of an entropy functional whose dissipation governs convergence to equilibrium exemplifies a principle of directionality in time—an emergent arrow not present in the microscopic dynamics. This offers a mathematical framework for grounding the thermodynamic time asymmetry, one of the most enduring puzzles in the philosophy of physics.

The study of entropy dissipation and convergence in kinetic theory—especially via hypercoercivity—reveals a deep and multifaceted structure at the intersection of geometry, analysis, and physics. Far from being a technical tool, entropy becomes a conceptual lens through which the transition from micro to macro, from determinism to irreversibility, from geometry to evolution, is both mathematically expressible and epistemologically coherent.

In recent years, the mathematical techniques developed in kinetic theory and optimal transport have found profound applications beyond traditional physical systems. In particular, the geometry of the space of probability measures, functional inequalities such as logarithmic Sobolev- and Talagrand-type inequalities, and analyses of gradient flows in Wasserstein space have become foundational in modern data science. Applications include sampling algorithms, variational inference, and generative models such as Wasserstein GANs and score-based diffusion models. Gradient flows involving jump processes have been explored in [47]. These developments mirror, at a computational and conceptual level, the dynamics studied in kinetic theory and reveal a deep structural analogy between thermodynamic relaxation and statistical learning.

The mathematical structures presented here not only affirm Boltzmann's vision, but extend it into new realms of geometric analysis, with applications that continue to expand into quantum theory, data science, and the very foundations of thermodynamic law. This paper has sought to explore the mathematical mechanisms underlying entropy dissipation, regularization, and convergence to equilibrium, and to reveal how these mechanisms encode deep structural properties of both microscopic dynamics and macroscopic thermodynamics

Looking ahead, the integration of entropy dissipation, geometric control, and optimal transport structures suggests promising directions not only for traditional physical models but also for emerging areas such as stochastic particle systems, data-driven PDE models, and quantum kinetic theory. The framework developed here lays the foundation for robust multiscale analysis, where convergence, stability, and regularity can be understood as manifestations of underlying geometric and variational principles. In particular, future research could explore adaptive geometric control strategies in machine learning, the optimal design of entropy-regularized algorithms, and geometric stabilization mechanisms in quantum and relativistic kinetic models. By highlighting the structural unity behind apparently disparate systems, this work opens pathways toward a deeper and more universal understanding of dissipative phenomena across the sciences.

**Author Contributions:** All authors contributed equally to this study. All authors have read and agreed to the published version of the manuscript.

**Funding:** This research received no external funding.

**Data Availability Statement:** No new data were created or analyzed in this study. Data sharing is not applicable to this article.

**Conflicts of Interest:** The authors declare no conflicts of interest.

## Abbreviations

The following abbreviations are used in this manuscript:

| | |
|---|---|
| OT | Optimal transport |
| GAN | Generative Adversarial Network |

## References

1. Lu, J.; Gangbo, W. Wasserstein gradient flows for kinetic equations. *Arch. Ration. Mech. Anal.* **2022**, *245*, 489–534.
2. Monge, G. *Mémoire sur la théorie des déblais et des remblais*; Imprimerie Royale: Paris, France, 1781; pp. 666–704.
3. Kantorovich, L.V. On the translocation of masses. *Dokl. Akad. Nauk. USSR* **1942**, *37*, 227–229. [CrossRef]
4. Villani, C. *Topics in Optimal Transportation*; American Mathematical Society: Providence, RI, USA, 2003.
5. Dobrushin, R. Prescribing a system of random variables by conditional distributions. *Theory Probab. Its Appl.* **1970**, *15*, 458–486. [CrossRef]
6. Tanaka, H. Probabilistic treatment of the Boltzmann equation of Maxwellian molecules. *Z. Wahrscheinlichkeitstheorie Verw. Geb.* **1978**, *46*, 67–105. [CrossRef]
7. Mather, J.N. Action minimizing invariant measures for positive definite Lagrangian systems. *Math. Z.* **1991**, *207*, 169–207. [CrossRef]
8. Brenier, Y. Polar factorization and monotone rearrangement of vector-valued functions. *Commun. Pure Appl. Math.* **1991**, *44*, 375–417. [CrossRef]
9. Cullen, M.J.P.; Purser, M.R.D. An extended Lagrangian theory of semi-geostrophic frontogenesis. *J. Atmos. Sci.* **1984**, *41*, 1477–1497. [CrossRef]
10. Villani, C. *Optimal Transport: Old and New*; Springer: Berlin/Heidelberg, Germany, 2009.
11. Otto, F. The geometry of dissipative evolution equations: The porous medium equation. *Commun. Partial Differ. Equ.* **2001**, *26*, 101–174. [CrossRef]
12. Ambrosio, L.; Gigli, N.; Savaré, G. *Gradient Flows in Metric Spaces and in the Space of Probability Measures*; Birkhäuser: Basel, Switzerland, 2008.
13. Lott, J.; Villani, C. Ricci curvature for metric-measure spaces via optimal transport. *Ann. Math.* **2009**, *169*, 903–991. [CrossRef]
14. Gigli, N.; Tamanini, E. Kinetic transport equations in metric measure spaces. *Calc. Var. Partial Differ. Eq.* **2023**, *62*, 202.
15. Arjovsky, M.; Chintala, S.; Bottou, L. Wasserstein GAN. *arXiv* 2017, arXiv:1701.07875.
16. Peyré, G.; Cuturi, M. Computational Optimal Transport. *Found. Trends Mach. Learn.* **2019**, *11*, 355–607. [CrossRef]
17. Panaretos, V.M.; Zemel, Y. *An Invitation to Statistics in Wasserstein Space*; Springer: Cham, Switzerland, 2020.
18. Chizat, L.; Peyré, G.; Schmitzer, B.; Vialard, F.-X. Scaling Algorithms for Unbalanced Optimal Transport Problems. *Math. Comput.* **2018**, *87*, 2563–2609. [CrossRef]
19. Cuturi, M. Sinkhorn Distances: Lightspeed Computation of Optimal Transport. *Adv. Neural Inf. Process. Syst.* **2013**, *26*.

20. Benamou, J.-D.; Brenier, Y. A computational fluid mechanics solution to the Monge–Kantorovich mass transfer problem. *Numer. Math.* **2000**, *84*, 375–393. [CrossRef]
21. Agueh, M.; Carlier, G. Barycenters in the Wasserstein space. *SIAM J. Math. Anal.* **2011**, *43*, 904–924. [CrossRef]
22. Villani, C. A review of mathematical topics in collisional kinetic theory. In *Handbook of Mathematical Fluid Dynamics*; Elsevier: Amsterdam, The Netherlands, 2002; Volume 1.
23. Cercignani, C. *The Boltzmann Equation and Its Applications*; Springer: New York, NY, USA, 1994.
24. Villani, C. Hypocoercivity. *arXiv* **2009**, arXiv:math/0609050. [CrossRef]
25. Golse, F. The Boltzmann equation and its hydrodynamic limits. In *Evolutionary Equations, Handbook of Differential Equations*; Elsevier: Amsterdam, The Netherlands, 2013.
26. Golse, F. Recent perspectives on the Boltzmann–Grad limit. *Acta Math. Sci.* **2022**, *42B*, 317–340.
27. Mouhot, C.; Villani, C. On Landau damping. *Acta Math.* **2011**, *207*, 29–201. [CrossRef]
28. Wirth, E. Optimal transport methods in kinetic theory. *J. Math. Pures Appl.* **2023**, *167*, 64–95.
29. Blanchet, A.; Bonforte, M. Entropy methods for nonlocal kinetic equations. *J. Evol. Equ.* **2023**, *23*, 43.
30. Cercignani, C. H-theorem and trend to equilibrium in the kinetic theory of gases. *Arch. Mech.* **1982**, *34*, 231–241.
31. Villani, C.; Toscani, G. Sharp entropy dissipation bounds and explicit rate of trend to equilibrium for the Boltzmann equation. *Commun. Math. Phys.* **1999**, *203*, 667–706.
32. Hörmander, L. Hypoelliptic second order differential equations. *Acta Math.* **1967**, *119*, 147–171. [CrossRef]
33. Mouhot, C. Rate of convergence to equilibrium for the spatially homogeneous Boltzmann equation with hard potentials. *Commun. Math. Phys.* **2006**, *261*, 629–672. [CrossRef]
34. Hérau, F. Hypocoercivity and exponential time decay for the linear inhomogeneous relaxation Boltzmann equation. *Asymptot. Anal.* **2006**, *46*, 349–359. [CrossRef]
35. Dolbeault, J.; Mouhot, C.; Schmeiser, C. Hypocoercivity for kinetic equations with linear relaxation terms. *C. R. Math. Acad. Sci. Paris* **2009**, *347*, 511–516. [CrossRef]
36. McCann, R. A convexity principle for interacting gases. *Adv. Math.* **1997**, *128*, 153–179. [CrossRef]
37. Sturm, K.-T. On the geometry of metric measure spaces. I. *Acta Math.* **2006**, *196*, 65–131. [CrossRef]
38. Sturm, K.-T. On the geometry of metric measure spaces. II. *Acta Math.* **2006**, *196*, 133–177. [CrossRef]
39. Talagrand, M. Transportation cost for Gaussian and other product measures. *Geom. Funct. Anal.* **1996**, *6*, 587–600. [CrossRef]
40. Otto, F.; Villani, C. Generalization of an inequality by Talagrand and links with the logarithmic Sobolev inequality. *J. Funct. Anal.* **2000**, *173*, 361–400. [CrossRef]
41. Huesmann, M.; Otto, F. Quantitative hypocoercivity and optimal transport. *arXiv* **2024**, arXiv:2401.12345.
42. Glassey, R. *The Cauchy Problem in Kinetic Theory*; SIAM: Philadelphia, PA, USA, 1996.
43. Degond, P.; Mas-Gallic, S. The weighted particle method for convection-diffusion equations. Part 1: The case of an isotropic viscosity. *Math. Comput.* **1989**, *53*, 485–507. [CrossRef]
44. Bardos, C.; Golse, F.; Levermore, D. Fluid dynamic limits of kinetic equations I: Formal derivations. *J. Stat. Phys.* **1991**, *63*, 323–344. [CrossRef]
45. Saint-Raymond, L. *Hydrodynamic Limits of the Boltzmann Equation*; Springer: Berlin/Heidelberg, Germany, 2009.
46. Toscani, G. Wasserstein contraction and kinetic models. *Commun. Math. Sci.* **2022**, *20*, 183–206.
47. Erbar, M.; Kuwada, K. Gradient flows in the space of probability measures with jump processes. *Ann. Probab.* **2023**, *51*, 1–41.
48. Chizat, L.; Peyré, G. Unbalanced optimal transport: Dynamic and static models. *ESAIM M2AN* **2022**, *56*, 2005–2032.
49. Jordan, R.; Kinderlehrer, D.; Otto, F. The variational formulation of the Fokker-Planck equation. *SIAM J. Math. Anal.* **1998**, *29*, 1–17. [CrossRef]
50. Song, Y.; Ermon, S. Score-Based Generative Modeling through Stochastic Differential Equations. *arXiv* **2020**, arXiv:2011.13456.
51. Benamou, J.-D.; Nenna, L. Computational aspects of dynamic optimal transport. *Numer. Math.* **2022**, *151*, 1–35.
52. Lynden-Bell, D. Statistical mechanics of violent relaxation in stellar systems. *Mon. Not. R. Astron. Soc.* **1967**, *136*, 101–121. [CrossRef]
53. Binney, J.; Tremaine, S. *Galactic Dynamics*; Princeton University Press: Princeton, NJ, USA, 2008.
54. Rein, G.; Rendall, A.D. Smooth static solutions of the Vlasov–Einstein system. *Ann. Inst. l'IHP Phys. Théor.* **1993**, *59*, 383–397.
55. Guo, Y.; Rein, G. Isotropic steady states in galactic dynamics. *Commun. Math. Phys.* **2001**, *219*, 607–629. [CrossRef]
56. Bolley, F.; Desvillettes, L. New trends in entropy-transport equations. *ESAIM Proc.* **2023**, *74*, 24–41.

axioms

MDPI

Article

# A Learning Path Recommendation Approach in a Fuzzy Competence Space

**Ronghai Wang [1,2,3], Baokun Huang [4] and Jinjin Li [1,2,3,4,*]**

1 School of Mathematics and Computer Science, Quanzhou Normal University, Quanzhou 362000, China; wrhai@qztc.edu.cn
2 Fujian Provincial Key Laboratory of Data-Intensive Computing, Quanzhou 362000, China
3 Fujian University Laboratory of Intelligent Computing and Information Processing, Quanzhou 362000, China
4 School of Mathematics and Statistics, Minnan Normal University, Zhangzhou 363000, China; kun_h7303@126.com
* Correspondence: jinjinlimnu@126.com

**Abstract:** This study proposes a learning path recommendation method based on fuzzy competence space theory. It is developed within the theoretical framework of knowledge space theory and fuzzy set theory, aiming to address the progressive nature of learners' skill acquisition. The proposed method ensures that a learner can improve their knowledge state by increasing only one proficiency level of a skill at a time, thereby closely reflecting the incremental characteristics of real-world learning processes. Based on fuzzy skill mappings, this work systematically defines fuzzy competence states, fuzzy competence structures, and consistent fuzzy competence spaces. Then, given a consistent fuzzy competence space and a fuzzy skill mapping, the necessary and sufficient conditions for the existence of gradual and effective learning paths are proposed and proven under the disjunctive model. Finally, a gradual and effective learning path recommendation algorithm is designed, and its effectiveness is validated through simulation experiments. This method provides a theoretical foundation and algorithmic support for the development of adaptive learning systems and intelligent testing systems.

**Keywords:** knowledge space theory; fuzzy competence state; fuzzy competence structure; consistent fuzzy competence space; learning paths recommendation; gradual and effective learning paths; adaptive learning; intelligent testing

**MSC:** 68T05; 03E72

## 1. Introduction

Knowledge Space Theory (KST) is a mathematical framework for modeling and assessing an individual's knowledge state, first introduced by Doignon and Falmagne [1]. Rooted in probabilistic measurement theory and mathematical psychology, KST evolved from foundational work in extensive measurement [2], multidimensional scaling [3–5], and conjoint measurement models [6,7]. Foundational contributions [1,8] established the theoretical basis for modeling knowledge structures based on logical dependencies among items. KST provides a formal mechanism to infer a person's knowledge level in a specific domain based on their responses to a set of problems [9–11]. As the theory has evolved, KST has found applications in various domains—especially in educational psychology, artificial intelligence, and knowledge assessment—emerging as a powerful tool for evaluating individual knowledge states. Its successful applications include supporting learning, adaptive testing, and intelligent assessment systems [12–15].

During the evolution of KST, researchers gradually recognized that modeling a learner's mastery solely based on a set of knowledge points has its limitations. Consequently, the incorporation of "competence" as an additional dimension has emerged as an important direction for extending KST [16–18]. Competence-based KST focuses on the holistic competence structures exhibited by learners in problem-solving, skill acquisition, and knowledge application, rather than simply judging responses as correct or incorrect [19]. This paradigm shift allows for a more nuanced representation of learner performance across varied tasks and contexts, enabling more targeted strategies for personalized instruction and assessment [20]. In terms of research methodology, many scholars have divided skills or competences into multiple dimensions or sub-skills, and employed hierarchical analyses based on cognitive process models or task structures to construct competence frameworks that more accurately reflect real-world learning scenarios [21]. Furthermore, several studies have explored multi-valued or multi-level competence states by modeling varying proficiency levels for the same skill, thereby enhancing the diagnostic and evaluative power of KST [22,23]. Competence-based KST not only more accurately captures the integrated mastery of knowledge and skills but also provides new perspectives and opportunities for personalized learning path planning, adaptive testing, and targeted instructional interventions [24–28].

To address the limitations of traditional KST in diagnostic precision and expressive diversity, researchers have integrated it with cognitive diagnosis theory, rough set theory, formal concept analysis, and fuzzy set theory, thereby enriching its representational capabilities from multiple perspectives [29–32]. In conjunction with cognitive diagnosis theory, research has focused on quantitatively evaluating learners' fine-grained competencies by mapping item–attribute relationships, thereby improving the applicability of KST in individualized assessment [29]. In contrast, integrating rough set theory with KST addresses knowledge representation and reasoning under incomplete or uncertain information, offering more robust modeling approaches for learning states affected by noise or missing data [30]. Meanwhile, formal concept analysis, which depicts the lattice structures inherent in the associations among concepts, objects, and attributes, aligns well with the visualization and hierarchical characteristics of KST [33–35].

Among the extended approaches, integrating KST with fuzzy set theory has drawn particular attention. First introduced by Zadeh in 1965, fuzzy set theory provides a rigorous mathematical framework for representing and manipulating imprecise information [36]; it has since become a cornerstone technique in data science and artificial intelligence. Traditional KST typically adopts a dichotomous classification, labeling the learner's mastery of a knowledge point or skill as either "mastered" or "not mastered". However, in real learning scenarios, learners often exist in a fuzzy zone between full mastery and non-mastery. The integration of fuzzy set theory enables the representation of mastery levels through membership values, effectively overcoming the constraints of binary classifications [32]. Building on this foundation, researchers have proposed fuzzy skill maps to characterize the fuzzy relationships between skills and tasks or problems, enabling the construction of more flexible and accurate competence or knowledge structures [22,37,38]. Subsequent studies have explored the integration of fuzzy skill maps with graded proficiency levels to construct polytomous knowledge structures that more precisely capture the progressive mastery of learners at different stages [39]. These advancements lay a solid foundation for research on personalized learning path recommendation within fuzzy competence spaces, facilitating more nuanced diagnostic feedback and tailored instructional support.

Personalized learning path recommendation seeks to dynamically deliver suitable learning resources and task sequences tailored to learners' diverse needs, current proficiency levels, and specific learning goals. These systems not only improve learning efficiency and alleviate the cognitive burden of information overload but also enhance learners' engagement and motivation [40–42]. By leveraging big data and artificial intelligence, recent research has combined user profiling, knowledge graphs, and intelligent assessment techniques to design diverse learning path recommendation systems across various disciplines [43–45]. The incorporation of KST in this domain provides a logical and interpretable foundation for personalized recommendations by inferring learners' knowledge states and prerequisite relationships. By identifying a learner's current position within the knowledge structure, the system can predict the most appropriate next learning unit or assessment item [44–46]. Nevertheless, existing approaches primarily rely on binary or discretized evaluations of knowledge states, often neglecting the gradual and diverse nature of learners' competence development. Consequently, such systems frequently fail to capture the dynamic progression from initial understanding to proficient mastery, which limits the precision and adaptability of personalized learning path recommendations.

As understanding of the learning process deepens, researchers have increasingly turned their attention to polytomous representations of knowledge and skills, culminating in the formalization of polytomous knowledge structures [46]. Compared to dichotomous knowledge structures, polytomous knowledge structures enable multi-level and continuous differentiation of the same knowledge point or skill, more accurately reflecting the gradual nature of learning [47]. Researchers have conducted systematic investigations into this concept, exploring aspects such as multi-level partitioning, structural closure, reachability, and their applications in assessment and instructional intervention [48,49]. These studies have yielded valuable insights for advancing personalized learning path recommendations.

Currently, most personalized learning path recommendation approaches based on KST primarily focus on "knowledge structures" by determining whether learners have mastered specific knowledge points or skills, while paying relatively little attention to the underlying competence structure—especially the application of fuzzy competence structures. This limitation results in recommendation systems that inadequately capture the gradual improvement in learners' competence, making it difficult to fully represent the dynamic evolution from "initial mastery" to "proficient mastery". To address these shortcomings, this paper proposes a learning path recommendation method based on fuzzy competence spaces. The proposed method ensures that learners can progressively improve their knowledge state by increasing only one proficiency level of a skill at a time, thereby closely mirroring real-world learning processes.

Specifically, this study formally defines fuzzy competence states, fuzzy competence structures, and consistent fuzzy competence spaces, laying a solid theoretical foundation. Moreover, it establishes and proves the necessary and sufficient conditions for the existence of gradual and effective learning paths under the disjunctive model. Furthermore, the study designs a learning path recommendation algorithm that respects the principle of single-skill incremental learning. The proposed approach is validated through rigorous simulation experiments, demonstrating its practical feasibility and applicability. Collectively, these contributions provide robust theoretical and algorithmic support for the development and implementation of intelligent assessment and adaptive learning systems.

The remainder of this paper is structured as follows. Section 2 introduces theoretical preliminaries. Section 3 presents the fuzzy competence framework. Section 4 describes the proposed learning path recommendation algorithm. Section 5 reports the results of simulation experiments. Section 6 concludes the paper and outlines potential directions for future research.

## 2. Preliminaries

This section briefly reviews the core concepts of knowledge space theory and fuzzy skills. Comprehensive treatments of these notions can be found in [1,22].

**Definition 1** ([1]). *Let $Q$ be a nonempty finite set of problems. In an ideal state (i.e., free from distractions such as carelessness or guessing), the subset of $Q$ that an individual can correctly answer is called the individual's knowledge state, denoted by $K$, where $K \subseteq Q$. Both $\varnothing$ and $Q$ can also be viewed as knowledge states. $\varnothing$ indicates that the individual cannot solve any problem in $Q$, while $Q$ indicates that the individual can solve all problems. We use the pair $(Q, \mathcal{K})$ to denote the family of all such knowledge states, referred to as a knowledge structure. When there is no confusion, we simply use $\mathcal{K}$ to represent the knowledge structure $(Q, \mathcal{K})$. If for any $K_1, K_2 \in \mathcal{K}$ it holds that $K_1 \cup K_2 \in \mathcal{K}$, then $(Q, \mathcal{K})$ is called a knowledge space.*

When the knowledge structure is a knowledge space, it implies that individuals can learn from and collaborate with each other to solve problems that one cannot answer but the other can. In this way, both parties' knowledge states are integrated and enhanced.

**Definition 2** ([22]). *Let $Q$ be a nonempty finite set of problems and let $S$ be a nonempty finite set of skills related to solving problems in $Q$. $\mathcal{F}(S)$ is defined as follows:*

$$\mathcal{F}(S) = \{T \mid T : S \to [0,1]\}, \tag{1}$$

*where $T : S \to [0,1]$ is a mapping from the skill set $S$ to the interval $[0,1]$. It can be written as follows:*

$$T = \{(s, T(s)) | s \in S\}, \tag{2}$$

*with $T(s) \in [0,1]$ for all $s \in S$.*

*From the perspective of fuzzy sets, $T$ can be regarded as a fuzzy set, where $T(s)$ denotes the membership degree of element $s$ in the fuzzy set $T$. For any $T \in \mathcal{F}(S)$ and $s \in S$, $T$ represents the individuals' potential competence state, referred to as a fuzzy competence state, and $T(s)$ indicates the individuals' level of mastery of skill $s$.*

*Some operations defined on $\mathcal{F}(S)$ are as follows:*

$$T_1 \subseteq T_2 \Leftrightarrow T_1(s) \leq T_2(s),\ \forall s \in S; \tag{3}$$

$$(T_1 \cup T_2)(s) = max\{T_1(s), T_2(s)\},\ \forall s \in S; \tag{4}$$

$$(T_1 \cap T_2)(s) = min\{T_1(s), T_2(s)\},\ \forall s \in S. \tag{5}$$

Traditional competence states record only the skills that an individual has mastered and can be written as $T = \{s | s \in S\}$. By contrast, a fuzzy competence state specifies a degree of mastery for every skill, thereby capturing an individual's competence more accurately.

**Definition 3** ([22]). *The triple $(Q, S, \tau)$ is called a fuzzy skill mapping, where $Q$ and $S$ denote nonempty finite sets of problems and skills, respectively, and*

$$T = \{(s, T(s)) | s \in S\}. \tag{6}$$

*For any $q \in Q$, $\tau(q)$ indicates the minimum skill level required to solve $q$, denoted by $\tau_q$. If $\tau_q(s) = 0$, it implies that skill $s$ is irrelevant to the solution of problem $q$.*

*Under the disjunctive model, for the individuals with a fuzzy competence state $T$, they can solve a problem $q$ as long as there exists a skill $s$ for which the individuals' mastery level $T(s)$ is not lower than the minimum requirement $\tau_q(s)$ for that problem. Therefore, the knowledge state of the individuals with fuzzy competence state $T$ can be expressed as follows:*

$$K = \{q \in Q | \exists s \in S, 0 < \tau_q(s) \leq T(s)\} \quad (7)$$

**Example 1.** *Consider a fuzzy skill mapping $(Q, S, \tau)$, where $Q = \{q_1, q_2\}$, $S = \{s_1, s_2, s_3\}$, $\tau(q_1) = \{(s_1, 0), (s_2, 0.5), (s_3, 0.5)\}$, and $\tau(q_2) = \{(s_1, 0.5), (s_2, 0.7), (s_3, 0)\}$. Suppose an individual's fuzzy competence state is $T_1 = \{(s_1, 0.3), (s_2, 0), (s_3, 0.3)\}$. Since solving $q_1$ does not require skill $s_1$, and the minimum mastery levels for $s_2$ and $s_3$ are both 0.5, this individual cannot solve $q_1$. Similarly, they cannot solve $q_2$, and thus their knowledge state is $\varnothing$. If another individual has a competence state $T_2 = \{(s_1, 0.5), (s_2, 0.5), (s_3, 0)\}$, they can solve both $q_1$ and $q_2$, and hence their knowledge state is $\{q_1, q_2\}$.*

In practice, fuzzy skill mappings are usually defined by domain experts. Nevertheless, there is no consistent standard for specifying the exact values of $\tau(q)$, and the values of $T(s)$ are often determined retrospectively. In Example 1, if we consider another competence state $T$ such that $T(s_1) = T(s_3) = 0$, but the individual can still solve $q_1$, it implies that there is a certain range constraint for $T(s_2)$ (for instance, $0.5 \leq T(s_2) < 0.7$). If we change $\tau_{q_2}(s_2)$ from 0.7 to 0.6, this range-based judgment remains unaffected, indicating that small adjustments to certain skill thresholds do not alter the individual's set of solvable problems.

## 3. Fuzzy Competence Space

In general, $T \in \mathcal{F}(S)$ is not necessarily a valid fuzzy competence state. For instance, consider an object-oriented programming context where skill $s_1$ represents "declaring a class" and skill $s_2$ represents "declaring a derived class". If an individual's competence state is $T = \{(s_1, 0.95), (s_2, 0)\}$, it indicates that the person has a solid grasp of "declaring a class" but has not begun learning "declaring a derived class". In this example, it is clear that $T = \{(s_1, 0), (s_2, 0.95)\}$ cannot be a valid fuzzy competence state because it conflicts with the learning progression required in object-oriented programming, where "declaring a class" is fundamental to "declaring a derived class". We next discuss the concept of a fuzzy competence structure.

**Definition 4** ([50]). *Let $U$ be a nonempty finite set and denote*

$$\mathcal{B} = \{B_i \subseteq U | i \in I\}. \quad (8)$$

*Here $I$ is an index set. A subset $X \subseteq U$ is called a transversal of the family $\mathcal{B}$. If there exists a bijection $\varphi : X \to I$ such that for every $x \in X$, it holds that $x \in B_{\varphi(x)}$.*

For example, let $U = \{u_1, u_2, u_3, u_4\}$ and $\mathcal{B} = \{B_1, B_2\}$, where $B_1 = \{u_1, u_2\}$ and $B_2 = \{u_3, u_4\}$. Suppose $X = \{u_1, u_3\}$ and there is a bijection $\varphi : X \to I$ with $I = \{1, 2\}$. Let $\varphi(u_1) = 1$ and $\varphi(u_3) = 2$. Then, $u_1 \in B_{\varphi(u_1)}$ and $u_3 \in B_{\varphi(u_3)}$, so $X$ is a transversal of $\mathcal{B}$. Similarly, $\{u_1, u_4\}$, $\{u_2, u_3\}$, and $\{u_2, u_4\}$ are also transversals of $\mathcal{B}$.

Given a skill set $S$, for each $s \in S$, let $(P_s, \leq_s)$ be a nonempty finite set of numerical values, where $P_s$ represents all possible "response values" (or proficiencies) of skill $s$, with 1 as the maximum element and 0 as the minimum element. The relation $\leq_s$ retains the usual ordering of real numbers. Define

$$S \times P_s = \bigcup_{s \in S} \{s\} \times P_s, \tag{9}$$

which is the set of all pairs formed by each skill and its possible proficiency values. Let $\{\{s\} \times P_s : s \in S\}$ be the family of subsets built from each skill and its proficiency values. A transversal of this family is denoted by $T$, with the requirement that there exists a bijection $\varphi : T \to S$ such that for any $(s, p_s) \in T$ we have $\varphi(s, p_s) = s$, where $p_s \in P_s$.

**Example 2.** *Let $S = \{s_1, s_2\}$, with $P_{s_1} = \{0, 0.5, 1\}$ and $P_{s_2} = \{0, 1\}$. Then*

$$S \times P_s = \{(s_1, 0), (s_1, 0.5), (s_1, 1), (s_2, 0), (s_2, 1)\} \text{ and}$$

$$\{\{s\} \times P_s : s \in S\} = \{\{(s_1, 0), (s_1, 0.5), (s_1, 1)\}, \{(s_2, 0), (s_2, 1)\}\}.$$

*Let $T$ be a transversal of $\{\{s\} \times P_s : s \in S\}$ and suppose there is a bijection $\varphi : T \to S$ such that for any $(s, p_s) \in T$ we have $\varphi(s, p_s) = s$. Denote by $P_s^S$ the family of all such transversals. Consequently, we obtain the following:*

$$P_s^S = \{\{(s_1,0),(s_2,0)\},\{(s_1,0),(s_2,1)\},\{(s_1,0.5),(s_2,0)\},\{(s_1,0.5),(s_2,1)\},\{(s_1,1),(s_2,0)\},\{(s_1,1),(s_2,1)\}\}$$

Based on the above, we now introduce the definition of a fuzzy competence structure.

**Definition 5.** *Let $S$ be a nonempty finite set of skills and for each $s \in S$, let $(P_s, \leq_s)$ be a finite set of numerical values whose minimum element is 0 and maximum element is 1. Let $P_s^S$ denote the family of all transversals of $\{\{s\} \times P_s | s \in S\}$. Suppose there exists a subset $\mathcal{C} \subseteq P_s^S$ satisfying $S \times \{0\} \in \mathcal{C}$, $S \times \{1\} \in \mathcal{C}$ and $\{(s, p_s) \in T | T \in \mathcal{C}\} = S \times P_s$. Then, the triple $(S, P_s, \mathcal{C})$ is called a fuzzy competence structure and any $T \in \mathcal{C}$ is referred to as a fuzzy competence state.*

**Example 3.** *Let $S = \{s_1, s_2, s_3\}$ with $P_{s_1} = P_{s_3} = \{0, 0.5, 1\}$ and $P_{s_2} = \{0, 0.4, 0.8, 1\}$. Let $P_s^S$ be the family of all transversals of $\{\{s\} \times P_s | s \in S\}$. There are 36 such transversals in total, and each corresponds to one state. Table 1 lists 23 of these states, denoted by $T_i \in P_s^S$ for $1 \leq i \leq 23$. In particular, $T_1 = S \times \{0\}$ and $T_{23} = S \times \{1\}$, and it holds that $\{(s, p_s) \in T_i | 1 \leq i \leq 23\} = S \times P_s$. By Definition 5, the family of these states forms a fuzzy competence structure $(S, P_s, \mathcal{C})$. Any $T_i \in \mathcal{C}$ is regarded as a fuzzy competence state in $(S, P_s, \mathcal{C})$.*

**Table 1.** A sample of fuzzy competence states.

| $T$ | Fuzzy Competence State | $T$ | Fuzzy Competence State |
|---|---|---|---|
| $T_1$ | $\{(s_1,0),(s_2,0),(s_3,0)\}$ | $T_{13}$ | $\{(s_1,1),(s_2,0.4),(s_3,0.5)\}$ |
| $T_2$ | $\{(s_1,0),(s_2,0),(s_3,0.5)\}$ | $T_{14}$ | $\{(s_1,1),(s_2,0.8),(s_3,0.5)\}$ |
| $T_3$ | $\{(s_1,0),(s_2,0),(s_3,1)\}$ | $T_{15}$ | $\{(s_1,1),(s_2,1),(s_3,0.5)\}$ |
| $T_4$ | $\{(s_1,0),(s_2,0.4),(s_3,0.5)\}$ | $T_{16}$ | $\{(s_1,0.5),(s_2,0),(s_3,1)\}$ |
| $T_5$ | $\{(s_1,0),(s_2,0.8),(s_3,0.5)\}$ | $T_{17}$ | $\{(s_1,0.5),(s_2,0.4),(s_3,1)\}$ |
| $T_6$ | $\{(s_1,0),(s_2,1),(s_3,0.5)\}$ | $T_{18}$ | $\{(s_1,0.5),(s_2,0.8),(s_3,1)\}$ |
| $T_7$ | $\{(s_1,0),(s_2,1),(s_3,1)\}$ | $T_{19}$ | $\{(s_1,0.5),(s_2,1),(s_3,1)\}$ |
| $T_8$ | $\{(s_1,0.5),(s_2,0),(s_3,0.5)\}$ | $T_{20}$ | $\{(s_1,1),(s_2,0),(s_3,1)\}$ |
| $T_9$ | $\{(s_1,0.5),(s_2,0.4),(s_3,0.5)\}$ | $T_{21}$ | $\{(s_1,1),(s_2,0.4),(s_3,1)\}$ |
| $T_{10}$ | $\{(s_1,0.5),(s_2,0.8),(s_3,0.5)\}$ | $T_{22}$ | $\{(s_1,1),(s_2,0.8),(s_3,1)\}$ |
| $T_{11}$ | $\{(s_1,0.5),(s_2,1),(s_3,0.5)\}$ | $T_{23}$ | $\{(s_1,1),(s_2,1),(s_3,1)\}$ |
| $T_{12}$ | $\{(s_1,1),(s_2,0),(s_3,0.5)\}$ | | |

**Definition 6.** *Let $(S, P_s, \mathcal{C})$ be a fuzzy competence structure and let $(Q, S, \tau)$ be a given fuzzy skill mapping. For any $T \in \mathcal{C}$, under the disjunctive model, define the following:*

$$K = \{q \in Q | \exists s \in S, 0 < \tau_q(s) \leq T(s)\}, \tag{10}$$

*and denote $m(T) = K$. Then, $m$ is called the fuzzy disjunctive problem function corresponding to $(Q, S, \tau)$. Moreover, define the following:*

$$\mathcal{K} = \{K | K = m(T), T \in \mathcal{C}\} \tag{11}$$

*as the knowledge structure induced by $(S, P_s, \mathcal{C})$ and $(Q, S, \tau)$ under the disjunctive model.*

**Proposition 1.** *Let $(S, P_s, \mathcal{C})$ be a fuzzy competence structure and let $(Q, S, \tau)$ be a fuzzy skill mapping. Suppose $m$ is the fuzzy disjunctive problem function corresponding to $(Q, S, \tau)$. Then, the following three properties hold:*

*(1)* $m : \mathcal{C} \to \mathcal{K}$ *is surjective;*
*(2)* $m(S \times \{0\}) = \varnothing$ *and* $m(S \times \{1\}) = Q$*;*
*(3)* *if* $T_1, T_2 \in \mathcal{C}$ *and* $T_1 \subseteq T_2$*, then* $m(T_1) \subseteq m(T_2)$.

**Proof.** (1) By Definition 6, $\mathcal{K} = \{K | K = m(T), T \in \mathcal{C}\}$. Hence, for every knowledge state $K \in \mathcal{K}$, there is at least one $T \in \mathcal{C}$ such that $m(T) = K$. Therefore, $m$ is surjective.

(2) When $T = S \times \{0\}$, for all $s \in S$, $T(s) = 0$. Thus, for all $q \in Q$, there is no $s \in S$ such that $0 < \tau_q(s) \leq T(s)$. Consequently, $m(S \times \{0\}) = \varnothing$. When $T = S \times \{1\}$, for all $q \in Q$ and $s \in S$, $\tau_q(s) \leq 1 = T(s)$. Therefore, $m(S \times \{1\}) = Q$.

(3) Suppose $T_1 \subseteq T_2$. Then, $T_1(s) \leq T_2(s)$ for all $s \in S$. If $q \in m(T_1)$, there exists some $s \in S$ such that $\tau_q(s) \leq T_1(s) \leq T_2(s)$. Hence, $q \in m(T_2)$, implying $m(T_1) \subseteq m(T_2)$. □

**Example 4 (Continuation of Example 3).** *Given $Q = \{q_1, q_2, q_3, q_4, q_5\}$, the fuzzy skill mapping is shown in Table 2, and the corresponding knowledge states and fuzzy competence states are presented in Table 3. As shown in Table 2, solving problem $q_1$ is independent of skills $s_1$ and $s_2$ and requires at least a proficiency level of 0.5 in skill $s_3$ to solve it. Therefore, individuals with fuzzy competence states $T_2$ and $T_4$ both have the knowledge state $\{q_1\}$. This case demonstrates that although individuals may have varying levels of proficiency in different skills, their knowledge state can be determined based on the fuzzy competence state. For instance, if an individual's proficiency in skill $s_3$ is 0.5 or higher, they are able to solve problem $q_1$, and no higher proficiency level is required.*

**Table 2.** Fuzzy skill mapping table.

| Q | $\tau(q)$ |
|---|---|
| $q_1$ | $\{(s_1,0),(s_2,0),(s_3,0.5)\}$ |
| $q_2$ | $\{(s_1,0),(s_2,0),(s_3,0.7)\}$ |
| $q_3$ | $\{(s_1,0.3),(s_2,0.5),(s_3,0)\}$ |
| $q_4$ | $\{(s_1,0.7),(s_2,0.5),(s_3,0.5)\}$ |
| $q_5$ | $\{(s_1,0),(s_2,0.8),(s_3,0)\}$ |

**Table 3.** Fuzzy Competence States and Corresponding Knowledge States.

| $T$ | $m(T)$ |
|---|---|
| $T_1$ | $\varnothing$ |
| $T_2, T_4$ | $\{q_1\}$ |
| $T_3$ | $\{q_1, q_2\}$ |
| $T_8, T_9$ | $\{q_1, q_3\}$ |
| $T_{12}, T_{13}$ | $\{q_1, q_3, q_4\}$ |
| $T_{16}, T_{17}$ | $\{q_1, q_2, q_3\}$ |
| $T_{20}, T_{21}$ | $\{q_1, q_2, q_3, q_4\}$ |
| $T_5, T_6, T_{10}, T_{11}, T_{14}, T_{15}$ | $\{q_1, q_3, q_4, q_5\}$ |
| $T_7, T_{18}, T_{19}, T_{22}, T_{23}$ | $Q$ |

The fuzzy competence structure is merely a pre-established evaluation criterion. For example, in the IELTS exam, some candidates achieve a score of 7 but do not reach 7.5. These candidates may have varying levels of English proficiency, but the IELTS exam cannot further differentiate their proficiency levels. Therefore, the form of the fuzzy competence structure and the specification of the fuzzy skill mapping are independent of each other. In Example 3, for an individual whose knowledge state is $\{q_1, q_2\}$, their fuzzy competence state will be determined as $T_3$. Naturally, since skill acquisition is a continuous process, a learner's proficiency in skill $s_1$ could be 0.2 or some other value; however, such granularity is not captured in this fuzzy competence structure.

**Definition 7.** *Given a fuzzy competence structure $(S, P_s, \mathcal{C})$, if for any $T_1, T_2 \in \mathcal{C}$, it holds that $T_1 \cup T_2 \in \mathcal{C}$, then $(S, P_s, \mathcal{C})$ is called a fuzzy competence space.*

**Proposition 2.** *Given a fuzzy competence structure$(S, P_s, \mathcal{C})$ and a defined fuzzy skill mapping $(Q, S, \tau)$, the knowledge structure $\mathcal{K}$ induced by $(S, P_s, \mathcal{C})$ and $(Q, S, \tau)$ is a knowledge space.*

**Proof.** For any $K_1, K_2 \in \mathcal{K}$, there exist $T_1, T_2 \in \mathcal{C}$. From Proposition 1(3), we obtain $m(T_1) \subseteq m(T_1 \cup T_2)$ and $m(T_2) \subseteq m(T_1 \cup T_2)$, so $m(T_1) \cup m(T_2) \subseteq m(T_1 \cup T_2)$ holds. For any $q \in m(T_1 \cup T_2)$, there exists a skill $s \in S$ such that $0< \tau_q(s) \leq (T_1 \cup T_2)(s) = max\{T_1(s), T_2(s)\}$, thus $0 < \tau_q(s) \leq T_1(s)$ or $0 < \tau_q(s) \leq T_2(s)$. Therefore $q \in m(T_1)$ or $q \in m(T_2)$, so $m(T_1 \cup T_2) \subseteq m(T_1) \cup m(T_2)$ holds. In conclusion, $K_1 \cup K_2 = m(T_1) \cup m(T_2) = m(T_1 \cup T_2) \in \mathcal{K}$. By Definition 1, $\mathcal{K}$ is a knowledge space. □

**Definition 8.** *Given a fuzzy competence structure $(S, P_s, \mathcal{C})$, we define the following operations and symbols:*

(1) *For any $T \in \mathcal{C}$, let*

$$|T| = |\{s \in S | T(s) > 0\}|, \tag{12}$$

*where the absolute value symbol indicates the number of elements in the set.*

(2) *For any $T_1, T_2 \in \mathcal{C}$, if $T_1 \subseteq T_2$, define*

$$T_2 \setminus T_1 = \{s \in S | T_2(s) - T_1(s) > 0\}; \tag{13}$$

(3) *For any $P_s = \left\{p_1, p_2, \ldots, p_{|P_s|}\right\}$, where $0 = p_1, p_2, \ldots, p_{|P_s|} = 1$ for $1 \leq i < j \leq |P_s|$, define*

$$\Delta(p_i, p_j) = j - i; \tag{14}$$

(4) *For any $T_1, T_2 \in \mathcal{C}$, if $T_1 \subseteq T_2$, define*

$$\Delta(T_1, T_2) = \sum_{s \in S} \Delta(T_1(s), T_2(s)). \tag{15}$$

In Example 3, a fuzzy competence state chain of the form $T_1 \subseteq T_2 \subseteq T_3 \subseteq T_{16} \subseteq T_{20} \subseteq T_{21} \subseteq T_{22} \subseteq T_{23}$, adjacent fuzzy competence states $T_i \subseteq T_j$ satisfy $|T_j \setminus T_i| = 1$, and $\Delta(T_i, T_j) = 1$.

**Definition 9.** *Given a fuzzy competence structure $(S, P_s, \mathcal{C})$, if $\mathcal{C}$ satisfies the following two properties, then $(S, P_s, \mathcal{C})$ is called consistent:*

(1) *For any* $T, T' \in \mathcal{C}$, *if* $T \subseteq T'$, *there exist* $T_0, T_1, \ldots, T_n \in \mathcal{C}$ *such that* $T = T_0 \subseteq T_1 \subseteq \ldots \subseteq T_n = T'$, *and* $|T_i \setminus T_{i-1}| = 1$, *where* $1 \leq i \leq n$;

(2) *For any* $T, T' \in \mathcal{C}$, *if* $T \subseteq T'$, *and* $|T' \setminus T| = 1$, *suppose* $(T' \setminus T)(s) > 0$, *then there exist* $T_0, T_1, \ldots, T_n \in \mathcal{C}$ *such that* $T = T_0 \subseteq T_1 \subseteq \ldots \subseteq T_n = T'$, *and* $\Delta(T_{i-1}(s), T_i(s)) = 1$, *where* $1 \leq i \leq n$.

*Given a fuzzy competence structure* $(S, P_s, \mathcal{C})$, *if it is consistent, then* $(S, P_s, \mathcal{C})$ *is called a consistent fuzzy competence space.*

A consistent fuzzy competence space has three educational learning principles similar to those of a knowledge space:

(1) Closure under union of competences: this guarantees that individuals can interact and learn from one another, enabling their fuzzy competence states to merge and improve;

(2) Gradualness of skill learning: for fuzzy competence states $T, T' \in \mathcal{C}$, if $T \subseteq T'$, there exists a chain of fuzzy competence states as described in Definition 8(1) and (2), meaning individuals can progressively learn skills;

(3) Consistency of skill learning: an individual's improvement in fuzzy competence states does not interfere with the learning of certain skills.

**Proposition 3.** *Given a fuzzy competence space* $(S, P_s, \mathcal{C})$ *and* $T, T' \in \mathcal{C}$, *where* $T \subseteq T'$, *and* $|T' \setminus T| = 1$. *Suppose* $(T' \setminus T)(s_0) > 0$. *For any* $T^* \in \mathcal{C}$, *and* $T \subseteq T^*$, *if* $T^*(s_0) < T'(s_0)$, *define* $\hat{T}(s) = \begin{cases} T^*(s) & s \neq s_0 \\ p & s = s_0 \end{cases}$, *where* $T^*(s_0) \leq p \leq T'(s_0)$, *and* $p \in P_{s_0}$, *then* $\hat{T} \in \mathcal{C}$.

**Proof.** Since $T^* \in \mathcal{C}$ and $T' \in \mathcal{C}$, and $(S, P_s, \mathcal{C})$ is a fuzzy competence, it follows that $T^* \cup T' \in \mathcal{C}$. For any $s \neq s_0$, we have $T'(s) = T(s) \leq T^*(s)$, so $\max\{T^*(s), T'(s)\} = T^*(s)$. For $s = s_0$ we have $T^*(s) < T'(s)$, so $\max\{T^*(s_0), T'(s_0)\} = T'(s_0)$. It follows that $|(T' \cup T^*) \setminus T^*| = 1$, and hence $T^* \subseteq \hat{T} \subseteq T' \cup T^*$. By Definition 8(2), it follows that $\hat{T} \in \mathcal{C}$. □

**Remark 1.** *Consider* $T$ *as the initial fuzzy competence state of an individual. Since* $|T' \setminus T| = 1$ *and* $(T' \setminus T)(s_0) > 0$, *the individual reaches fuzzy competence state* $T'$ *by learning skill* $s_0$. *For another individual, whose fuzzy competence state is* $T^*$, *and* $T \subseteq T^*$, *this individual can also improve their fuzzy competence state by learning skill* $s_0$, *which shows that the improvement in competence does not interfere with the learning of skills.*

## 4. Learning Paths of Fuzzy Skills

As shown in Example 3, the fuzzy disjunctive problem function $m : \mathcal{C} \rightarrow \mathcal{K}$ is not necessarily a bijection, meaning that the potential competence level of an individual cannot be uniquely inferred from their knowledge state. The following proposition provides a method for determining the upper bound of an individual's potential competence level in a fuzzy competence space.

**Proposition 4.** *Given a fuzzy competence space* $(S, P_s, \mathcal{C})$ *and fuzzy skill mapping* $(Q, S, \tau)$, *let* $m$ *be the fuzzy disjunctive problem function corresponding to* $(Q, S, \tau)$. $\mathcal{K} = \{K | K = m(T), T \in \mathcal{C}\}$ *is the knowledge space induced by* $(S, P_s, \mathcal{C})$ *and* $(Q, S, \tau)$ *under the disjunctive model. For* $K \in \mathcal{K}$, *let* $[T]_K = \{T \in \mathcal{C} | m(T) = K\}$, *then the following two properties hold:*

(1) $\bigcup [T]_K \in \mathcal{C}$, *and* $m(\bigcup [T]_K) = K$;

(2) *For any* $s \in S$, $(\bigcup[T]_K)(s) < \bigcap_{q \notin K} \tau_q(s)$.

**Proof.** (1) $\bigcup[T]_K$ represents the family of fuzzy competence states of all individuals with knowledge state $K$. Since $(S, P_s, \mathcal{C})$ is a fuzzy competence space, $\bigcup[T]_K \in \mathcal{C}$ always holds. As in the proof of Proposition 2, we have $m(\bigcup[T]_K) = \bigcup_{T \in [T]_K} m(T) = K$.

(2) If there exists $s_0 \in S$ such that $(\bigcup[T]_K)(s_0) \geq \bigcap_{q \notin K} \tau_q(s_0)$, i.e., there exists $q_0 \notin K$ such that $(\bigcup[T]_K)(s_0) \geq \tau_{q_0}(s_0)$, then there exists $T \in [T]_K$ such that $T(s_0) \geq \tau_{q_0}(s_0)$. This implies that $q_0 \in m(T) = K$, which contradicts $q_0 \notin K$. □

While consistent fuzzy competence spaces ensure gradual skill learning, they do not guarantee changes in knowledge states. For instance, in Example 4, although $T_8 \subset T_9$, but $T_8, T_9 \in [T]_{\{q_1,q_3\}}$, i.e., $m(T_8) = m(T_9)$. This indicates that an improvement in competence does not necessarily lead to an improvement in the knowledge state. The literature [24] refers to such a learning method or learning path as "ineffective". The following proposition explores the existence of effective learning paths.

**Proposition 5.** *Given a consistent fuzzy competence space* $(S, P_s, \mathcal{C})$ *and a fuzzy skill mapping* $(Q, S, \tau)$, *let* $m$ *be the fuzzy disjunctive problem function corresponding to* $(Q, S, \tau)$. $\mathcal{K}$ *is the knowledge space induced by* $(S, P_s, \mathcal{C})$ *and* $(Q, S, \tau)$ *under the disjunctive model. Define* $\hat{\mathcal{C}} = \{\bigcup[T]_K | K \in \mathcal{K}\}$, *and if* $|\hat{\mathcal{C}}| = |\mathcal{C}|$, *the following two propositions hold:*

(1) *The fuzzy disjunctive problem function* $m : \mathcal{C} \to \mathcal{K}$ *is a bijection;*
(2) *Given* $T \in \mathcal{C}$ *and* $m(T) = K$, *for any knowledge state* $K' \in \mathcal{K}$ *with* $K \subset K'$, *there exist* $T_0, T_1, \ldots, T_n \in \mathcal{C}$ *such that* $T = T_0 \subseteq T_1 \subseteq \ldots \subseteq T_n$, *and* $m(T_n) = K'$, *and the following conditions hold:* $m(T_{i-1}) \subseteq m(T_i)$ *and* $\Delta(T_{i-1}, T_i) = 1$, *where* $1 \leq i \leq n$.

**Proof.** (1) Since $\bigcup[T]_K \in \mathcal{C}$, and by Proposition 4(1), we know that $\bigcup[T]_K \in [T]_K$, and since $|\hat{\mathcal{C}}| = |\mathcal{C}|$, for any $K \in \mathcal{K}$, we have $|[T]_K| = 1$, so $m : \mathcal{C} \to \mathcal{K}$ is a bijection.

(2) Since $m : \mathcal{C} \to \mathcal{K}$ is a bijection, for any $K, K' \in \mathcal{K}$, there exist $T, T' \in \mathcal{C}$ such that $m(T) = K$ and $m(T') = K'$. For any $K \in \mathcal{K}$, we have $|[T]_K| = 1$, so $K \subset K' \Leftrightarrow T \subset T'$. This is consistent with the definition of a consistent fuzzy competence structure. Therefore, the proposition holds. □

If for any fuzzy competence state $T \in \mathcal{C}$, and any knowledge state $K' \supset m(T)$, there exists a gradual and effective learning path as shown in Proposition 5(2), such a learning model benefits all learners. We call such a learning model "effective". Proposition 5 provides a sufficient condition for the validity of the learning model, namely that $(S, P_s, \mathcal{C})$ is a consistent fuzzy competence space and $|\hat{\mathcal{C}}| = |\mathcal{C}|$. The following proposition provides a more general case.

**Proposition 6.** *Given a consistent fuzzy competence space* $(S, P_s, \mathcal{C})$ *and a fuzzy skill mapping* $(Q, S, \tau)$, *let* $m$ *be the fuzzy disjunctive problem function corresponding to* $(Q, S, \tau)$. $\mathcal{K}$ *is the knowledge space induced by* $(S, P_s, \mathcal{C})$ *and* $(Q, S, \tau)$ *under the disjunctive model. If the learning model is effective, then for any knowledge states* $K, K' \in \mathcal{K}$ *with* $K \subset K'$, *we have* $|[T]_K| \leq |[T]_{K'}|$.

**Proof.** Assume there exist $K, K' \in \mathcal{K}$, such that $K \subset K'$, and $|[T]_K| > |[T]_{K'}|$. Suppose $K'$ is the smallest knowledge state containing $K$, i.e., there does not exist $K^* \in \mathcal{K}$ such that $K \subset K^* \subset K'$. Let $|[T]_K| = m + n$, and $|[T]_{K'}| = m$. Define $[T]_K = \{T_1, T_2, \ldots, T_{m+n}\}$ and $[T]_{K'} = \{T_1{}', T_2{}', \ldots, T_m{}'\}$. If the learning model is effective, there exist $T_1, T_2 \in [T]_K$ and $T_K{}' \in [T]_{K'}$, such that $\Delta(T_i, T_K{}') = \Delta(T_j, T_K{}') = 1$. Clearly, in this case, $T_i$ and $T_j$ do not have an inclusion relationship, so $T_i \cup T_j = T_K'$. Since $T_i \cup T_j \in [T]_K$, this contradicts the assumption. □

The preceding theoretical investigation establishes the foundation for a learning-path recommendation method within fuzzy competence spaces. Building on this foundation, Figure 1 presents the overall research framework of the proposed method. The upper-left quadrant contains the fundamental concepts used throughout the paper, namely the problem set $Q$, the skill set $S$, the fuzzy skill mapping $(Q, S, \tau)$, and the fuzzy competence structure $(S, P_s, \mathcal{C})$. The lower-left quadrant provides the theoretical underpinning: The definition of a consistent fuzzy competence space given in Definition 9, and the necessary and sufficient conditions for the existence of gradual and effective learning paths stated in Propositions 5 and 6. The upper-right quadrant corresponds to the algorithmic layer, including the validation and construction of a consistent fuzzy competence space and the generation of gradual and effective learning paths. Finally, the lower-right quadrant covers simulation and discussion, comprising dataset construction, algorithm implementation, analysis of simulation results, and discussion of application scenarios. Arrows illustrate the dependencies among these components.

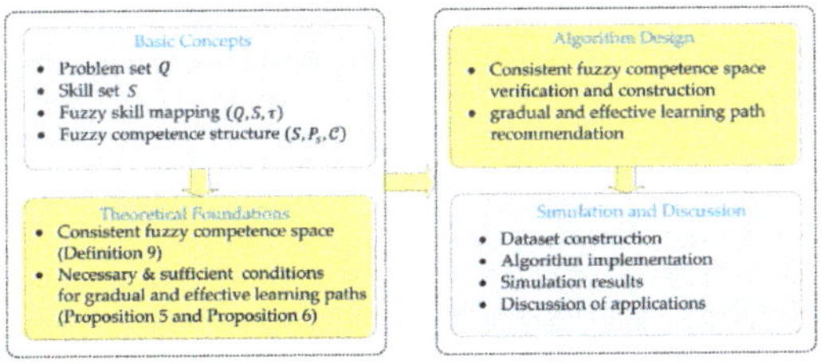


**Figure 1.** The overall research framework.

When the conditions of Proposition 5 are satisfied, every pair of knowledge states in the knowledge space induced by a consistent fuzzy competence space $(S, P_s, \mathcal{C})$ and a fuzzy skill mapping $(Q, S, \tau)$ can be connected by a gradual and effective learning path. In practical learning environments, the path of greatest interest is the one that starts from the initial knowledge state $\varnothing$ and ends at the final knowledge state $Q$. Such a path upgrades exactly one skill-proficiency level at each step and guarantees a simultaneous improvement in the knowledge state until $Q$ is reached, thereby minimizing learning time and markedly enhancing learning efficiency.

According to Proposition 5, if $(S, P_s, \mathcal{C})$ is a consistent fuzzy competence space and $|\hat{\mathcal{C}}| = |\mathcal{C}|$, a gradual and effective learning path from $\varnothing$ to $Q$ is assured to exist; if $|\hat{\mathcal{C}}| \neq |\mathcal{C}|$, the existence of such a path cannot be determined a priori. Algorithm 1 outlines the overall procedure for searching a gradual and effective learning path from $\varnothing$ to $Q$ given $(S, P_s, \mathcal{C})$ and $(Q, S, \tau)$. Algorithm 2 refines Steps 1–2 of Algorithm 1 by deciding whether the given fuzzy competence structure is a consistent fuzzy competence space. Algorithm 3 refines Steps 3–5 by verifying whether the equality $|\hat{\mathcal{C}}| = |\mathcal{C}|$ in Proposition 5 holds. Algorithm 4 further refines Step 6 and is responsible for finding the gradual and effective learning path. It is important to emphasize that Algorithm 4 is executed regardless of whether $|\hat{\mathcal{C}}| = |\mathcal{C}|$ holds; if a gradual and effective learning path from $\varnothing$ to $Q$ is found, it is reported, otherwise an informative message is returned.

**Algorithm 1** Learning path recommendation algorithm

**Input:** A fuzzy competence structure $(S, P_s, \mathcal{C})$ and a fuzzy skill mapping $(Q, S, \tau)$.
**Output:** One of the following two outcomes:

(1) A gradual and effective learning path from the initial knowledge state $\varnothing$ to $Q$.
(2) A determination that no gradual and effective learning path exists from $\varnothing$ to $Q$.

1: Check whether $(S, P_s, \mathcal{C})$ is a fuzzy competence space. If yes, continue to Step 2; otherwise, $flag$ = FALSE, go to Step 7.
2: Check whether $(S, P_s, \mathcal{C})$ is a consistent fuzzy competence space. If yes, proceed to Step 3; otherwise, $flag$ = FALSE, go to Step 7.
3: Compute the knowledge space $\mathcal{K} = \{K | K = m(T), T \in \mathcal{C}\}$ induced by the fuzzy competence space $(S, P_s, \mathcal{C})$ and the fuzzy skill mapping $(Q, S, \tau)$.
4: Compute $\hat{\mathcal{C}} = \{\cup[T]_K | K \in \mathcal{K}\}$.
5: Compute the set cardinalities of $\hat{\mathcal{C}}$ and $\mathcal{C}$ denoted as $c1$ and $c2$.
6: Finding and drawing the gradual and effective learning path.
7: IF $flag$ = FALSE then Output "No gradual and effective learning path exists".
8: End.

**Algorithm 2** Refines Steps 1–2 of Algorithm 1. Deciding whether the given fuzzy competence structure is a consistent fuzzy competence space.

**Input:** A fuzzy competence structure $(S, P_s, \mathcal{C})$.
**Output:** TRUE if $(S, P_s, \mathcal{C})$ is a consistent fuzzy competence space; FALSE otherwise

```
for each pair (T1, T2) in C × C do
    if (T1 ∪ T2) ∉ C then
        return FALSE
    end if
end for
create empty directed graph G = (C, Adj)
for each pair (T, U) in C × C with T ⊂ U do
    if |diff(T, U)| = 1 then
        add edge (T → U) to Adj
    end if
end for
for each pair (T, U) in C × C with T ⊂ U
    if no path from T to U in G then
        return FALSE
    end if
end for
for each pair(T, U) in C × C with T ⊂ U and |diff(T, U)| = 1 do
    let s0 ← the unique skill in diff(T, U)
    t0 ← T(s0)
    U0 ← U(s0)
    for p from next t0 to U0 in P_s0 do
        TP ← T, TP(s0)= p
        if TP ∉ C then
            return FALSE
        end if
    end for
end for
return TRUE
```

**Algorithm 3** Refines Steps 3–5 of Algorithm 1.

**Input:** A consistent fuzzy competence space $(S, P_s, \mathcal{C})$ and a fuzzy skill mapping $(Q, S, \tau)$.
**Output:** $c1,\ c2, \mathcal{K}, \hat{\mathcal{C}},\ Kmap$

```
n = |C|
CSET ← C
create empty dictionary Kmap//key: knowledge state K
for i = 1 to n do
    T ← CSET[i]
    K ← ∅
    for each problem q ∈ Q do
        for each skill s ∈ S do
            if (τ_q(s) > 0 and τ_q(s) <= T(s)) then
                K ← K ∪ {q} ; break
            end if
        end for
        m(i) ← K
        if K not in Kmap then
            Kmap[K] ← empty list
        end if
        append i to Kmap[K]
    end for
end for
𝒦 ← keys(Kmap)
Ĉ ← ∅
for each K in 𝒦 do
    classIdx ← Kmap[K]
    U ← CSET[classIdx(1)]
    for j = 2 to length(classIdx) do
        U ← max(U, CSET[classIdx(j)])
    end for
    Ĉ ← Ĉ ∪ {U}
end for
c1 ← |Ĉ|
c2 ← n
return c1, c2, 𝒦, Ĉ, Kmap
```

**Algorithm 4** Refines Step 6 of Algorithm 1. Finding and drawing the gradual and effective learning path.

**Input:** $c1,\ c2, \mathcal{K}, \hat{\mathcal{C}},\ Kmap$
**Output:** $flag$

```
if c1 = c2 then
    flag ← TRUE
else
    flag ← FALSE
end if
CS ← sort C by each skill's proficiency in lexicographical order
KS ← {∅}
FP ← {first(CS)}
KT ← ∅
i ← 2
while i <= |CS| do
    FTprev ← FP.last
    FTcur ← CS[i]
    if diffSkillCount(FTprev, FTcur) ≠ 1 then
        i ← i + 1
        continue
    end if
    Kcur ← induceKnowledge(FTcur, τ)
    if KT ⊂ Kcur then
        append(KS, Kcur)
        append(FP, Fcur)
```

**Algorithm 4** *Cont.*

```
            KT ← Kcur
            if KT = Q then
                break
            end if
        end if
        i ← i + 1
    end while
    if KS.last = Q
        flag ← TRUE
        Output FP, KS
        drawPathDiagram(FP, KS)
        STOP
    end if
    return flag
```

## 5. Simulation Experiments

To verify the effectiveness of Algorithm 1, we carried out a set of simulation experiments. The experiments were executed on an Intel® Core™ i7-9700 CPU @ 3.00 GHz with 16 GB RAM under Windows 10, and the simulator that implements Algorithm 1 was written in Python 3.13.2.

First, we built ten datasets of different sizes, denoted d01–d10. Each dataset consists of three parts: (i) the skills together with their proficiency levels, (ii) the fuzzy competence states, and (iii) the fuzzy skill mapping; the basic statistics are listed in Table 4.

**Table 4.** Basic information of the first group of 10 datasets.

| ds | $\|S\|$ | $\|P_s\|$ | $\|Q\|$ | $\|C\|$ |
|---|---|---|---|---|
| d01 | 2 | 3 | 4 | 9 |
| d02 | 3 | 3 | 6 | 27 |
| d03 | 3 | 3 or 4 | 9 | 36 |
| d04 | 4 | 3 or 4 | 12 | 144 |
| d05 | 5 | 3 or 4 | 15 | 432 |
| d06 | 5 | 3 or 4 or 5 | 18 | 900 |
| d07 | 6 | 3 or 4 | 20 | 1296 |
| d08 | 6 | 3 or 4 or 5 | 23 | 1620 |
| d09 | 7 | 3 | 25 | 2187 |
| d10 | 8 | 3 | 28 | 6561 |

For every dataset, the fuzzy competence states comprise all possible states, which guarantees that the dataset forms a consistent fuzzy competence space and that a gradual and effective learning path from $\varnothing$ to $Q$ always exists.

All datasets are stored as Excel workbooks. The ps sheet stores the skills and their proficiency levels, the fcs sheet stores the fuzzy competence states, and the fsm sheet stores the fuzzy skill mapping. Taking dataset d03 as an example, the three sheets are shown in Tables 5–7.

**Table 5.** Dataset d03—ps worksheet.

| s | p1 | p2 | p3 | p4 |
|---|---|---|---|---|
| s1 | 0 | 0.6 | 1 | |
| s2 | 0 | 0.6 | 1 | |
| s3 | 0 | 0.2 | 0.4 | 1 |

**Table 6.** Dataset d03—fcs worksheet.

| T | s1 | s2 | s3 | T | s1 | s2 | s3 |
|---|---|---|---|---|---|---|---|
| T0 | 0 | 0 | 0 | T18 | 0.6 | 0.6 | 0.4 |
| T1 | 0 | 0 | 0.2 | T19 | 0.6 | 0.6 | 1 |

**Table 6.** *Cont.*

| T | s1 | s2 | s3 | T | s1 | s2 | s3 |
|---|---|---|---|---|---|---|---|
| T2 | 0 | 0 | 0.4 | T20 | 0.6 | 1 | 0 |
| T3 | 0 | 0 | 1 | T21 | 0.6 | 1 | 0.2 |
| T4 | 0 | 0.6 | 0 | T22 | 0.6 | 1 | 0.4 |
| T5 | 0 | 0.6 | 0.2 | T23 | 0.6 | 1 | 1 |
| T6 | 0 | 0.6 | 0.4 | T24 | 1 | 0 | 0 |
| T7 | 0 | 0.6 | 1 | T25 | 1 | 0 | 0.2 |
| T8 | 0 | 1 | 0 | T26 | 1 | 0 | 0.4 |
| T9 | 0 | 1 | 0.2 | T27 | 1 | 0 | 1 |
| T10 | 0 | 1 | 0.4 | T28 | 1 | 0.6 | 0 |
| T11 | 0 | 1 | 1 | T29 | 1 | 0.6 | 0.2 |
| T12 | 0.6 | 0 | 0 | T30 | 1 | 0.6 | 0.4 |
| T13 | 0.6 | 0 | 0.2 | T31 | 1 | 0.6 | 1 |
| T14 | 0.6 | 0 | 0.4 | T32 | 1 | 1 | 0 |
| T15 | 0.6 | 0 | 1 | T33 | 1 | 1 | 0.2 |
| T16 | 0.6 | 0.6 | 0 | T34 | 1 | 1 | 0.4 |
| T17 | 0.6 | 0.6 | 0.2 | T35 | 1 | 1 | 1 |

**Table 7.** Dataset d03—fsm worksheet.

| q | s1 | s2 | s3 |
|---|---|---|---|
| q1 | 0 | 0 | 0.2 |
| q2 | 0.6 | 0 | 0.2 |
| q3 | 0 | 0 | 0.4 |
| q4 | 0.6 | 0.6 | 0 |
| q5 | 1 | 0.6 | 0.4 |
| q6 | 0 | 1 | 0 |
| q7 | 1 | 1 | 1 |
| q8 | 0.6 | 0 | 0.4 |
| q9 | 0.6 | 0 | 0 |

The simulator read the ten datasets and successfully located a gradual and effective learning path from ∅ to $Q$ for each of them, which confirms the validity of the algorithms proposed in Section 3 of this paper. Using dataset d03 as an example, the knowledge structure obtained by the simulation program is presented in Table 8. The gradual and effective learning path found from ∅ to $Q$ is depicted in Figure 2.

**Table 8.** Knowledge structure derived for dataset d03.

| id | Knowledge State | Fuzzy Competence State |
|---|---|---|
| 1 | {} | [T0] |
| 2 | {q1,q2} | [T1] |
| 3 | {q1,q2,q3,q5,q8} | [T2] |
| 4 | {q1,q2,q3,q5,q7,q8} | [T3] |
| 5 | {q4,q5} | [T4] |
| 6 | {q1,q2,q4,q5} | [T5] |
| 7 | {q1,q2,q3,q4,q5,q8} | [T6] |
| 8 | {q1,q2,q3,q4,q5,q7,q8} | [T7] |
| 9 | {q4,q5,q6,q7} | [T8] |
| 10 | {q1,q2,q4,q5,q6,q7} | [T9] |
| 11 | {q1,q2,q3,q4,q5,q6,q7,q8} | [T10, T11] |
| 12 | {q2,q4,q8,q9} | [T12] |
| 13 | {q1,q2,q4,q8,q9} | [T13] |

**Table 8.** *Cont.*

| id | Knowledge State | Fuzzy Competence State |
|---|---|---|
| 14 | {q1,q2,q3,q4,q5,q8,q9} | [T14, T18] |
| 15 | {q1,q2,q3,q4,q5,q7,q8,q9} | [T15, T19, T26, T27, T30, T31] |
| 16 | {q2,q4,q5,q8,q9} | [T16] |
| 17 | {q1,q2,q4,q5,q8,q9} | [T17] |
| 18 | {q2,q4,q5,q6,q7,q8,q9} | [T20, T32] |
| 19 | {q1,q2,q4,q5,q6,q7,q8,q9} | [T21, T33] |
| 20 | {q1,q2,q3,q4,q5,q6,q7,q8,q9} | [T22, T23, T34, T35] |
| 21 | {q2,q4,q5,q7,q8,q9} | [T24, T28] |
| 22 | {q1,q2,q4,q5,q7,q8,q9} | [T25, T29] |

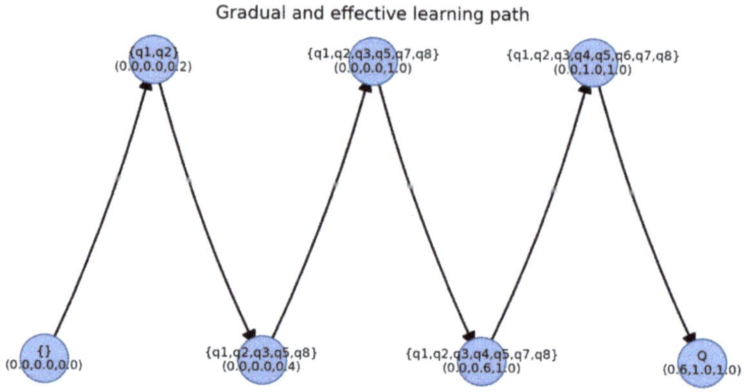


**Figure 2.** Gradual and effective learning path for dataset d03.

Table 9 reports the simulation results for the first ten datasets; the column $|\hat{C}|$ gives the cardinality of $\hat{C}$, while columns t_alg2, t_alg3 and t_alg4 give, respectively, the execution time of Algorithms 2–4. columns %A2, %A3 and %A4 show their percentages of the total time given by column t_sum. It is clear that, as $|C|$ grows, the total running time is dominated by Algorithm 2. The same trend can be seen in Figure 3, which plots the running time against the number of fuzzy competence states. It is worth noting that, as the number of fuzzy competence states grows, the running-time of Algorithm 2 is several orders of magnitude larger than those of Algorithms 3 and 4. Consequently, the curves for Algorithms 3 and 4 overlap and almost degenerate into a straight horizontal line; therefore, only the curve representing Algorithm 4 is visually discernible in Figure 3.

**Table 9.** Simulation results for the first dataset group.

| ds | $|\hat{C}|$ | t_alg2 (s) | t_alg3 (s) | t_alg4 (s) | %A2 | %A3 | %A4 | t_sum (s) |
|---|---|---|---|---|---|---|---|---|
| d01 | 8 | 0.0029588 | 0.0002256 | 0.0001866 | 87.772 | 6.692 | 5.535 | 0.003371 |
| d02 | 12 | 0.0195838 | 0.0004235 | 0.0001666 | 97.075 | 2.099 | 0.826 | 0.0201739 |
| d03 | 22 | 0.0338597 | 0.0005785 | 0.0002373 | 97.647 | 1.668 | 0.684 | 0.0346755 |
| d04 | 72 | 0.468807 | 0.0020978 | 0.0005439 | 99.440 | 0.445 | 0.115 | 0.4714487 |
| d05 | 168 | 3.9694118 | 0.0055021 | 0.0006219 | 99.846 | 0.138 | 0.016 | 3.9755358 |
| d06 | 296 | 17.1784075 | 0.015804 | 0.0019423 | 99.897 | 0.092 | 0.011 | 17.1961538 |
| d07 | 672 | 34.2429477 | 0.0176207 | 0.0025812 | 99.941 | 0.051 | 0.008 | 34.2631496 |
| d08 | 427 | 53.6230973 | 0.0194081 | 0.0014302 | 99.961 | 0.036 | 0.003 | 53.6439356 |
| d09 | 869 | 98.782046 | 0.0305387 | 0.0034947 | 99.966 | 0.031 | 0.004 | 98.8160794 |
| d10 | 1991 | 889.9205651 | 0.0865662 | 0.0173953 | 99.988 | 0.010 | 0.002 | 890.0245266 |

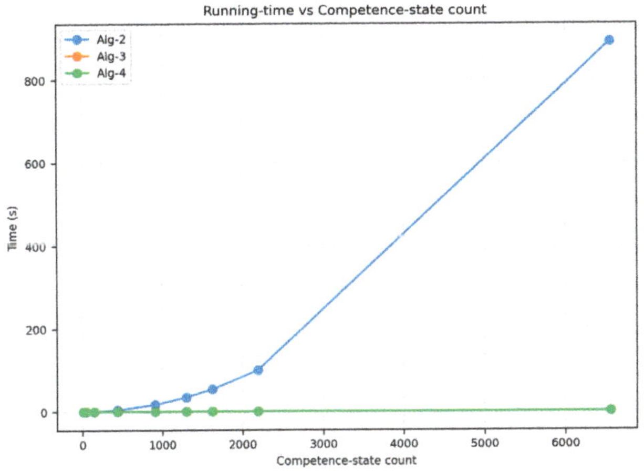


**Figure 3.** Running-time versus the number of fuzzy competence states.

To study how the numbers of skills and problems affect the running time, we constructed another group of ten datasets with different skill and problem scales, as summarized in Table 10.

**Table 10.** Basic information of the second group of 10 datasets.

| ds | $\|S\|$ | $\|P_s\|$ | $\|Q\|$ | $\|\mathcal{C}\|$ |
|---|---|---|---|---|
| d01 | 3 | 3 or 4 | 8 | 9 |
| d02 | 10 | 3 or 4 or 5 | 28 | 29 |
| d03 | 20 | 3 or 4 or 5 | 63 | 64 |
| d04 | 30 | 3 or 4 | 76 | 77 |
| d05 | 40 | 3 or 4 or 5 | 130 | 131 |
| d06 | 50 | 3 or 4 or 5 | 146 | 147 |
| d07 | 55 | 3 or 4 or 5 | 166 | 167 |
| d08 | 60 | 3 or 4 or 5 | 182 | 183 |
| d09 | 65 | 3 or 4 or 5 | 202 | 203 |
| d10 | 75 | 3 or 4 or 5 | 216 | 217 |

The simulation results of this second group are summarized in Table 11.

**Table 11.** Simulation results for the second dataset group.

| ds | $\|\hat{C}\|$ | t_alg2 (s) | t_alg3 (s) | t_alg4 (s) | %A2 | %A3 | %A4 | t_sum (s) |
|---|---|---|---|---|---|---|---|---|
| d01 | 5 | 0.0025003 | 0.0002202 | 0.0001701 | 86.498 | 7.618 | 5.885 | 0.0028906 |
| d02 | 20 | 0.0204677 | 0.0006195 | 0.000432 | 95.114 | 2.879 | 2.008 | 0.0215192 |
| d03 | 35 | 0.0965181 | 0.0012357 | 0.0004883 | 98.245 | 1.258 | 0.497 | 0.0982421 |
| d04 | 42 | 0.1401482 | 0.0015445 | 0.0005962 | 98.496 | 1.085 | 0.419 | 0.1422889 |
| d05 | 74 | 0.3952275 | 0.003094 | 0.0004799 | 99.104 | 0.776 | 0.120 | 0.3988014 |
| d06 | 81 | 0.5022423 | 0.0037556 | 0.0007904 | 99.103 | 0.741 | 0.156 | 0.5067883 |
| d07 | 91 | 0.6776541 | 0.0046647 | 0.000595 | 99.230 | 0.683 | 0.087 | 0.6829138 |
| d08 | 103 | 0.7992948 | 0.0051466 | 0.0009669 | 99.241 | 0.639 | 0.120 | 0.8054083 |
| d09 | 112 | 0.975403 | 0.0062941 | 0.0007262 | 99.285 | 0.641 | 0.074 | 0.9824233 |
| d10 | 127 | 1.1444909 | 0.0069527 | 0.0007232 | 99.334 | 0.603 | 0.063 | 1.1521668 |

Figures 4 and 5 plot the running time versus the number of skills and the number of problems, respectively.

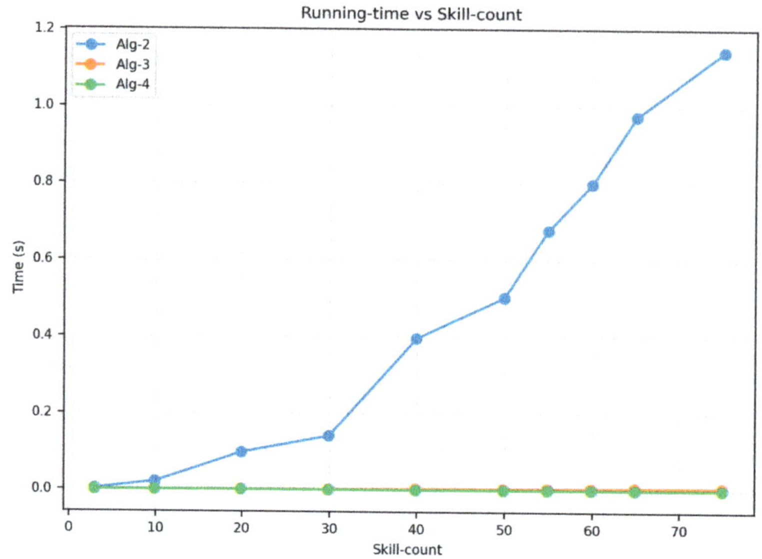


**Figure 4.** Running time versus the number of skills.

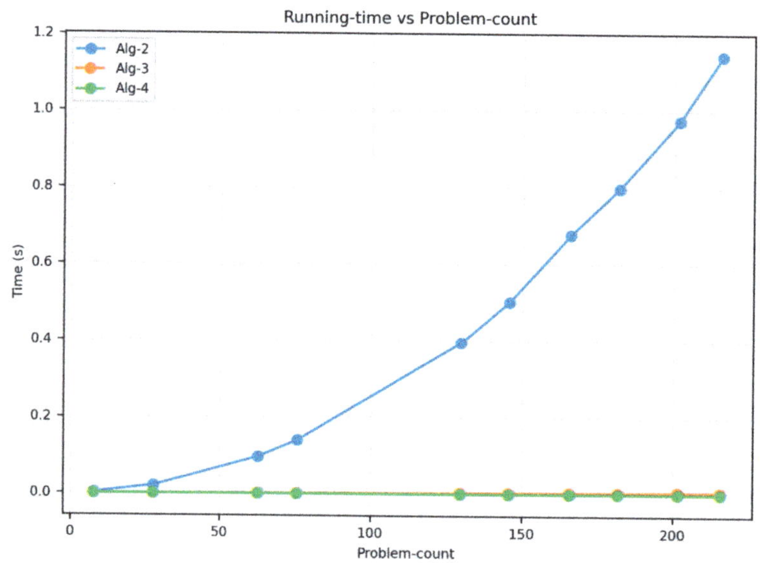


**Figure 5.** Running time versus the number of problems.

From Table 11 and Figures 4 and 5, we observe that the running time also increases with the numbers of skills and problems. Comparing the two groups of datasets, we conclude that $|\mathcal{C}|$ is the predominant factor that affects the overall running time of the algorithms. It is worth noting that the execution times of Algorithms 3 and 4 remain below 0.02 s for all test cases, which is negligible compared with Algorithm 2. Therefore, any optimization effort should mainly target Algorithm 2.

The simulation results show that when the number of fuzzy competence states is kept below 200, the overall running-time of the algorithms can be limited to less than one second. It should be noted that, in the second group of simulations, the fuzzy competence states of the ten datasets were randomly selected under the prerequisite that they form a consistent fuzzy competence space. The experimental outcomes reveal that, except for dataset d01, none of the remaining datasets possesses a gradual and effective learning path from the initial knowledge state ∅ to the target knowledge state $Q$.

In practical applications, the number of test items is usually no more than 100. Therefore, constructing a consistent fuzzy competence space with fewer than 200 fuzzy competence states—while guaranteeing, under the corresponding fuzzy skill mapping, the existence of a gradual and effective learning path from ∅ to $Q$—would be highly desirable. Therefore, beyond further optimizing Algorithm 2, an important avenue for future research is to devise ways to construct a consistent fuzzy competence space with as few competence states as possible while still guaranteeing that the associated fuzzy skill mapping admits a gradual and effective learning path from ∅ to $Q$.

## 6. Conclusions

Personalized, gradual, and effective learning paths have direct relevance to two major application domains.

(1) Adaptive Learning Systems. In adaptive learning platforms, the recommended sequence of learning activities must accommodate fine-grained differences in learners' mastery. Representing each learner's state as a fuzzy competence state allows the system to assign membership degrees to every skill, so that content delivery, formative assessment and feedback can be aligned with the learner's exact proficiency. The single-skill-increment principle ensures that the recommended path advances competence step-by-step without cognitive overload, thereby supporting mastery-based progression and just-in-time remediation.

(2) Intelligent Testing Systems. In computerized adaptive testing or intelligent tutoring, the test-engine repeatedly selects the next item that is most informative with respect to the learner's fuzzy knowledge state. A gradual and effective learning (or testing) path guarantees that item difficulty increases in tandem with skill levels, which safeguards measurement precision while avoiding abrupt jumps that may discourage test-takers.

Within this context, our study formulates personalized learning path recommendation inside the mathematical framework of fuzzy competence structures and consistent fuzzy competence spaces. By replacing the binary notion of mastery with fuzzy membership functions, the proposed approach captures incremental skill acquisition, and Algorithm 1—refined into Algorithms 2–4—systematically searches for a path that increases exactly one skill level at each step.

The current implementation handles small- and medium-scale datasets efficiently ($\leq$200 competence states, total runtime < 1 s). Experimental results indicate that Algorithm 2—the consistency checker—accounts for the major share of computation as the number of competence states increases; when the state space reaches several thousand, runtime becomes prohibitive and limits immediate deployment in very-large-scale scenarios. Ongoing work therefore focuses on optimizing Algorithm 2 through parallel union-closure computation, incremental cover-graph construction, and heuristic state-selection strategies that keep the working set compact.

Future work will evaluate the method on large MOOC platforms by combining cognitive-diagnostic models with log-data analytics; incorporate learner traits such as preferences, metacognition and self-regulation into the fuzzy competence representation to achieve fully adaptive recommendation; extend the technique to cross-disciplinary curricula where skills have complex interdependencies; and investigate theoretical issues—including minimality, redundancy, and path pruning—under consistency constraints. Through these efforts, learning-path recommendation grounded in fuzzy competence space theory is expected to play an increasingly important role in next-generation adaptive learning and intelligent testing technologies.

**Author Contributions:** Writing—original draft preparation, R.W., B.H. and J.L.; writing—review and editing, R.W., B.H. and J.L.; visualization, R.W. All authors have read and agreed to the published version of the manuscript.

**Funding:** This research was funded in part by the National Natural Science Foundation of China, grant number "12271191", and in part by the Natural Science Foundation of Fujian Province, China, grant number "2024J01793", as well as the Education Research Project for Young and Middle-aged Teachers in Fujian Province, grant number "JAT220280".

**Data Availability Statement:** The dataset format is illustrated with examples in the article; further details can be obtained from the first author upon request.

**Acknowledgments:** The authors extend their heartfelt gratitude to the anonymous reviewers and editors for their meticulous review and valuable suggestions.

**Conflicts of Interest:** The authors declare no conflict of interest.

## Abbreviations

The following abbreviations are used in this manuscript:

KST Knowledge space theory

## References

1. Doignon, J.-P.; Falmagne, J.-C. Spaces for the assessment of knowledge. *Int. J. Man-Mach. Stud.* **1985**, *23*, 175–196. [CrossRef]
2. Falmagne, J.C. A probabilistic theory of extensive measurement. *Philos. Sci.* **1980**, *47*, 277–296. [CrossRef]
3. Kruskal, J.B. Multidimensional scaling by optimizing goodness of fit to a non-metric hypothesis. *Psychometrika* **1964**, *29*, 1–27. [CrossRef]
4. Kruskal, J.B. Non metric multidimensional scaling: A numerical method. *Psychometrika* **1964**, *29*, 28–42. [CrossRef]
5. Carroll, J.D.; Chang, J.J. Analysis of individual differences in multidimensional scaling via an N-way generalization of 'Eckart–Young' decomposition. *Psychometrika* **1970**, *35*, 283–319. [CrossRef]
6. Falmagne, J.C. Random conjoint measurement and loudness summation. *Psychol. Rev.* **1976**, *83*, 65–79. [CrossRef]
7. Falmagne, J.C. On a class of probabilistic conjoint measurement models: Some diagnostic properties. *J. Math. Psychol.* **1979**, *19*, 73–88. [CrossRef]
8. Falmagne, J.C.; Doignon, J.-P. *Learning Spaces*; Springer: New York, NY, USA, 1999.
9. Falmagne, J.C.; Doignon, J.P. A class of stochastic procedures for the assessment of knowledge. *Br. J. Math. Stat. Psychol.* **1988**, *41*, 1–23. [CrossRef]
10. Falmagne, J.-C.; Koppen, P.; Villano, M.; Doignon, J.-P. Introduction to knowledge spaces: How to build, test, and search them. *Psychol. Rev.* **1990**, *97*, 201. [CrossRef]
11. Schrepp, M. A generalization of knowledge space theory to problems with more than two answer alternatives. *J. Math. Psychol.* **1997**, *41*, 237–243. [CrossRef]
12. Heller, J.; Mayer, B.; Hockemeyer, C.; Albert, D. Competence-based knowledge structures for personalised learning. *Int. J. E-Learn.* **2006**, *5*, 75–88.
13. Steiner, C.M.; Albert, D.; Nussbaumer, A. Supporting self-regulated personalised learning through competence-based knowledge space theory. *Policy Futures Educ.* **2009**, *7*, 645–661. [CrossRef]
14. Reddy, A.A.; Harper, M. ALEKS-based placement at the University of Illinois. In *Knowledge Spaces: Applications in Education*; Falmagne, J.C., Albert, D., Doble, C., Eppstein, D., Hu, X., Eds.; Springer: Berlin/Heidelberg, Germany, 2013; pp. 51–68.
15. Doble, C.; Matayoshi, J.; Cosyn, E.; Uzun, H.; Karami, A. A data-based simulation study of reliability for an adaptive assessment based on knowledge space theory. *Int. J. Artif. Intell. Educ.* **2019**, *29*, 258–282. [CrossRef]
16. Doignon, J.-P. Knowledge spaces and skill assignments. In *Contributions to Mathematical Psychology, Psychometrics, and Methodology*; Springer: New York, NY, USA, 1994; pp. 111–121.
17. Düntsch, I.; Gediga, G. Skills and knowledge structures. *Br. J. Math. Stat. Psychol.* **1995**, *48*, 9–27. [CrossRef]
18. Gediga, G.; Düntsch, I. Skill set analysis in knowledge structures. *Br. J. Math. Stat. Psychol.* **2002**, *55*, 361–384. [CrossRef]
19. Stefanutti, L.; Albert, D. Skill assessment in problem solving and simulated learning environments. *J. Univers. Comput. Sci.* **2003**, *9*, 1455–1468.
20. Heller, J.; Augustin, T.; Hockemeyer, C.; Stefanutti, L.; Albert, D. Recent developments in competence-based knowledge space theory. In *Knowledge Spaces: Applications in Education*; Springer: Berlin/Heidelberg, Germany, 2013; pp. 243–286.
21. Suck, R. Skills first—An alternative approach to construct knowledge spaces. *J. Math. Psychol.* **2021**, *101*, 102517. [CrossRef]
22. Zhou, Y.; Li, J.; Wang, H.; Sun, W. Skills and fuzzy knowledge structures. *J. Intell. Fuzzy Syst.* **2022**, *42*, 2629–2645. [CrossRef]
23. Stefanutti, L.; Anselmi, P.; de Chiusole, D. Towards a competence-based polytomous knowledge structure theory. *J. Math. Psychol.* **2023**, *115*, 102781. [CrossRef]

24. Stefanutti, L.; de Chiusole, D. On the assessment of learning in competence based knowledge space theory. *J. Math. Psychol.* **2017**, *80*, 22–32. [CrossRef]
25. Anselmi, P.; de Chiusole, D.; Stefanutti, L. The assessment of knowledge and learning in competence spaces: The gain–loss model for dependent skills. *Br. J. Math. Stat. Psychol.* **2017**, *70*, 457–479. [CrossRef] [PubMed]
26. de Chiusole, D.; Anselmi, P.; Stefanutti, L. Stat-Knowlab. Assessment and learning of statistics with competence-based knowledge space theory. *Int. J. Artif. Intell. Educ.* **2020**, *30*, 668–700. [CrossRef]
27. Anselmi, P.; Stefanutti, L.; de Chiusole, D. Constructing, improving, and shortening tests for skill assessment. *J. Math. Psychol.* **2022**, *106*, 102621. [CrossRef]
28. Anselmi, P.; de Chiusole, D.; Stefanutti, L. Constructing tests for skill assessment with competence-based test development. *Br. J. Math. Stat. Psychol.* **2024**, *77*, 429–458. [CrossRef]
29. Heller, J.; Stefanutti, L.; Anselmi, P.; Robusto, E. On the link between cognitive diagnostic models and knowledge space theory. *Psychometrika* **2015**, *80*, 995–1019. [CrossRef]
30. Liu, G. Rough set approaches in knowledge structures. *Int. J. Approx. Reason.* **2021**, *138*, 78–88. [CrossRef]
31. Xie, X.; Xu, W.; Li, J. A novel concept-cognitive learning method: A perspective from competences. *Knowl. Based Syst.* **2023**, *265*, 110382. [CrossRef]
32. Sun, W.; Li, J.; Ge, X.; Lin, Y. Knowledge structures delineated by fuzzy skill maps. *Fuzzy Sets Syst.* **2021**, *407*, 50–66. [CrossRef]
33. Zhou, Y.; Li, J.; Yang, H.; Xu, Q.; Yang, T.; Feng, D. Knowledge structures construction and learning paths recommendation based on formal contexts. *Int. J. Mach. Learn. Cybern.* **2024**, *15*, 1605–1620. [CrossRef]
34. Yang, H.-L.; Xie, X.; Li, J. A concept fringe-based concept-cognitive learning method in skill context. *Knowl. Based Syst.* **2024**, *305*, 112618. [CrossRef]
35. Zhou, Y.F.; Yang, H.L.; Li, J.J.; Wang, D.L. Skill assessment method: A perspective from concept-cognitive learning. *Fuzzy Sets Syst.* **2025**, *508*, 109331. [CrossRef]
36. Zadeh, L.A. Fuzzy sets. *Inf. Control* **1965**, *8*, 338–353. [CrossRef]
37. Xu, B.; Li, J. The inclusion degrees of fuzzy skill maps and knowledge structures. *Fuzzy Sets Syst.* **2023**, *465*, 108540. [CrossRef]
38. Xu, B.; Li, J.; Sun, W.; Wang, B. On delineating forward-and backward-graded knowledge structures from fuzzy skill maps. *J. Math. Psychol.* **2023**, *117*, 102819. [CrossRef]
39. Sun, W.; Li, J.; Lin, F.; He, Z. Constructing polytomous knowledge structures from fuzzy skills. *Fuzzy Sets Syst.* **2023**, *461*, 108395. [CrossRef]
40. Nabizadeh, A.H.; Leal, J.P.; Rafsanjani, H.N.; Shah, R.R. Learning path personalization and recommendation methods: A survey of the state-of-the-art. *Expert Syst. Appl.* **2020**, *159*, 113596. [CrossRef]
41. Zhu, F.; Wen, Y.; Fu, Q. A survey on learning path recommendation. In *CCF Conference on Computer Supported Cooperative Work and Social Computing*; Springer: Singapore, 2021; pp. 577–589.
42. Bayly-Castaneda, K.; Ramirez-Montoya, M.S.; Morita-Alexander, A. Crafting personalized learning paths with AI for lifelong learning: A systematic literature review. *Front. Educ.* **2024**, *9*, 1424386. [CrossRef]
43. Peng, H.; Ma, S.; Spector, J.M. Personalized adaptive learning: An emerging pedagogical approach enabled by a smart learning environment. *Smart Learn. Environ.* **2019**, *6*, 1–14. [CrossRef]
44. Raj, N.S.; Renumol, V.G. A systematic literature review on adaptive content recommenders in personalized learning environments from 2015 to 2020. *J. Comput. Educ.* **2022**, *9*, 113–148. [CrossRef]
45. Raj, N.S.; Renumol, V.G. An improved adaptive learning path recommendation model driven by real-time learning analytics. *J. Comput. Educ.* **2024**, *11*, 121–148. [CrossRef]
46. Stefanutti, L.; de Chiusole, D.; Anselmi, P. On the polytomous generalization of knowledge space theory. *J. Math. Psychol.* **2020**, *94*, 102306. [CrossRef]
47. Heller, J. Generalizing quasi-ordinal knowledge spaces to polytomous items. *J. Math. Psychol.* **2021**, *101*, 102515. [CrossRef]
48. Sun, W.; Li, J.; Xu, B.; Wang, B. Well-graded polytomous knowledge structures. *J. Math. Psychol.* **2023**, *114*, 102770. [CrossRef]
49. Wang, B.; Li, J. Exploring well-gradedness in polytomous knowledge structures. *J. Math. Psychol.* **2024**, *119*, 102840. [CrossRef]
50. Mirsky, L. *Transversal Theory: An Account of Some Aspects of Combinatorial Mathematics*; Academic Press: New York, NY, USA, 1971.

*axioms*

MDPI

*Article*

# Change-Point Estimation and Detection for Mixture of Linear Regression Models

**Wenzhi Zhao [1], Tian Cheng [2] and Zhiming Xia [2,*]**

[1] School of Science, Xi'an Polytechnic University, Xi'an 710048, China; zhaowenzhi@xpu.edu.cn
[2] School of Mathematics, Northwest University, Xi'an 710127, China; 201820540@nwu.edu.cn
* Correspondence: statxzm@nwu.edu.cn

**Abstract:** This paper studies the estimation and detection problems in the mixture of linear regression models with change point. An improved Expectation–Maximization (EM) algorithm is devised specifically for multi-classified mixture data with change points. Under appropriate conditions, the large-sample properties of the estimator are rigorously proven. This improved EM algorithm not only precisely locates the change points but also yields accurate parameter estimates for each class. Additionally, a detector grounded in the score function is proposed to identify the presence of change points in mixture data. The limiting distributions of the test statistics under both the null and alternative hypotheses are systematically derived. Extensive simulation experiments are conducted to assess the effectiveness of the proposed method, and comparative analyses with the conventional EM algorithm are performed. The results clearly demonstrate that the EM algorithm without considering change points exhibits poor performance in classifying data, often resulting in the misclassification or even omission of certain classes. In contrast, the estimation method introduced in this study showcases remarkable accuracy and robustness, with favorable empirical sizes and powers.

**Keywords:** change point; mixture of linear regression model; multi-classification; EM algorithm

**MSC:** 62F10; 62J05

## 1. Introduction

Mixture models have found extensive applications in econometrics and social sciences, and the associated theoretical frameworks have been thoroughly investigated. Among them, finite mixtures of linear regression models, a particularly valuable class of mixture models, have been widely employed across diverse fields, including econometrics, marketing, epidemiology, and biology. Simultaneously, the statistical inference and parameter estimation based on mixture models play a pivotal role in practical applications. On another front, the change point problem remains a focal point in statistical research. Conceptually, a change point denotes the specific location or instant at which a sudden alteration in a statistical property occurs. Change point phenomena are pervasive in both natural and social systems, and have enabled crucial advancements in numerous domains such as industrial control, financial economics, biomedicine, and signal processing. The detection and estimation of change points within mixture datasets are essential for discerning underlying patterns and making informed decisions, thereby holding significant practical implications.

In recent decades, remarkable progress has been achieved in the analysis of mixture models. Goldfeld and Quandt provided an outstanding introduction to mixtures of linear regression models [1] . They delved into the parameter estimation problem of such mixtures and applied it to analyze the imbalance in the housing price market. Frühwirth and Schnatter summarized the Bayesian approach for mixtures of linear regression models in their paper [2]. Hurn and Justel proposed a generalized linear finite mixture model and overcame the label switching issue by normalizing the loss function [3]. Li, Chen, and their collaborators (Chen, Li, and Fu) concentrated on the hypothesis testing problem regarding the order of the mixture model and derived the limiting distribution of the test statistics [4,5]. Huang and Yao introduced a semiparametric mixture regression model, where the mixing proportion is a smooth function of covariates [6]. Huang, Li, and Wang developed a non-parametric finite mixture method for regression models and demonstrated the estimation procedure through an analysis of U.S. Housing Price Index (HPI) data [7].

The change point problem has attracted extensive research attention, with a vast body of literature accumulated over the years. It was first introduced by Page during his study of continuous inspection schemes, who proposed the Cumulative Sum (CUSUM) test method [8]. Subsequently, scholars like Sen and Srivastava, Hawkins, James et al., and Srivastava and Worsley investigated the detection of change points in the mean of normal random variable sequences [9–13]. Basseville and Nikiforov systematically expounded the theoretical foundation of change point detection and estimation algorithms [14]. Wang, Zou, and Yin delved into change point detection in multinomial data as the number of categories approaches infinity, rigorously proving the statistical properties of relevant test statistics [15]. Xia and Qiu proposed the JIC criterion to tackle the multi-change point problem in non-parametric regression models [16]. Bai employed the least squares method to estimate the mean change point of linear processes, deriving the consistency and convergence rate of the change point estimator [17]. Baranowski et al. utilized grid search algorithms based on binary segmentation to accurately determine the number and positions of change points [18]. Follain et al. developed a novel approach for estimating change points in partially observed, high-dimensional time series with simultaneous mean shifts in sparse coordinate subsets [19]. Gong et al. redefined the graph-based change point detection problem as a prediction task and proposed an innovative change point detection (CPD) method for dynamic graphs through a latent evolution model. Drabech et al. introduced a Markov Random Field (MRF) model to detect slope changes [20], while Ratnasingam et al. proposed an empirical likelihood-based non-parametric procedure for identifying structural changes in quantile regression models [21]. Notably, despite these abundant studies, the statistical analysis of change points within finite mixtures of linear models remains a relatively overlooked area [22].

This paper delves into the estimation and detection problems of the finite mixture of linear regression models with change points. Specifically, for multi-classified mixture data incorporating change points, we ingeniously propose an improved Expectation–Maximization (EM) algorithm. This algorithm is meticulously designed to accurately compute parameter estimators, such as the location of change points and regression coefficients. Through rigorous mathematical proofs, we firmly establish the consistency and asymptotic normality of these parameter estimators, providing a solid theoretical foundation. Moreover, to effectively detect the presence of change points in the mixture of linear regression models, we innovatively develop a detector based on the score function. By conducting in-depth analyses, we systematically derive the limiting distributions under both the null hypothesis and the alternative hypothesis, which significantly contributes to the theoretical framework of this study. To thoroughly verify the practical effectiveness of the proposed method, we carefully design and execute a series of simulation experiments.

The remaining sections of this paper are structured as follows. In Section 2, we introduce the estimation and detection methods, statistical models, along with their associated assumptions. In Section 3 is dedicated to the development of the estimation and detection techniques for change points within the mixture of linear regression models. Additionally, we obtain the large sample properties of the estimators and test statistics. In Section 4, the simulation results are presented. Section 5 provides some concluding remarks and discussions. In Section 6, the limitations and future research directions are presented. The proofs of the theorems are included in the appendix.

## 2. Statistical Model and Assumptions

Assume that $\{(X_i, Y_i), i = 1, \cdots, n\}$ are independent random samples from the following data generating process:

$$Y_i \sim \begin{cases} \sum\limits_{c=1}^{C} \pi_c^{*-} N(X_i^T \beta_c^{*-}, \sigma_c^{2*-}), & 1 \le i \le k^*, \\ \sum\limits_{c=1}^{C} \pi_c^{*+} N(X_i^T \beta_c^{*+}, \sigma_c^{2*+}), & k^*+1 \le i \le n, \quad k^* \in [1, n-1], \end{cases} \tag{1}$$

where $k^*$ is a change point, $X_i$ is a p-dimensional random covariate, C is the number of components, $\beta_c^{*-}, \pi_c^{*-}, \sigma_c^{*-}$, $\beta_c^{*+}, \pi_c^{*+}, \sigma_c^{*+}$ are mixture coefficients for the $c$th component, $1 \ge \pi_c^{*-} \ge 0$, $\pi_c^{*+} \ge 0$, $\sum\limits_{c=1}^{C} \pi_c^{*-} = \sum\limits_{c=1}^{C} \pi_c^{*+} = 1$. $\pi_c^{*-}$ and $\pi_c^{*+}$ are called mixing proportions or weights. $\beta_c^{*-}, \beta_c^{*+} \in R^p, \sigma_c^{2*-}, \sigma_c^{2*+} \in R^+$ and the parameters are unknown. Equivalently speaking, $\{Y_i, i = 1, \cdots, n\}$ follow a finite mixture of normals,

$$Y_i \sim \sum_{c=1}^{C} \pi_c^{*-} N(X_i^T \beta_c^{*-}, \sigma_c^{2*-}) \cdot I_{\{i \le k^*\}} + \sum_{c=1}^{C} \pi_c^{*+} N(X_i^T \beta_c^{*+}, \sigma_c^{2*+}) \cdot I_{\{i \ge k^*+1\}}.$$

Naturally, the log-likelihood function corresponding to the dataset $\{(X_i, Y_i), i = 1, \cdots, n\}$ can be expressed as

$$\begin{aligned} &l(k, \pi_c^-, \beta_c^-, \sigma_c^{2-}, \pi_c^+, \beta_c^+, \sigma_c^{2+}) = \\ &\sum_{i=1}^{n} \log \left[ \sum_{c=1}^{C} \left\{ \pi_c^- \phi\left(Y_i | X_i^T \beta_c^-, \sigma_c^{2-}\right) \cdot I_{\{i \le k\}} + \pi_c^+ \phi\left(Y_i | X_i^T \beta_c^+, \sigma_c^{2+}\right) \cdot I_{\{i \ge k+1\}} \right\} \right] \end{aligned} \tag{2}$$

where $\phi(y|\mu, \sigma^2)$ denotes the normal density.

For later use, we introduce some notations. Let $\theta^* = ((\pi^*)^T, (\beta^*)^T, (\sigma^{2*})^T)^T$ denote the true parameter, where $\pi^* = (\pi_1^*, \cdots, \pi_{C-1}^*)^T$, $\beta^* = (\beta_1^{*T}, \cdots, \beta_C^{*T})^T$, $\sigma^{2^*} = (\sigma_1^{2^*}, \cdots, \sigma_C^{2^*})^T$ and $\beta_i^* \in R^P$, $i = 1, \cdots, C$. Let $\theta^{*-}, \theta^{*+}$ represent the parameters on the left and right sides of the change point, respectively. Similarly, we can define $\theta$, $\theta^-, \theta^+$.

Let $\hat{k}_n$ and $\hat{\theta}_n$ be the maximum likelihood estimator of $k^*$ and $\theta$, which can be obtained by maximizing (2). In Section 3.1, an improved EM algorithm is proposed to carry out the estimation. The following assumptions are imposed.

**Assumption 1.** $\frac{k^*}{n} \to \tau^*, n \to \infty$ *and* $\tau^* \in (0, 1)$.

The above assumption requires that $k^*$ depends on the sample size $n$ and is approximately proportional to $n$.

**Assumption 2.** *We suppose that* $\theta \in \Theta$ *and parameter space* $\Theta \subset R^q$ *is a compact set,* $q = (p+2) \cdot C - 1$.

Assumption 2 restricts the parameter space to be compact, which means any open cover of $\Theta$ has a finite subcover.

**Assumption 3.** $\{(X_i, Y_i),\ i = 1, 2, \cdots, n\}$ *are independent.*

## 3. Parameter Inference

### 3.1. Estimation Procedure

In this subsection, we propose an effective EM algorithm to deal with the parameter estimation problem. We take $i \geq k+1$ as an example to illustrate the derivation of the iterative formula ( $i < k$ can be obtained in the same way). At this time, the log-likelihood function corresponding to the data is

$$\sum_{i=k+1}^{n} \log\left[\sum_{c=1}^{C} \pi_c^{+} \phi\{Y_i | X_i^T \beta_c^{+}, \sigma_c^{2+}\}\right]. \tag{3}$$

In the EM framework, the mixture problem is described as an incomplete-data problem. We view the observed data $(X_i, Y_i, i = 1, 2, \cdots, n)$ as being incomplete, and then introduce unobserved *Bernoulli* random variables

$$z_{ic} = \begin{cases} 1, & if (X_i, Y_i) \text{ is in the cth group}, \\ 0, & otherwise, \end{cases}$$

$$i = 1, 2, \cdots, n, \quad c = 1, 2, \cdots, C.$$

and $z_i = (z_{i1}, \cdots, z_{iC})^T$, which is the component label of $(X_i, Y_i)$. Therefore, the complete data are $\{(X_i, Y_i, z_i)\}_{i=1}^n$, and the complete log-likelihood function corresponding to (3) is

$$\sum_{i=k+1}^{n} \sum_{c=1}^{C} z_{ic} \left[\log \pi_c^{+} + \log \phi\{Y_i | X_i^T \beta_c^{+}, \sigma_c^{2+}\}\right].$$

Supposing in the $l$th cycle of the EM algorithm iteration, we have $\pi_c^{+(l)}, \beta_c^{+(l)}, \sigma_c^{2+(l)}$; then, in the $E$-step of $(l+1)$th cycle, the expectation of the latent variable $z_{ic}$ can be calculated by

$$r_{ic}^{(l+1)} = \frac{\pi_c^{+(l)} \phi\{Y_i | X_i^T \beta_c^{+(l)}, \sigma_c^{2+(l)}\}}{\sum_{c=1}^{C} \pi_c^{+(l)} \phi\{Y_i | X_i^T \beta_c^{+(l)}, \sigma_c^{2+(l)}\}}.$$

In the $M$-step of the $(l+1)$th cycle, we maximize

$$\sum_{i=k+1}^{n} \sum_{c=1}^{C} r_{ic}^{(l+1)} \left[\log \pi_c^{+} + \log \phi\{Y_i | X_i^T \beta_c^{+}, \sigma_c^{2+}\}\right]. \tag{4}$$

The maximization of Equation (4) is equivalent to separately maximize $\sum_{i=k+1}^{n} \sum_{c=1}^{C} r_{ic}^{(l+1)} \log \pi_c^{+}$ and $\sum_{i=k+1}^{n} \sum_{c=1}^{C} r_{ic}^{(l+1)} \log \phi\{Y_i | X_i^T \beta_c^{+}, \sigma_c^{2+}\}$. Furthermore, the iterative formula can be easily derived as follows:

$$\pi_c^{+(l+1)} = \frac{\sum_{i=k+1}^{n} r_{ic}^{(l+1)}}{n},$$

$$\beta_c^{+(l+1)} = \left(\sum_{i=k+1}^{n} X_i r_{ic}^{(l+1)} X_i^T\right)^{-1} \left(\sum_{i=k+1}^{n} X_i r_{ic}^{(l+1)} Y_i\right),$$

$$\sigma_c^{2+(l+1)} = \frac{\sum_{i=k+1}^{n} r_{ic}^{(l+1)} (Y_i - X_i^T \beta_c^{+(l)})(Y_i - X_i^T \beta_c^{+(l)})^T}{\sum_{i=k+1}^{n} r_{ic}^{(l+1)}}, \quad c = 1, 2, \cdots, C$$

Let the initial value be $\pi_c^{+(0)}, \boldsymbol{\beta}_c^{+(0)}, \sigma_c^{+(0)}, c = 1, \cdots, C$, repeat the above iteration algorithm, and when the iteration converges, we obtain the estimator of mixture parameters, denoted as $\pi_c^{+}(k), \boldsymbol{\beta}_c^{+}(k), \sigma_c^{2+}(k), c = 1, \cdots, C$. At this time, the log-likelihood function corresponding to the data $\{(X_i, Y_i)\}_{i=k+1}^{n}$ is

$$l^{+}(k, \pi_c^{+}, \boldsymbol{\beta}_c^{+}, \sigma_c^{2+}) = \sum_{i=k+1}^{n} \log\left[\sum_{c=1}^{C} \pi_c^{+}(k)\phi\{Y_i|X_i^T\boldsymbol{\beta}_c^{+}(k), \sigma_c^{2+}(k)\}\right].$$

Whenever a value of $k$ is determined, the mixture data are divided into two parts: $\{(X_i, Y_i)\}_{i=1}^{k}$ and $\{(X_i, Y_i)\}_{i=k+1}^{n}$. Let the initial value be $\pi_c^{\pm(0)}, \boldsymbol{\beta}_c^{\pm(0)}, \sigma_c^{\pm(0)}$, $c = 1, \cdots, C$, and we can obtain the estimations of change point and mixture parameter according to Algorithm 1:

$$(\hat{k}, \hat{\boldsymbol{\theta}^{-}}, \hat{\boldsymbol{\theta}^{+}}) = \underset{k, \pi_c^{\pm}, \boldsymbol{\beta}_c^{\pm}, \sigma_c^{\pm}}{\arg\max}\ l(k, \pi_c^{-}, \boldsymbol{\beta}_c^{-}, \sigma_c^{2-}, \pi_c^{+}, \boldsymbol{\beta}_c^{+}, \sigma_c^{2+}),$$

where $\hat{\boldsymbol{\theta}}^{\pm} = ((\hat{\boldsymbol{\pi}}^{\pm})^T, (\hat{\boldsymbol{\beta}}^{\pm})^T, (\hat{\boldsymbol{\sigma}}^{2\pm})^T)^T$, $\hat{\boldsymbol{\pi}}^{\pm} = (\hat{\pi}_1^{\pm}, \cdots, \hat{\pi}_C^{\pm})^T$ and $\hat{\boldsymbol{\beta}}^{\pm} = (\hat{\beta}_1^{\pm}, \cdots, \hat{\beta}_C^{\pm})^T$, $\hat{\boldsymbol{\sigma}}^{2\pm} = (\hat{\sigma}_1^{2\pm}, \cdots, \hat{\sigma}_C^{2\pm})^T$, $l(k, \pi_c^{-}, \boldsymbol{\beta}_c^{-}, \sigma_c^{2-}, \pi_c^{+}, \boldsymbol{\beta}_c^{+}, \sigma_c^{2+}) = l^{+}(k, \pi_c^{+}, \boldsymbol{\beta}_c^{+}, \sigma_c^{2+}) + l^{-}(k, \pi_c^{-}, \boldsymbol{\beta}_c^{-}, \sigma_c^{2-})$.

**Algorithm 1** EM algorithm considering change point

**Intput:** $\{X_i, Y_i\}_{i=1}^{n}$, the number of mixture component $C$, the maximum iterations $T$.
**Output:** $\hat{k}, \hat{\boldsymbol{\theta}}^{-}, \hat{\boldsymbol{\theta}}^{+}$

1: **for** $k = 1, 2, \cdots, n-1$ **do**

2: For any given $k$, the mixture data are divided into two parts: $\{(X_i, Y_i)\}_{i=1}^{k}$ and $\{(X_i, Y_i)\}_{i=k+1}^{n}$. Using EM algorithm separately for two parts of data. For $\{(X_i, Y_i)\}_{i=1}^{k}$, let the initial value be $\pi_c^{-(0)}, \boldsymbol{\beta}_c^{-(0)}, \sigma_c^{-(0)}, c = 1, \cdots, C$.

3: **for** $t = 1, 2, \cdots, T$ **do**

4: *E*-step: calculate $r_{ic}^{(l+1)}(k)$,

$$r_{ic}^{(l+1)}(k) = \frac{\pi_c^{-(l)}\phi\{Y_i|X_i^T\boldsymbol{\beta}_c^{-(l)}, \sigma_c^{2-(l)}\}}{\sum_{c=1}^{C}\pi_c^{-(l)}\phi\{Y_i|X_i^T\boldsymbol{\beta}_c^{-(l)}, \sigma_c^{2-(l)}\}},\ i = 1, \cdots, k, c = 1, \cdots, C$$

5: *M*-step: calculate

$$\pi_c^{-(l+1)}(k) = \frac{\sum_{i=1}^{n} r_{ic}^{(l+1)}}{n},\quad \boldsymbol{\beta}_c^{-(l+1)}(k) = (\sum_{i=1}^{n} X_i r_{ic}^{(l+1)} X_i^T)^{-1}(\sum_{i=1}^{n} X_i r_{ic}^{(l+1)} Y_i)$$

$$\sigma_c^{2-(l+1)}(k) = \frac{\sum_{i=1}^{n} r_{ic}^{(l+1)}(Y_i - X_i^T\boldsymbol{\beta}_c^{-(l)})(Y_i - X_i^T\boldsymbol{\beta}_c^{-(l)})^T}{\sum_{i=1}^{n} r_{ic}^{(l+1)}}$$

6: **end for**

7: When the iteration reaches convergence, we obtain the estimator $\pi_c^{-}(k), \boldsymbol{\beta}_c^{-}(k), \sigma_c^{2-}(k), c = 1, \cdots, C$ and the log-likelihood function value $l^{-}(k)$

8: For $\{(X_i, Y_i)\}_{i=k+1}^{n}$, repeat steps 3–7 and obtain $\pi_c^{+}(k), \boldsymbol{\beta}_c^{+}(k), \sigma_c^{2+}(k)$, $c = 1, \cdots, C$ and $l^{+}(k)$

9: **end for**

10: $\hat{k} = \underset{1 \le k \le n-1}{\arg\max}(l^{-}(k) + l^{+}(k))$, $\hat{\boldsymbol{\theta}}^{-} = \hat{\boldsymbol{\theta}^{-}}(\hat{k})$, $\hat{\boldsymbol{\theta}}^{+} = \hat{\boldsymbol{\theta}^{+}}(\hat{k})$,

### 3.2. Hypothesis Test

Define the following notations for later use:

$$\eta(Y|\boldsymbol{\theta}) = \sum_{c=1}^{C} \pi_c \phi\{X, Y|\beta_c, \sigma_c^2\}, \quad \ell(\boldsymbol{\theta}, Y) = \log \eta(Y|\boldsymbol{\theta}),$$

$$q_1\{\boldsymbol{\theta}, Y\} = \frac{\partial \ell\{\boldsymbol{\theta}, Y\}}{\partial \boldsymbol{\theta}}, \quad q_2\{\boldsymbol{\theta}, Y\} = \frac{\partial^2 \ell\{\boldsymbol{\theta}, Y\}}{\partial \partial \boldsymbol{\theta}^T},$$

$$\mathcal{I}(\boldsymbol{\theta}) = -E[q_2\{\boldsymbol{\theta}, Y\}], \quad \mathcal{B}(\boldsymbol{\theta}) = Var[q_1\{\boldsymbol{\theta}, Y\}] = E[q_1\{\boldsymbol{\theta}, Y\} q_1^T\{\boldsymbol{\theta}, Y\}].$$

In the following, we are interested in testing the null hypothesis:

$$H_0: \ \boldsymbol{\theta}_i = \boldsymbol{\theta}^* \quad (i = 1, \cdots, n)$$

against the local alternative hypothesis:

$$H_A: \boldsymbol{\theta}_i = \boldsymbol{\theta}^* + \frac{1}{\sqrt{n}} \cdot \boldsymbol{g}(\frac{i}{n}),$$

where $\boldsymbol{g} = (g_1, g_2, \cdots, g_q)^T$ is a function of bounded variation on [0,1] which describes the patter of departure from stability of the parameter $\boldsymbol{\theta}^*$.

Firstly, we give the following lemmas and then we build an empirical process and infer its limiting process under the $H_0$ and $H_1$ hypothesis, respectively, as described by Theorem 1.

**Theorem 1.** *Under $H_0$ and Lemma A3 in the Appendix A, given by*

$$\Delta_n(t, \hat{\boldsymbol{\theta}}_n) = \frac{1}{\sqrt{n}} \sum_{i=1}^{[nt]} q_1(\hat{\boldsymbol{\theta}}_n, Y_i), \quad t \in (0,1), \tag{5}$$

*then, we have*

*(1). under $H_0$,*

$$\hat{\mathcal{B}}_n^{-1/2} \Delta_n(t, \hat{\boldsymbol{\theta}}_n) \xrightarrow{d} \mathbf{W}^0(t), n \to \infty,$$

*where $\mathbf{W}^0(t)$ is a q-dimensional standard Brownian bridge with $\mathbf{W}^0(t) = \mathbf{W}(t) - t\mathbf{W}(1)$ and $\hat{\mathcal{B}}_n$ some consistent covariance matrix estimation, such as $\hat{\mathcal{B}}_n = \frac{1}{n}\sum_{i=1}^{n} q_1(\hat{\boldsymbol{\theta}}_n, Y_i) q_1(\hat{\boldsymbol{\theta}}_n, Y_i)^T$.*

*(2). Under $H_A$,*

$$\hat{\mathcal{B}}_n^{-1/2} \Delta_n(t, \hat{\boldsymbol{\theta}}_n) \xrightarrow{d} W^0(t) + \mathcal{B}(\boldsymbol{\theta}^*)^{1/2} \mathbf{G}^0(t), n \to \infty,$$

*where $\mathbf{G}^0(t) = \mathbf{G}(t) - t\mathbf{G}(1)$ with $\mathbf{G}(t) = \int_0^t \boldsymbol{g}(y) dy$.*

Next, we construct test statistics according to the empirical process (5) stated above. The key idea is that the empirical process reflects some symptoms of structural changes, and its performance under $H_0$ and $H_A$ is significantly different; then, the test statistics can be constructed as follows:

$$T_n = \sup_{1 \le k \le n} \left\| \hat{\mathcal{B}}_n^{-1/2} \Delta_n(k/n, \hat{\boldsymbol{\theta}}_n) \right\|^2.$$

Further from Theorem 1 and continuous mapping theorem, the following corollary can be obtained:

**Corollary 1.** *Given the empirical process* (5) *in Theorem 1, we have*

*(1). under* $H_0$,

$$T_n \xrightarrow{d} \sup_{t\in[0,1]} \left\| \mathbf{W}^0(t) \right\|^2 = \sup_{t\in[0,1]} \left\{ \sum_{i=1}^{q} W_i^0(t)^2 \right\}, \quad n \to \infty. \tag{6}$$

*(2). Under* $H_A$,

$$T_n \xrightarrow{d} \sup_{t\in[0,1]} \left\| \mathbf{W}^0(t) + \mathcal{B}(\boldsymbol{\theta}^*)^{1/2} \mathbf{G}^0(t) \right\|^2, \quad n \to \infty$$

The above results show that the limiting distributions of the test statistics are different under the null and alternative hypothesis; thus, we can judge the existence of the change point according to it.

### 3.3. Consistency

In order to prove the consistency of the estimator, we first construct a function $\mathcal{L}_n$ as follows:

$$\mathcal{L}_n(\tau, \boldsymbol{\theta}) = \frac{1}{n} \sum_{i=1}^{n} \tilde{f}(X_i, Y_i|t, \boldsymbol{\theta}) = \frac{1}{n} \sum_{i=1}^{[n\tau]} \tilde{f}(X_i, Y_i|t, \boldsymbol{\theta}) + \frac{1}{n} \sum_{i=[n\tau]+1}^{n} \tilde{f}(X_i, Y_i|t, \boldsymbol{\theta}), \tag{7}$$

where $[n\tau] = k$, $[a]$ means the integer part of $a$ and

$$\tilde{f}(X_i, Y_i|t, \boldsymbol{\theta}) = \log \Bigg[ \sum_{c=1}^{C} \{ \pi_c^- \phi(Y_i|X_i^T \beta_c^-, \sigma_c^{2-}) I_{\{i \le [nt]\}} + \\ \pi_c^+ \phi(Y_i|X_i^T \beta_c^+, \sigma_c^{2+}) I_{\{i \ge [nt]+1\}} \} \Bigg].$$

Without loss of generality, we only consider the case $k \le k^*$ for brevity; then, by *Kolmogorov*'s Law of Large Numbers and *Jessen* inequality, the Formula (7) can be rewritten as

$$\begin{aligned}
\mathcal{L}_n(\tau, \boldsymbol{\theta}) &= \frac{1}{n} \sum_{i=1}^{[n\tau]} f(X_i, Y_i|\tau, \boldsymbol{\theta}^-) + \frac{1}{n} \sum_{i=[n\tau]+1}^{[n\tau^*]} f(X_i, Y_i|\tau, \boldsymbol{\theta}^-) + \frac{1}{n} \sum_{i=[n\tau^*]+1}^{n} f(X_i, Y_i|\tau, \boldsymbol{\theta}^+) \\
&= \frac{[n\tau]}{n} \cdot \frac{1}{[n\tau]} \sum_{i=1}^{[n\tau]} f(X_i, Y_i|\tau, \boldsymbol{\theta}^-) + \frac{[n\tau^*] - [n\tau]}{n} \cdot \frac{1}{[n\tau^*] - [n\tau]} \sum_{i=[n\tau]+1}^{[n\tau^*]} f(X_i, Y_i|\tau, \boldsymbol{\theta}^-) \\
&\quad + \frac{n - [n\tau^*]}{n} \cdot \frac{1}{n - [n\tau^*]} \sum_{i=[n\tau^*]+1}^{n} f(X_i, Y_i|\tau, \boldsymbol{\theta}^+) \\
&\xrightarrow{p} \tau \cdot E_{(\tau^*, \boldsymbol{\theta}^{*-})} f(X, Y|\tau, \boldsymbol{\theta}^-) + (\tau^* - \tau) \cdot E_{(\tau^*, \boldsymbol{\theta}^{*-})} f(X, Y|\tau, \boldsymbol{\theta}^-) \\
&\quad + (1 - \tau^*) \cdot E_{(\tau^*, \boldsymbol{\theta}^{*+})} f(X, Y|\tau, \boldsymbol{\theta}^+) \\
&\triangleq \mathcal{L}(\tau, \boldsymbol{\theta}|\tau^*, \boldsymbol{\theta}^*)
\end{aligned}$$

where

$$f(X_i, Y_i|\tau, \boldsymbol{\theta}^-) = \tilde{f}(X_i, Y_i|\tau, \boldsymbol{\theta})|_{\boldsymbol{\theta}=\boldsymbol{\theta}^-}, \quad f(X_i, Y_i|\tau, \boldsymbol{\theta}^+) = \tilde{f}(X_i, Y_i|\tau, \boldsymbol{\theta})|_{\boldsymbol{\theta}=\boldsymbol{\theta}^+}.$$

Now, we state our second theoretical result, which is the consistency of the obtained estimator.

**Theorem 2.** *Let $\hat{\tau} = \frac{\hat{k}_n}{n}$ and under the conditions of the Lemmas A1 and A2 in Appendix A; then, we have*

$$(\hat{\tau}, \hat{\boldsymbol{\theta}}_n) \xrightarrow{p} (\tau^*, \boldsymbol{\theta}^*).$$

## 4. Simulation

To assess the performance of our proposed method, we shall consider two simulation experiments as follows.

### 4.1. Estimation Experiment

In Experiment 1, we focus on the scenario where the vector $\boldsymbol{\beta}$ is two-dimensional and the value of $C$ is set to 2. Additionally, when dealing with the parameter estimation problem of mixed models that incorporate change points, the conventional approach is to overlook the presence of these change points. Instead, the Expectation–Maximization (EM) algorithm is directly employed to estimate the unknown parameters, as if the data were generated from a mixed model consisting of 2C components. Consequently, we conduct a comparison between the estimation results obtained by the EM method that does not take change points into account (referred to as "NCPEM") and those derived from our improved EM method ("CPEM"). We utilize the data generation mechanism of Model (1) to generate the data. Subsequently, we construct a two-component mixed model with a change point and proceed to specify the parameters as follows:

$$(\boldsymbol{\beta}_1^{*-})^T = (1,2),\ \sigma_1^{2*-} = 0.1,\ \pi_1^{*-} = 0.4,\ (\boldsymbol{\beta}_2^{*-})^T = (1,3),\ \sigma_2^{2*-} = 0.2,\ \pi_2^{*-} = 0.6.$$
$$(\boldsymbol{\beta}_1^{*+})^T = (3,4),\ \sigma_1^{2*+} = 0.2,\ \pi_1^{*+} = 0.7,\ (\boldsymbol{\beta}_2^{*+})^T = (3,5),\ \sigma_2^{2*+} = 0.2,\ \pi_2^{*+} = 0.3.$$

$\mathbf{X}_i^T = (1, X_i)$ and $X_i \sim U(0,1)$ for $i = 1,2,\cdots,n$. Let the total sample size $n$ from $\{500, 1000, 2000\}$ and the change point $k^*$ be $\{250, 500, 1000\}$, respectively. The change point estimators and the corresponding standard errors are $\hat{k} = 250.45(0.730), 500.18(0.458), 1000.5(0.759)$ over 100 simulations. It can be seen that the change point estimator is close to the true value. The mixture parameter estimators and the corresponding standard errors are presented in Tables 1–3.

**Table 1.** Estimated value and standard error of $\boldsymbol{\beta}^*$.

| | $\boldsymbol{\beta}^*$ | $(\boldsymbol{\beta}_1^{*-})^T = (\mathbf{1}, \mathbf{2})$ | $(\boldsymbol{\beta}_2^{*-})^T = (\mathbf{1}, \mathbf{3})$ | $(\boldsymbol{\beta}_1^{*+})^T = (\mathbf{3}, \mathbf{4})$ | $(\boldsymbol{\beta}_2^{*+})^T = (\mathbf{3}, \mathbf{5})$ |
|---|---|---|---|---|---|
| $n = 500$ | CPEM | (0.994, 2.004)<br>(0.045, 0.029) | (0.975, 3.023)<br>(0.150, 0.129) | (2.993, 4.004)<br>(0.064, 0.041) | (2.999, 4.999)<br>(0.085, 0.057) |
| | NCPEM | (2.235, 1.911)<br>(9.906, 1.624) | (0.988, 3.048)<br>(7.933, 1.290) | (3.086, 3.874)<br>(9.285, 1.609) | (3.022, 1.941)<br>(0.511, 0.278) |
| $n = 1000$ | CPEM | (0.982, 2.054)<br>(0.042, 0.017) | (1.006, 2.993)<br>(0.104, 0.077) | (2.992, 4.005)<br>(0.039, 0.024) | (2.996, 5.001)<br>(0.058, 0.038) |
| | NCPEM | (0.452, 2.220)<br>(8.490, 1.664) | (0.884, 3.044)<br>(3.710, 0.678) | (1.550, 4.192)<br>(8.211, 1.367) | (3.187, 4.939)<br>(2.540, 0.484) |
| $n = 2000$ | CPEM | (1.000, 1.999)<br>(0.022, 0.014) | (1.014, 2.995)<br>(0.069, 0.046) | (2.930, 4.017)<br>(0.030, 0.019) | (3.001, 4.997)<br>(0.041, 0.035) |
| | NCPEM | (1.225, 2.054)<br>(4.212, 0.624) | (1.318, 2.975)<br>(2.383, 0.505) | (2.880, 3.921)<br>(0.557, 0.342) | (3.009, 4.975)<br>(0.182, 0.107) |

**Table 2.** Estimated value and standard error of $\sigma^{2*}$.

| | $\sigma^{2*}$ | $\sigma_1^{2*-}=0.1$ | $\sigma_2^{2*-}=0.2$ | $\sigma_1^{2*+}=0.1$ | $\sigma_2^{2*+}=0.2$ |
|---|---|---|---|---|---|
| $n$ = 500 | CPEM | 0.099 (0.006) | 0.199 (0.012) | 0.100 (0.008) | 0.197 (0.011) |
| | NCPEM | 0.193 (0.466) | 0.346 (0.626) | 0.171 (0.436) | 0.441 (0.786) |
| $n$ = 1000 | CPEM | 0.098 (0.011) | 0.200 (0.005) | 0.099 (0.006) | 0.199 (0.008) |
| | NCPEM | 0.143 (0.287) | 0.375 (0.686) | 0.147 (0.338) | 0.376 (0.661) |
| $n$ = 2000 | CPEM | 0.100 (0.003) | 0.203 (0.015) | 0.099 (0.011) | 0.204 (0.005) |
| | NCPEM | 0.153 (0.339) | 0.333 (0.616) | 0.096 (0.022) | 0.376 (0.687) |

**Table 3.** Estimated value and standard error of $\pi^*$.

| | $\pi^*$ | $\pi_1^{*-}=0.6$ | $\pi_2^{*-}=0.4$ | $\pi_1^{*+}=0.3$ | $\pi_2^{*+}=0.7$ |
|---|---|---|---|---|---|
| $n$ = 500 | CPEM | 0.601 (0.031) | 0.399 (0.031) | 0.301 (0.030) | 0.699 (0.030) |
| | NCPEM | 0.182 (0.053) | 0.310 (0.050) | 0.189 (0.045) | 0.320 (0.062) |
| $n$ = 1000 | CPEM | 0.594 (0.063) | 0.406 (0.063) | 0.295 (0.019) | 0.705 (0.019) |
| | NCPEM | 0.189 (0.060) | 0.310 (0.044) | 0.193 (0.039) | 0.308 (0.056) |
| $n$ = 2000 | CPEM | 0.599 (0.014) | 0.401 (0.013) | 0.298 (0.033) | 0.702 (0.033) |
| | NCPEM | 0.194 (0.035) | 0.311 (0.058) | 0.186 (0.049) | 0.310 (0.045) |

As is evident from Table 1, the estimation results obtained by the Change Point Expectation–Maximization (CPEM) method are much closer to the true parameter values compared to those derived from the Non-Change Point Expectation–Maximization (NCPEM) method. Moreover, the CPEM method yields a significantly smaller standard error. Based on the estimations of $\sigma^{2*}$ and $\pi^*$ presented in Tables 2 and 3, it is clear that the estimation results of the NCPEM method deviate substantially from the true parameter values. Additionally, as the sample size increases, the majority of the estimation results tend to converge more closely to the true parameter values, accompanied by a smaller standard error. These findings strongly indicate that our improved CPEM method exhibits superior accuracy and enhanced robustness.

*4.2. Detection Experiment*

In experiment 2, we explore the performance of the detection procedure. Let $p = 1$ and consider the following mixture model:

$$Y_i \sim \begin{cases} \sum\limits_{c=1}^{2} \pi_c^{*-} N(\mu_c^{*}-, \sigma_c^{2*-}), & 1 \le i \le k^*, \\ \sum\limits_{c=1}^{2} \pi_c^{*+} N(\mu_c^{*+}, \sigma_c^{2*+}), & k^*+1 \le i \le n, \quad k^* \in [1, n], \end{cases} \tag{8}$$

where

$$\mu_1^{*-} = 1,\ \sigma_1^{2*-} = 0.1,\ \pi_1^{*-} = 0.6,\ \mu_2^{*-} = 2,\ \sigma_2^{2*-} = 0.2,\ \pi_2^{*-} = 0.4,$$
$$\mu_1^{*+} = 3,\ \sigma_1^{2*+} = 0.2,\ \pi_1^{*+} = 0.3,\ \mu_2^{*+} = 4,\ \sigma_2^{2*+} = 0.3,\ \pi_2^{*+} = 0.7.$$

The limiting distribution function in (6) is well known and tabulated by Kiefer [23]. In model (8), $q = 5$, at the significance level of 0.05, the critical value is 2.0005. We set the values of n to be 500, 1000, 2000, k to be $n/4$, $n/2$, and $3n/4$ to represent the case where the change point is located in the front, middle, and back end of the data. The empirical sizes and powers are shown in Tables 4 and 5 under 100 simulations.

**Table 4.** Empirical sizes.

| $n$ | **500** | **1000** | **2000** |
|---|---|---|---|
| size | 0.07 | 0.06 | 0.05 |

**Table 5.** Empirical powers.

| $n$ \ $k^*$ | $\frac{n}{4}$ | $\frac{n}{2}$ | $\frac{3n}{4}$ |
|---|---|---|---|
| 500 | 0.60 | 0.83 | 0.59 |
| 1000 | 0.96 | 0.88 | 0.67 |
| 2000 | 1 | 0.98 | 0.94 |

Based on the analysis of the data in the tables, the performance of the method proposed in this paper under large-sample scenarios can be summarized as follows:

(1) Empirical Level Performance: As clearly shown in Table 4, with the continuous increase in the sample size $n$, the empirical level gradually approaches the significance level of 0.05. This indicates that, under large sample conditions, the actual test level of this method is in good agreement with the preset theoretical level.

(2) Empirical Power Performance: According to the data results in Table 5, there is a significant positive correlation between the increase in sample size and the improvement in empirical power. That is, the larger the sample size, the closer the value of empirical power is to 1, suggesting that the method can more effectively detect true change point situations in large samples.

(3) Influence of Change Point Location: The position of the change point in the data sequence has an impact on the detection effect. When the change point is located in the middle or front part of the data, the detection effect of this method is significantly better than when the change point is located at the end of the data.

(4) Comprehensive Performance Advantages: In large sample scenarios, the method proposed in this paper demonstrates good empirical size and power.

## 5. Concluding Remarks

This paper proposes an improved EM method to solve the parameter estimation problem with a mixture of the linear regression model and change point. This method is more accurate and robust against usual EM algorithms. Furthermore, a detection method based on score function is obtained to test the change point in mixture data. Simulations demonstrate the effectiveness of the proposed methodology.

## 6. Limitations and Future Research Directions

The method presented in this article also has certain limitations and challenges. Firstly, there is the issue of robustness in complex noisy scenarios. The method proposed in this article performs well in dealing with normal noise, but the detection accuracy remains to be studied under complex noise interference. The algorithm mentioned in the article still needs further research in dealing with high-dimensional data point detection and estimation problems. Finally, the computational complexity of the method proposed in this article is relatively high, and it is worth studying whether there is a simpler and faster processing method. The above issues are also possible research directions for the future.

**Author Contributions:** Methodology, Z.X.; Software, W.Z.; Writing—original draft, T.C.; Writing—review & editing, W.Z. All authors have read and agreed to the published version of the manuscript.

**Funding:** This work was supported by the National Natural Science Foundation of China (Grant No. 12171391) and the Natural Science Basic Research Program of Shaanxi (Grant No. 2024JC-YBQN-0039), Shaanxi Fundamental Science Research Project for Mathematics and Physics (Grant No. 23JSY043).

**Data Availability Statement:** Data are contained within the article.

**Conflicts of Interest:** The authors declare no conflicts of interest.

## Appendix A. Appendix for Proof

**Lemma A1.** *Under the Assumption 3 and Cramér-Rao regular conditions, we have*

$$E[q_1(\boldsymbol{\theta}^*, Y)] = 0,$$

$$E[q_2(\boldsymbol{\theta}^*, Y)] = -E[q_1(\boldsymbol{\theta}^*, Y)q_1^T(\boldsymbol{\theta}^*, Y)].$$

**Proof.** See McLachlan and Peel [24]. □

**Lemma A2.** *For the process given by*

$$\Delta_n(t, \boldsymbol{\theta}^*) = \frac{1}{\sqrt{n}} \sum_{i=1}^{[nt]} q_1(\boldsymbol{\theta}^*, Y_i), \quad t \in (0, 1). \tag{A1}$$

*and under the conditions of Lemma A1 and under $H_0$ the following functional central limit theorem holds:*

$$\Delta_n(\cdot, \boldsymbol{\theta}^*) \xrightarrow{d} Z(\cdot),$$

*where $Z(\cdot)$ is the Gaussian process whose mean is $E[Z(t)] = 0$ and variance function is $Var[Z(t)] = \mathcal{B}(\boldsymbol{\theta}^*)$.*

*Furthermore, if $\mathcal{B}(\boldsymbol{\theta}^*)$ is reversible, then we have*

$$\mathcal{B}(\boldsymbol{\theta}^*)^{-1/2}\Delta_n(\cdot, \boldsymbol{\theta}^*) \xrightarrow{d} W(\cdot),$$

*where $W(\cdot)$ is standard Brownian motion.*

**Proof.** The proof follows by direct application of Donsker's theorem (Billingsley [25]). □

Usually in applications, the parameters $\boldsymbol{\theta}^*$ under the null hypothesis are not known but have to be estimated. Let $\hat{\boldsymbol{\theta}}_n$ is the maximum likelihood estimator of $\boldsymbol{\theta}^*$; therefore,

$$\sum_{i=1}^{n} q_1(\hat{\boldsymbol{\theta}}_n, Y_i) = 0.$$

Taylor expansion of $\Gamma_n(\boldsymbol{\theta}) = \frac{1}{n} \sum_{i=1}^{n} q_1(\boldsymbol{\theta}, Y_i)$ at $\boldsymbol{\theta}^*$ when $\boldsymbol{\theta} = \hat{\boldsymbol{\theta}}_n$; then,

$$0 = \Gamma_n(\hat{\boldsymbol{\theta}}_n) = \Gamma_n(\boldsymbol{\theta}^*) + \Gamma_n'(\boldsymbol{\theta}^*)(\hat{\boldsymbol{\theta}}_n - \boldsymbol{\theta}^*) + R_n.$$

Under suitable regularity conditions

$$-\Gamma_n'(\boldsymbol{\theta}^*) = \frac{1}{n} \sum_{i=1}^{n} -q_2(\boldsymbol{\theta}^*, Y_i) \xrightarrow{p} \mathcal{I}(\boldsymbol{\theta}^*),$$

$$\sqrt{n}\Gamma_n(\boldsymbol{\theta}^*) \xrightarrow{d} \mathcal{N}(0, \mathcal{B}(\boldsymbol{\theta}^*)),$$

$$\sqrt{n}R_n \xrightarrow{p} 0.$$

Therefore, the following holds:

$$\sqrt{n}(\hat{\boldsymbol{\theta}}_n - \boldsymbol{\theta}^*) \xrightarrow{d} \mathcal{N}(0, \mathcal{V}(\boldsymbol{\theta}^*)),$$

where $\mathcal{V}(\boldsymbol{\theta}^*) = \mathcal{I}(\boldsymbol{\theta}^*)^{-1}\mathcal{B}(\boldsymbol{\theta}^*)\{\mathcal{I}(\boldsymbol{\theta}^*)^{-1}\}^T$. Equivalently, we can write

$$\sqrt{n}(\hat{\boldsymbol{\theta}}_n - \boldsymbol{\theta}^*) \doteq \mathcal{I}(\boldsymbol{\theta}^*)^{-1}\Delta_n(1, \boldsymbol{\theta}^*).$$

**Lemma A3.** *Under $H_0$, the following holds:*

$$\Delta_n(\cdot, \hat{\boldsymbol{\theta}}_n) \xrightarrow{d} Z^0(\cdot),$$

*where $Z^0(t) = Z(t) - tZ(1)$.*

**Proof.** Taylor expansion of $\Delta_n(t, \hat{\boldsymbol{\theta}}_n)$ at $\boldsymbol{\theta}^*$,

$$\begin{aligned}
\Delta_n(t, \hat{\boldsymbol{\theta}}_n) &\doteq \frac{1}{\sqrt{n}}\sum_{i=1}^{[nt]} q_1(\boldsymbol{\theta}^*, Y_i) + \frac{1}{n}\sum_{i=1}^{[nt]} q_2(\boldsymbol{\theta}^*, Y_i) \cdot \sqrt{n}(\hat{\boldsymbol{\theta}}_n - \boldsymbol{\theta}^*) \\
&\doteq \Delta_n(t, \boldsymbol{\theta}^*) - \frac{[nt]}{n}\mathcal{I}(\boldsymbol{\theta}^*) \cdot \mathcal{I}(\boldsymbol{\theta}^*)^{-1}\Delta_n(1, \boldsymbol{\theta}^*) \\
&\xrightarrow{d} Z(t) - tZ(1).
\end{aligned}$$

□

Next, we will provide the proof process for Theorem 1.

**Proof.** (1) On the basis of the three lemmas stated above and if $\mathcal{B}(\boldsymbol{\theta}^*)$ is reversible, we can obtain the first conclusion in Theorem 1:

$$\hat{\mathcal{B}}_n^{-1/2}\Delta_n(\cdot, \hat{\boldsymbol{\theta}}_n) \xrightarrow{d} W^0(\cdot),$$

where $W^0(\tau) = W(\tau) - \tau W(1)$ is a standard Brownian bridge, $\hat{\mathcal{B}}_n$ is the variance estimation, such as $\hat{\mathcal{B}}_n = \frac{1}{n}\sum_{i=1}^{n} q_1(\hat{\boldsymbol{\theta}}_n, Y_i) q_1(\hat{\boldsymbol{\theta}}_n, Y_i)^T$.

(2) Next, we prove the second conclusion. $Y_i$ has the probability density function under $H_A$ hypothesis:

$$\begin{aligned}
\eta(Y|\boldsymbol{\theta}_i) &\doteq \eta(Y|\boldsymbol{\theta}^*) + \frac{\partial \eta(Y|\boldsymbol{\theta})}{\partial \boldsymbol{\theta}}|_{\boldsymbol{\theta}=\boldsymbol{\theta}_0} \\
&= \eta(Y|\boldsymbol{\theta}^*) + \frac{\partial \log \eta(Y|\boldsymbol{\theta})}{\partial \boldsymbol{\theta}} \cdot \eta(Y|\boldsymbol{\theta})|_{\boldsymbol{\theta}=\boldsymbol{\theta}_0} \cdot \frac{1}{\sqrt{n}} \cdot I_{\{i \geq [n\tau]+1\}} \\
&= \eta(Y|\boldsymbol{\theta}^*)\{1 + q_1(\boldsymbol{\theta}^*, Y)^T \cdot \frac{1}{\sqrt{n}} \cdot I_{\{i \geq [n\tau]+1\}}\},
\end{aligned}$$

which can be derived from the Taylor expansion of $\eta$. Therefore, under the alternative hypothesis, the process (A1) no longer has zero mean in general but

$$\begin{aligned}
E[q_1(\boldsymbol{\theta}_i, Y)] &\doteq \int q_1(\boldsymbol{\theta}^* \eta(y|\boldsymbol{\theta}^*)dy + \int q_1(\boldsymbol{\theta}^*, y) q_1(\boldsymbol{\theta}^*, y)^T \eta(y|\boldsymbol{\theta}^*) \frac{1}{\sqrt{n}} \cdot I_{\{i \geq [nt]+1\}} dy \\
&= 0 + \frac{1}{\sqrt{n}}\mathcal{B}(\boldsymbol{\theta}^*) \cdot I_{\{i \geq [nt]+1\}}.
\end{aligned}$$

Similar to the Lemmas A2 and A3, we can deduce

$$\Delta_n(\cdot, \boldsymbol{\theta}^*) \xrightarrow{d} W^A(\cdot),$$

where $W^A(t) = W(t) + \mathcal{B}(\theta^*)G(t)$, $(G(t) = \int_0^t \cdot I_{\{\frac{i}{n} \geq t + \frac{1}{n}\}} d(\frac{i}{n}) = t(1-t) + o(1))$.

Finally, the following limiting process can be derived, which is our second conclusion:

$$
\begin{aligned}
\hat{\mathcal{B}}_n^{-1/2}\Delta_n(\tau, \hat{\theta}_n) &\doteq \hat{\mathcal{B}}_n^{-1/2}\{\Delta_n(\tau, \theta^*) - \tau\Delta_n(1, \theta^*)\} \\
&\doteq W^0(\tau) + \hat{\mathcal{B}}(\hat{\theta}_n)^{1/2} G^0(\tau) \\
&\xrightarrow{d} W^0(t) + \mathcal{B}(\theta^*)^{1/2} G^0(t).
\end{aligned}
$$

□

Next, we prove Theorem 2 and first give two useful lemmas.

**Lemma A4.** *Under the conditions of model* (8) *and Assumptions 1 and 2, $\mathcal{L}_n$ uniformly converges to $\mathcal{L}$ with probability.*

**Proof.** According to the structure of the function $\mathcal{L}$, we can show that $\mathcal{L}_n$ converges to $\mathcal{L}$ point by point. Next, we prove uniform convergence.

Due to the fact that the parameter space $\Theta$ is a compact set, $\forall i, \delta_i > 0, \Theta \subseteq \bigcup_{i=1}^{m} U((\tau_i, \theta_i), \delta_i), m \in R$, where $U((\tau_i, \theta_i), \delta_i)$ is the neighborhood with center $(\tau_i, \theta_i)$ and radius $\delta_i$. According to the continuity of $\mathcal{L}_n$, $\forall \epsilon > 0$,

$$
|(\tau_i, \theta_i) - (\tau, \theta)| < \delta_i \Rightarrow |\mathcal{L}_n(\tau_i, \theta_i) - \mathcal{L}_n(\tau, \theta)| < \epsilon, \ \forall (\tau, \theta) \in U((\tau_i, \theta_i), \delta_i).
$$

Consequently,

$$
\begin{aligned}
|\mathcal{L}_n(\tau, \theta) - \mathcal{L}(\tau, \theta)| &= |\mathcal{L}_n(\tau, \theta) - \mathcal{L}_n(\tau_i, \theta_i) + \mathcal{L}_n(\tau_i, \theta_i) - \mathcal{L}(\tau_i, \theta_i) + \mathcal{L}(\tau_i, \theta_i) - \mathcal{L}(\tau, \theta)| \\
&\leq |\mathcal{L}_n(\tau, \theta) - \mathcal{L}_n(\tau_i, \theta_i)| + |\mathcal{L}_n(\tau_i, \theta_i) - \mathcal{L}(\tau_i, \theta_i)| + |\mathcal{L}(\tau_i, \theta_i) - \mathcal{L}(\tau, \theta)| \\
&< 3\epsilon.
\end{aligned}
$$

□

**Lemma A5.** *Under the condition of model* (8) *and Assumptions 1 and 3, the parameters are identifiable.*

**Proof.** From the *Jessen* inequality,

$$
\begin{aligned}
&\mathcal{L}(\tau, \theta|\tau^*, \theta^*) - \mathcal{L}(\tau^*, \theta^*|\tau^*, \theta^*) \\
&= \tau \cdot E_{(\tau^*, \theta^{*-})} f(X, Y|\tau, \theta^-) + (\tau^* - \tau) \cdot E_{(\tau^*, \theta^{*-})} f(X, Y|\tau, \theta^+) \\
&\quad + (1 - \tau^*) \cdot E_{(\tau^*, \theta^{*+})} f(X, Y|\tau, \theta^+) - (\tau \cdot E_{(\tau^*, \theta^{*-})} f(X, Y|\tau^*, \theta^{*-}) \\
&\quad + (\tau^* - \tau) \cdot E_{(\tau^*, \theta^{*-})} f(X, Y|\tau^*, \theta^{*-}) + (1 - \tau^*) \cdot E_{(\tau^*, \theta^{*+})} f(X, Y|\tau^*, \theta^{*+})) \\
&= \tau \cdot [E_{(\tau^*, \theta^{*-})} f(X, Y|\tau, \theta^-) - E_{(\tau^*, \theta^{*-})} f(X, Y|\tau^*, \theta^{*-})] + (\tau^* - \tau)[E_{(\tau^*, \theta^{*-})} f(X, Y|\tau, \theta^+) \\
&\quad - E_{(\tau^*, \theta^{*-})} f(X, Y|\tau^*, \theta^{*-})] + (1 - \tau^*) \cdot [E_{(\tau^*, \theta^{*+})} f(X, Y|\tau, \theta^+) - E_{(\tau^*, \theta^{*+})} f(X, Y|\tau^*, \theta^{*+})] \\
&= \tau \cdot E_{(\tau^*, \theta^{*-})}[\log g_1(X, Y|\theta^-, \theta^{*-})] + (\tau^* - \tau) \cdot E_{(\tau^*, \theta^{*-})}[\log g_2(X, Y|\theta^+, \theta^{*-})] \\
&\quad + (1 - \tau^*) \cdot E_{(\tau^*, \theta^{*+})}[\log g_3(X, Y|\theta^+, \theta^{*+})] \\
&\leq \tau \cdot \log\{E_{(\tau^*, \theta^{*-})}[g_1(X, Y|\theta^-, \theta^{*-})]\} + (\tau^* - \tau) \cdot \log\{E_{(\tau^*, \theta^{*-})}[g_2(X, Y|\theta^+, \theta^{*-})]\} \\
&\quad + (1 - \tau^*) \cdot \log\{E_{(\tau^*, \theta^{*+})}[g_3(X, Y|\theta^+, \theta^{*+})]\} \\
&= 0,
\end{aligned}
$$

where

$$g_1(X,Y|\boldsymbol{\theta}^-,\boldsymbol{\theta}^{*-}) = \frac{\sum\limits_{c=1}^{C} \frac{\pi_c}{\sqrt{2\pi\sigma_c^{2-}}} \exp\{-\frac{(Y-X^T\beta_c^-)^2}{2\sigma_c^{2-}}\}}{\sum\limits_{c=1}^{C} \frac{\pi_c^*}{\sqrt{2\pi\sigma_c^{2*-}}} \exp\{-\frac{(Y-X^T\beta_c^{*-})^2}{2\sigma_c^{2*-}}\}},$$

$$g_2(X,Y|\boldsymbol{\theta}^+,\boldsymbol{\theta}^{*-}) = \frac{\sum\limits_{c=1}^{C} \frac{\pi_c}{\sqrt{2\pi\sigma_c^{2+}}} \exp\{-\frac{(Y-X^T\beta_c^+)^2}{2\sigma_c^{2+}}\}}{\sum\limits_{c=1}^{C} \frac{\pi_c^*}{\sqrt{2\pi\sigma_c^{2*}}} \exp\{-\frac{(Y-X^T\beta_c^{*-})^2}{2\sigma_c^{2*}}\}},$$

$$g_3(X,Y|\boldsymbol{\theta}^+,\boldsymbol{\theta}^{*+}) = \frac{\sum\limits_{c=1}^{C} \frac{\pi_c}{\sqrt{2\pi\sigma_c^{2+}}} \exp\{-\frac{(Y-X^T\beta_c^+)^2}{2\sigma_c^{2+}}\}}{\sum\limits_{c=1}^{C} \frac{\pi_c^*}{\sqrt{2\pi\sigma_c^{2*+}}} \exp\{-\frac{(Y-X^T\beta_c^{*+})^2}{2\sigma_c^{2*+}}\}}.$$

Therefore, we have $\mathcal{L}(\tau,\boldsymbol{\theta}|\tau^*,\boldsymbol{\theta}^*) \leq \mathcal{L}(\tau^*,\boldsymbol{\theta}^*|\tau^*,\boldsymbol{\theta}^*)$, and the equal sign holds only when $(\tau,\boldsymbol{\theta}) = (\tau^*,\boldsymbol{\theta}^*)$; that is, $\mathcal{L}$ maximizes at $(\tau^*,\boldsymbol{\theta}^*)$. Next, we prove that the maximum point is unique.

According to *Jessen* inequality, the three terms on the left side of the inequality are all less than or equal to 0. Therefore, the left side is equal to 0 if and only if the three terms are equal to 0. Since $\tau,\tau^* \in (0,1)$, both $g_1(X,Y|\boldsymbol{\theta}^-,\boldsymbol{\theta}^{*-})$ and $g_3(X,Y|\boldsymbol{\theta}^+,\boldsymbol{\theta}^{*+})$ are equal to 1 if and only if $(\pi_c,\beta_c^-,\sigma_c^{2-}) = (\pi_c^*,\beta_c^{*-},\sigma_c^{2*-})$ and $(\pi_c,\beta_c^+,\sigma_c^{2+}) = (\pi_c^*,\beta_c^{*+},\sigma_c^{2*+})$; meanwhile, because of $\beta_c^+ \neq \beta_c^{*-},\sigma_c^{2+} \neq \sigma_c^{2*-}$, $g_2(X,Y|\boldsymbol{\theta}^+,\boldsymbol{\theta}^{*-})$ is equal to 1 if and only if $\tau = \tau^*$. Therefore, $\mathcal{L}(\tau,\boldsymbol{\theta}|\tau^*,\boldsymbol{\theta}^*)$ obtains the unique maximum at $(\tau^*,\boldsymbol{\theta}^*)$. □

The proof of Theorem 2 is as follows.

**Proof.** For any $\epsilon > 0$, let

$$\begin{aligned} A &= \{\mathcal{L}_n(\tau^*,\boldsymbol{\theta}^*) > \mathcal{L}(\tau^*,\boldsymbol{\theta}^*) - \epsilon/3\}, \\ B &= \{\mathcal{L}_n(\hat{\tau},\hat{\boldsymbol{\theta}}_n) > \mathcal{L}_n(\tau^*,\boldsymbol{\theta}^*) - \epsilon/3\}, \\ C &= \{\mathcal{L}(\hat{\tau},\hat{\boldsymbol{\theta}}_n) > \mathcal{L}_n(\hat{\tau},\hat{\boldsymbol{\theta}}_n) - \epsilon/3\}. \end{aligned}$$

From Lemmas A4 and A5, $\mathcal{L}_n$ uniformly converges to $\mathcal{L}$; furthermore, $(\hat{\tau},\hat{\boldsymbol{\theta}}_n)$ and $(\tau^*,\boldsymbol{\theta}^*)$ are the maximum points of $\mathcal{L}_n$ and $\mathcal{L}$, respectively; therefore, when $n \to \infty$, $P(A), P(B), P(C)$ all tend to 1. So when the event $A \cap B \cap C$ occurs,

$$\begin{aligned} \mathcal{L}(\tau^*,\boldsymbol{\theta}^*) - \mathcal{L}(\hat{\tau},\hat{\boldsymbol{\theta}}_n) &= (\mathcal{L}(\tau^*,\boldsymbol{\theta}^*) - \mathcal{L}_n(\tau^*,\boldsymbol{\theta}^*)) + (\mathcal{L}_n(\tau^*,\boldsymbol{\theta}^*) - \mathcal{L}_n(\hat{\tau},\hat{\boldsymbol{\theta}}_n)) \\ &\quad + (\mathcal{L}_n(\hat{\tau},\hat{\boldsymbol{\theta}}_n) - \mathcal{L}(\hat{\tau},\hat{\boldsymbol{\theta}}_n)) \\ &< \frac{\epsilon}{3} + \frac{\epsilon}{3} + \frac{\epsilon}{3} = \epsilon. \end{aligned}$$

Furthermore, the parameter space $\Theta$ is a compact set and $\mathcal{L}$ is continuous, so for a sufficiently small $\delta$, let $N = U((\tau^*,\boldsymbol{\theta}^*),\delta)$, we have

$$\sup_{(\tau,\boldsymbol{\theta})\in\Theta\cap N^c} \mathcal{L}(\tau,\boldsymbol{\theta}) \triangleq \mathcal{L}(\tau_0,\boldsymbol{\theta}_0) < \mathcal{L}(\tau^*,\boldsymbol{\theta}^*).$$

We might as well take $\epsilon = \mathcal{L}(\tau^*,\boldsymbol{\theta}^*) - \mathcal{L}(\tau_0,\boldsymbol{\theta}_0) > 0$, then $-\epsilon < \mathcal{L}(\tau^*,\boldsymbol{\theta}^*) - \mathcal{L}(\hat{\tau},\hat{\boldsymbol{\theta}}_n) < \epsilon$ holds with probability 1.

Therefore, the following holds:

$$P(|\mathcal{L}(\tau^*,\boldsymbol{\theta}^*) - \mathcal{L}(\hat{\tau},\hat{\boldsymbol{\theta}}_n)| < \epsilon) \to 1.$$

In other words, when $(\hat{\tau}, \hat{\boldsymbol{\theta}}_n) \in N^c$ and $|(\tau^*, \boldsymbol{\theta}^*) - (\hat{\tau}, \hat{\boldsymbol{\theta}}_n)| \geq \delta$, then $|\mathcal{L}(\tau^*, \boldsymbol{\theta}^*) - \mathcal{L}(\hat{\tau}, \hat{\boldsymbol{\theta}}_n)| \geq \epsilon$. It can be shown that

$$P(|(\tau^*, \boldsymbol{\theta}^*) - (\hat{\tau}, \hat{\boldsymbol{\theta}}_n)| \geq \delta) \leq P(|\mathcal{L}(\tau^*, \boldsymbol{\theta}^*) - \mathcal{L}(\hat{\tau}, \hat{\boldsymbol{\theta}}_n)| \geq \epsilon) \rightarrow 0.$$

i.e., $P(|(\tau^*, \boldsymbol{\theta}^*) - (\hat{\tau}, \hat{\boldsymbol{\theta}}_n)| \geq \delta) \rightarrow 0$. Therefore, we obtain the desired result:

$$(\hat{\tau}, \hat{\boldsymbol{\theta}}_n) \xrightarrow{p} (\tau^*, \boldsymbol{\theta}^*).$$

□

## References


1. Goldfeld, S.M.; Quandt, R.E. A Markov model for switching regressions. *J. Econom.* **1973**, *1*, 3–15. [CrossRef]
2. Frühwirth-Schnatter, S. *Finite Mixture and Markov Switching Models*; Springer: New York, NY, USA, 2006; pp. 241–275.
3. Hurn, M.; Justel, A.; Robert, C.P. Estimating Mixtures of Regressions. *J. Comput. Graph. Stat.* **2003**, *12*, 55–79. [CrossRef]
4. Li, P.; Chen, J. Testing the Order of a Finite Mixture. *J. Am. Stat. Assoc.* **2010**, *105*, 1084–1092. [CrossRef]
5. Chen, J.; Li, P.; Fu, Y. Inference on the Order of a Normal Mixture. *J. Am. Stat. Assoc.* **2012**, *107*, 1096–1105. [CrossRef]
6. Huang, M.; Yao, W. Mixture of Regression Models With Varying Mixing Proportions: A Semiparametric Approach. *J. Am. Stat. Assoc.* **2012**, *107*, 711–724. [CrossRef]
7. Huang, M.; Li, R.; Wang, S. Nonparametric Mixture of Regression Models. *J. Am. Stat. Assoc.* **2013**, *108*, 929–941. [CrossRef]
8. Page, E.S. Continuous inspection schemes. *Biometrika* **1954**, *41*, 100–115. [CrossRef]
9. Sen, A.; Srivastava, M.S. On tests for detecting change in mean. *Ann. Stat.* **1975**, *3*, 98–108. [CrossRef]
10. Sen, A.; Srivastava, M.S. Some one-sided tests for change in level. *Technometrics* **1975**, *17*, 61–64. [CrossRef]
11. Hawkins, D.M. Testing a sequence of observations for a shift in location. *J. Am. Stat. Assoc.* **1977**, *72*, 180–186. [CrossRef]
12. James, B.; James, K.; Siegmund, D. Tests for a change-point. *Biometrika* **1987**, *74*, 71–83. [CrossRef]
13. Srivastava, M.S.; Worsley, K.J. Likelihood ratio tests for a change in the multivariate normal mean. *J. Am. Stat. Assoc.* **1986**, *81*, 199–204. [CrossRef]
14. Bassevile, M.; Nikiforov, I. *Detection of Abrupt Changes: Theory and Applications*; Prentice Hall: Hoboken, NJ, USA, 1993.
15. Wang, G.; Zou, C.; Yin, G. Change-point detection in multinomial data with a large number of categories. *Ann. Stat.* **2018**, 46, 2020–2044. [CrossRef]
16. Xia, Z.; Qiu, P. Jump information criterion for statistical inference in estimating discontinuous curves. *Biometrika* **2015**, *102*, 397–408. [CrossRef]
17. Bai, J. Least squares estimation of a shift in linear processes. *J. Time Ser. Anal.* **1994**, *15*, 453–472. [CrossRef]
18. Baranowski, R.; Chen, Y.; Fryzlewicz, P. Narrowest-over-threshold detection of multiple change points and change-point-like features. *J. R. Stat. Soc. Ser. Stat. Methodol.* **2019**, *81*, 649–672. [CrossRef]
19. Follain, B.; Wang, T.; Samworth, R.J. High-dimensional changepoint estimation with heterogeneous missingness. *J. R. Stat. Soc. Ser. Stat. Methodol.* **2022**, *84*, 1023–1055. [CrossRef]
20. Drabech, Z.; Douimi, M.; Zemmouri, E. A Markov random field model for change points detection. *J. Comput. Sci.* **2024**, *83*, 102429. [CrossRef]
21. Ratnasingam, S.; Gamage, R. Empirical likelihood change point detection in quantile regression models. *Comput. Stat.* **2025**, *40*, 999–1020. [CrossRef]
22. Gong, Y.; Dong, X.; Zhang, J.; Chen, M. Latent evolution model for change point detection in time-varying networks. *Inf. Sci.* **2023**, *646*, 119376. [CrossRef]
23. Kiefer, J. K-sample analogues of the Kolmogorov-Smirnov and Cramér-Von Mises tests. *Ann. Math. Stat.* **1959**, *30*, 420–447. [CrossRef]
24. McLachlan, G.; Peel, D. *Finite Mixture Models*; Wiley: New York, NY, USA, 2000.
25. Billingsley, P. *Convergence of Probability Measures*, 2nd ed.; Wiley: New York, NY, USA, 1999.

axioms

*Article*

# Integrated Production, EWMA Scheme, and Maintenance Policy for Imperfect Manufacturing Systems of Bolt-On Vibroseis Equipment Considering Quality and Inventory Constraints

**Nuan Xia [1,2,*], Zilin Lu [1,2], Yuling Zhang [1,2] and Jundong Fu [1,2]**

[1] Shandong Earthquake Disaster Prevention Center, Shandong Earthquake Agency, Jinan 250014, China; lvlin3956@163.com (Z.L.); zyt202@163.com (Y.Z.); 19905414656@163.com (J.F.)
[2] Shandong Institute of Earthquake Engineering, Jinan 250021, China
* Correspondence: xianuan3816@126.com

**Abstract:** In recent years, the synergistic effect among production, maintenance, and quality control within manufacturing systems has garnered increasing attention in academic and industrial circles. In high-quality production settings, the real-time identification of minute process deviations holds significant importance for ensuring product quality. Traditional approaches, such as routine quality inspections or Shewhart control charts, exhibit limitations in sensitivity and response speed, rendering them inadequate for meeting the stringent requirements of high-precision quality control. To address this issue, this paper presents an integrated framework that seamlessly integrates stochastic process modeling, dynamic optimization, and quality monitoring. In the realm of quality monitoring, an exponentially weighted moving average (EWMA) control chart is employed to monitor the production process. The statistic derived from this chart forms a Markov process, enabling it to more acutely detect minor shifts in the process mean. Regarding maintenance strategies, a state-dependent preventive maintenance (PM) and corrective maintenance (CM) mechanism is introduced. Specifically, preventive maintenance is initiated when the system is in a statistically controlled state and the inventory level falls below a predefined threshold. Conversely, corrective maintenance is triggered when the EWMA control chart generates an out-of-control (OOC) signal. To facilitate continuous production during maintenance activities, an inventory buffer mechanism is incorporated into the model. Building upon this foundation, a joint optimization model is formulated, with system states, including equipment degradation state, inventory level, and quality state, serving as decision variables and the minimization of the expected total cost (ETC) per unit time as the objective. This problem is formalized as a constrained dynamic optimization problem and is solved using the genetic algorithm (GA). Finally, through a case study of the production process of vibroseis equipment, the superiority of the proposed model in terms of cost savings and system performance enhancement is empirically verified.

**Keywords:** imperfect manufacturing systems; EWMA scheme; maintenance; inventory constraints; joint design model; expected total cost

**MSC:** 62P30; 62-08

## 1. Introduction and Literature Review

Rapidly changing market demands, varying production plans in the short run, and increasing complexity of manufacturing systems have posed a challenge for improving the quality and efficiency of production processes. Production (production plan and inventory control), maintenance, and quality are three main operational areas in manufacturing. Mathematical modeling assumes a pivotal role in tackling these intricate problems, facilitating the integration of production and maintenance, implementing statistical process control, and achieving optimization (Zhang et al. [1]; Alhidairah et al. [2]; Jafari et al. [3]). In the past, many studies dealt with the optimal design of the three operation areas separately. However, this may severely affect the global optimality (Frahani and Tohidi [4]; Hafidi et al. [5]). In light of this, this research endeavors to develop an optimal integrated model for production, maintenance, and quality control. It is anticipated that, through this model, process variation can be reduced, process quality can be enhanced, the reliability of the production system can be strengthened, and production costs can be effectively saved. During this process, mathematical modeling will function as a core instrument, enabling us to precisely depict the relationships among various factors and accomplish the integrated optimization of production and maintenance. Developing an optimal integration of production, maintenance, and quality control models is the object of this study, which can reduce the process variation, improve process quality, increase the reliability of the production system, and save production costs.

In the joint design literature, some studies were developed based on the two-aspect integration of three functions (production, maintenance and quality) in manufacturing systems, for example, production and maintenance policies (Slameh and Ghattas [6], Goel, Grievink, and Weijnen [7], El-Ferik [8], Nahas [9]) and quality and maintenance (Ben-Daya and Rahim [10], Charongrattanasakul and Pongpullponsak [11], Xiang et al. [12], Duan et al. [13], Huang et al. [14]). However, the three functions interact mutually, and practitioners need to find the optimal management method to balance the three tasks by considering them simultaneously (Salmasnia et al. [15], Salmasnia et al. [16], Hadian et al. [17], Frahani and Tohidi [4], Zhang et al. [18]). Mathematical modeling is capable of integrating these three functions into a unified framework for analysis by constructing functional relationships among multiple variables. This approach enables the realization of more efficient integrated management.

During the last twenty years, many integrated models have been proposed to examine assignable causes based on Shewhart type control charts. These models demonstrate distinct characteristics in the realm of mathematical modeling. Ben-Daya and Makhdoum [19] presented a joint optimization economic production quantity (EPQ) and quality model under various PM policies, and a Shewhart $\overline{X}$ chart was used to monitor the main characteristic. Rahim and Ben-Daya [20] proposed an economic production quantity and quality control design under the surveillance of an $\overline{X}$ control chart. In this study, mathematical models were also utilized to ascertain the optimal production and quality control parameters. Pandey et al. [21] developed an integrated cost model for jointly optimizing the PM interval and some design parameters of the $\overline{X}$ control chart, where two failure models were introduced for machine failures. By combining probability distributions and cost functions, mathematical modeling of maintenance and quality control was achieved. Pan et al. [22] introduced the EPQ model into the integrated quality control and maintenance policy, further enriching the mathematical model system of production and maintenance integration. Noting the possible presence of multiple assignable causes, Salmasnia et al. [15] proposed a joint design of production, maintenance, and control charts. In this design, a variable sampling interval scheme was employed, and the dynamic changes of the sampling interval were considered in the mathematical modeling process. Recently, Bahria et al. [23] modeled a joint maintenance and quality control strategy for which quality control was again performed by an $\overline{\text{X}}$ control chart to analyze process data. Salmasnia et al. [24] provided a joint determination of production cycle length, maintenance policy, and several parameters of the control chart, where the time value of money and the stochastic shift size were considered. To keep the reliability of the system, they also adopted the strategy of non-uniform sampling. Hadian et al. [17] developed a joint model of maintenance planning, inventory, and quality control policy. Recently, Shi et al. [25] proposed an optimal model for optimizing production, maintenance, and quality control of imperfect manufacturing systems considering timely replenishment. Although they suggested that, when designing the integrated model, a proper control chart should be considered, the $\overline{\text{X}}$ charting scheme is still applied in their numerical study. It is clear that the $\overline{\text{X}}$ chart still stands as a popular statistical process monitoring (SPM) tool used in different integrated production, maintenance, and quality control policies.

When implementing a control chart for monitoring the non-conforming fraction, it is worth pointing out that choosing an efficient online monitoring scheme is crucial to undertake the corresponding maintenance action. The Shewhart type control charts are easy to implement and efficient in detecting large variations in a process, but they are relatively inefficient in monitoring small and moderate changes (Serel and Moskowitz [26], Ardakan, [27], Hesamian et al. [28], Sukparungsee et al. [29]). In the literature, Serel and Moskowitz [26] presented an EWMA cost minimization model, and it can be regarded as a type of economic–statistical design. Charongrattanasakul and Pongpullponsak [8] investigated the integrated system approach to model quality control and maintenance policy using the EWMA scheme. Six conditions, namely, in-control alert signal, out-of-control signal, in-control no signal, out-of-control no signal, warning limit alert signal, and warning limit no signal, are given in the integrated model. After that, an EWMA chart was adopted to combine PM and CM actions on the process. Ardakan et al. [27] provided a hybrid model to connect the control chart with the planned and reactive maintenance. Yin et al. [30] considered a production process with multiple quality characteristics, and a cost model based on a multivariate EWMA chart is established. Noman et al. [31] presented an integrated optimization method that addresses both maintenance policies and quality control practices, which investigated the optimal integrated design for maintenance and quality control, yet the production and inventory control policies are not considered. To the best of our knowledge, there is no literature on the joint design production, maintenance, and quality policy based on the EWMA scheme. Therefore, this paper considers the EWMA monitoring scheme in the optimal integrated design to increase the scheme's sensitivity in small to moderate shifts.

In actual situations, production processes are subject to assignable causes, which mainly lead to producing defective products. A proper maintenance policy is necessary for restoring the system to a good situation or an as-good-as-new state to maintain the production process at a high quality level. However, maintenance without taking the quality control information or production requirements into consideration may increase the process variability, risk of machine failure, and production costs. The choice of maintenance is constrained by the maintenance plan, quality monitoring information, and inventory size. Some researchers investigated PM, CM, age-based maintenance policies, etc. in the integrated model based on the signal given by the control chart and the equipment state. For instance, Nourelfath et al. [32] performed an imperfect PM policy in the integrated production, maintenance, and quality model for an imperfect production process. They employed a linear relationship between the PM cost and the improvement of the conditions.

Bouslah et al. [33] considered imperfect maintenance as a part of the setup activity at the beginning of each lot production and major maintenance when the proportion of defectives in a rejected lot reaches or exceeds a given threshold. They offered an integrated production, preventive maintenance, and quality control strategy. In the mathematical modeling, factors such as the threshold of the proportion of non-conforming products and the number of batches were taken into account. Salmasnia et al. [16] provided an integrated EPQ method, maintenance, and quality control policy based on a $\mathrm{VP} - \mathrm{T}^2$ Hotelling chart, where PM and CM are conducted under different production scenorios. Rivera-Gómez et al. [34] presented a joint optimization design of production and maintenance policy, where an adaptive sampling plan and the minimal repair and PM policies are considered. Besides the above discussion, many researchers have made contributions to providing maintenance policy for improving the quality and reliability of machines (see Bahria et al. [23], Baria et al. [35], He et al. [36], Hadian et al. [17]), which can be referred to in the integrated model. Since the production capacity and machine availability are significantly influenced by the maintenance, a proper maintenance policy should be determined and adjusted according to the actual condition of the production process in the integrated production, maintenance, and quality control model.

To satisfy the continuous demand of customers, the production and inventory control policies are also of concern to managers. The inventory size is usually limited in many factories, therefore, the optimization of production scheduling and inventory control should be considered in the integrated production, maintenance and quality control model (Pan et al. [22], Fakher et al. [37], Salmasnia et al. [15], Salmasnia et al. [16], Hadian et al. [17]). In mathematical modeling, inventory levels can be described by production rate, demand rate, and time, while taking into account the constraints of upper and lower inventory limits. However, one can find that few researchers considered the viewpoint of inventory constraints. To this end, in this paper, we consider the inventory to be constrained.

In addition, most of the inventory policies considered in the integrated model are based on the assumption that the products monitored by the control chart are perfect before the control chart triggers a signal. The rejection of defective products is not clarified in the previous integrated optimal studies. The control chart may generally not reflect the OOC situation in actual production processes due to its self-limit. Bahria et al. [35] once pointed out that the number of defective items is proportional to the quantity produced before the control chart signals. Mokhtari and Asadkhani [38] proposed an economic production quantity model, and two rejection of defective items policies are compared. Their comparison results showed that the decision of removing the faulty items once per subproduction cycle would cost less than the decision of disposing of the defective items once per cycle. For some production processes, for example, the high-voltage rotor bolts' hot upsetting process, the defective items cannot be reworked or will be reworked at a relatively larger additional cost, resulting in that the defective items are not suitable to put into inventory for sale at a later time from the economic viewpoint. Therefore, in this paper, we considered the discarding defective items strategy instead of putting defective items into inventory.

Table 1 summarizes the work related to this paper. To the best of our knowledge, the existing integrated model based on the EWMA chart has not considered the inventory constraints for carrying out PM in various integrated optimal designs. To give scientific and efficient guidance for production management, we present an integrated EWMA chart to control and improve the quality of the process and reduce the number of defects. According to the information from the EWMA control chart and inventory level, a proper maintenance action is carried out to restore the machine to an as-good-as-new state. Considering conditions of shortage and without shortage and the rejection of defective items, the inventory level is evaluated. Finally, the joint design for production, EWMA control, and maintenance policy is established to bridge the research gap.

**Table 1.** Summary and Comparison of related contributions.

| Author(s) | Type of Control Chart | | Failure Mechanism | Maintenance Policy | | Inventory Control | | |
|---|---|---|---|---|---|---|---|---|
| | $\overline{X}$ | EWMA | | Preventive Maintenance | Corrective Maintenance | Without Shortage | With Shortage | Reject Defective Items |
| Pandey et al. [21] | √ | | √ | √ | √ | | | |
| Charongrattanasakul, Pongpullponsak [11] | | √ | √ | √ | √ | | | |
| Pan et al. [22] | √ | | √ | √ | √ | | | |
| Xiang [9] | √ | | √ | √ | √ | | | |
| Yin et al. [30] | | √ | √ | √ | √ | | | |
| Ardakan et al. [27] | | √ | √ | √ | √ | | | |
| Nourelfath et al. [32] | | | √ | √ | | | | |
| Lin et al. [39] | | | √ | √ | | √ | | |
| Salmasnia et al. [15] | √ | | √ | √ | √ | | | |
| Fakher et al. [37] | | | √ | √ | | | | |
| Bahria et al. [23] | √ | | | √ | √ | √ | √ | √ |
| Duffuaa et al. [40] | √ | | √ | √ | √ | √ | | |
| Salmasnia et al. [24] | √ | | √ | √ | | √ | | |
| Rivera-Gómez et al. [34] | | | | √ | | √ | | √ |
| Hadian et al. [17] | √ | | √ | √ | √ | √ | √ | |
| Wan et al. [41] | √ | | √ | √ | √ | √ | | |
| Zhang et al. [18] | | | √ | √ | √ | √ | | √ |
| Lv et al. [42] | | | √ | √ | √ | | √ | |
| **The proposed model** | | √ | √ | √ | √ | √ | √ | √ |

With respect to the available literature, the proposed integrated design of EWMA monitoring scheme, maintenance, and inventory policies for optimizing the production process has the following benefits:

(1) To suit the need of monitoring moderate and small shifts, the EWMA charting scheme is adopted to replace the Shewhart $\overline{X}$ charting scheme, which can better control and improve the quality of the production process.
(2) To suit the actual conditions of factories, a preventive maintenance action is carried out to improve the machine's state based on its usage time, comprehensively considering quality condition and inventory levels.
(3) To accurately model the inventory, both scenarios with and without shortages are considered.

A new integrated optimal design of production, maintenance, and quality control is established for guiding the production management, where the joint design is connected by the expected total cost (ETC) per unit time in one production cycle.

The rest of this paper is organized as follows. Section 2 describes the notations, problems, and assumptions of this study. In Section 3, we briefly introduce the EWMA chart for quality control. Afterwards, in Section 4, we define three scenarios in a production cycle. Section 5 gives the cost analysis of the proposed joint design of the production, maintenance, and quality control model. Section 6 is devoted to establishing the integrated model for the production (production plan and inventory control), maintenance, and quality policy. Section 7 gives a real case study to demonstrate the implementation of the proposed integrated model. Finally, some conclusions and discussions are given in Section 8.

## 2. Notations, Problem Description, and Assumptions

### 2.1. Notations

| Decision Variables | Description |
|---|---|
| $k$ | Number of samplings in one production cycle |
| $h$ | Sampling interval |
| $n$ | Sample size |
| $L$ | Coefficient of control limits of the EWMA chart |
| $r$ | Smoothing parameter |
| Parameters | Description |
| $m$ | Lower critical inventory level |
| $M$ | Upper critical inventory level |
| $e_1$ | Lower production rate |
| $e_2$ | Upper production rate |
| $\lambda$ | The occurrence rate of quality shifts |
| $u_0, \sigma$ | The mean and standard deviation of the key quality characteristic |
| $u_1$ | The mean of the key characteristic when the process shifts |
| $\delta$ | The magnitude of shifts in process mean |
| $UCL$ | The upper control limit |
| $LCL$ | The lower control limit |
| $ARL$ | Average run length |
| $\alpha$ | The false alarm rate of the EWMA control chart |
| $p(t\|\delta)$ | Probability of the control chart signals at the $t$-th sample when the process is OOC with shift $\delta$ |
| $\tau$ | The average time between the last sampling taken in the IC process to the occurrence of the assignable cause |
| $P$ | Production rate |
| $D$ | Demand rate |
| $I$ | Inventory level |
| $I_{max}$ | Maximum inventory level |
| $C_I$ | Cost of the quality loss per time unit when the process is IC |
| $C_O$ | Cost of the quality loss per time unit when the process is OOC |
| $C_F$ | Fixed inspection cost of sampling |
| $C_s$ | Variable inspection cost of sampling |
| $C_1$ | Cost of preventive maintenance (PM) |
| $C_2$ | Cost of corrective maintenance (CM) |
| $C_3$ | Maintenance cost when PM is replaced by CM |
| $C_f$ | Cost of inspecting a false alarm |
| $S$ | The setup cost per production cycle |
| $B$ | The inventory holding cost per unit time |
| $B_1$ | The unit shortage cost per time unit |
| $\beta$ | The proportion of defective items produced in OOC processes |
| $t_1$ | The duration of PM |
| $t_2$ | The duration of CM |
| $t_3$ | The maintenance time when PM is replaced by CM |
| $E(O)$ | The expected cost of setup |
| $E(I)$ | The expected inventory holding cost |
| $E(Q)$ | The expected quality loss cost |
| $E(S)$ | The expected sampling inspection cost |
| $E(M)$ | The expected maintenance cost |
| $E(C_{Fa})$ | The expected false alarm cost |
| $EC$ | The average total cost per production cycle |
| $ET$ | Expected operating time per production cycle |

### 2.2. Problem Description

In this paper, a single-unit imperfect manufacturing system is considered, where three main tasks, production and inventory scheduling, quality control, and maintenance, are involved. The key problems concerned in each part are described as follows.

**(a). Production and inventory**

We assume that one machine produces a single product in batches at rate $P$ to satisfy a constant market demand rate $D$. When $P \leq D$, the products flow from the factory into the market directly. When $P > D$, demands are fully satisfied and the inventory is built up at the rate $P - D$. Similar to Salmasnia et al. [15], the production rate $P$ is set larger than the demand rate $D$ in this paper. In production–inventory control issues, a two-critical-number policy $(m, M)$ with $0 \leq m \leq M$ for the production operational mechanism has been studied by many researchers (Gaver [43], Sobel [44], Lin [45]).

We defined $e_1$ as the production rate when the inventory level reaches its maximum $M$ and $e_2$ as the rate when the level is below the minimum inventory threshold $m$ $(0 \leq e_1 < e_2)$. Specifically, when the inventory level rises from $m$ to $M$, the production rate switches from $e_2$ to $e_1$, and the production rate switches from $e_1$ to $e_2$ when the inventory level falls from $M$ to $m$. In this study, we consider that the production run process starts at a zero inventory level with a production rate $e_2 = P$. When the inventory is at a full level, the production ends with a production rate $e_1 = 0$. In addition, to ensure the quality of products, a 100% inspection of products is performed before they flow into the market or the inventory.

**(b). Quality control**

Since the production system is imperfect, some assignable causes may occur due to the deterioration of the machine and some external environmental factors, resulting in defective (or non-conforming) items being produced. The manufacturer will give an additional cost to rework or scrap the defective products. To reduce the rate of defective products, quickly detecting the occurrence of assignable causes is needed. To this end, the EWMA control chart is adopted by monitoring the quality characteristic of products to reflect whether an assignable cause occurs.

The process operates in an in-control (IC) state when production starts, and a sampling policy with sampling interval $h$ and sample size $n$ is adopted to plot the EWMA control chart. The quality characteristic of products to be monitored is assumed to follow a normal distribution with mean $u_0$ and standard deviation $\sigma$. When an assignable cause occurs, the process mean may shift from $u_0$ to $u_1 = u_0 + \delta\sigma$. In this paper, the standard deviation is assumed to be known and remains always the same (Hadian et al. [17]). When the control chart signals and practitioners check that an assignable cause occurs, the production ends. Otherwise, the production will end at the time of the kth sampling when no signal is triggered.

**(c). Maintenance**

The process ends when the control chart detects an assignable cause, otherwise, the process continues with no signal alert of a process shift until the kth sampling inspection. Therefore, based on the comprehensive consideration of the production–inventory and quality control, PM will be carried out both considering the process operates after the $k$th sampling inspection and inventory level reaches the critical value $I_{max}$, where $I_{max} = kh * (P - D)$. It is noted that PM is carried out here to improve the machine's condition under the constraints of inventory level. Moreover, once the control chart gives an alarm signal before the $k$th sampling inspection when an assignable cause occurs, CM action will be taken. Both PM and CM actions considered here are perfect.

A production cycle contains the production uptime for producing items and production downtime for maintenance. Two possible conditions, with shortage and without shortage, are considered in this paper as follows.

- Without shortage: (1) Production uptime: The process starts at a zero inventory level, then, the inventory is built up to the maximum inventory level $I_{max}$ at time $kh$ or the inventory reaches the level $I'$ $(I' < I_{max})$ when an alarm is triggered by the control chart. (2) Production downtime: The process develops from the inventory level $I_{max}(or\ I')$ to zero.

- With shortage: (1) Production uptime: The production uptime in the case of shortage is the same as the production time in the case of without shortage. (2) Production downtime: The process develops from the inventory level $I_{max}$ $(or\ I')$ to backorder.

In the above two conditions, we assume that the maintenance duration in the condition of without shortage (with shortage) is less (longer) than the inventory depletion period, then, no shortage (shortage) will happen in one production cycle.

Moreover, the classical evolution method of the inventory level is based on the assumption that products are all perfect (or all conforming) (Pan et al. [19]). However, the control chart may be unable to reflect the OOC process due to its self-limit. Considering that the rejection of defective items can reduce the occupancy of storage space and management cost, therefore, defective products will be rejected in this paper, and the corresponding description can be found in Section 5.

Finally, the integration design of production, EWMA control, and maintenance policy is investigated in this study, and the objective is to minimize the expected total cost per unit time (ETC) under the constraints of the inventory size, the sample size, the sampling interval, the sampling number, the false alarm rate, and the run length of the OOC process and provide the optimal decision variables: sampling inspection number $k$, sampling interval $h$, sample size $n$, coefficient $L$ of control limits of the EWMA control chart, and smoothing parameter $r$.

### 2.3. Assumptions

The following assumptions and definitions are used to develop the proposed model:

(1) The time to the occurrence of an assignable cause follows the exponential distribution with parameter $\lambda$ (Salmasnia et al. [16], Seif [46], Duffuaa et al. [40], Huang et al. [14]).
(2) The PM and CM restore the production system to an as-good-as-new condition (Salmasnia et al. [15], Salmasnia et al. [16], Hadian et al. [17]).
(3) The time of finding a false alarm, the time of sampling, and the time to validate the assignable cause can be ignored, since they are relatively small in comparison with the total operation time in one production cycle (Huang et al. [14]).

The proportion of defective items of the OOC process is assumed to be a constant. (Bahria et al. [35]).

Subsequently, the study will elaborate on the design of the EWMA control chart and its implementation within the production process. Building on this foundation, we will analyze three distinct scenarios: firstly, when an assignable cause is detected by the control chart, triggering corrective maintenance; secondly, when a drift remains undetected by the chart but is discovered during periodic preventive maintenance; and thirdly, when only routine preventive maintenance is performed without any detected drift. For each scenario, the calculation methods for various production costs—including inspection, quality control, maintenance, and downtime costs—will be derived in detail. Finally, the corresponding expected total cost per unit time (ETC) expressions will be formulated to form the basis of the integrated optimization model.

## 3. The EWMA Control Charting Scheme

Note that most existing studies focus on using the $\overline{X}$ control chart to reduce the complexity of designing the integrated model for production, maintenance, and quality control policy, regardless of the detection efficiency. Therefore, the EWMA charting scheme is considered in this paper.

First, the EWMA control chart is briefly introduced in this section. Assume that $(X_1, X_2, \ldots, X_n)$ is a group of random samples collected from a normally distributed process with mean $u_0$ and standard deviation $\sigma$. $\overline{X_t}$ is the sample mean, and it can be denoted as

$$\overline{X_t} = \frac{1}{n}\sum_{j=1}^{n} x_j, j = 1, \ldots n,\ t = 1, 2, \ldots.$$

It is clear that $\overline{X_t} \sim N\left(u_0, \frac{\sigma^2}{n}\right)$. Then, the EWMA statistic can be established as follows:

$$Z_t = r\overline{X_t} + (1-r)Z_{t-1}, t = 1, 2, \ldots,$$

where $Z_0 = u_0$, and the asymptotic upper and lower control limits of the EWMA control chart are

$$UCL = u_0 + L\frac{\sigma}{\sqrt{n}}\sqrt{\frac{r}{2-r}},\ \text{and}\ LCL = u_0 - L\frac{\sigma}{\sqrt{n}}\sqrt{\frac{r}{2-r}}$$

The design of an EWMA control chart consists of sample size ($n$), coefficient of control limits ($L$), smoothing parameter ($r$). Further, the probability can be calculated by the Markov chain method. When the EWMA control chart signals at the $i$-th sample, we obtained

$$p(rl = i|\delta) = p_{initial}(R_{i-1} - R_i)\mathbf{1}, \tag{1}$$

where $rl$ is the run length of the control chart under the shift $\delta$, $p_{initial}$ is a vector of initial probabilities, $R$ is a $(t-1, t-1)$ matrix containing transient states. $\mathbf{1}$ is the $(t-1) \times 1$ vector of unities. Detailed calculation of Equation (1) can be found in the Supplementary Materials. Moreover, the expected average run length ($ARL$) can be expressed by

$$ARL = E(rl|\delta) = \sum_{rl=1}^{\infty} rl \times p(rl|\delta).$$

Thus, the $ARL$ for the IC process ($ARL_0$) can be calculated by setting $\delta = 0$, and $ARL$ for the OOC process ($ARL_1$) can also be computed when shift $\delta$ is not equal to zero.

## 4. Different Scenarios in One Production Run Process

In manufacturing processes, the system is affected by some assignable causes, and usually, the time to the occurrence of an assignable cause is assumed to follow a continuous distribution, where an exponential distribution is commonly used in modeling the occurrence of quality shifts (Salmasnia et al. [16], Seif [46], Duffuaa et al. [40], Huang et al. [14]. Note that, in Bahria et al. [35], the failure mechanism has not been considered, resulting in that the corresponding effect of the frequency of assignable causes on the production cost is not clear. Therefore, the failure mechanism is considered in this paper, and possible scenarios due to an assignable cause that happen in one production cycle are described close to real production processes. Especially, we adopted three scenarios which have been considered in Pan et al. [22], Salmasnia et al. [15], Salmasnia et al. [16], Huang et al. [14], and Hadian et al. [17].

**Scenario 1:**

As shown in Figure 1, the production process starts in the IC state, and the quality shift does not occur from the beginning of the production cycle to the time when the inventory is built up to the maximum level $I_{max}$, where the number of sampling inspections $k$ is taken in this period. In this situation, PM action is carried out to guarantee the reliability of the manufacturing equipment. The occurrence probability of scenario 1 ($S_1$) is expressed as follows:

$$p(S_1) = 1 - F(kh) = e^{-\lambda kh}. \quad (2)$$

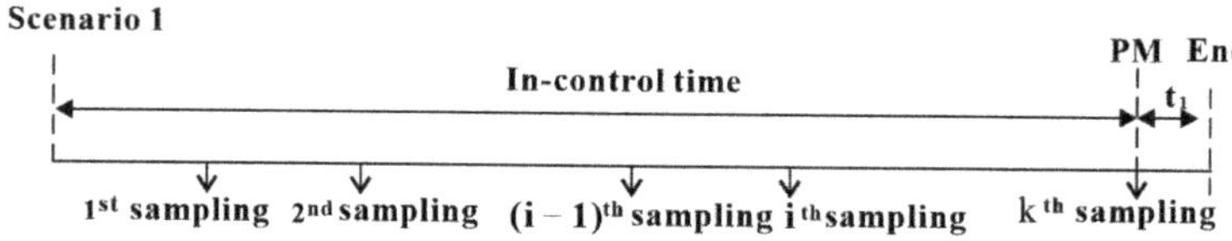


**Figure 1.** The process of EWMA monitoring and maintenance in Scenario 1.

The expected IC and OOC time in $S_1$ can be obtained as

$$E(t_{IC}|S_1) = kh,\ E(t_{OOC}|S_1) = 0. \quad (3)$$

and the expected total time $E(t|S_1)$ is

$$E(t|S_1) = E(t_{IC}|S_1) + E(t_{OOC}|S_1) = kh \quad (4)$$

**Scenario 2:**

Figure 2 shows that the production process starts in the IC state and shifts to the OOC state at time $t$ between interval $[(i-1)h,\ ih]$ when an assignable cause occurs, and the process parameter changes from $\mu_0$ to $\mu_1$ with $\mu_1 = \mu_0 + \delta\sigma$. The chart can detect the shift before the end of the $k^{\text{th}}$ sampling, that is, the control chart first gives alarm at the $(i+j-1)^{\text{th}}$ sampling, $j = 1, 2, \ldots, k-i+1$. When the process shift is detected, CM is adopted to restore the machine to an as-good-as-new state. The occurrence probability of scenario 2 ($S_2$) is given as follows:

$$\begin{aligned} p(S_2) &= \textstyle\sum_{i=1}^{k} \sum_{j=1}^{k-i+1} \int_{(i-1)h}^{ih} \lambda e^{-\lambda t} dt p(j|\delta) \\ &= \textstyle\sum_{i=1}^{k} \sum_{j=1}^{k-i+1} \left(e^{-\lambda(i-1)h} - e^{-\lambda ih}\right) p(j|\delta). \end{aligned} \quad (5)$$

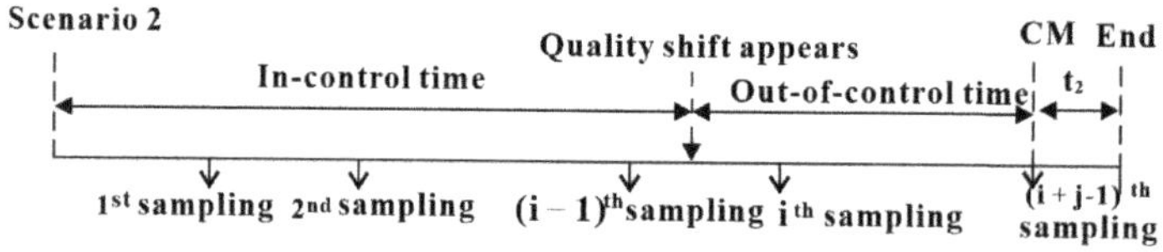


**Figure 2.** The process of EWMA monitoring and maintenance in scenario 2.

The expected IC and OOC time in $S_2$ are

$$E(t_{IC}|S_2) = \frac{\sum_{i=1}^{k} \sum_{j=1}^{k-i+1} \left(e^{-\lambda(i-1)h} - e^{-\lambda ih}\right) p(j|\delta)((i-1)h + \tau)}{P(S_2)} \quad (6)$$

and

$$E(t_{OOC}|S_2) = \frac{\sum_{i=1}^{k} \sum_{j=1}^{k-i+1} \left(e^{-\lambda(i-1)h} - e^{-\lambda ih}\right) p(j|\delta)(jh - \tau)}{P(S_2)}, \quad (7)$$

and the expected total time $E(t|S_2)$ is

$$E(t|S_2) = E(t_{IC}|S_2) + E(t_{OOC}|S_2), \quad (8)$$

where $\tau$ is the average time from the last sampling to the occurrence of the shift, and according to the assumption that the time to the occurrence of an assignable cause follows the exponential distribution with parameter $\lambda$, therefore, $\tau$ is derived as follows:

$$\tau = \frac{\int_h^{2h} (t-h)\lambda e^{-\lambda h} dt}{\int_h^{2h} \lambda e^{-t} dt} = \frac{1-(1+\lambda h)e^{-\lambda h}}{\lambda(1-e^{-\lambda h})}. \tag{9}$$

**Scenario 3:**

Figure 3 shows that the production process starts in an IC state and shifts to an OOC state at time $t$ between interval $[(i-1)h,\ ih]$ when an assignable cause occurs, and the process parameter changes from $\mu_0$ to $\mu_1$ with $\mu_1 = \mu_0 + \delta\sigma$. However, due to the limits of the control chart's capability, the monitoring scheme is unable to detect the quality shift until the end of the $k^{\text{th}}$ sampling inspection and the inventory level reaches the maximum value $I_{max}$. The process continues with no signal alert until the PM is scheduled. But, after checking and finding the true quality shift, a CM is carried out to replace the PM for repairing the machine to an as-good-as-new state. In this case, the occurrence probability of scenario 3 ($S_3$) can be given as

$$\begin{aligned} p(S_3) &= \textstyle\sum_{i=1}^{k} \int_{(i-1)h}^{ih} \lambda e^{-\lambda t} dt \left(1 - \sum_{j=1}^{k-i+1} p(j|\delta)\right) \\ &= \textstyle\sum_{i=1}^{k} \left(e^{-\lambda(i-1)h} - e^{-\lambda ih}\right)\left(1 - \sum_{j=1}^{k-i+1} p(j|\delta)\right). \end{aligned} \tag{10}$$

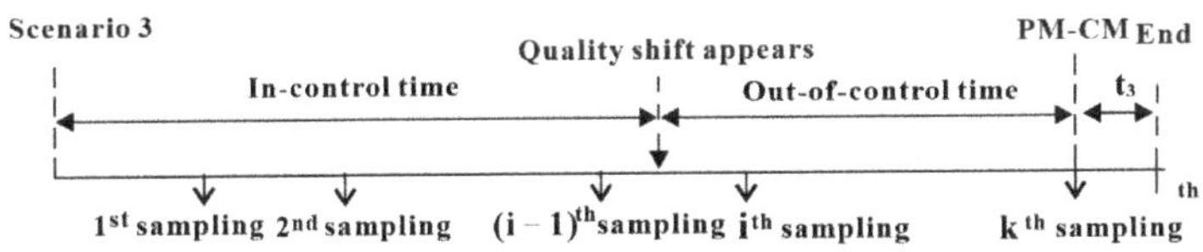


**Figure 3.** The process of EWMA monitoring and maintenance in scenario 3.

The expected IC and OOC time in $S_3$ are easily obtained as

$$E(t_{IC}|S_3) = \frac{\sum_{i=1}^{k} \left(e^{-\lambda(i-1)h} - e^{-\lambda ih}\right)\left(1 - \sum_{j=1}^{k-i+1} p(j|\delta)\right)((i-1)h + \tau)}{p(S_3)} \tag{11}$$

and

$$E(t_{OOC}|S_3) = \frac{\sum_{i=1}^{k} \left(e^{-\lambda(i-1)h} - e^{-\lambda ih}\right)\left(1 - \sum_{j=1}^{k-i+1} p(j|\delta)\right)((i+j-1)h - \tau)}{p(S_3)}. \tag{12}$$

and the expected total time $E(t|S_3)$ is

$$E(t|S_3) = E(t_{IC}|S_3) + E(t_{OOC}|S_3). \tag{13}$$

## 5. Production Cost and Production Cycle Time Analysis

The issue of production costs has long been the core concern for enterprises due to limited human, material, and financial resources, which motivates many researchers to establish an economic integration design of the production, maintenance, and quality control policy. Therefore, the production cost and production cycle time will be analyzed in this section for constructing the integrated model.

The expected production cost of one production cycle contains the expected quality loss cost, the expected sampling cost, the expected maintenance cost, the expected false alarm cost, the expected setup cost, and the expected cost of inventory control. As the production run time and the probability of each scenario are given in Section 4, the expected production cost and expected production cycle time for one production cycle will be introduced through the following expressions.

**(1) Expected quality loss cost**

The defective items (or the non-conforming products) continues even when the process is monitored by the control chart. However, when the process is in the IC state, the proportion of the defective products is very low. When a process shift occurs, the key characteristic parameters of the products may deviate from the designed value, resulting in defective products being produced. There is an obvious fact that the quality loss cost of the OOC process is higher than that of the IC process. The quality loss cost can be expressed as

$$E(C_Q) = \sum_{i=1}^{3} E(C_{Qi}|S_i)p(S_i), i = 1,2,3, \tag{14}$$

and

$$E(C_{Qi}|S_i) = \begin{cases} C_I E(t_{IC}|S_i), & for\ i = 1, \\ C_I E(t_{IC}|S_i) + C_O E(t_{OOC}|S_i), & for\ i = 2,3, \end{cases} \tag{15}$$

where $C_I$ and $C_O$ are the quality loss per time unit in the IC state and OOC state, and $C_I$ and $C_O$ can be estimated by the Taguchi quality loss function (Pan et al. [19]).

**(2) Expected sampling cost**

Sampling cost happens when the control chart plots based on the sampling data to see whether the production process is in the IC state. To compute the sampling cost in each scenario, the average number of samplings needs to be found. From Figures 1–3, we obtained that the numbers of samplings in scenario 1 and scenario 3 are $k$. However, the number of samplings for scenario 2 is equal to $\frac{(E(t_{IC}|S_3) + E(t_{OOC}|S_3))}{h}$, where a true signal is detected before the $k$th sampling. Thus, the average cost of sampling is given by

$$E(C_s) = \sum_{i=1}^{3} E(C_{si}|S_i)p(S_i),\ i = 1,2,3, \tag{16}$$

and

$$E(C_{si}|S_i)p(S_i) = \begin{cases} k(C_F + C_S n), & for\ i = 1,3, \\ (C_F + C_S n)\dfrac{(E(t_{IC}|S_3) + E(t_{OOC}|S_3))}{h}, & for\ i = 2, \end{cases} \tag{17}$$

where $(C_F + C_S n)$ is the summation of the fixed and variable cost of each sampling.

**(3) Expected maintenance cost**

The maintenance cost is different in three scenarios. As shown in Figure 3, the process is always in an IC state until the production stops and the PM cost will be included in scenario 1. However, in scenario 2, the process shift occurs and the control chart gives an alarm signal, therefore, the cost of CM should be considered. The maintenance cost of scenario 3 will be higher than the maintenance cost of scenario 2 because the process experiences both PM and CM actions. Therefore, the maintenance cost can be obtained as follows:

$$E(C_M) = \sum_{i=1}^{3} E(C_{Mi}|S_i)p(S_i), for\ i = 1,2,3, \tag{18}$$

where

$$E(C_{Mi}|S_i) = C_i,\ for\ i = 1,2,3, \tag{19}$$

and $C_i$ represents the cost of maintenance in scenario $i$.

**(4) Expected false alarm cost**

A false alarm happens when the EWMA monitoring statistic exceeds the surveillance limits but the process is in the IC state. The false alarm exists because the control chart is constructed based on the theory of hypothesis testing, therefore, the cost of the false alarm should be taken into account, and it can be expressed as follows:

$$E(C_{Fa}) = \sum_{i=1}^{3} E(C_{Fai}|S_i)p(S_i), \tag{20}$$

where

$$E(C_{Fai}|S_i) = \begin{cases} C_f k\alpha, & for\ i = 1, \\ C_f\left[\dfrac{\sum_{i=1}^{k}\left(e^{-\lambda(i-1)h} - e^{-\lambda ih}\right)\left(\sum_{j=1}^{k-i+1} p(j|u_0,\delta)\right)(i-1)\alpha}{p(S_2)}\right], & for\ i = 2, \\ C_f\left[\dfrac{\sum_{i=1}^{k}\left(e^{-\lambda(i-1)h} - e^{-\lambda ih}\right)\left(1 - \sum_{j=1}^{k-i+1} p(j|u_0,\delta)\right)(i-1)\alpha}{p(S_3)}\right], & for\ i = 3, \end{cases} \tag{21}$$

and $C_f$ represents the cost of inspecting a false alarm, and $\alpha$ is the false alarm rate.

**(5) Expected setup cost**

The expected setup cost in one production cycle can be given as

$$E(C_o) = \sum_{i=1}^{3} E(C_{oi}|S_i)p(S_i), for\ i = 1, 2, 3, \tag{22}$$

where

$$E(C_{oi}|S_i) = S, \tag{23}$$

$S$ is the setup cost per production cycle.

**(6) Expected inventory control cost**

A machine produces items at a rate of P. The products will be 100% inspected and defective products are discarded. We assume that the proportion of average defective items of the OOC process is a constant $\beta$, where $\beta$ can be estimated from historical data (Bahria et al. [35]). However, for the IC process it is reasonably assumed that a very low proportion of defective products are produced, and we can ignore defective products. The expected average inventory control cost will be calculated for all possible conditions in one production cycle. Depending on whether the maintenance duration is less or longer than the inventory depletion period, two cases consisting of shortage and without shortage in one production process are considered, and each case under different production scenarios will be given as follows.

**(a) Scenario 1**

■ **Case: without shortage:**

Figure 4a shows the evolution of the average inventory level for the case without shortage in scenario 1. The expected inventory level contains two parts, $Z_1$ and $Z_2$, which are respectively the average inventory holding level during the production uptime and production downtime. The duration of PM $t_1$ is smaller than $\frac{kh(P-D)}{D}$, where $\frac{kh(P-D)}{D}$ represents the time from the inventory level $I_{max}$ to zero. Therefore, we have the following calculations:

$$t_1 \leq \frac{kh(P-D)}{D},$$

$$Z_1 = \frac{(P-D)(kh)^2}{2},\ Z_2 = \frac{[kh(P-D)]^2}{2D}. \tag{24}$$

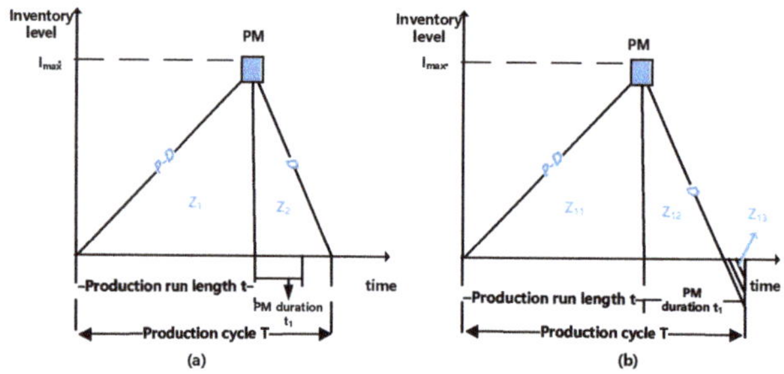


**Figure 4.** Evolution of the inventory level in scenario 1: (**a**) case: without shortage; (**b**) case: with shortage.

The average inventory level in case (a) for scenario 1 is given by $\Gamma_1 = Z_1 + Z_2$.

- **Case: with shortage**

Figure 4b shows the evolution of the expected inventory level for the case of shortage in scenario 1. In this scenario, the PM period is larger than the inventory consumption period, which can be expressed by

$$t_1 > \frac{kh(P-D)}{D}$$

Let $\Gamma_1'$ be the average inventory level. $\Gamma_1'$ contains the inventory holding level $Z_{11}$ and $Z_{12}$. Three functions, $Z_{11}$, $Z_{12}$, and $Z_{13}$, are given as

$$Z_{11} = \frac{(P-D)(kh)^2}{2},\ Z_{12} = \frac{[kh(P-D)]^2}{2D},\ Z_{13} = D\left[t_1 - \frac{kh(P-D)}{D}\right]. \tag{25}$$

Therefore, the average inventory level in case (b) of scenario 1 is $\Gamma_1' = Z_{11} + Z_{12}$, and $\Psi_1 = Z_{13}$ denotes the average shortage level.

**(b) Scenario 2**

- **Case: without shortage:**

From Figure 5a, we can see that the duration of CM $t_2$ is less than or equal to the duration of the inventory consumption, and it can be expressed by

$$t_2 \leq \frac{E(t|S_2)(P-D) - \beta P E(t_{OOC}|S_2)}{D},$$

where $E(t_{OOC}|S_2)$ and $E(t|S_2)$ can be found in Equations (7) and (8). Let $Z_3$ and $Z_4$ respectively be the average inventory level during the production uptime and production downtime. $Z_3$ and $Z_4$ are described as

$$Z_3 = \frac{kh(P-D)E(t|S_2)}{2}, \tag{26}$$

$$Z_4 = \frac{[(P-D)E(t|S_2) - \beta P E(t_{OOC}|S_2)]^2}{2D} \tag{27}$$

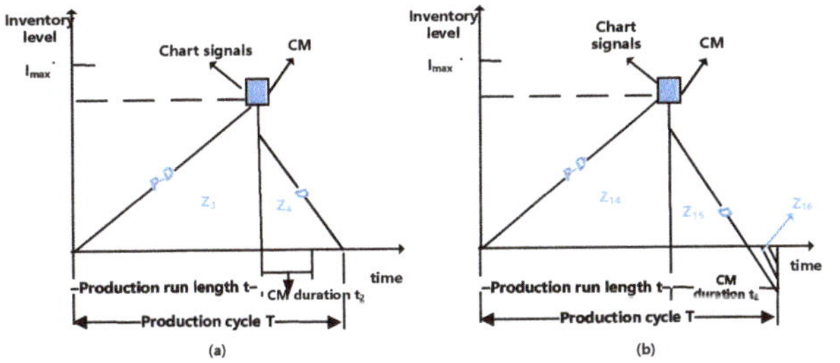


**Figure 5.** Evolution of the inventory level in scenario 2: (**a**) case: without shortage; (**b**) case: with shortage.

The average inventory level is $\Gamma_2 = Z_3 + Z_4$ for the case of without shortage in scenario 2.

- **Case: with shortage**

For the case of shortage in scenario 2, the production process is disrupted by CM, and the period of CM $t_2$ is longer than the period of inventory consumption (see Figure 5b).

$$t_2 > \frac{E(t|S_2)(P-D) - \beta PE(t_{OOC}|S_2)}{D},$$

The average inventory level $Z_{14}$, $Z_{15}$ and the average shortage level $Z_{16}$ are respectively expressed by

$$Z_{14} = \frac{(P-D)E(t|S_2)^2}{2}, \tag{28}$$

$$Z_{15} = \frac{[(P-D)E(t|S_2) - \beta PE(t_{OOC}|S_2)]^2}{2D}, \tag{29}$$

$$Z_{16} = D\left[t_2 - \frac{(P-D)E(t|S_2) - \beta PE(t_{OOC}|S_2)}{D}\right]. \tag{30}$$

Finally, the average inventory level in case (b) for scenario 2 is $\Gamma_2' = Z_{14} + Z_{15}$, and $\Psi_2 = Z_{16}$ is the average shortage level.

**(c) Scenario 3**

- **Case: without shortage:**

As we can see from Figure 6a, the expected inventory level in one production cycle can be divided into two parts, $Z_5$ and $Z_6$, and the maintenance duration is less than or equal to $\frac{kh(P-D)-\beta PE(t_{OOC}|S_3)}{D}$. The $\frac{kh(P-D)-\beta PE(t_{OOC}|S_3)}{D}$ denotes the inventory consumption period starting from the time that the inventory is built up to the maximum value to the end of the production cycle.

$$t_3 \le \frac{kh(P-D) - \beta PE(t_{OOC}|S_3)}{D},$$

$Z_5$ and $Z_6$ are respectively obtained as

$$Z_5 = \frac{(P-D)(kh)^2}{2}, \tag{31}$$

$$Z_6 = \frac{[kh(P-D) - \beta PE(t_{OOC}|S_3)]^2}{2D}. \tag{32}$$

Therefore, the average inventory level in case (a) for scenario 3 is $\Gamma_3 = Z_4 + Z_5$.

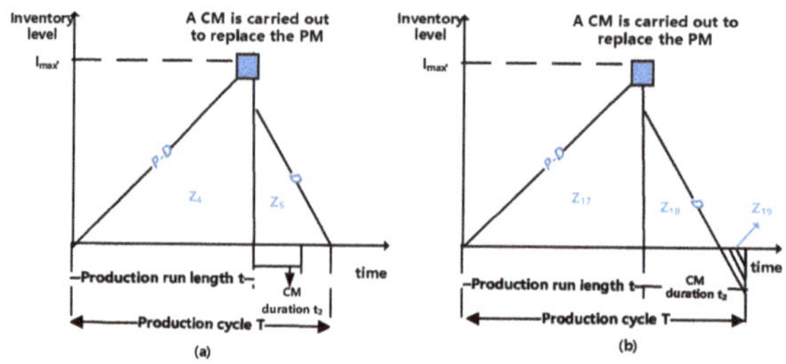


**Figure 6.** Evolution of the inventory level in scenario 3: (**a**) case: without shortage; (**b**) case: with shortage.

■ **Case: with shortage**

From Figure 6b, we can find that the period of maintenance $t_3$ is longer than the period of inventory consumption, where the relationship between $t_3$ and the period of the consumption of the inventory can be defined as

$$t_3 > \frac{kh(P-D) - \beta PE(t_{OOC}|S_3)}{D}.$$

The equation for the average inventory level and shortage level is obtained using the following formula,

$$Z_{17} = \frac{(P-D)(kh)^2}{2}, \tag{33}$$

$$Z_{18} = \frac{[(P-D)kh - \beta PE(t_{OOC}|S_3)]^2}{2}, \tag{34}$$

$$Z_{19} = D\left[t_3 - \frac{(P-D)kh - \beta PE(t_{OOC}|S_3)}{D}\right]. \tag{35}$$

Therefore, the average inventory level in case (b) of scenario 3 is $\Gamma_3' = Z_{15} + Z_{16}$, and $\Psi_3 = Z_{19}$ is the average shortage level.

Following the above analysis of the average inventory level, we define $E(I)$ as the average inventory control cost, where $E(I)$ contains the average inventory holding cost and the average shortage cost. For easy expression, we give three indicators in three scenarios as follows:

$$\phi_1 = \begin{cases} 1,\ if\ t_1 \le \dfrac{kh(P-D)}{D}, \\ 0,\ if\ t_1 > \dfrac{kh(P-D)}{D}, \end{cases} \tag{36}$$

$$\phi_2 = \begin{cases} 1,\ if\ t_2 \le \dfrac{E(t|S_2)(P-D) - \beta PE(t_{OOC}|S_2)}{D}, \\ 0,\ if\ t_2 > \dfrac{E(t|S_2)(P-D) - \beta PE(t_{OOC}|S_2)}{D}, \end{cases} \tag{37}$$

$$\phi_3 = \begin{cases} 1,\ if\ t_3 \le \dfrac{kh(P-D) - \beta PE(t_{OOC}|S_3)}{D}, \\ 0,\ if\ t_3 > \dfrac{kh(P-D) - \beta PE(t_{OOC}|S_3)}{D}, \end{cases} \tag{38}$$

Finally, we define $E(I)$ as follows:

$$E(I) = \sum_{i=1}^{3} \phi_i B\Gamma_i p(S_i) + \sum_{i=1}^{3} (1-\phi_i)\left(B\Gamma_i' p(S_i) + B_1 \Psi_i p(S_i)\right). \tag{39}$$

**(7) Expected production cycle time**

In different scenarios, we can find that the expected production cycle time depends on the production uptime, the maintenance duration, and the period of the inventory consumption. Therefore, the expected production cycle time $ET$ can be given as

$$ET = \sum_{i=1}^{3} E(T_i|S_i)p(S_i), \, for \; i = 1, 2, 3, \tag{40}$$

where $E(T_i|S_i)$ is the average length of one production cycle in the occurrence of scenario $i$, and $E(T_i|S_i)$ can be expressed as follows:

$$E(T_1|S_1) = \begin{cases} kh + \dfrac{kh(P-D)}{D}, & if \; t_1 \leq \dfrac{kh(P-D)}{D}, \\ kh + t_1, & if \; t_1 > \dfrac{kh(P-D)}{D}, \end{cases} \tag{41}$$

$$E(T_2|S_2) = \begin{cases} E(t|S_2) + \dfrac{E(t|S_2)(P-D) - \beta P E(t|S_2)}{D}, & if \; t_2 \leq \dfrac{E(t|S_2)(P-D) - \beta P E(t|S_2)}{D}, \\ E(t|S_2) + t_2, & if \; t_2 > \dfrac{E(t|S_2)(P-D) - \beta P E(t|S_2)}{D}, \end{cases} \tag{42}$$

$$E(T_3|S_3) = \begin{cases} kh + \dfrac{kh(P-D) - \beta Pkh}{D}, & if \; t_3 \leq \dfrac{kh(P-D) - \beta Pkh}{D}, \\ kh + t_3, & if \; t_3 > \dfrac{kh(P-D) - \beta Pkh}{D}. \end{cases} \tag{43}$$

## 6. Integrated Model of Production, EWMA Control, and Maintenance Policy

In this section, the integrated model of the production, EWMA control, and maintenance policy will be established based on the expected total cost per time unit (ETC), namely, the ETC model. Based on the ETC model, the objective is to minimize the ETC to achieve an optimal production level under the given constraints of the inventory size, the false alarm rate, the ARL of the OOC process, the sampling interval, the sample size, and sampling number. Further, the solution method will be introduced to deal with this optimization problem.

**(1) The objective function and constraints**

The expected total cost $EC$ per production cycle consists of expected quality loss cost $E(Q)$, expected sampling inspection cost $E(S)$, expected maintenance cost $E(M)$ and expected false alarm cost $E(C_{Fa})$, expected cost of setup cost $E(O)$, and expected inventory control cost $E(I)$, and $EC$ can be expressed by

$$EC = E(Q) + E(S) + E(M) + E(C_{Fa}) + E(O) + E(I). \tag{44}$$

The average expected total cost of one production cycle per time unit (ETC) is

$$ETC = \frac{EC}{ET}, \tag{45}$$

To make the integrated model close to the real production process, sampling number $k$, sampling interval $h$, sample size $n$, smooth parameter, inventory size $I$, and type I error $\alpha$ (Salmasnia et al. [16]; Zhou et al. [47]; Wan et al. [48]) and ARL of OOC processes $ARL_1$ are limited. Especially, the maximum value of the false alarm $\alpha_0$ (Salmasnia et al. [16]) and the maximum ARL of the OOC process $ARL_{1,max}$ (Pan et al. [22], Salmasnia et al. [15]) should be prefixed. The optimization problem of the integrated model is formulated as follows:

$$Min\{ETC\}, \tag{46}$$

subject to

$$k_{min} \leq k \leq k_{max}, \tag{47}$$

$$h_{min} \leq h \leq h_{max}, \tag{48}$$

$$n_{min} \leq n \leq n_{max}, \tag{49}$$

$$0 < r < 1, \tag{50}$$

$$I \leq I_{max}, \tag{51}$$

$$\alpha \leq \alpha_0, \tag{52}$$

$$ARL_1 < ARL_{1,max}, \tag{53}$$

$$h > 0, L > 0, n \in N^+, k \in N^+, \tag{54}$$

where $I = kh(P - D)$.

**(2) Solution approach**

The complexity of the presented integrated model leads to the difficulty of solving the objective function, where both the non-linear target and non-linear constraint functions increase the complexity of the model. In the literature, many efficient algorithms were developed to solve the optimization problem when establishing an integrated design of production, maintenance, and quality control policy, for example, Pan et al. [22] used Pattern Search Tool in MATLAB 7.0. Charongrattanasakul and Pongpullponsak [11], Yin et al. [30], and Huang et al. [14] adopted the genetic algorithm (GA). Salmasnia et al. [15] and Salmasnia et al. [16] applied meta-heuristic algorithms, etc. Without loss of generality, the GA is adopted to solve the optimization problem defined in Equations (46)–(54). The solution steps using the GA are shown in Table 2:

**Table 2.** Genetic Algorithm for Optimal ETC.

| | |
|---|---|
| Step 1 | **Set model parameters. Specify the process parameters: quality shift rate** $\lambda$, initial mean $u_0$, standard deviation $\sigma$, mean shift magnitude $\delta$, and other relevant values. |
| Step 2 | **Configure GA parameters.** The iteration time, the population size, the crossover fraction, and the mutation probability parameters are predetermined. In this paper, we set (iteration time, population size, crossover fraction, mutation probability) = (200,100,0.8,0.1). |
| Step 3 | **Initialize population.** The procedure starts at randomly generating 100 solutions that satisfy the constraints (Equations (47)–(54)) described in Section 6. |
| Step 4 | **Evolute fitness.** For each individual, compute the fitness value using the objective function $ETC = \frac{EC}{ET}$. |
| Step 5 | While stopping criterion is not met:<br>1. **Select parents** using roulette wheel selection based on fitness.<br>2. **Perform crossover** on selected parents with probaility 0.8.<br>3. **Apply mutation** to offspring with probability 0.1.<br>4. **Evaluate new population** and compute fitness for each offspring.<br>5. **Replace population** with new offspring.<br>6. **Check stopping criterion:** halt if no improvement in ETC over 50 consecutive generations. |
| Step 6 | Return the best solution found and its corresponding ETC value. |

## 7. Case Study and Analysis

In Section 6, an integrated model for production, EWMA control, and maintenance policy is established, and the GA solution method is also provided. To show the application of the proposed model, first, a real example of a vibroseis equipment production process is introduced. Then, a comparative study is conducted between the integrated model established using the $\overline{X}$ control chart and the proposed model. Finally, the sensitivity analysis is performed to investigate the influence of key input parameters on the objective function and decision parameters.

**(1) Case study**

In this subsection, a real example of a vibroseis equipment production process is adopted to illustrate the application of the proposed model, where the vibroseis equipment's bolt is one of the widespread parts used in vibroseis equipment. Vibrators installed on trucks of a vibroseis continuously impact the ground to generate seismic waves. The bolts play a crucial role in fixing various structures. Therefore, the quality and lifespan of vibroseis bolts are of great importance. The hardness is one of the key quality characteristics of the vibroseis equipment's bolt and is mainly influenced by the heating temperature. Due to some assignable causes, the heating temperature will deviate from the target value, resulting in the hardness being unqualified and further leading to an increase in the proportion of defective bolts. Therefore, the EWMA control chart is adopted to monitor the heating temperature of the high-voltage rotor bolt production process.

To provide an optimal design of production, maintenance, and quality control policy for this bolt production process and minimize the production cost, the proposed integrated model is applied. According to the historical data and the information collected from engineers of the vibroseis equipment's bolt production process, some input parameters are given in Table 3.

**Table 3.** Input parameters for the vibroseis equipment's bolt production process.

| Parameter | $\lambda$ | $u_0$ | $\sigma$ | $C_F$ | $C_S$ | $C_I$ | $t_1$ | $\beta$ |
|---|---|---|---|---|---|---|---|---|
| value | 0.001/h | 800 °C | 1.5 | 30$ | 3$ | 300$ | 0.5h | 0.2 |
| Parameter | $C_O$ | $C_f$ | $C_1$ | $C_2$ | $C_3$ | $n_{max}$ | $t_2$ | $k_{max}$ |
| Value | 600$ | 800$ | 2000$ | 4000$ | 3500$ | 20 | 1.0h | 100 |
| Parameter | $\alpha_{max}$ | P | D | S | B | $t_3$ | $h_{max}$ | $B_1$ |
| Value | 0.01 | 100 | 60 | 100$ | 0.001$ | 1.1h | 20 | 0.1 |

From Table 3, we can see that the production process stays in an IC state for an average of 100 h because of the shift parameter $\lambda = 0.01$. Moreover, the average magnitude of the shift when the process goes OOC is approximately 0.25 standard variance. With variables detailed and constraints specified, the ETC and decision variables $\{k, h, n, L, r\}$ can be obtained by solving Expression (47) subject to

$$\alpha \leq 0.01, \tag{55}$$

$$ARL_1 < 10, \tag{56}$$

$$0 < r < 1, \tag{57}$$

$$5 \leq n \leq 20, \tag{58}$$

$$0 \leq h \leq 20, \tag{59}$$

$$0 \le k \le 100, \tag{60}$$

$$kh * (P - D) \le I_{max} = 12000, \tag{61}$$

$$h > 0, L > 0, n \in N^{+}, k \in N^{+}. \tag{62}$$

Figure 7 shows the iteration process of the GA for calculating the optimal ETC with $\delta = 0.25$. It can be seen that the values of the ETC under iterations 146–196 are approximately the same, which means that the ETC has not been remarkably improved during iterations 146–196. Therefore, it can be concluded with high confidence that the obtained results are very close to the real optimal solution. Finally, the optimal solution of decision parameters is $\{k, h, n, L, r\} = \{75, 4, 20, 1.6429, 0.3952\}$, and the ETC is 242.6404. It is suggested by these results that, during one production cycle, 75 sampling instances are needed, and one should take one sample of size 20 every 4 h. The coefficient of the control limits of the EWMA control chart should be set at 1.6429 and the smooth parameter is recommended to be 0.3952. Moreover, the economic production quantity (EPQ) for one production cycle is $EPQ = khP = 30000$, and the maximum inventory level is $E(I) = kh(P - D) = 12,000$, which means that the utilization rate of inventory capacity is 100%.

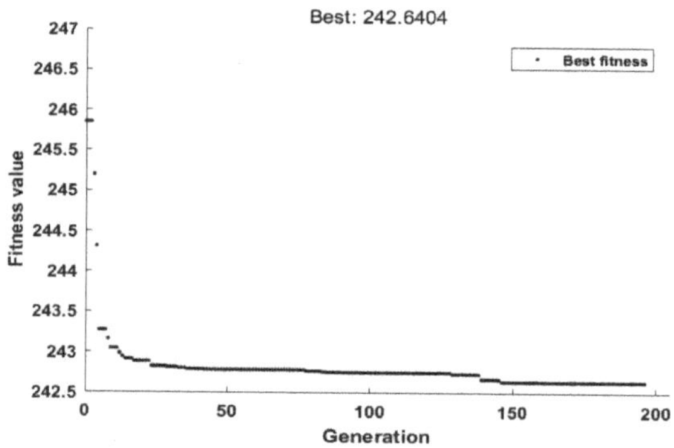


**Figure 7.** The iteration process of the GA for the case of $\delta = 0.25$.

**(2) Comparison**

Since there is no existing design for performing preventive maintenance (PM) based on information from the EWMA control chart and inventory level, a comparative study is conducted among three models: the model without monitoring, the model using the $\overline{X}$ chart, and the proposed method. The comparison results are presented in Table 4. In the model using the $\overline{X}$ chart, the assumptions, maintenance policies, and inventory control strategy are consistent with those of the proposed model using the EWMA chart. However, the decision parameters for the $\overline{X}$ control chart model include the sampling number sampling number $k_1$, sampling interval $h_1$, sample size $n_1$, and coefficient of the control limits $L_1$ of $\overline{X}$ control chart. As shown in Table 4, the proposed model is the most economical. Furthermore, the proposed model is superior to the model without monitoring.

It can also be concluded that the economic performance of the proposed integrated method based on the EWMA control chart is superior to the traditional integrated model based on the $\overline{X}$ control chart, because the ETC of our model is consistently less than the model of using the $\overline{X}$ control chart. For example, the ETC of our proposed model based on the EWMA control chart is 242.6404 when shift $\delta$ is 0.25, while the ETC of the model based on the $\overline{X}$ control chart is 250.7435.

**Table 4.** The comparison results of the proposed model, the model without monitoring, and the model based on the $\overline{X}$ chart.

| $\delta$ | Model Without Monitoring | | Model Using the $\overline{X}$ Chart | | The Proposed Model | |
|---|---|---|---|---|---|---|
| | $[k,h]$ | ETC | $[k_1,h_1,n_1,L_1]$ | ETC | $[k,h,n,L,r]$ | ETC |
| 0.25 | [15,19.9750] | 337.3120 | [62,4.8185,20,1.5455] | 250.7435 | [75,4,20,1.6429,0.3952] | **242.6404** |
| 0.5 | [15,19.9998] | 335.5869 | [69,4.3336,20,2.1574] | 235.2727 | [68,4.4118,20,2.2311,0.5931] | **226.8182** |
| 0.75 | [22,13.6364] | 335.9043 | [67,4.4662,16,2.4176] | 228.8077 | [71,4.2254,16,2.6863,0.5738] | **220.0941** |
| 1.0 | [18,16.6667] | 335.2473 | [73,4.0978,12,2.6348] | 225.4887 | [78,3.8462,11,2.7786,0.4579] | **216.4485** |
| 1.5 | [16,18.7501] | 335.0049 | [79,3.7927,7,2.8231] | 222.1195 | [88,3.4091,12,2.8021,0.1592] | **212.0050** |
| 2.0 | [15,20] | 334.9024 | [81,3.6933,5,2.9877] | 220.5056 | [72,4.1667,18,2.4179,0.0421] | **207.0293** |
| 3.0 | [16,18.7501] | 335.0047 | [80,3.7500,5,2.9997] | 220.0562 | [79,3.7975,7,2.3978,0.0473] | **203.2866** |

**(3) Sensitivity analysis**

In this subsection, the effect of parameters on the ETC is investigated. To quickly capture the relationship between the input parameters and the ETC under the same shift $\delta$, the experiment design is first considered. Second, the effects of $\delta$ on the ETC and decision parameters are also given.

The orthogonal experimental design (ODE) method is a well-known experimental design method, where both the characteristics of the uniformly dispersed and symmetrical comparability exist, and the ODE can significantly reduce the number of experiments when there are many influence factors and levels. Salmasnia et al. [13] once adopted a Taguchi ODE to analyze the effect of input parameters on two comparative models. Motivated by Salmasnia et al. [13] and Wan [45], a numerical experiment using the ODE is also taken in this subsection.

For exploring the effect of eleven parameters $\left\{\lambda, B, C_I, C_0, C_1, C_2, C_3,\ C_F, C_S, C_f, B_1\right\}$ on the ETC adequately, the number of parameter levels is set to 3. Detailed arrangements of experiments by ODE $L_{27}(3^{11})$ under the case of $\delta = 0.25$ are listed in Table 5, and corresponding results of decision parameters and the ETC are recorded. Especially, to better understand the influence of eleven input parameters on the ETC, the results of the range analysis are also summarized in the last line of Table 5. The values of I, II, and III are prepared for calculating the range value R, and W represents the summarization of I, II, and III under the same parameter. The range value R is expressed as $\mathrm{R} = \max\{\mathrm{I}, \mathrm{II}, \mathrm{III}\} - \min\{\mathrm{I}, \mathrm{II}, \mathrm{III}\}$ under the same parameter. We define that $ETC_{si}$ is the summation of ETC under the same parameter level $i$ $(i = 1, 2, 3)$ and I, II, and III are respectively the mean of $ETC_{si}$. For example, the first value 149.38 for row 29 in Table 4 is the mean of $ETC_{s1}$ under $\lambda = 0.001$ and $\mathrm{R} = \max\{149.38, 177.50, 200.01\} - \min\{149.38, 177.50, 200.01\} = 50.64$.

**Table 5.** The Orthogonal experimental $L_{27}(3^{11})$ design for sensitivity analysis when $\delta = 0.25$.

| Exp.No. | $\lambda$ | $B$ | $C_I$ | $C_0$ | $C_1$ | $C_2$ | $C_3$ | $C_F$ | $C_S$ | $C_f$ | $B_1$ | Decision Parameters | ETC |
|---|---|---|---|---|---|---|---|---|---|---|---|---|---|
| 1 | 0.001 | 0.0005 | 150 | 500 | 1500 | 3000 | 3000 | 25 | 3 | 700 | 0.1 | [32,9.375,20,1.7093,0.3505] | 113.0511 |
| 2 | 0.001 | 0.0005 | 150 | 500 | 2000 | 4000 | 3500 | 30 | 15 | 800 | 0.5 | [4,20,5,1.5440,0.0859] | 117.5981 |
| 3 | 0.001 | 0.0005 | 150 | 500 | 2500 | 5000 | 4000 | 35 | 27 | 900 | 0.9 | [5,19.9416,5,1.6281] | 123.2958 |
| 4 | 0.001 | 0.001 | 200 | 600 | 1500 | 3000 | 3000 | 30 | 15 | 800 | 0.9 | [3,19.9999,5,1.1947,0.0396] | 144.3174 |
| 5 | 0.001 | 0.001 | 200 | 600 | 2000 | 4000 | 3500 | 35 | 27 | 900 | 0.1 | [4,19.9969,5,1.2230,0.0421] | 149.8485 |
| 6 | 0.001 | 0.001 | 200 | 600 | 2500 | 5000 | 4000 | 25 | 3 | 700 | 0.5 | [35,8.5715,20,1.7263,0.3548] | 150.0100 |
| 7 | 0.001 | 0.0015 | 250 | 700 | 1500 | 3000 | 3000 | 35 | 27 | 900 | 0.5 | [3,20,5,1.2175,0.0416] | 178.0378 |
| 8 | 0.001 | 0.0015 | 250 | 700 | 2000 | 4000 | 3500 | 25 | 3 | 700 | 0.9 | [38,7.8947,5,1,0.6070] | 188.7280 |
| 9 | 0.001 | 0.0015 | 250 | 700 | 2500 | 5000 | 4000 | 30 | 15 | 800 | 0.1 | [4,19.9996,6,2.0237,0.5255] | 179.5152 |
| 10 | 0.005 | 0.0005 | 200 | 700 | 1500 | 4000 | 4000 | 25 | 15 | 900 | 0.1 | [4,19.9983,5,1.9427,0.4053] | 184.9048 |
| 11 | 0.005 | 0.0005 | 200 | 700 | 2000 | 5000 | 3000 | 30 | 27 | 700 | 0.5 | [3,16.4487,5,1.3739,0.0586] | 180.7463 |
| 12 | 0.005 | 0.0005 | 200 | 700 | 2500 | 3000 | 3500 | 35 | 3 | 800 | 0.9 | [40,7.5,20,1.2132,0.3855] | 172.0500 |

**Table 5.** *Cont.*

| Exp.No. | $\lambda$ | $B$ | $C_I$ | $C_0$ | $C_1$ | $C_2$ | $C_3$ | $C_F$ | $C_S$ | $C_f$ | $B_1$ | Decision Parameters | ETC |
|---|---|---|---|---|---|---|---|---|---|---|---|---|---|
| 13 | 0.005 | 0.001 | 250 | 500 | 1500 | 4000 | 4000 | 30 | 27 | 700 | 0.9 | [39,7.6923,5,1.1119,0.4922] | 210.2503 |
| 14 | 0.005 | 0.001 | 250 | 500 | 2000 | 5000 | 3000 | 35 | 3 | 800 | 0.1 | [40,7.5,20,1.4423,0.3591] | 199.7689 |
| 15 | 0.005 | 0.001 | 250 | 500 | 2500 | 3000 | 3500 | 25 | 15 | 900 | 0.5 | [38,7.8947,5,1.0406,0.3265] | 205.9329 |
| 16 | 0.005 | 0.0015 | 150 | 600 | 1500 | 4000 | 4000 | 35 | 3 | 800 | 0.5 | [40,7.1221,20,1.3005,0.3833] | 144.6626 |
| 17 | 0.005 | 0.0015 | 150 | 600 | 2000 | 5000 | 3000 | 25 | 15 | 900 | 0.9 | [3,16.8316,5,1.2092,0.0409] | 147.0074 |
| 18 | 0.005 | 0.0015 | 150 | 600 | 2500 | 3000 | 3500 | 30 | 27 | 700 | 0.1 | [3,19.8754,5,1.1997,0.004] | 152.1716 |
| 19 | 0.009 | 0.0005 | 250 | 600 | 1500 | 5000 | 3500 | 25 | 27 | 800 | 0.1 | [40, 7.5, 5.0, 1.0, 0.6614] | 239.3768 |
| 20 | 0.009 | 0.0005 | 250 | 600 | 2000 | 3000 | 4000 | 30 | 3 | 900 | 0.5 | [40,6.8831,20,1.2637,0.3776] | 212.8657 |
| 21 | 0.009 | 0.0005 | 250 | 600 | 2500 | 4000 | 3000 | 35 | 15 | 700 | 0.9 | [40,7.5,5,1.016,0.7822] | 228.5852 |
| 22 | 0.009 | 0.001 | 150 | 700 | 1500 | 5000 | 3500 | 30 | 3 | 900 | 0.9 | [40,5.4348,20,1.2776,0.3800] | 172.8708 |
| 23 | 0.009 | 0.001 | 150 | 700 | 2000 | 3000 | 4000 | 35 | 15 | 700 | 0.1 | [40,6.440603,5,1,0.8483] | 176.3145 |
| 24 | 0.009 | 0.001 | 150 | 700 | 2500 | 4000 | 3000 | 25 | 27 | 800 | 0.5 | [40,7.296,5,1,0.8625] | 188.4005 |
| 25 | 0.009 | 0.0015 | 200 | 500 | 1500 | 5000 | 3500 | 35 | 15 | 700 | 0.5 | [40,7.5,5,1.0181,0.6538] | 200.5966 |
| 26 | 0.009 | 0.0015 | 200 | 500 | 2000 | 3000 | 4000 | 25 | 27 | 800 | 0.9 | [40,7.5,5,1.0029,0.5732] | 197.0845 |
| 27 | 0.009 | 0.0015 | 200 | 500 | 2500 | 4000 | 3000 | 30 | 3 | 900 | 0.1 | [40,7.4725,20,1.1916,0.3786] | 184.0319 |
| I | 149.38 | 174.72 | 148.37 | 172.40 | 176.45 | 172.43 | 173.77 | 179.39 | 170.89 | 177.83 | 175.44 | | |
| II | 177.50 | 177.52 | 173.73 | 174.32 | 174.44 | 177.45 | 177.69 | 149.06 | 176.09 | 175.86 | 175.43 | W = 526.89 | |
| III | 200.01 | 174.65 | 204.78 | 180.17 | 176.00 | 177.02 | 175.43 | 174.80 | 179.91 | 173.20 | 176.02 | | |
| R | **50.64** | 2.88 | **56.41** | 7.77 | 2.01 | 5.02 | 3.91 | **30.33** | 9.02 | 4.63 | 0.59 | | |

For clear observation, the analysis of the effect of input parameters on the ETC is reported in Figure 8. Furthermore, the effects of $\delta$ on the ETC and decision parameters are plotted in Figure 9. The results of sensitivity analysis can be concluded as follows.

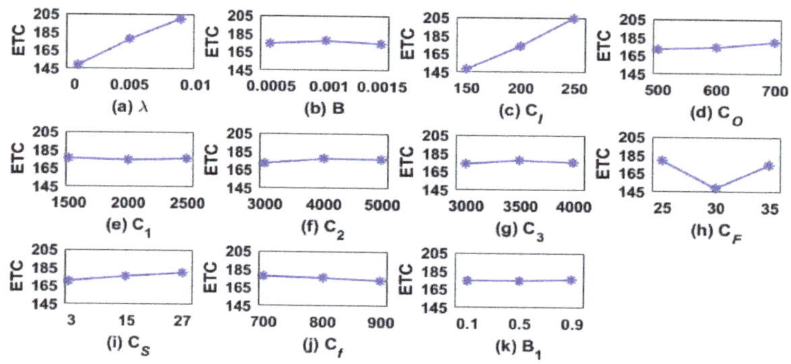


**Figure 8.** The graphical representation of the main effects of eleven input parameters on the ETC.

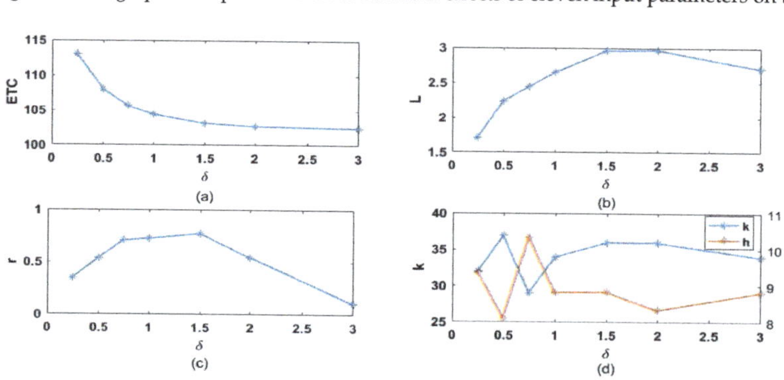


**Figure 9.** The sensitivity analysis: (**a**) The effect of $\delta$ on ETC; (**b**) The effect of $\delta$ on $L$; (**c**) The effect of $\delta$ on $r$; (**d**) The effect of $\delta$ on $k,\ h$.

- **Effect of eleven key parameters on the ETC**

From Figure 8, the following conclusions are obtained.

(1) As we can see in Figure 8, the parameter $\lambda$, the quality loss per time $C_I$ in IC processes, and the cost of fixed sampling $C_F$ are three of the most effective input parameters on the ETC. Moreover, the range analysis results show that the order of three influence factors is $C_I > \lambda > C_F$ (see the last line in Table 4).

(2) Eight parameters $B, C_o, C_1, C_2, C_3, C_s, C_{INSP}, B_1$ have a smaller effect on the ETC.

(3) Moreover, one can find that the increase in the parameters $\lambda$, $C_I$, $C_o$, and $C_s$ can lead to an increase in the ETC. This phenomenon is consistent with the common knowledge that the occurrence rate of shift $\lambda$ increases will increase the production cost per unit time. It is also obvious that increasing the quality loss cost parameter $C_I$ in the IC process, the quality loss cost parameter $C_o$ in the OOC process, and the varied sampling cost parameter $C_s$ will also increase the ETC.

(4) It is worth pointing out that the increase in $C_f$ can reduce the ETC because the decision parameters can be adjusted to compensate the impact of the increase in the $C_f$ on ETC.

- **Effect of $\delta$ on decision parameters and the ETC**

From Figure 9, we can obtain the following conclusions.

(1) When the magnitude of shift increases, the ETC decreases.

(2) Figure 9b shows that, as $\delta$ increases, the coefficient of the control limits of the EWMA control chart $L$ increases under moderate and small shifts $\delta \leq 1.5$.

(3) One can also conclude from Figure 9c that, as $\delta$ increases, the value of the smooth parameter $r$ increases under moderate and small shifts $\delta \leq 1.5$. However, the value of the smooth parameter shows a downward trend when $\delta > 1.5$.

There exists strong interaction between parameters $k$ and $h$ (see Figure 9d). The decision parameter $k$ increases (decreases), the parameter $h$ decreases (increases). It is because the process needs to satisfy the constraint $kh(P - D) \leq I_{max}$ that two decision parameters $(k, h)$ are adjusted to realize the minimized ETC.

## 8. Conclusions

In this paper, considering production quality and inventory constraints, we developed an integrated model of the production, EWMA control, and maintenance policy. The EWMA charting scheme is adopted to guarantee the process quality, efficiently detect moderate and small shifts, and reduce the quality loss cost. Considering the inventory size of the production process is finite in practice, a limited inventory size is considered in the proposed model. From the viewpoint of taking the opportunity to improve the state of the system, the PM action is carried out both considering the IC information given by the EWMA control chart and the inventory state. Finally, the proposed integrated model is applied to a vibroseis equipment's bolt production process, and the decision parameters are given for arranging high-quality production. The corresponding results show that the production costs for the bolt production process are greatly reduced, which demonstrates the proposed model is more economic. Therefore, the proposed model is more suitable to be recommended to production decision-makers.

Despite the above contributions, this study has several limitations that suggest valuable directions for future research. First, the model relies on the assumption of perfect detection, where faults are always identified once they occur. In practice, detection systems may exhibit varying reliability, and incorporating imperfect detection processes represents an important extension. Second, parameters such as the failure rate are treated as fixed, while in real settings they may change over time or be influenced by external factors; developing more dynamic models would enhance practical applicability. Furthermore, the current work assumes that the occurrence of an assignable cause does not affect the process variance, and the quality characteristic follows a normal distribution. Future studies could investigate joint monitoring schemes for both mean and variance under non-normal distributions. Moreover, this study focuses on a single quality characteristic and a single-machine system. Research could be extended to incorporate multiple quality characteristics and multimachine manufacturing environments, which pose greater complexity but are more representative of actual industrial systems. Finally, relaxing other simplifying assumptions, such as immediate maintenance resource availability, would further improve the model's robustness and broaden its applicability.

**Supplementary Materials:** The following supporting information can be downloaded at: https://www.mdpi.com/article/10.3390/axioms14090703/s1, Markov chain method for calculating run-length (RL) of the EWMA chart.

**Author Contributions:** Methodology, N.X.; Software, Z.L.; Writing—original draft, Y.Z. and N.X.; Writing—review and editing, N.X. and J.F. All authors have read and agreed to the published version of the manuscript.

**Funding:** This work was supported by Special project for cultivating scientific and technological innovation teams of Shandong Earthquake Agency (TD202303), Key tasks and special projects of Shandong Earthquake Agency (YW2305).

**Data Availability Statement:** Data are contained within the article.

**Conflicts of Interest:** The authors declare no conflicts of interest.

## References

1. Zhang, Y.Z.; Cai, H.; Zhang, J.J. Weighted-Likelihood-Ratio-Based EWMA Schemes for Monitoring Geometric Distributions. *J. Axioms* **2024**, *13*, 392. [CrossRef]
2. Alhidairah, S.; Alam, F.M.A.; Nassar, M. Failure Cause Analysis Under Progressive Type-II Censoring Using Generalized Linear Exponential Competing Risks Model with Medical and Industrial Applications. *Axioms* **2025**, *14*, 595. [CrossRef]
3. Jafari, N.; Lopes, A.M. Fault Detection and Identification with Kernel Principal Component Analysis and Long Short-Term Memory Artificial Neural Network Combined Method. *Axioms* **2023**, *12*, 583. [CrossRef]
4. Farahani, A.; Tohidi, H. Integrated optimization of quality and maintenance: A literature review. *Comput. Ind. Eng.* **2021**, *151*, 106924. [CrossRef]
5. Hafidi, N.; EI Barkany, A.; EI Mhamedi, A. Joint optimization of production, maintenance, and quality: A review and research trends. *Int. J. Ind. Eng. Manag.* **2023**, *14*, 282–296. [CrossRef]
6. Salameh, M.K.; Ghattas, R.E. Optimal just-in-time inventory for regular preventive maintenance. *J. Prod. Econ.* **2001**, *74*, 157–161. [CrossRef]
7. Goel, H.D.; Grievink, J.; Weijnen, M.P.C. Integrated optimal reliable design, production, and maintenance planning for multipurpose process plants. *Comput. Chem. Eng.* **2003**, *27*, 1543–1555. [CrossRef]
8. El-Ferik, S. Economic production lot-sizing for an unreliable machine under imperfect age-based maintenance policy. *Eur. J. Oper. Res.* **2008**, *186*, 150–163. [CrossRef]
9. Nahas, N. Buffer allocation and preventive maintenance optimization in unreliable production lines. *J. Intell. Manuf.* **2017**, *28*, 85–93. [CrossRef]
10. Ben-Daya, M.; Rahim, M. Effect of maintenance on the economic design of x control chart. *Eur. J. Oper. Res.* **2000**, *120*, 131–143. [CrossRef]
11. Charongrattanasakul, P.; Pongpullponsak, A. Minimizing the cost of integrated systems approach to process control and maintenance model by EWMA control chart using genetic algorithm. *Expert Syst. Appl.* **2011**, *38*, 5178–5186. [CrossRef]
12. Xiang, Y. Joint optimization of X-control chart and preventive maintenance policies: A discrete-time Markov chain approach. *Eur. J. Oper. Res.* **2013**, *229*, 382–390. [CrossRef]

13. Duan, C.Q.; Deng, C.; Gharaei, A.; Wu, J.; Wang, B.R. Selective maintenance scheduling under stochastic maintenance quality with multiple maintenance actions. *Int. J. Prod. Res.* **2018**, *56*, 7160–7178. [CrossRef]
14. Huang, S.; Yang, J.; Xie, M. A double-sampling SPM scheme for simultaneously monitoring of location and scale shifts and its joint design with maintenance strategies. *J. Manuf. Syst.* **2020**, *54*, 94–102. [CrossRef]
15. Salmasnia, A.; Abdzadeh, B.; Namdar, M. A joint design of production run length, maintenance policy and control chart with multiple assignable causes. *J. Manuf. Syst.* **2017**, *42*, 44–56. [CrossRef]
16. Salmasnia, A.; Kaveie, M.; Namdar, M. An integrated production and maintenance planning model under VP-T2 Hotelling chart. *Comput. Ind. Eng.* **2018**, *118*, 89–103. [CrossRef]
17. Hadian, S.M.; Farughi, H.; Rasay, H. Joint planning of maintenance, buffer stock and quality control for unreliable imperfect manufacturing systems. *Comput. Ind. Eng.* **2021**, *157*, 107304. [CrossRef]
18. Zhang, N.; Tian, S.; Xu, J.T.; Deng, Y.J.; Cai, K.Q. Optimal production lot-sizing and condition-based maintenance policy considering imperfect manufacturing process and inspection errors. *Comput. Ind. Eng.* **2023**, *177*, 108929. [CrossRef]
19. Ben-Daya, M.; Makhdoum, M. Integrated production and quality model under various preventive maintenance policies. *J. Oper. Res. Soc.* **1998**, *49*, 840–853. [CrossRef]
20. Rahim, M.A.; Ben-Daya, M. A generalized economic model for joint determination of production run: Inspection schedule and control chart design. *Int. J. Prod. Res.* **1998**, *36*, 277–289. [CrossRef]
21. Pandey, D.; Kulkarni, M.S.; Vrat, P. A methodology for joint optimization for maintenance planning, process quality and production scheduling. *Comput. Ind. Eng.* **2011**, *61*, 1098–1106. [CrossRef]
22. Pan, E.; Jin, Y.; Wang, S.H.; Cang, T. An integrated EPQ model based on a control chart for an imperfect production process. *Int. J. Prod. Res.* **2012**, *50*, 6999–7011. [CrossRef]
23. Bahria, N.; Chelbi, A.; Dridi, I.H.; Bouchriha, H. Maintenance and quality control integrated strategy for manufacturing systems. *Eur. J. Ind. Eng.* **2018**, *12*, 307–331. [CrossRef]
24. Salmasnia, A.; Hajihosseini, Z.; Namdar, M.; Mamashli, F. A joint determination of production cycle length, maintenance policy, and control chart parameters considering time value of money under stochastic shift size. *Sci. Iran.* **2020**, *27*, 427–447. [CrossRef]
25. Shi, L.X.; Lv, X.L.; He, Y.D.; He, Z. Optimising production, maintenance, and quality control for imperfect manufacturing systems considering timely replenishment. *Int. J. Prod. Res.* **2024**, *62*, 3504–3525. [CrossRef]
26. Serel, D.A.; Moskowitz, H. Joint economic design of EWMA control charts for mean and variance. *Eur. J. Oper. Res.* **2008**, *184*, 157–168. [CrossRef]
27. Ardakan, M.A.; Hamadani, A.Z.; Sima, M.; Reihaneh, M. A hybrid model for economic design of MEWMA control chart under maintenance policies. *Int. J. Adv. Manuf. Technol.* **2016**, *83*, 2101–2110. [CrossRef]
28. Hesamian, G.; Akbari, M.G.; Ranjbar, E. Exponentially weighted moving average control chart based on normal fuzzy random variables. *Int. J. Fuzzy Syst.* **2019**, *21*, 1187–1195. [CrossRef]
29. Sukparungsee, S.; Areepong, Y.; Taboran, R. Exponentially weighted moving average-moving average charts for monitoring the process mean. *PLoS ONE* **2020**, *15*, e0228208.
30. Yin, H.; Zhu, H.; Zhang, G.; Deng, Y. Design of MEWMA control chart for process subject to quality shift and equipment failure. In Proceedings of the 2015 9th International Conference on Application of Information and Communication Technologies (ICAICT), Rostov on Don, Russia, 14–16 October 2015; pp. 404–407.
31. Noman, M.A.; Al-Shayea, A.; Nasr, E.A.; Kaid, H.; Mahmoud, H.A. A model for maintenance planning and process quality control optimization based on EWMA and CUSUM control charts. *Trans. Famena* **2021**, *45*, 95–116. [CrossRef]
32. Nourelfath, M.; Nahas, N.; Ben-Daya, M. Integrated preventive maintenance and production decisions for imperfect processes. *Reliab. Eng. Syst. Saf.* **2016**, *148*, 21–31. [CrossRef]
33. Bouslah, B.; Gharbi, A.; Pellerin, R. Integrated production, sampling quality control and maintenance of deteriorating production systems with AOQL constraint. *Omega* **2016**, *61*, 110–126. [CrossRef]
34. Rivera-Gómez, H.; Gharbi, A.; Kenné, J.P.; Montaño-Arango, O.; Corona-Armenta, J.R. Joint optimization of production and maintenance strategies considering a dynamic sampling strategy for a deteriorating system. *Comput. Ind. Eng.* **2020**, *140*, 106273. [CrossRef]
35. Bahria, N.; Chelbi, A.; Bouchriha, H.; Dridi, I.H. Integrated production, statistical process control, and maintenance policy for unreliable manufacturing systems. *Int. J. Prod. Res.* **2019**, *57*, 2548–2570. [CrossRef]
36. He, Y.; Liu, F.; Cui, J.; Han, X.; Zhao, Y.; Chen, Z.; Zhang, A. Reliability-oriented design of integrated model of preventive maintenance and quality control policy with time-between-events control chart. *Comput. Ind. Eng.* **2019**, *129*, 228–238. [CrossRef]
37. Fakher, H.B.; Mourelfath, M.; Gendreau, M. A cost minimisation model for joint production and maintenance planning under quality constraints. *Int. J. Prod. Res.* **2017**, *55*, 2163–2176. [CrossRef]

38. Mokhtari, H.; Asadkhani, J. Extended economic production quantity models with preventive maintenance. *Sci. Iran.* **2020**, *27*, 3253–3264.
39. Lin, Y.H.; Chen, Y.C.; Wang, W.Y. Optimal Production Model for Imperfect Process with Imperfect Maintenance, Minimal Repair and Rework. *Int. J. Syst. Sci. Oper. Logist.* **2016**, *4*, 229–240. [CrossRef]
40. Duffuaa, S.; Kolus, A.; Al-Turki, U.; El-Khalifa, A. An Integrated Model of Production Scheduling, Maintenance and Quality for a Single Machine. *Comput. Ind. Eng.* **2020**, *142*, 106239. [CrossRef]
41. Wan, Q.; Zhu, M.; Qiao, H. A joint design of production, maintenance planning and quality control for continuous flow processes with multiple assignable causes. *CIRP J. Manuf. Sci. Technol.* **2023**, *43*, 214–226. [CrossRef]
42. Lv, X.; Shi, L.; He, Y.; He, Z. Joint optimization of production, inspection, and maintenance under finite time for smart manufacturing systems. *Reliab. Eng. Syst. Saf.* **2025**, *253*, 110490. [CrossRef]
43. Gaver, D.P. Operating Characteristics of a Simple Production, Inventory-Control Model. *Oper. Res.* **1961**, *9*, 635–649. [CrossRef]
44. Sobel, M.J. Optimal Average-cost Policy for a Queue with Start-up and Shut-down Costs. *Oper. Res.* **1969**, *17*, 145–162. [CrossRef]
45. Lin, H.J. An Economic Production Quantity Model with Backlogging and Imperfect Rework Process for Uncertain Demand. *Int. J. Prod. Res.* **2019**, *59*, 467–482. [CrossRef]
46. Seif, A. A New Markov Chain Approach for the Economic Statistical Design of the VSS T2 Control Chart. *Commun. Stat.-Simul. Comput.* **2019**, *48*, 200–218. [CrossRef]
47. Zhou, P.; Wei, H.; Zhang, H. Selective Reviews of Bandit Problems in AI via a Statistical View. *Mathematics* **2025**, *13*, 665. [CrossRef]
48. Wan, Q. Economic-statistical Design of Integrated Model of VSI Control Chart and Maintenance Incorporating Multiple Dependent State Sampling. *IEEE Access* **2020**, *8*, 87609–87620. [CrossRef]

axioms

MDPI

*Article*

# Performance Evaluation of Shiryaev–Roberts and Cumulative Sum Schemes for Monitoring Shape and Scale Parameters in Gamma-Distributed Data Under Type I Censoring

**He Li [1], Peile Chen [2], Ruicheng Ma [1,*] and Jiujun Zhang [1,*]**

1 School of Mathematics and Statistics, Liaoning University, Shenyang 110036, China; lihe@lnu.edu.cn
2 School of Mathematics and Statistics, Changchun University of Technology, Changchun 130012, China; peile145325@163.com
* Correspondence: maruicheng@lnu.edu.cn (R.M.); zjjly790816@163.com (J.Z.)

**Abstract:** This paper proposes two process monitoring schemes, namely the Shiryaev–Roberts (SR) procedure and the cumulative sum (CUSUM) procedure, to detect shifts in the shape and scale parameters of Type I right-censored Gamma-distributed lifetime data. The performance of the proposed schemes is compared with that of an exponentially weighted moving average (EWMA) control chart based on deep learning networks. The performance of the proposed schemes is evaluated under various censoring rates using Monte Carlo simulations, with the average run length (ARL) as the primary metric. Furthermore, the SR and CUSUM schemes are compared for both zero-state and steady-state shifts. Simulation results indicate that the SR and CUSUM procedures exhibit superior performance, with the SR scheme showing particular advantages when the actual shift is small, while the CUSUM chart proves more effective for identifying larger shifts. The shape parameter has a significant effect on the performance of the control charts such that a reduction in the shape parameter effectively improves the ability to capture early offsets. Increased censoring rates reduce detection sensitivity. To maintain $ARL_0$= 370, control limits $h$ adapt differentially. The SR and CUSUM charts with different censoring rates need to recalibrate the parameter to mitigate performance losses under higher censoring conditions. The monitoring performance of the SR and CUSUM chart is enhanced by an increase in sample size. Finally, a practical example is provided to illustrate the application of the proposed monitoring schemes.

**Keywords:** Type I censored; Shiryaev–Roberts; cumulative sum; statistical process monitoring; Gamma distribution

**MSC:** 62P30

## 1. Introduction

Statistical process monitoring (SPM) has been widely applied in various fields, including manufacturing, healthcare, environmental monitoring, energy, transportation, supply chain management, telecommunications, education, agriculture, and more. Among the tools used for SPM, control charts are particularly prominent for detecting changes in process parameters. The concept of control charts was first introduced by Dr. Shewhart in 1931 Shewhart [1], followed by Page's proposal of the cumulative sum (CUSUM) chart

Page [2]. Over the years, extensive research on control charts has yielded significant social and economic benefits. Their user-friendly nature and simplicity have contributed to their widespread adoption across numerous industries. Traditionally, control charts are designed under the assumption that quality characteristics follow a normal distribution. However, in practice, the variables of interest often deviate from normality and may instead follow non-normal distributions. In such cases, an alternative strategy is to monitor the inter-arrival time of nonconforming events, which may exhibit a skewed distribution, such as the Gamma distribution, rather than focusing solely on the occurrence of nonconforming events.

The Gamma distribution plays a pivotal role in SPM for monitoring time-to-event data, reliability analysis, and non-negative continuous processes. Its flexibility in modeling skewed data with shape and scale parameters makes it indispensable for industrial and healthcare applications. In recent decades, significant advancements have been made in Gamma-based control chart methodologies to enhance sensitivity in detecting process shifts. Zhang et al. [3] pioneered a Gamma control chart for monitoring the time of the $r$-th event using a stochastic shift model. Alevizakos and Koukouvinos [4] subsequently developed a one-sided double exponential weighted moving average chart, demonstrating superior performance over conventional EWMA and Shewhart charts in detecting downward shifts. For parameter-specific scenarios, Yang et al. [5] proposed an average time to signal unbiased Gamma chart through scale parameter hypothesis testing, while also introducing an ATS-unbiased version for unknown parameter single-phase monitoring. Hybrid methodologies have further expanded the toolkit: Chakraborty et al. [6] introduced a generally weighted moving average chart, later enhanced by Alevizakos et al. [7] through a double GWMA design that outperforms DEWMA and GWMA charts in detecting moderate-to-large shifts. Shah et al. [8] innovatively employed exact probability distributions of monitoring statistics for Gamma chart design. Recent advancements include triple-smoothing techniques: Alevizakos et al. [9] proposed triple EWMA charts where bilateral and lower-unilateral schemes excel in detecting small-to-medium downward shifts, while upper-unilateral schemes show heightened sensitivity to minor upward shifts. Complementing this, Lone and Shahab [10] developed triple homogeneously weighted moving average charts with both unilateral and bilateral implementations.

With the advancement of production processes, many products now exhibit superior quality and extended lifespans. Consequently, lifetime data are often collected under censoring to reduce testing time and costs. For instance, when testing the lifetime of electronic products, practitioners may set a predetermined termination time to conclude the test, thereby minimizing resource expenditure. However, since some units may not fail by the termination time, the resulting data are incomplete; these are known as Type I right-censored data. This area has attracted significant research attention. Steiner and Mackay [11] proposed an SPM scheme based on the concept of replacing each censored observation with a conditional expected value (CEV) to detect changes in the mean of censored lifetime data. Dickinson et al. [12] developed a CUSUM scheme for monitoring censored Weibull lifetimes, while ChoiMin-jae and LeeJaeheon [13] introduced a binomial CUSUM scheme for Type I right-censored Weibull lifetimes. Xu and Jeske [14] proposed a Shewhart-type SPM scheme based on the likelihood ratio test statistic. Yu et al. [15] proposed a modified EWMA control chart for monitoring the Weibull scale parameter based on Type I censored data. Zhang et al. [16] introduced an enhanced monitoring approach, the weighted adaptive cumulative sum (WACUSUM) chart, which integrates exponential weighting with maximum likelihood estimation to effectively track reliability processes characterized by Type I censored Weibull-distributed data. Ali et al. [17] developed EWMA and CUSUM control charts for monitoring Type I censored generalized exponential distributed data. More recently, Pei-Hsi [18] combined the EWMA CEV and conditional median (CM) chart with deep learning methods to enhance efficiency for monitoring Type I right-censored Gamma-distributed data. Jiang et al. [19] proposed a new adaptive exponentially weighted moving average control chart, called the AEWMA-LR control chart, for monitoring the quality characteristics of two-parameter exponential distributions based on Type II censored data. Nadi et al. [20] introduced two Shewhart-type control charts for monitoring the relative risk rate when the lifetimes of competing risks are independent Weibull random variables. Aditi et al. [21] developed Shewhart-type control charts for monitoring the percentiles of an inverse Pareto distribution (IPD) using the complete and middle-censored data sets.

The Shiryaev–Roberts (SR) procedure is a statistical method designed for detecting changes in process parameters, particularly in scenarios where early detection of shifts is critical. Initially proposed by Shiryaev [22] for Brownian motion, the SR procedure is based on the conditional average delay time criterion, which aims to minimize the expected delay in detecting a change while controlling the rate of false alarms. Due to its robustness and efficiency, the SR procedure has been widely studied and extended to various applications. Pollak and Siegmund [23] compared the performance of the CUSUM and SR procedures in detecting shifts in the mean of a Gaussian process when the in-control (IC) value of the mean is unknown. Additionally, Kenett and Pollak [24] introduced an SR scheme for monitoring non-homogeneous Poisson distributions. Srivastava and Wu [25] conducted a comparative study of the EWMA, CUSUM, and SR procedures for detecting mean shifts. Zhang et al. [26] proposed an SR-based program for the simultaneous detection of shifts in both the process mean and variability. Furthermore, Zhang et al. [27] developed adaptive-type SR procedures designed to monitor the process mean and variance across a range of shift sizes. Moustakides et al. [28] explored integral equations for performance metrics and utilized numerical approximations to evaluate the efficiency of SR procedures. Ottenstreuer [29] investigated SR control charts for Markovian counting time series. Lastly, Yu et al. [30] investigated an SR control chart scheme for monitoring the Weibull scale parameter based on Type I censored data.

In this paper, the CUSUM and SR methods are applied to Type I right-censored Gamma-distributed data. The primary objectives of this study are threefold: (1) to systematically evaluate the adaptability of traditional control charts in censored data environments, (2) to address the performance limitations of deep learning-based monitoring approaches in practical reliability engineering scenarios, and (3) to develop simultaneous monitoring strategies for both scale and shape parameters of Gamma distributions under censoring mechanisms. The performance of the proposed methods is compared with that of an EWMA control chart based on deep learning networks, using both zero-state average run length (ARL) and steady-state average run length as performance metrics. The results demonstrate that both the CUSUM and SR control charts outperform the EWMA chart. Specifically, the SR scheme exhibits superior performance for small shifts, while for medium shifts, the SR and CUSUM schemes each show distinct advantages depending on the scenario.

We use the adaptation and application of the SR and CUSUM schemes for the joint monitoring of shape and scale parameters in Gamma-distributed processes subject to Type I censoring. This addresses a significant gap in SPM literature, where traditional control charts often assume complete data. We conduct the thorough performance evaluation that systematically compares the effectiveness of the SR and CUSUM procedures in a censored data environment. Our study moves beyond a simple comparison by evaluating their performance under a wide range of censoring rates and shift magnitudes, providing crucial insights into their relative strengths and weaknesses.

The remainder of the paper is organized as follows: Section 2 provides a review of the necessary background information, including the Gamma distribution, Type I right-censored Gamma distribution, and related work such as the EWMA CEV and CM chart combined with deep learning methods. Section 3 details the proposed CUSUM and SR methods for monitoring Type I right-censored Gamma-distributed data. Section 4 introduces the algorithm for determining the UCL and estimating $ARL_1$. Section 5 presents a comparative analysis of the proposed methods with existing EWMA approaches. Section 6 illustrates the implementation of the CUSUM and SR charts through a real-world example. Finally, Section 7 concludes the paper with a summary of the findings.

## 2. Preamble and Existing Work

This section presents a systematic analysis of fundamental characteristics pertaining to the Gamma distribution, along with two existing EWMA CEV and CM schemes integrated with deep learning architectures.

### 2.1. The Gamma Distribution and Censoring

Let $T_1, T_2, \ldots, T_n$ denote a sequence of independent and identically distributed (i.i.d.) random variables following a Gamma distribution. The distribution is parametrized by a shape parameter $\beta > 0$ and a scale parameter $\eta > 0$. The probability density function (PDF) governing the lifetime measurement $T$ is formally expressed as:

$$f(t|\beta,\eta) = \frac{\eta^\beta}{\Gamma(\beta)} t^{\beta-1} \exp(-\eta t), \tag{1}$$

The cumulative distribution function (CDF) of the Gamma distribution is given by

$$F(t \mid \beta,\eta) = \int_0^t \frac{\eta^\beta}{\Gamma(\beta)} x^{\beta-1} \exp(-\eta x) dx, \tag{2}$$

Let C represent the random variable corresponding to the censoring time. The censoring probability $P_c$, defined as the likelihood of data truncation prior to observing the terminal event, is mathematically expressed as:

$$P_c = 1 - F(\mu = c_T \mid \beta,\eta), \tag{3}$$

where $c_T$ is the censoring time.

### 2.2. The EWMA CEV and CM Charts with Deep Learning Method

The CEV and CM metrics for the Gamma distribution are formulated as:

$$\text{CEV} = \mathbb{E}[U \mid U \geq c_T] = \frac{\beta\eta[1 - F(c_T \mid \beta+1,\eta)]}{1 - F(c_T \mid \beta,\eta)}, \tag{4}$$

$$\text{CM} = F^{-1}(0.5 - 0.5F(c_T \mid \beta,\eta)|\beta,\eta), \tag{5}$$

where $F^{-1}(\cdot \mid \beta,\eta)$ denotes the inverse CDF of the Gamma distribution parametrized by $\beta$ and $\eta$.

Through reliability life testing, $n$ independent observations are collected. Let $u_j$ represent the lifetime measurement of the $j$-th sample. The processed data $x_j$ in the sample mean $\bar{X} = n^{-1}\sum_{j=1}^{n} x_j$ follows:

$$x_j = \begin{cases} u_j, & u_j \le c_T \\ \text{Cd}, & u_j > c_T \end{cases}, \tag{6}$$

where Cd corresponds to either CEV or CM values depending on the adopted estimation method. The IC process parameters are characterized by:

$$M_0 = \beta\eta, \quad V_0 = \beta\eta^2. \tag{7}$$

For decreased mean shift detection, the EWMA statistics with smoothing constant $\lambda \in (0,1]$ proposed by Pei-Hsi [18] are computed recursively as:

$$E_i = \min\{V_0, \lambda\bar{X}_i + (1-\lambda)E_{i-1}\}, \tag{8}$$
$$Z_i = \min\{M_0, \lambda\bar{X}_i + (1-\lambda)Z_{i-1}\}. \tag{9}$$

A process is deemed statistically unstable if either control limit is violated:

$$\begin{cases} E_i < h, \\ Z_i < h. \end{cases} \tag{10}$$

Recent work by Pei-Hsi [18] has developed an innovative approach combining EWMA control charts with deep learning techniques. Their methodology integrates two variants of EWMA charts (CEV and CM) with convolutional neural networks (CNNs) and long short-term memory (LSTM) networks. The CEV and CM components provide traditional process monitoring capabilities, while the CNN layers extract spatial patterns and LSTM networks capture temporal dependencies in the data. This hybrid framework enhances detection sensitivity by leveraging both statistical process control principles and deep learning's pattern recognition strengths. The complete implementation details, including network architectures and training procedures, are thoroughly documented in the original work Pei-Hsi [18].

## 3. The Proposed Control Charts

This section proposes two independent SPM frameworks for Gamma-distributed systems operating under Type I censoring conditions. The first methodology employs a CUSUM control chart designed to detect deviations in both the shape and the scale parameters. The second approach utilizes an SR control chart to monitor parameter shifts through likelihood ratio evaluation.

### 3.1. The CUSUM Control Chart

Let $T_{i1}, T_{i2}, \ldots, T_{in}$ be independent random variables following a Gamma distribution with shape parameter $\beta$ and scale parameter $\eta$, denoted as $\Gamma(\beta, \eta)$. Here, $C$ represents the predetermined censoring time, and $P_c$ denotes the censoring rate, as defined in Equation (3).

For statistical distributions involving right-censored data, the general form of the likelihood function can be expressed as proposed by Meeker [31]:

$$L(T|\beta,\eta) = \prod_{j=1}^{n} f(T_{ij}|\beta,\eta)^{\delta_{ij}} \left[1 - F(T_{ij}|\beta,\eta)\right]^{1-\delta_{ij}}, \tag{11}$$

where $\delta_{ij} = 0$ indicates a censored observation, and $\delta_{ij} = 1$ represents an exact failure time. Here, $f(\cdot)$ denotes the PDF of the underlying distribution, and $F(\cdot)$ corresponds to its CDF. Under IC conditions, the lifetime variable $T$ follows a Gamma distribution $\Gamma(\beta_0, \eta_0)$, characterized by the PDF $f_0(\cdot)$ and CDF $F_0(\cdot)$. Under out-of-control (OOC) conditions, the lifetime variable $T$ follows a Gamma distribution $\Gamma(\beta_1, \eta_1)$, characterized by the PDF $f_1(\cdot)$ and CDF $F_1(\cdot)$. This study addresses both Phase I (retrospective analysis) and Phase II (online monitoring) scenarios under standard assumptions. Specifically, the initial parameters $\beta_0$ and $\eta_0$ are assumed to be known during the monitoring process. Then, the log-likelihood ratio statistic $Z_i$ for the $i$-th sample can be expressed as:

$$\begin{aligned} Z_i &= \log\left(\frac{L(T_i|\beta_1,\eta_1)}{L(T_i|\beta_0,\eta_0)}\right) \\ &= \sum_{j=1}^{n} \delta_{ij} \log\left[\frac{f_1(x_{ij}|\beta_1,\eta_1)}{f_0(x_{ij}|\beta_0,\eta_0)}\right] + \sum_{j=1}^{n} (1-\delta_{ij}) \log\left[\frac{1 - F_1(x_{ij}|\beta_1,\eta_1)}{1 - F_0(x_{ij}|\beta_0,\eta_0)}\right], \end{aligned} \tag{12}$$

For a given random sample $\mathbf{x}_i = (x_{i1}, x_{i2}, \ldots, x_{in})$ from the Type I right-censored Gamma-distributed process, the log-likelihood ratio statistic can be derived from Equation (12) as:

$$\begin{aligned} Z_i = \delta_i &\left(\beta_1 \log(\eta_1) - \beta_0 \log(\eta_0) + \log\left[\frac{\Gamma(\beta_0)}{\Gamma(\beta_1)}\right] + (\beta_1 - \beta_0) \sum_{j=1}^{n} \log x_{ij} - (\eta_1 - \eta_0) \sum_{j=1}^{n} x_{ij}\right) \\ &+ (1-\delta_i) \sum_{j=1}^{n} \log\left[\frac{1 - F_1(x_{ij}|\beta_1,\eta_1)}{1 - F_0(x_{ij}|\beta_0,\eta_0)}\right], \end{aligned} \tag{13}$$

where $\delta_i = \sum_{j=1}^{n} \delta_{ij}$ represents the total number of uncensored observations in the $i$-th batch.

Under the hypothesis of a parameter shift from the IC state $(\beta_0, \eta_0)$ to the out-of-control state $(\beta_1, \eta_1)$, the likelihood ratio-based CUSUM control chart can be constructed as:

$$D_i^- = \max(0, D_i^- + Z_i), D_0^- = 0, i = 1, 2, 3, \ldots, \tag{14}$$

### 3.2. The SR Control Chart

Following Moustakides et al. [28], for $i \geq 1$, the instantaneous likelihood ratio $\Lambda_i$ between the post-change and pre-change hypotheses is defined as:

$$\Lambda_i = \frac{f_1(T_{ij})}{f_0(T_{ij})} = \exp(Z_i), \tag{15}$$

where $f_0(T_{ij})$ and $f_1(T_{ij})$ denote the probability density functions under the pre-change and post-change hypotheses, respectively. Based on this definition, the SR-type plotting statistic can be constructed as follows:

$$R_i = \sum_{k=1}^{i} \prod_{j=k}^{i} \Lambda_j. \tag{16}$$

The monitoring scheme triggers an OOC signal when $R_i > h$, where the control limit $h$ is determined by setting the IC $\text{ARL}_0$ to a predefined target value. Furthermore, the SR statistic admits the following recursive representation:

$$R_i = (1 + R_{i-1})\Lambda_i, \tag{17}$$

where $R_0 = 0$. According to Equation (12), $\Lambda_i$ can be converted into:

$$\Lambda_i = \exp(Z_i) = \exp\left\{\sum_{j=1}^{n} \delta_{ij} \log\left[\frac{f_1(x_{ij}|\beta_1, \eta_1)}{f_0(x_{ij}|\beta_0, \eta_0)}\right] + \sum_{j=1}^{n}(1 - \delta_{ij}) \log\left[\frac{1 - F_1(x_{ij}|\beta_1, \eta_1)}{1 - F_0(x_{ij}|\beta_0, \eta_0)}\right]\right\}. \tag{18}$$

## 4. Simulation Studies

The ARL measures the performance of a control chart, defined as the expected number of samples before an OOC signal appears Montgomery [32]. A sufficiently large IC ARL ($\text{ARL}_0$) minimizes false alarms, while a small OOC ARL ($\text{ARL}_1$) ensures rapid shift detection. The ARL is estimated via Monte Carlo simulations using an algorithm implemented in R, assuming fixed and known IC values for the shape parameter $\beta$ and the scale parameter $\eta$.

Comprehensive evaluation of control chart efficacy necessitates dual examination of ARL metrics: zero-state (ZS-ARL) and steady-state (SS-ARL) analyses. The ZS-ARL metric assumes instantaneous process parameter deviations upon Phase II monitoring commencement, calculated as $\mathbb{E}[N|\beta = \beta_1, \eta = \eta_1]$ where $N$ denotes the run length post-shift. Conversely, SS-ARL addresses delayed shift scenarios through $\lim_{k\to\infty} \mathbb{E}[N - k|N > k, \beta = \beta_1, \eta = \eta_1]$, modeling processes that initially maintain IC ($\beta = \beta_0, \eta = \eta_0$) conditions before transitioning to OOC states at unknown change points. Empirical applications predominantly align with SS-ARL assumptions given the probabilistic nature of shift occurrence timing. Zwetsloot and Woodall [33] substantiate this preference through Markov chain analyses, demonstrating that control charts with headstart features exhibit ZS-ARL superiority but SS-ARL degradation ratios exceeding 40% in Monte Carlo simulations. This performance dichotomy underscores the criticality of SS-ARL incorporation for robust SPM scheme validation.

To ensure equitable performance benchmarking across monitoring schemes, all control charts were calibrated to maintain an IC zero-state $\text{ARL}_0 = 370$ through parameter-specific design thresholds $d_P$. Numerical simulations employed Monte Carlo algorithms to generate 50,000 trial sequences, yielding empirical ARL estimates via $\widehat{\text{ARL}} = \mathbb{E}[RL]$ where RL represents run length realizations. Steady-state ARL estimation protocol incorporated a 50-observation IC phase prior to parameter shift initiation. Figure 1 shows the algorithm for Monte Carlo simulation to determine the UCL of the SR control chart.

Taking the SR control chart as an example, the algorithm for Monte Carlo simulation to determine the UCL of the SR control chart is:

1. Initialization:
    - Set the process parameters for the IC state: sample size $n$, censoring rate $P_C$, predetermined percent change $d_P$, shape parameter $\beta$, and scale parameter $\eta$.
    - Define the total number of simulation replications as 50,000.
    - Initialize the upper control limit with a provisional value $h$.
2. Data Generation:
    - Draw a sample of size $n$ from a Gamma distribution parameterized by $\beta$ and $\eta$.
3. Computation of the Statistic:

- Compute the statistic $R_i$ for the current sample.
- If $R_i \leq h$, generate a new sample (return to Step 2).
- If $R_i > h$, note the sample index at which this first OOC event is detected, and record it as the RL.

4. Iteration and Calibration:
   - Repeat Steps 2 and 3 until 50,000 run lengths are collected.
   - Calculate the mean of these run lengths to estimate the IC $ARL_0$ corresponding to the current $h$.
   - Adjust $h$ iteratively until the target $ARL_0$ is achieved.
   - Finally, set the UCL equal to the calibrated $h$.

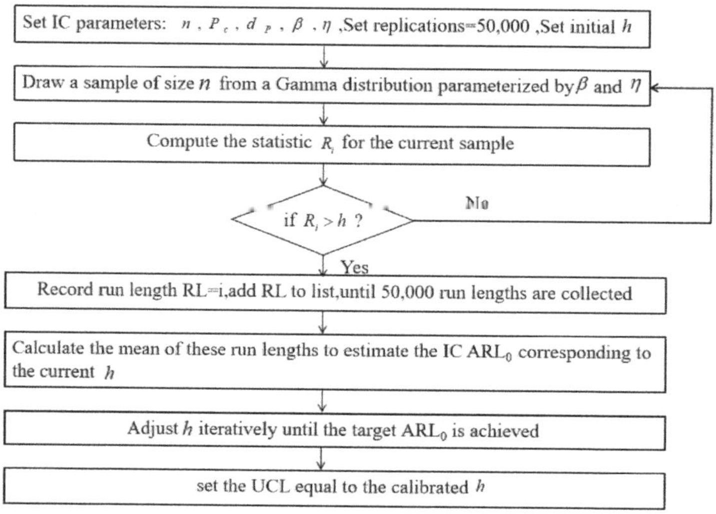


**Figure 1.** The algorithm for Monte Carlo simulation to determine the UCL of the SR control chart.

When the process experiences a shift, the OOC performance of the chart is assessed using $ARL_1$. We assume that the occurrence of an OOC condition modifies the IC scale parameter from $\eta_0$ to $\eta_1 = d_{T_1}\eta_0$ and $\beta_0$ to $\beta_1 = d_{T_2}\beta_0$, where $d_{T_1}$ and $d_{T_2}$ represent the true shift magnitude. Note that $d_{T_j}$ differs from the pre-specified $d_{P_j}$, which is known prior to monitoring, while $d_{T_j}$ is unknown until the shift occurs. Figure 2 shows the algorithm to estimate $ARL_1$.The following algorithm, implemented in R, can be used to estimate $ARL_1$:

Step 1: Define the parameters $n, \beta, \eta, P_C, d_{P_j}$ and determine the corresponding control limits.

Step 2: Generate a sample of size $n$ incorporating a shift of size $d_{T_j}$. Compute the plotting statistic $R_t$ using Equation (17).

Step 3: If the control chart signals an OOC condition, record the RL; otherwise, return to Step 2.

Step 4: After executing Steps 2 and 3 for 50,000 replications, calculate $ARL_1$ as the average of the recorded RL values.

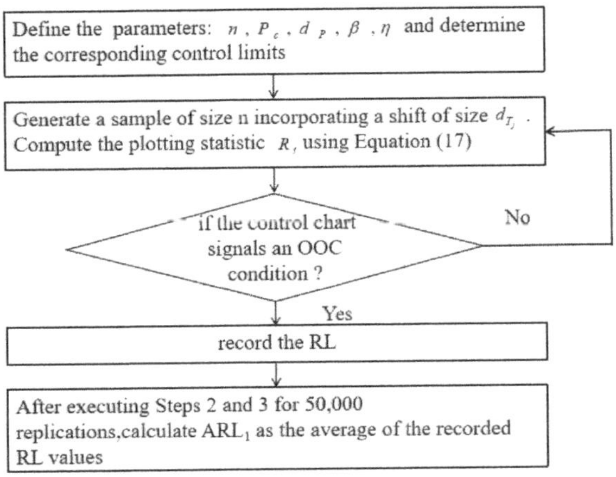


**Figure 2.** The algorithm estimates $ARL_1$.

## 5. Comparison and Discussion with Existing Charts

We compare the performance of the CUSUM and SR charts with the deep learning-based EWMA chart. To ensure a fair comparison, all control charts are calibrated to achieve an IC $ARL_0$ of approximately 370 with a sample size of $n = 5, 10$. The SS-ARL values, incorporating a warm-up period of 50, are estimated using Monte Carlo simulations with 50,000 iterations. The charts are evaluated under 12 parameter configurations, considering shape parameters ($\beta = 0.5, 1, 2$), scale parameters ($\eta = 0.5, 1, 2$), censoring rates ($P_c = 0.15, 0.25$), and pre-specified shift magnitudes ($d_P = 0.15, 0.25$).

In practical applications, the exact magnitude of a process shift is often unknown. Thus, it is crucial to evaluate the robustness of control charts designed for a specific pre-specified shift when the actual shift deviates. Table 1 presents the ZS-ARL values for the SR and CUSUM charts under various conditions ($P_c = 0.15, 0.25$), assuming $n = 5$ and parameter settings such as ($\beta = 2, \eta = 1$), ($\beta = 0.5, \eta = 1$), ($\beta = 1, \eta = 0.5$), and ($\beta = 1, \eta = 2$). Three pre-specified shift values ($d_P = 0.2, 0.5, 0.8$) are examined. Table 2 presents the SS-ARL values for the SR and CUSUM charts under the same conditions as in Table 1. Table 3 and Table 4 present the ZS-ARL and SS-ARL values for $n = 10$, under the same conditions as in Table 1 and Table 2, respectively.

For $P_c = 0.15$, the SR chart exhibits superior performance in detecting small-to-moderate shifts. Specifically, when the pre-specified shift is $d_{P_1} = d_{P_2} = 0.2$, the SR chart demonstrates a slightly lower ARL compared to the CUSUM chart in out-of-control scenarios. This advantage persists when $d_{P_1} = d_{P_2} = 0.5$, provided that the actual shift remains small. However, as the shift magnitude increases, the CUSUM chart, designed for $d_{P_1} = d_{P_2} = 0.5$, surpasses the SR chart in performance. When $d_{P_1} = d_{P_2} = 0.8$, the CUSUM chart consistently outperforms the SR chart. A similar trend is observed for $P_c = 0.25$ (Table 1). When the pre-specified shift is small (e.g., $d_{P_1} = d_{P_2} = 0.2$), the SR chart remains marginally more effective. However, as $d_{P_1} = d_{P_2} = 0.8$ and the actual shift magnitude increases, the CUSUM chart demonstrates better detection capability. Overall, the SR chart proves to be more effective in identifying small-to-moderate shifts.

In the steady-state scenario, the SR chart retains its advantage for $d_{P_1} = d_{P_2} = 0.2$, irrespective of the censoring rate. However, for larger shifts ($d_{P_1} = d_{P_2} = 0.8$), the CUSUM chart consistently outperforms the SR chart. When $d_{P_1} = d_{P_2} = 0.5$, the relative performance of the two methods depends on the true shift magnitude: the SR chart excels for small shifts, whereas the CUSUM chart becomes more effective as the shift magnitude increases. Figure 3 displays SS-ARL comparison between the SR and CUSUM charts ($n = 5$, $P_c = 0.15$, $\text{ARL}_0 = 370$. These findings align with the patterns observed in the zero-state case, reinforcing the conclusion that the SR chart is preferable for detecting small process shifts, while the CUSUM chart is better suited for larger deviations.

The shape parameter $\beta$ has a significant effect on the performance of the control charts: when $\beta$ is decreased from 2 to 0.5, the detection sensitivity increases for both the SR and CUSUM schemes, indicating that the reduction in $\beta$ effectively improves the ability to capture early offsets. The effect of the scale $\eta$ parameter on the performance of the control charts is not significant: when $\eta$ is decreased from 2 to 0.5, the performance of both the SR and CUSUM schemes is almost identical.

Comparative analysis of ZS-ARL results between censoring rates $P_c = 0.15$ and $P_c = 0.25$ (Table 1) under fixed $n = 5$ and $\text{ARL}_0 = 370$ reveals systematic performance variations. Increased censoring rates generally elevate ARL values across most shift magnitudes $d_{T_1}$, indicating reduced detection sensitivity. For instance, the SR chart exhibits a 1.5% ARL increase (153.75 $\rightarrow$ 156.11) at $d_{T_1} = 0.90$, while the CUSUM chart shows a 2.3% degradation (7.34 $\rightarrow$ 7.51) for $d_{T_1} = 0.50$, highlighting amplified impacts on small shift detection. To maintain $\text{ARL}_0 = 370$, control limits $h$ adapt differentially: SR limits increase slightly from 33.45 ($P_c = 0.15$) to 33.65 ($P_c = 0.25$), whereas CUSUM limits decrease marginally from 3.28 to 3.265, suggesting distinct compensation strategies. Notably, moderate shifts ($d_{T_1} = 0.75$) demonstrate greater ARL degradation (SR: 43.60 $\rightarrow$ 44.39, +1.8%; CUSUM: 19.24 $\rightarrow$ 20.42, +6.1%), emphasizing the need for parameter recalibration to mitigate performance losses under higher censoring conditions.

**Table 1.** ZS-ARL comparison for $n = 5, P_c = 0.15,\ 0.25,\ d_{T_1} = d_{T_2}$, $\text{ARL}_0 = 370$.

| | $P_c = 0.15, \eta = 1, \beta = 2$ | | | | | | $P_c = 0.25, \eta = 1, \beta = 2$ | | | | | |
|---|---|---|---|---|---|---|---|---|---|---|---|---|
| $d_T$ | $d_{P_1} = d_{P_2} = 0.2$ | | $d_{P_1} = d_{P_2} = 0.5$ | | $d_{P_1} = d_{P_2} = 0.8$ | | $d_{P_1} = d_{P_2} = 0.2$ | | $d_{P_1} = d_{P_2} = 0.5$ | | $d_{P_1} = d_{P_2} = 0.8$ | |
| | **SR** | **CUSUM** | **SR** | **CUSUM** | **SR** | **CUSUM** | **SR** | **CUSUM** | **SR** | **CUSUM** | **SR** | **CUSUM** |
| | **h = 33.45** | **h = 3.28** | **h = 144.26** | **h = 3.86** | **h = 274.85** | **h = 2.80** | **h = 33.65** | **h = 3.27** | **h = 143.95** | **h = 3.81** | **h = 274.35** | **h = 2.75** |
| | 370.99 | 369.82 | 370.08 | 370.75 | 370.27 | 369.28 | 370.61 | 369.99 | 370.65 | 370.46 | 369.39 | 371.00 |
| 0.90 | 153.75 | 161.07 | 113.00 | 121.71 | 90.33 | 88.99 | 156.11 | 160.41 | 115.97 | 124.99 | 93.93 | 92.17 |
| 0.85 | 100.86 | 105.89 | 67.58 | 73.30 | 57.55 | 52.26 | 101.69 | 106.57 | 69.03 | 74.94 | 59.83 | 54.41 |
| 0.80 | 66.39 | 70.22 | 42.10 | 45.37 | 40.62 | 34.31 | 67.38 | 71.31 | 43.70 | 46.90 | 42.37 | 35.93 |
| 0.75 | 43.60 | 47.06 | 27.47 | 29.32 | 30.43 | 24.35 | 44.39 | 47.41 | 28.64 | 30.33 | 31.95 | 25.28 |
| 0.70 | 29.31 | 31.34 | 19.19 | 19.69 | 23.88 | 18.08 | 29.92 | 32.15 | 20.04 | 20.42 | 25.04 | 18.91 |
| 0.65 | 19.84 | 21.28 | 13.89 | 13.75 | 19.20 | 13.97 | 20.30 | 21.92 | 14.41 | 14.35 | 20.15 | 14.50 |
| 0.60 | 13.73 | 14.72 | 10.37 | 10.14 | 15.83 | 10.99 | 14.19 | 15.09 | 10.79 | 10.43 | 16.42 | 11.50 |
| 0.55 | 9.71 | 10.30 | 8.05 | 7.62 | 13.09 | 8.87 | 9.92 | 10.54 | 8.35 | 7.83 | 13.61 | 9.16 |
| 0.50 | 6.99 | 7.34 | 6.36 | 5.86 | 10.87 | 7.19 | 7.13 | 7.51 | 6.52 | 6.06 | 11.28 | 7.39 |

| | $P_c = 0.15, \eta = 1, \beta = 0.5$ | | | | | | $P_c = 0.25, \eta = 1, \beta = 0.5$ | | | | | |
|---|---|---|---|---|---|---|---|---|---|---|---|---|
| $d_T$ | $d_{P_1} = d_{P_2} = 0.2$ | | $d_{P_1} = d_{P_2} = 0.5$ | | $d_{P_1} = d_{P_2} = 0.8$ | | $d_{P_1} = d_{P_2} = 0.2$ | | $d_{P_1} = d_{P_2} = 0.5$ | | $d_{P_1} = d_{P_2} = 0.8$ | |
| | **SR** | **CUSUM** | **SR** | **CUSUM** | **SR** | **CUSUM** | **SR** | **CUSUM** | **SR** | **CUSUM** | **SR** | **CUSUM** |
| | **h = 23.43** | **h = 3.03** | **h = 128.43** | **h = 3.953** | **h = 265.43** | **h = 3.00** | **h = 23.55** | **h = 3.02** | **h = 128.55** | **h = 3.94** | **h = 265.68** | **h = 2.97** |
| | 370.43 | 370.91 | 370.68 | 370.72 | 370.89 | 370.96 | 370.24 | 370.97 | 370.64 | 369.98 | 370.62 | 370.55 |
| 0.90 | 144.35 | 150.43 | 104.34 | 112.02 | 77.73 | 77.38 | 145.03 | 150.23 | 104.26 | 111.96 | 79.28 | 77.97 |
| 0.85 | 91.67 | 96.24 | 58.90 | 64.09 | 47.55 | 43.84 | 91.94 | 96.32 | 59.59 | 65.14 | 48.42 | 44.46 |
| 0.80 | 58.41 | 61.62 | 35.34 | 38.24 | 32.80 | 28.13 | 58.30 | 61.31 | 36.18 | 38.88 | 33.28 | 28.70 |
| 0.75 | 37.71 | 39.48 | 22.69 | 24.09 | 24.18 | 19.55 | 37.63 | 39.88 | 23.07 | 24.45 | 24.78 | 19.91 |
| 0.70 | 24.36 | 26.38 | 15.27 | 15.89 | 18.78 | 14.46 | 24.73 | 26.16 | 15.49 | 16.08 | 19.15 | 14.69 |
| 0.65 | 16.29 | 17.35 | 10.89 | 11.04 | 14.96 | 11.04 | 16.37 | 17.44 | 11.13 | 11.13 | 15.30 | 11.23 |
| 0.60 | 11.01 | 11.76 | 8.05 | 7.95 | 12.22 | 8.71 | 11.10 | 11.84 | 8.20 | 8.03 | 12.41 | 8.85 |
| 0.55 | 7.65 | 8.04 | 6.19 | 5.96 | 10.05 | 7.01 | 7.75 | 8.15 | 6.30 | 6.01 | 10.22 | 7.08 |
| 0.50 | 5.45 | 5.74 | 4.91 | 4.56 | 8.30 | 5.69 | 5.52 | 5.79 | 4.93 | 4.62 | 8.44 | 5.73 |

| | $P_c = 0.15, \eta = 0.5, \beta = 1$ | | | | | | $P_c = 0.25, \eta = 0.5, \beta = 1$ | | | | | |
|---|---|---|---|---|---|---|---|---|---|---|---|---|
| $d_T$ | $d_{P_1} = d_{P_2} = 0.2$ | | $d_{P_1} = d_{P_2} = 0.5$ | | $d_{P_1} = d_{P_2} = 0.8$ | | $d_{P_1} = d_{P_2} = 0.2$ | | $d_{P_1} = d_{P_2} = 0.5$ | | $d_{P_1} = d_{P_2} = 0.8$ | |
| | **SR** | **CUSUM** | **SR** | **CUSUM** | **SR** | **CUSUM** | **SR** | **CUSUM** | **SR** | **CUSUM** | **SR** | **CUSUM** |
| | **h = 27.66** | **h = 3.15** | **h = 134.95** | **h = 3.90** | **h = 269.35** | **h = 2.90** | **h = 27.78** | **h = 3.15** | **h = 135.85** | **h = 3.87** | **h = 270.54** | **h = 2.86** |
| | 369.77 | 370.32 | 370.81 | 370.98 | 370.67 | 369.87 | 370.75 | 370.82 | 369.87 | 370.93 | 370.17 | 370.50 |
| 0.90 | 150.26 | 156.67 | 108.05 | 117.61 | 84.32 | 83.36 | 149.63 | 155.98 | 110.38 | 118.70 | 86.27 | 85.28 |
| 0.85 | 95.55 | 100.10 | 63.58 | 68.84 | 52.57 | 48.12 | 96.43 | 101.55 | 64.46 | 70.09 | 54.08 | 49.69 |
| 0.80 | 61.93 | 66.21 | 38.58 | 41.81 | 36.51 | 31.26 | 62.72 | 66.88 | 39.72 | 42.52 | 37.95 | 32.16 |
| 0.75 | 40.73 | 43.18 | 24.97 | 26.46 | 27.29 | 21.87 | 40.94 | 43.85 | 25.77 | 27.08 | 28.34 | 22.63 |
| 0.70 | 26.93 | 28.95 | 17.09 | 17.61 | 21.26 | 16.22 | 27.09 | 29.18 | 17.60 | 18.27 | 21.94 | 16.68 |
| 0.65 | 18.02 | 19.40 | 12.28 | 12.34 | 17.05 | 12.47 | 18.36 | 19.49 | 12.62 | 12.67 | 17.56 | 12.79 |
| 0.60 | 12.27 | 13.07 | 9.12 | 8.94 | 13.90 | 9.84 | 12.51 | 13.37 | 9.42 | 9.19 | 14.35 | 10.07 |
| 0.55 | 8.58 | 9.15 | 7.03 | 6.71 | 11.48 | 7.87 | 8.71 | 9.30 | 7.21 | 6.86 | 11.77 | 8.03 |
| 0.50 | 6.15 | 6.44 | 5.51 | 5.13 | 9.47 | 6.40 | 6.27 | 6.57 | 5.66 | 5.27 | 9.73 | 6.49 |

| | $P_c = 0.15, \eta = 2, \beta = 1$ | | | | | | $P_c = 0.25, \eta = 2, \beta = 1$ | | | | | |
|---|---|---|---|---|---|---|---|---|---|---|---|---|
| $d_T$ | $d_{P_1} = d_{P_2} = 0.2$ | | $d_{P_1} = d_{P_2} = 0.5$ | | $d_{P_1} = d_{P_2} = 0.8$ | | $d_{P_1} = d_{P_2} = 0.2$ | | $d_{P_1} = d_{P_2} = 0.5$ | | $d_{P_1} = d_{P_2} = 0.8$ | |
| | **SR** | **CUSUM** | **SR** | **CUSUM** | **SR** | **CUSUM** | **SR** | **CUSUM** | **SR** | **CUSUM** | **SR** | **CUSUM** |
| | **h = 27.75** | **h = 3.15** | **h = 136.75** | **h = 3.90** | **h = 269.27** | **h = 2.90** | **h = 27.85** | **h = 3.14** | **h = 135.15** | **h = 3.88** | **h = 269.15** | **h = 2.86** |
| | 369.63 | 369.52 | 370.88 | 370.86 | 369.67 | 370.25 | 370.26 | 369.31 | 370.83 | 369.76 | 370.36 | 370.68 |
| 0.90 | 150.28 | 155.32 | 110.37 | 117.56 | 84.18 | 83.23 | 152.20 | 156.20 | 109.35 | 118.93 | 86.40 | 84.69 |
| 0.85 | 96.05 | 102.05 | 63.73 | 68.82 | 52.38 | 48.33 | 97.03 | 101.17 | 64.56 | 69.70 | 53.98 | 49.65 |
| 0.80 | 62.57 | 66.10 | 38.67 | 41.94 | 36.39 | 31.19 | 62.51 | 65.95 | 39.56 | 42.84 | 37.74 | 32.27 |
| 0.75 | 40.31 | 43.61 | 25.21 | 26.41 | 27.40 | 21.90 | 40.91 | 43.49 | 25.73 | 27.23 | 28.15 | 22.58 |
| 0.70 | 26.95 | 28.79 | 17.23 | 17.65 | 21.23 | 16.24 | 27.12 | 29.27 | 17.57 | 18.14 | 21.99 | 16.58 |
| 0.65 | 17.96 | 19.31 | 12.25 | 12.33 | 17.04 | 12.48 | 18.27 | 19.50 | 12.55 | 12.56 | 17.53 | 12.81 |
| 0.60 | 12.31 | 13.11 | 9.18 | 8.93 | 13.93 | 9.82 | 12.43 | 13.38 | 9.41 | 9.13 | 14.29 | 10.07 |
| 0.55 | 8.56 | 9.14 | 7.02 | 6.73 | 11.42 | 7.87 | 8.79 | 9.27 | 7.24 | 6.88 | 11.77 | 8.04 |
| 0.50 | 6.14 | 6.46 | 5.583 | 5.15 | 9.50 | 6.39 | 6.26 | 6.53 | 5.65 | 5.29 | 9.71 | 6.47 |

**Table 2.** SS-ARL comparison for $n = 5, P_c = 0.15,\ 0.25,\ d_{T_1} = d_{T_2}$, $\text{ARL}_0 = 370$.

| | **$P_c = 0.15, \eta = 1, \beta = 2$** | | | | | | **$P_c = 0.25, \eta = 1, \beta = 2$** | | | | | |
|---|---|---|---|---|---|---|---|---|---|---|---|---|
| $d_T$ | **$d_{P_1} = d_{P_2} = 0.2$** | | **$d_{P_1} = d_{P_2} = 0.5$** | | **$d_{P_1} = d_{P_2} = 0.8$** | | **$d_{P_1} = d_{P_2} = 0.2$** | | **$d_{P_1} = d_{P_2} = 0.5$** | | **$d_{P_1} = d_{P_2} = 0.8$** | |
| | **SR** | **CUSUM** | **SR** | **CUSUM** | **SR** | **CUSUM** | **SR** | **CUSUM** | **SR** | **CUSUM** | **SR** | **CUSUM** |
| | **h = 33.71** | **h = 3.28** | **h = 158.25** | **h = 3.94** | **h = 443.85** | **h = 3.34** | **h = 33.85** | **h = 3.27** | **h = 158.55** | **h = 3.92** | **h = 445.52** | **h = 3.25** |
| | 370.37 | 369.95 | 369.98 | 370.86 | 369.16 | 369.53 | 369.21 | 369.02 | 370.21 | 369.12 | 369.37 | 371.98 |
| 0.90 | 152.41 | 159.31 | 94.97 | 101.90 | 36.56 | 35.76 | 153.75 | 159.76 | 96.25 | 102.83 | 37.29 | 33.81 |
| 0.85 | 99.52 | 104.73 | 53.01 | 58.49 | 19.95 | 18.74 | 101.06 | 105.77 | 53.91 | 58.62 | 20.64 | 17.79 |
| 0.80 | 64.56 | 69.43 | 30.94 | 33.16 | 13.04 | 11.41 | 66.00 | 70.40 | 31.32 | 34.33 | 13.53 | 12.41 |
| 0.75 | 42.22 | 45.61 | 18.76 | 20.32 | 9.54 | 8.37 | 43.03 | 45.88 | 19.49 | 21.01 | 9.88 | 7.83 |
| 0.70 | 28.22 | 30.31 | 12.41 | 12.90 | 7.42 | 4.93 | 28.46 | 30.83 | 12.95 | 13.45 | 7.71 | 4.81 |
| 0.65 | 18.93 | 20.36 | 8.54 | 8.73 | 6.08 | 4.49 | 19.31 | 20.87 | 8.91 | 9.05 | 6.27 | 4.09 |
| 0.60 | 12.67 | 13.81 | 6.33 | 6.23 | 5.17 | 2.95 | 13.11 | 14.21 | 6.52 | 6.46 | 5.33 | 2.57 |
| 0.55 | 8.81 | 9.51 | 4.91 | 4.72 | 4.46 | 2.57 | 9.06 | 9.81 | 5.09 | 4.83 | 4.58 | 2.43 |
| 0.50 | 6.29 | 6.71 | 3.96 | 3.73 | 3.88 | 2.09 | 6.46 | 6.81 | 4.09 | 3.80 | 3.99 | 1.92 |

| | **$P_c = 0.15, \eta = 1, \beta = 0.5$** | | | | | | **$P_c = 0.25, \eta = 1, \beta = 0.5$** | | | | | |
|---|---|---|---|---|---|---|---|---|---|---|---|---|
| $d_T$ | **$d_{P_1} = d_{P_2} = 0.2$** | | **$d_{P_1} = d_{P_2} = 0.5$** | | **$d_{P_1} = d_{P_2} = 0.8$** | | **$d_{P_1} = d_{P_2} = 0.2$** | | **$d_{P_1} = d_{P_2} = 0.5$** | | **$d_{P_1} = d_{P_2} = 0.8$** | |
| | **SR** | **CUSUM** | **SR** | **CUSUM** | **SR** | **CUSUM** | **SR** | **CUSUM** | **SR** | **CUSUM** | **SR** | **CUSUM** |
| | **h = 23.58** | **h = 3.08** | **h = 137.53** | **h = 4.01** | **h = 400.43** | **h = 3.02** | **h = 23.61** | **h = 3.07** | **h = 137.83** | **h = 3.98** | **h = 403.58** | **h = 2.99** |
| | 370.92 | 370.92 | 370.00 | 370.73 | 369.40 | 370.95 | 369.47 | 370.98 | 370.63 | 369.99 | 369.71 | 370.53 |
| 0.90 | 144.24 | 149.58 | 90.17 | 97.78 | 32.81 | 32.01 | 144.39 | 148.65 | 90.94 | 97.92 | 33.70 | 31.26 |
| 0.85 | 90.55 | 96.08 | 48.94 | 53.37 | 17.49 | 14.61 | 91.64 | 94.61 | 48.57 | 53.54 | 17.81 | 16.76 |
| 0.80 | 57.82 | 60.81 | 27.51 | 30.08 | 11.29 | 9.19 | 57.61 | 60.70 | 27.58 | 30.76 | 11.40 | 9.27 |
| 0.75 | 36.91 | 39.01 | 16.40 | 17.73 | 8.16 | 6.17 | 37.05 | 39.54 | 16.42 | 18.01 | 8.24 | 6.24 |
| 0.70 | 23.96 | 25.48 | 10.39 | 11.10 | 6.42 | 4.52 | 24.12 | 25.73 | 10.66 | 11.30 | 6.51 | 4.58 |
| 0.65 | 15.77 | 17.00 | 7.19 | 7.39 | 5.23 | 3.30 | 15.75 | 16.97 | 7.29 | 7.56 | 5.31 | 3.47 |
| 0.60 | 10.44 | 11.30 | 5.28 | 5.31 | 4.42 | 2.57 | 10.61 | 11.36 | 5.38 | 5.37 | 4.47 | 2.78 |
| 0.55 | 7.18 | 7.65 | 4.11 | 4.01 | 3.81 | 2.09 | 7.26 | 7.71 | 4.17 | 4.03 | 3.86 | 2.25 |
| 0.50 | 5.10 | 5.38 | 3.31 | 3.14 | 3.35 | 1.84 | 5.16 | 5.43 | 3.37 | 3.19 | 3.37 | 1.89 |

| | **$P_c = 0.15, \eta = 0.5, \beta = 1$** | | | | | | **$P_c = 0.25, \eta = 0.5, \beta = 1$** | | | | | |
|---|---|---|---|---|---|---|---|---|---|---|---|---|
| $d_T$ | **$d_{P_1} = d_{P_2} = 0.2$** | | **$d_{P_1} = d_{P_2} = 0.5$** | | **$d_{P_1} = d_{P_2} = 0.8$** | | **$d_{P_1} = d_{P_2} = 0.2$** | | **$d_{P_1} = d_{P_2} = 0.5$** | | **$d_{P_1} = d_{P_2} = 0.8$** | |
| | **SR** | **CUSUM** | **SR** | **CUSUM** | **SR** | **CUSUM** | **SR** | **CUSUM** | **SR** | **CUSUM** | **SR** | **CUSUM** |
| | **h = 27.73** | **h = 3.17** | **h = 145.25** | **h = 3.91** | **h = 419.35** | **h = 2.91** | **h = 27.79** | **h = 3.18** | **h = 146.15** | **h = 3.89** | **h = 423.85** | **h = 2.90** |
| | 369.71 | 370.33 | 370.53 | 370.97 | 369.77 | 369.85 | 370.64 | 370.83 | 369.07 | 370.91 | 369.10 | 370.48 |
| 0.90 | 149.03 | 153.79 | 93.43 | 99.42 | 34.62 | 25.97 | 148.32 | 154.35 | 93.79 | 101.19 | 35.83 | 27.22 |
| 0.85 | 95.20 | 99.92 | 50.63 | 55.83 | 18.71 | 12.75 | 95.85 | 99.97 | 51.89 | 56.53 | 19.33 | 16.98 |
| 0.80 | 61.23 | 64.69 | 28.96 | 31.84 | 12.09 | 9.50 | 62.22 | 65.56 | 29.64 | 32.55 | 12.54 | 11.17 |
| 0.75 | 39.69 | 42.52 | 17.67 | 19.00 | 8.83 | 6.21 | 40.06 | 43.51 | 18.07 | 19.60 | 9.14 | 6.25 |
| 0.70 | 25.94 | 27.97 | 11.44 | 11.94 | 6.92 | 4.78 | 26.26 | 28.56 | 11.64 | 12.31 | 7.11 | 5.46 |
| 0.65 | 17.18 | 18.79 | 7.90 | 8.06 | 5.66 | 3.37 | 17.48 | 19.07 | 8.09 | 8.21 | 5.82 | 3.55 |
| 0.60 | 11.66 | 12.50 | 5.80 | 5.71 | 4.80 | 2.91 | 11.85 | 12.68 | 5.96 | 5.85 | 4.88 | 3.18 |
| 0.55 | 8.02 | 8.62 | 4.48 | 4.32 | 4.11 | 2.24 | 8.18 | 8.69 | 4.60 | 4.39 | 4.20 | 2.35 |
| 0.50 | 5.67 | 6.01 | 3.63 | 3.42 | 3.61 | 2.09 | 5.78 | 6.14 | 3.70 | 3.47 | 3.66 | 2.10 |

| | **$P_c = 0.15, \eta = 2, \beta = 1$** | | | | | | **$P_c = 0.25, \eta = 2, \beta = 1$** | | | | | |
|---|---|---|---|---|---|---|---|---|---|---|---|---|
| $d_T$ | **$d_{P_1} = d_{P_2} = 0.2$** | | **$d_{P_1} = d_{P_2} = 0.5$** | | **$d_{P_1} = d_{P_2} = 0.8$** | | **$d_{P_1} = d_{P_2} = 0.2$** | | **$d_{P_1} = d_{P_2} = 0.5$** | | **$d_{P_1} = d_{P_2} = 0.8$** | |
| | **SR** | **CUSUM** | **SR** | **CUSUM** | **SR** | **CUSUM** | **SR** | **CUSUM** | **SR** | **CUSUM** | **SR** | **CUSUM** |
| | **h = 27.85** | **h = 3.17** | **h = 145.86** | **h = 3.93** | **h = 425.57** | **h = 2.92** | **h = 28.13** | **h = 3.19** | **h = 146.75** | **h = 3.88** | **h = 426.85** | **h = 2.89** |
| | 370.29 | 370.02 | 369.88 | 370.83 | 369.44 | 370.15 | 370.51 | 370.21 | 370.08 | 370.14 | 370.32 | 369.98 |
| 0.90 | 148.73 | 154.72 | 93.30 | 100.28 | 34.64 | 31.24 | 149.05 | 152.72 | 93.54 | 101.63 | 35.29 | 30.25 |
| 0.85 | 95.43 | 100.21 | 50.89 | 55.50 | 18.95 | 13.36 | 95.72 | 100.19 | 51.16 | 56.49 | 19.42 | 22.45 |
| 0.80 | 61.48 | 65.21 | 29.11 | 32.08 | 12.08 | 9.53 | 61.41 | 65.05 | 29.66 | 32.48 | 12.56 | 8.81 |
| 0.75 | 40.01 | 42.61 | 17.76 | 19.11 | 8.81 | 6.29 | 40.06 | 42.62 | 18.12 | 19.51 | 9.04 | 6.09 |
| 0.70 | 26.09 | 27.97 | 11.47 | 12.27 | 6.90 | 4.73 | 26.28 | 28.30 | 11.78 | 12.28 | 7.13 | 5.09 |
| 0.65 | 17.11 | 18.63 | 7.91 | 8.12 | 5.67 | 3.13 | 17.42 | 18.73 | 8.05 | 8.26 | 5.81 | 2.90 |
| 0.60 | 11.59 | 12.64 | 5.78 | 5.80 | 4.80 | 2.89 | 11.84 | 12.68 | 5.94 | 5.87 | 4.88 | 2.77 |
| 0.55 | 8.05 | 8.53 | 4.50 | 4.32 | 4.12 | 2.47 | 8.15 | 8.67 | 4.57 | 4.43 | 4.19 | 2.41 |
| 0.50 | 5.66 | 6.02 | 3.63 | 3.42 | 3.61 | 2.16 | 5.76 | 6.11 | 3.71 | 3.48 | 3.66 | 1.98 |

**Table 3.** ZS-ARL comparison for $n = 10, P_c = 0.15,\ 0.25, d_{T_1} = d_{T_2}$, $ARL_0 = 370$.

| | $P_c = 0.15, \eta = 1, \beta = 2$ | | | | | | $P_c = 0.25, \eta = 1, \beta = 2$ | | | | | |
|---|---|---|---|---|---|---|---|---|---|---|---|---|
| $d_T$ | $d_{P_1} = d_{P_2} = 0.2$ | | $d_{P_1} = d_{P_2} = 0.5$ | | $d_{P_1} = d_{P_2} = 0.8$ | | $d_{P_1} = d_{P_2} = 0.2$ | | $d_{P_1} = d_{P_2} = 0.5$ | | $d_{P_1} = d_{P_2} = 0.8$ | |
| | **SR** | **CUSUM** | **SR** | **CUSUM** | **SR** | **CUSUM** | **SR** | **CUSUM** | **SR** | **CUSUM** | **SR** | **CUSUM** |
| | **h = 12.15** | **h = 2.44** | **h = 111.61** | **h = 4.03** | **h = 254.63** | **h = 3.27** | **h = 12.63** | **h = 2.48** | **h = 112.63** | **h = 4.01** | **h = 255.68** | **h = 3.21** |
| | 370.87 | 370.83 | 370.96 | 370.46 | 370.52 | 370.56 | 370.50 | 370.52 | 370.73 | 370.23 | 370.21 | 370.20 |
| 0.90 | 135.90 | 138.68 | 92.84 | 100.64 | 63.01 | 63.82 | 136.34 | 140.33 | 95.45 | 102.72 | 65.78 | 65.51 |
| 0.85 | 83.10 | 86.56 | 50.54 | 55.03 | 36.95 | 34.72 | 83.39 | 87.34 | 51.71 | 56.71 | 38.59 | 36.31 |
| 0.80 | 51.45 | 54.03 | 29.16 | 31.62 | 24.81 | 21.85 | 52.25 | 54.79 | 30.18 | 33.07 | 26.11 | 22.64 |
| 0.75 | 32.39 | 34.02 | 17.97 | 19.24 | 18.26 | 15.11 | 32.65 | 34.54 | 18.78 | 20.04 | 19.13 | 15.77 |
| 0.70 | 20.46 | 21.63 | 11.92 | 12.34 | 14.08 | 11.14 | 21.02 | 22.02 | 12.30 | 12.92 | 14.74 | 11.65 |
| 0.65 | 13.25 | 14.10 | 8.29 | 8.47 | 11.19 | 8.57 | 13.76 | 14.38 | 8.70 | 8.81 | 11.70 | 8.92 |
| 0.60 | 8.86 | 9.25 | 6.13 | 6.11 | 9.09 | 6.82 | 9.11 | 9.59 | 6.37 | 6.30 | 9.52 | 6.99 |
| 0.55 | 6.03 | 6.30 | 4.70 | 4.54 | 7.49 | 5.45 | 6.17 | 6.53 | 4.85 | 4.73 | 7.79 | 5.63 |
| 0.50 | 4.23 | 4.40 | 3.66 | 3.51 | 6.18 | 4.43 | 4.36 | 4.55 | 3.80 | 3.62 | 6.43 | 4.57 |
| | $P_c = 0.15, \eta = 1, \beta = 0.5$ | | | | | | $P_c = 0.25, \eta = 1, \beta = 0.5$ | | | | | |
| $d_T$ | $d_{P_1} = d_{P_2} = 0.2$ | | $d_{P_1} = d_{P_2} = 0.5$ | | $d_{P_1} = d_{P_2} = 0.8$ | | $d_{P_1} = d_{P_2} = 0.2$ | | $d_{P_1} = d_{P_2} = 0.5$ | | $d_{P_1} = d_{P_2} = 0.8$ | |
| | **SR** | **CUSUM** | **SR** | **CUSUM** | **SR** | **CUSUM** | **SR** | **CUSUM** | **SR** | **CUSUM** | **SR** | **CUSUM** |
| | **h = 5.26** | **h = 1.63** | **h = 94.56** | **h = 4.04** | **h = 240.66** | **h = 3.45** | **h = 5.46** | **h = 1.67** | **h = 95.32** | **h = 4.03** | **h = 241.33** | **h = 3.42** |
| | 370.46 | 369.66 | 370.16 | 370.52 | 370.46 | 370.43 | 370.54 | 369.84 | 370.26 | 370.13 | 370.14 | 370.26 |
| 0.90 | 123.35 | 124.66 | 85.20 | 92.44 | 53.06 | 54.00 | 124.91 | 125.02 | 85.59 | 92.68 | 53.80 | 54.80 |
| 0.85 | 72.46 | 73.59 | 44.00 | 48.75 | 29.95 | 28.42 | 73.17 | 73.93 | 44.59 | 49.16 | 30.57 | 29.03 |
| 0.80 | 43.01 | 44.25 | 24.51 | 26.88 | 19.72 | 17.46 | 43.38 | 44.99 | 25.06 | 27.41 | 20.18 | 17.97 |
| 0.75 | 26.25 | 27.03 | 14.70 | 15.73 | 14.29 | 11.99 | 26.44 | 27.29 | 14.99 | 16.12 | 14.62 | 12.19 |
| 0.70 | 16.26 | 16.78 | 9.48 | 9.93 | 10.92 | 8.81 | 16.48 | 17.18 | 9.63 | 10.12 | 11.18 | 9.00 |
| 0.65 | 10.23 | 10.70 | 6.53 | 6.62 | 8.65 | 6.77 | 10.52 | 10.95 | 6.64 | 6.79 | 8.78 | 6.86 |
| 0.60 | 6.80 | 7.07 | 4.73 | 4.74 | 6.95 | 5.31 | 6.91 | 7.14 | 4.84 | 4.78 | 7.10 | 5.41 |
| 0.55 | 4.56 | 4.74 | 3.61 | 3.53 | 5.71 | 4.29 | 4.65 | 4.82 | 3.67 | 3.61 | 5.81 | 4.35 |
| 0.50 | 3.23 | 3.32 | 2.83 | 2.74 | 4.69 | 3.49 | 3.28 | 3.36 | 2.87 | 2.76 | 4.79 | 3.54 |
| | $P_c = 0.15, \eta = 0.5, \beta = 1$ | | | | | | $P_c = 0.25, \eta = 0.5, \beta = 1$ | | | | | |
| $d_T$ | $d_{P_1} = d_{P_2} = 0.2$ | | $d_{P_1} = d_{P_2} = 0.5$ | | $d_{P_1} = d_{P_2} = 0.8$ | | $d_{P_1} = d_{P_2} = 0.2$ | | $d_{P_1} = d_{P_2} = 0.5$ | | $d_{P_1} = d_{P_2} = 0.8$ | |
| | **SR** | **CUSUM** | **SR** | **CUSUM** | **SR** | **CUSUM** | **SR** | **CUSUM** | **SR** | **CUSUM** | **SR** | **CUSUM** |
| | **h = 7.91** | **h = 2.03** | **h = 102.51** | **h = 4.05** | **h = 246.52** | **h = 3.35** | **h = 8.28** | **h = 2.07** | **h = 103.58** | **h = 4.02** | **h = 247.58** | **h = 3.31** |
| | 369.97 | 370.87 | 370.68 | 370.10 | 370.67 | 369.77 | 370.87 | 369.13 | 370.08 | 370.60 | 370.03 | 369.89 |
| 0.90 | 129.48 | 131.85 | 89.76 | 96.99 | 58.14 | 59.06 | 131.87 | 133.20 | 90.82 | 98.24 | 59.75 | 60.64 |
| 0.85 | 78.10 | 79.76 | 47.22 | 51.96 | 33.54 | 31.54 | 78.81 | 79.98 | 48.38 | 52.84 | 34.63 | 32.44 |
| 0.80 | 47.35 | 48.73 | 26.76 | 29.56 | 22.21 | 19.68 | 48.29 | 49.33 | 27.53 | 30.03 | 23.07 | 20.28 |
| 0.75 | 29.12 | 30.33 | 16.30 | 17.56 | 16.23 | 13.61 | 29.70 | 30.72 | 16.65 | 18.06 | 16.77 | 13.96 |
| 0.70 | 18.27 | 19.02 | 10.65 | 11.20 | 12.46 | 9.92 | 18.73 | 19.39 | 11.01 | 11.46 | 12.86 | 10.23 |
| 0.65 | 11.75 | 12.21 | 7.37 | 7.51 | 9.87 | 7.60 | 11.98 | 12.49 | 7.58 | 7.76 | 10.12 | 7.83 |
| 0.60 | 7.74 | 8.08 | 5.35 | 5.39 | 7.98 | 5.99 | 7.86 | 8.22 | 5.51 | 5.53 | 8.22 | 6.14 |
| 0.55 | 5.25 | 5.50 | 4.07 | 4.00 | 6.52 | 4.81 | 5.38 | 5.57 | 4.20 | 4.09 | 6.71 | 4.91 |
| 0.50 | 3.68 | 3.82 | 3.22 | 3.09 | 5.40 | 3.91 | 3.77 | 3.87 | 3.28 | 3.15 | 5.53 | 3.99 |
| | $P_c = 0.15, \eta = 2, \beta = 1$ | | | | | | $P_c = 0.25, \eta = 2, \beta = 1$ | | | | | |
| $d_T$ | $d_{P_1} = d_{P_2} = 0.2$ | | $d_{P_1} = d_{P_2} = 0.5$ | | $d_{P_1} = d_{P_2} = 0.8$ | | $d_{P_1} = d_{P_2} = 0.2$ | | $d_{P_1} = d_{P_2} = 0.5$ | | $d_{P_1} = d_{P_2} = 0.8$ | |
| | **SR** | **CUSUM** | **SR** | **CUSUM** | **SR** | **CUSUM** | **SR** | **CUSUM** | **SR** | **CUSUM** | **SR** | **CUSUM** |
| | **h = 7.99** | **h = 2.04** | **h = 102.95** | **h = 4.04** | **h = 245.95** | **h = 3.36** | **h = 8.26** | **h = 2.07** | **h = 103.21** | **h = 4.03** | **h = 247.28** | **h = 3.31** |
| | 369.84 | 370.53 | 370.09 | 370.89 | 370.20 | 370.00 | 370.05 | 369.57 | 370.82 | 370.53 | 370.84 | 370.02 |
| 0.90 | 130.95 | 132.27 | 89.92 | 96.82 | 57.54 | 58.79 | 131.69 | 132.88 | 90.32 | 97.91 | 59.66 | 60.40 |
| 0.85 | 78.49 | 80.59 | 47.35 | 51.54 | 33.36 | 31.49 | 78.79 | 80.69 | 48.36 | 52.74 | 34.55 | 32.53 |
| 0.80 | 47.62 | 48.85 | 26.93 | 29.48 | 22.25 | 19.68 | 47.98 | 49.38 | 27.36 | 29.85 | 23.09 | 20.22 |
| 0.75 | 29.42 | 30.59 | 16.23 | 17.45 | 16.22 | 13.56 | 29.65 | 30.84 | 16.65 | 17.91 | 16.81 | 13.88 |
| 0.70 | 18.39 | 19.23 | 10.66 | 11.17 | 12.43 | 9.92 | 18.65 | 19.56 | 10.96 | 11.48 | 12.84 | 10.20 |
| 0.65 | 11.88 | 12.38 | 7.39 | 7.51 | 9.81 | 7.64 | 11.93 | 12.57 | 7.56 | 7.75 | 10.15 | 7.80 |
| 0.60 | 7.84 | 8.13 | 5.39 | 5.37 | 7.96 | 6.01 | 7.87 | 8.26 | 5.52 | 5.53 | 8.18 | 6.13 |
| 0.55 | 5.24 | 5.50 | 4.11 | 4.01 | 6.53 | 4.82 | 5.39 | 5.57 | 4.21 | 4.09 | 6.71 | 4.92 |
| 0.50 | 3.69 | 3.79 | 3.22 | 3.08 | 5.40 | 3.94 | 3.77 | 3.91 | 3.27 | 3.17 | 5.52 | 3.99 |

**Table 4.** SS-ARL comparison for $n = 10, P_c = 0.15,\ 0.25, d_{T_1} = d_{T_2}$, $\text{ARL}_0 = 370$.

| | $P_c = 0.15, \eta = 1, \beta = 2$ | | | | | | $P_c = 0.25, \eta = 1, \beta = 2$ | | | | | |
|---|---|---|---|---|---|---|---|---|---|---|---|---|
| $d_T$ | $d_{P_1} = d_{P_2} = 0.2$ | | $d_{P_1} = d_{P_2} = 0.5$ | | $d_{P_1} = d_{P_2} = 0.8$ | | $d_{P_1} = d_{P_2} = 0.2$ | | $d_{P_1} = d_{P_2} = 0.5$ | | $d_{P_1} = d_{P_2} = 0.8$ | |
| | **SR** | **CUSUM** | **SR** | **CUSUM** | **SR** | **CUSUM** | **SR** | **CUSUM** | **SR** | **CUSUM** | **SR** | **CUSUM** |
| | **h = 12.21** | **h = 2.44** | **h = 116.43** | **h = 4.08** | **h = 357.48** | **h = 3.66** | **h = 12.78** | **h = 2.47** | **h = 117.69** | **h = 4.06** | **h = 363.62** | **h = 3.61** |
| | 370.58 | 369.38 | 370.74 | 370.35 | 370.81 | 369.84 | 370.15 | 370.59 | 370.37 | 370.11 | 370.05 | 369.12 |
| 0.90 | 136.49 | 139.05 | 86.15 | 94.15 | 33.20 | 33.04 | 137.22 | 139.63 | 88.66 | 95.89 | 33.92 | 32.90 |
| 0.85 | 83.21 | 85.55 | 44.44 | 48.97 | 15.78 | 14.07 | 85.20 | 87.10 | 45.31 | 50.19 | 16.47 | 14.96 |
| 0.80 | 51.75 | 53.41 | 23.90 | 26.63 | 9.82 | 8.33 | 52.29 | 54.00 | 24.48 | 27.48 | 10.27 | 8.33 |
| 0.75 | 32.13 | 33.49 | 13.97 | 15.03 | 7.01 | 5.43 | 33.05 | 34.17 | 14.30 | 15.68 | 7.31 | 5.48 |
| 0.70 | 20.46 | 21.24 | 8.67 | 9.31 | 5.51 | 3.95 | 20.84 | 21.94 | 9.01 | 9.49 | 5.76 | 3.99 |
| 0.65 | 13.14 | 13.84 | 5.91 | 6.13 | 4.59 | 3.09 | 13.45 | 14.11 | 6.14 | 6.37 | 4.71 | 3.12 |
| 0.60 | 8.68 | 9.11 | 4.33 | 4.36 | 3.89 | 2.56 | 8.86 | 9.39 | 4.48 | 4.51 | 4.00 | 2.55 |
| 0.55 | 5.87 | 6.13 | 3.37 | 3.30 | 3.38 | 2.19 | 5.99 | 6.30 | 3.47 | 3.40 | 3.48 | 2.14 |
| 0.50 | 4.09 | 4.30 | 2.74 | 2.64 | 2.98 | 1.86 | 4.22 | 4.42 | 2.81 | 2.71 | 3.05 | 1.89 |
| | $P_c = 0.15, \eta = 1, \beta = 0.5$ | | | | | | $P_c = 0.25, \eta = 1, \beta = 0.5$ | | | | | |
| $d_T$ | $d_{P_1} = d_{P_2} = 0.2$ | | $d_{P_1} = d_{P_2} = 0.5$ | | $d_{P_1} = d_{P_2} = 0.8$ | | $d_{P_1} = d_{P_2} = 0.2$ | | $d_{P_1} = d_{P_2} = 0.5$ | | $d_{P_1} = d_{P_2} = 0.8$ | |
| | **SR** | **CUSUM** | **SR** | **CUSUM** | **SR** | **CUSUM** | **SR** | **CUSUM** | **SR** | **CUSUM** | **SR** | **CUSUM** |
| | **h = 5.24** | **h = 1.63** | **h = 97.04** | **h = 4.07** | **h = 318.98** | **h = 3.77** | **h = 5.42** | **h = 1.66** | **h = 97.78** | **h = 4.07** | **h = 321.51** | **h = 3.75** |
| | 370.23 | 369.45 | 370.84 | 370.35 | 370.60 | 370.21 | 370.60 | 369.92 | 370.83 | 370.98 | 370.48 | 370.00 |
| 0.90 | 123.45 | 123.91 | 80.82 | 87.72 | 28.52 | 29.52 | 124.48 | 125.32 | 81.61 | 89.24 | 29.17 | 29.09 |
| 0.85 | 72.02 | 73.77 | 39.93 | 44.33 | 13.50 | 12.59 | 73.14 | 74.07 | 40.09 | 45.01 | 13.80 | 12.85 |
| 0.80 | 43.17 | 44.09 | 20.86 | 23.30 | 8.26 | 6.94 | 43.42 | 44.63 | 21.27 | 23.61 | 8.41 | 7.15 |
| 0.75 | 26.17 | 27.00 | 11.83 | 12.07 | 5.95 | 4.72 | 26.49 | 27.11 | 12.14 | 13.21 | 6.11 | 4.79 |
| 0.70 | 16.15 | 16.73 | 7.34 | 7.79 | 4.71 | 3.49 | 16.33 | 17.02 | 7.45 | 7.99 | 4.79 | 3.55 |
| 0.65 | 10.24 | 10.73 | 4.93 | 5.10 | 3.89 | 2.79 | 10.40 | 10.77 | 5.01 | 5.22 | 3.97 | 2.83 |
| 0.60 | 6.66 | 6.96 | 3.62 | 3.66 | 3.33 | 2.31 | 6.82 | 7.06 | 3.67 | 3.71 | 3.38 | 2.32 |
| 0.55 | 4.54 | 4.69 | 2.82 | 2.80 | 2.91 | 1.99 | 4.56 | 4.74 | 2.85 | 2.84 | 2.93 | 1.99 |
| 0.50 | 3.20 | 3.29 | 2.29 | 2.25 | 2.56 | 1.73 | 3.22 | 3.31 | 2.33 | 2.27 | 2.58 | 1.71 |
| | $P_c = 0.15, \eta = 0.5, \beta = 1$ | | | | | | $P_c = 0.25, \eta = 0.5, \beta = 1$ | | | | | |
| $d_T$ | $d_{P_1} = d_{P_2} = 0.2$ | | $d_{P_1} = d_{P_2} = 0.5$ | | $d_{P_1} = d_{P_2} = 0.8$ | | $d_{P_1} = d_{P_2} = 0.2$ | | $d_{P_1} = d_{P_2} = 0.5$ | | $d_{P_1} = d_{P_2} = 0.8$ | |
| | **SR** | **CUSUM** | **SR** | **CUSUM** | **SR** | **CUSUM** | **SR** | **CUSUM** | **SR** | **CUSUM** | **SR** | **CUSUM** |
| | **h = 7.97** | **h = 2.04** | **h = 105.47** | **h = 4.07** | **h = 337.52** | **h = 3.70** | **h = 8.24** | **h = 2.07** | **h = 106.67** | **h = 4.06** | **h = 342.67** | **h = 3.68** |
| | 370.27 | 370.83 | 370.01 | 370.07 | 370.15 | 370.39 | 370.15 | 369.91 | 370.77 | 370.11 | 370.64 | 369.91 |
| 0.90 | 130.29 | 132.33 | 83.55 | 91.23 | 30.90 | 30.83 | 130.79 | 132.70 | 84.67 | 92.52 | 32.15 | 31.55 |
| 0.85 | 77.84 | 80.29 | 42.36 | 46.95 | 14.60 | 13.46 | 78.24 | 80.82 | 42.88 | 47.98 | 15.07 | 13.77 |
| 0.80 | 47.49 | 49.30 | 22.53 | 24.96 | 9.09 | 7.53 | 47.89 | 49.52 | 23.02 | 25.29 | 9.30 | 7.83 |
| 0.75 | 29.10 | 30.25 | 12.86 | 14.17 | 6.49 | 5.13 | 29.68 | 30.78 | 13.20 | 14.37 | 6.67 | 5.32 |
| 0.70 | 18.33 | 18.98 | 8.03 | 8.59 | 5.10 | 3.69 | 18.40 | 19.37 | 8.17 | 8.69 | 5.25 | 3.77 |
| 0.65 | 11.66 | 12.27 | 5.39 | 5.64 | 4.22 | 2.92 | 11.83 | 12.38 | 5.52 | 5.78 | 4.33 | 2.96 |
| 0.60 | 7.57 | 8.05 | 3.96 | 3.96 | 3.61 | 2.41 | 7.74 | 8.16 | 4.04 | 4.07 | 3.68 | 2.45 |
| 0.55 | 5.17 | 5.42 | 3.06 | 3.05 | 3.13 | 2.06 | 5.28 | 5.49 | 3.13 | 3.10 | 3.18 | 2.06 |
| 0.50 | 3.61 | 3.75 | 2.51 | 2.43 | 2.75 | 1.78 | 3.68 | 3.82 | 2.55 | 2.47 | 2.80 | 1.78 |
| | $P_c = 0.15, \eta = 2, \beta = 1$ | | | | | | $P_c = 0.25, \eta = 2, \beta = 1$ | | | | | |
| $d_T$ | $d_{P_1} = d_{P_2} = 0.2$ | | $d_{P_1} = d_{P_2} = 0.5$ | | $d_{P_1} = d_{P_2} = 0.8$ | | $d_{P_1} = d_{P_2} = 0.2$ | | $d_{P_1} = d_{P_2} = 0.5$ | | $d_{P_1} = d_{P_2} = 0.8$ | |
| | **SR** | **CUSUM** | **SR** | **CUSUM** | **SR** | **CUSUM** | **SR** | **CUSUM** | **SR** | **CUSUM** | **SR** | **CUSUM** |
| | **h = 7.96** | **h = 2.04** | **h = 106.11** | **h = 4.07** | **h = 338.31** | **h = 3.71** | **h = 8.24** | **h = 2.07** | **h = 107.23** | **h = 4.06** | **h = 341.46** | **h = 3.68** |
| | 370.47 | 370.25 | 370.19 | 369.87 | 370.49 | 369.96 | 370.37 | 370.67 | 370.44 | 370.36 | 370.59 | 369.62 |
| 0.90 | 129.45 | 133.10 | 83.61 | 90.66 | 30.52 | 30.04 | 130.72 | 131.52 | 84.66 | 92.12 | 31.45 | 31.38 |
| 0.85 | 78.04 | 80.04 | 41.92 | 47.13 | 14.62 | 13.32 | 78.42 | 80.97 | 43.18 | 48.38 | 15.14 | 14.07 |
| 0.80 | 47.71 | 48.99 | 22.54 | 25.01 | 9.04 | 7.64 | 48.24 | 49.27 | 23.09 | 25.48 | 9.30 | 7.65 |
| 0.75 | 29.21 | 30.51 | 12.87 | 14.15 | 6.52 | 5.12 | 29.46 | 30.73 | 13.18 | 14.32 | 6.65 | 5.26 |
| 0.70 | 18.04 | 18.97 | 8.05 | 8.55 | 5.11 | 3.72 | 18.50 | 19.45 | 8.22 | 8.76 | 5.24 | 3.75 |
| 0.65 | 11.79 | 12.20 | 5.42 | 5.59 | 4.22 | 2.90 | 11.88 | 12.38 | 5.60 | 5.71 | 4.33 | 2.97 |
| 0.60 | 7.61 | 7.98 | 3.95 | 3.99 | 3.60 | 2.43 | 7.78 | 8.17 | 4.05 | 4.07 | 3.67 | 2.42 |
| 0.55 | 5.13 | 5.40 | 3.08 | 3.04 | 3.14 | 2.05 | 5.23 | 5.50 | 3.14 | 3.09 | 3.18 | 2.03 |
| 0.50 | 3.62 | 3.77 | 2.51 | 2.45 | 2.75 | 1.77 | 3.67 | 3.80 | 2.55 | 2.48 | 2.79 | 1.80 |

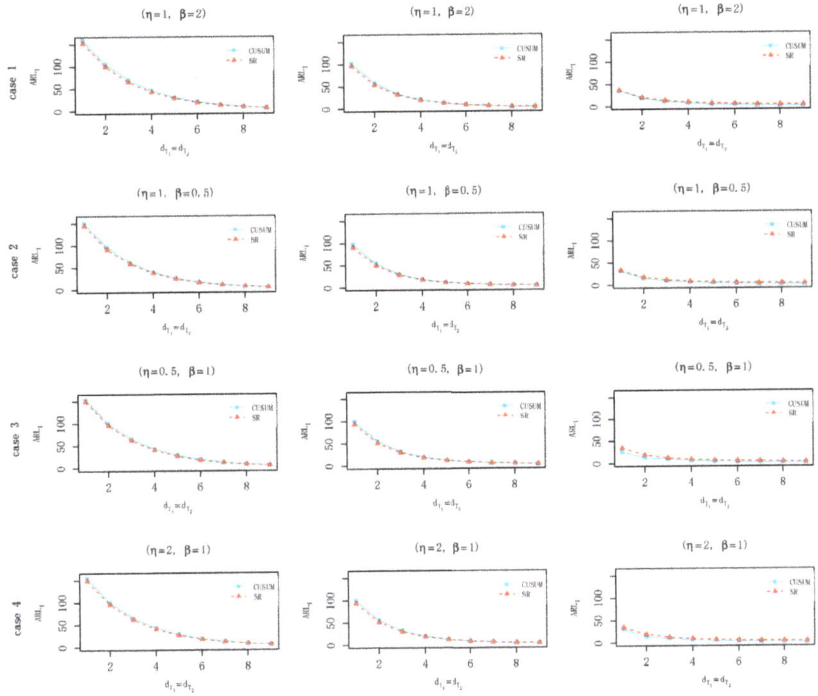


**Figure 3.** SS-ARL comparison between the SR and CUSUM charts ($n = 5$, $P_c = 0.15$, $\text{ARL}_0 = 370$).

A comparative analysis of ZS-ARL results between Table 1 ($n = 5$) and Table 3 ($n = 10$) demonstrates that increased sample size enhances control chart monitoring performance. Under identical process shift conditions ($d_{T_1} = d_{T_2}$), expanding the sample size from $n = 5$ to $n = 10$ yields significant reductions in ARL for both control charts. Specifically, the SR chart exhibits ARL reductions from 153.75 to 135.90 (11.6% decrease) for $d_{T_1} = 0.90$ and from 6.99 to 4.23 (39.5% decrease) for $d_{T_1} = 0.50$. Similarly, the CUSUM chart shows improved responsiveness with ARL decreasing from 161.07 to 138.68 (13.9% reduction) at $d_{T_1} = 0.90$, and a substantial 40.1% improvement (7.34 to 4.40) for $d_{T_1} = 0.50$. These results highlight the amplified detection capability of larger samples, particularly for smaller process shifts where statistical power gains are most pronounced.

To ensure a fair comparison benchmarked against Pei-Hsi [18], we evaluated the ZS-ARL performance of the proposed SR and CUSUM control charts alongside existing EWMA methods under identical operating conditions ($\eta = 1, \beta = 1, n = 5, \text{ARL}_0 = 200$). Final comparisons with existing depth-based EWMA control charts reveal that both the proposed SR and CUSUM charts demonstrate superior performance for detecting small shifts. Only for large shift detection does the CNN-based EWMA control chart outperform both SR and CUSUM control charts (see Table 5).The SR and CUSUM schemes exhibit pronounced advantages in computational efficiency, interpretability, and unsupervised statistical process control. In contrast, machine learning methods offer a formidable capability for managing high-dimensional and complex data, as well as for identifying subtle, non-linear patterns where traditional parametric assumptions may fail.

**Table 5.** SS-ARL comparison for $\eta = 1, \beta = 1, n = 5$, $ARL_0 = 200$.

| $d_{T_2}$ | $d_{P_2} = 0.2$ | | $d_{P_2} = 0.5$ | | $d_{P_2} = 0.8$ | | $\lambda = 0.1$ | | | | | | $\lambda = 0.2$ | | | | | |
|---|---|---|---|---|---|---|---|---|---|---|---|---|---|---|---|---|---|---|
| | SR | CUSUM | SR | CUSUM | SR | CUSUM | EWMA | | CNN | | LSTM | | EWMA | | CNN | | LSTM | |
| | | | | | | | CEV | CM | CEV | CM | CEV | CM | CEV | CM | CEV | CM | CEV | CM |
| **$P_c = 0.2$** | | | | | | | | | | | | | | | | | | |
| | **h = 6.08** | **h = 1.76** | **h = 57.02** | **h = 3.54** | **h = 177.91** | **h = 3.29** | **h = 0.78** | **h = 0.41** | **h = −0.11** | **h = −0.03** | **h = −0.81** | **h = −0.40** | **h = 0.69** | **h = 0.36** | **h = −0.06** | **h = −0.05** | **h = −0.79** | **h = −0.40** |
| 0.80 | 27.36 | 28.75 | 14.87 | 16.29 | 7.08 | 6.29 | 15.52 | 17.85 | 21.59 | 21.86 | 32.63 | 95.62 | 15.50 | 17.21 | 18.01 | 23.91 | 26.72 | 130.62 |
| 0.70 | 11.52 | 12.10 | 5.97 | 6.47 | 4.21 | 3.20 | 8.78 | 9.73 | 7.38 | 8.80 | 12.53 | 41.08 | 8.08 | 8.57 | 7.30 | 8.87 | 11.48 | 45.06 |
| 0.60 | 5.42 | 5.67 | 3.29 | 3.34 | 3.10 | 2.22 | 4.99 | 6.78 | 3.71 | 4.88 | 6.51 | 16.26 | 5.27 | 5.50 | 3.01 | 4.39 | 6.30 | 16.46 |
| 0.50 | 2.87 | 2.99 | 2.21 | 2.17 | 2.44 | 1.70 | 3.64 | 4.16 | 2.36 | 2.75 | 3.72 | 7.92 | 3.90 | 3.92 | 2.25 | 2.06 | 3.88 | 9.34 |
| 0.20 | 1.07 | 1.07 | 1.09 | 1.07 | 1.28 | 1.05 | 2.38 | 2.55 | 1.19 | 1.17 | 1.29 | 2.44 | 2.07 | 2.26 | 1.13 | 1.00 | 1.23 | 2.52 |
| **$P_c = 0.5$** | | | | | | | | | | | | | | | | | | |
| | **h = 6.23** | **h = 1.77** | **h = 58.43** | **h = 3.56** | **h = 179.86** | **h = 3.27** | **h = 0.83** | **h = 0.27** | **h = −0.06** | **h = −0.02** | **h = −0.80** | **h = −0.15** | **h = 0.73** | **h = 0.25** | **h = −0.06** | **h = −0.02** | **h = −0.79** | **h = −0.15** |
| 0.80 | 28.22 | 28.86 | 15.21 | 17.45 | 7.30 | 6.19 | 10.96 | 12.37 | 15.82 | 13.60 | 29.42 | 20.26 | 12.28 | 10.34 | 14.71 | 13.20 | 23.71 | 19.39 |
| 0.70 | 11.81 | 12.24 | 6.15 | 6.61 | 4.26 | 3.24 | 5.48 | 5.19 | 5.32 | 4.31 | 13.53 | 6.95 | 6.54 | 5.26 | 4.75 | 4.03 | 12.07 | 7.68 |
| 0.60 | 5.44 | 5.74 | 3.36 | 3.41 | 3.14 | 2.20 | 3.49 | 3.55 | 3.04 | 1.86 | 7.03 | 3.60 | 4.09 | 3.36 | 2.58 | 2.01 | 5.87 | 3.58 |
| 0.50 | 2.96 | 3.09 | 2.24 | 2.18 | 2.46 | 1.68 | 3.73 | 3.61 | 2.05 | 1.26 | 3.70 | 2.08 | 3.14 | 2.48 | 1.42 | 1.27 | 3.78 | 1.97 |
| 0.20 | 1.07 | 1.08 | 1.10 | 1.08 | 1.28 | 1.05 | 1.68 | 2.21 | 1.26 | 1.00 | 1.27 | 1.04 | 1.84 | 1.39 | 1.00 | 1.00 | 1.30 | 1.02 |
| **$P_c = 0.8$** | | | | | | | | | | | | | | | | | | |
| | **h = 6.38** | **h = 1.80** | **h = 58.95** | **h = 3.49** | **h = 184.91** | **h = 3.17** | **h = 0.88** | **h = 0.39** | **h = −0.06** | **h = −0.03** | **h = −0.65** | **h = −0.21** | **h = 0.82** | **h = 0.37** | **h = −0.05** | **h = −0.01** | **h = −0.66** | **h = −0.22** |
| 0.80 | 29.32 | 30.49 | 16.17 | 17.34 | 7.95 | 6.73 | 9.78 | 9.23 | 10.03 | 8.88 | 20.20 | 18.41 | 9.49 | 8.21 | 8.83 | 7.80 | 22.51 | 21.44 |
| 0.70 | 12.12 | 12.90 | 6.62 | 6.96 | 4.55 | 3.55 | 4.78 | 5.99 | 4.46 | 3.61 | 9.51 | 8.11 | 4.85 | 4.49 | 3.69 | 3.15 | 9.23 | 9.22 |
| 0.60 | 5.81 | 5.95 | 3.56 | 3.59 | 3.31 | 2.17 | 4.48 | 3.96 | 1.98 | 1.51 | 4.39 | 3.39 | 3.09 | 2.92 | 2.43 | 1.68 | 4.71 | 4.10 |
| 0.50 | 3.06 | 3.19 | 2.34 | 2.26 | 2.54 | 1.60 | 2.11 | 2.70 | 1.38 | 1.14 | 2.45 | 1.90 | 2.27 | 2.23 | 1.58 | 1.31 | 2.71 | 2.35 |
| 0.20 | 1.08 | 1.08 | 1.10 | 1.07 | 1.28 | 1.02 | 2.58 | 1.28 | 1.00 | 1.00 | 1.06 | 1.01 | 1.25 | 1.31 | 1.00 | 1.01 | 1.05 | 1.00 |

## 6. Example

To validate the proposed methodology, we adopt the liquid-crystal display module (LCM) reliability test dataset from Pei-Hsi [18], comprising 30 batches of accelerated life testing data under 70 °C and 80% relative humidity conditions, with a sample size of $n = 5$ per batch. Historical IC phase analysis confirms that the LCM lifetime follows a Gamma distribution with shape parameter $\beta_0 = 5.72$ and scale parameter $\eta_0 = 0.48$. To optimize testing efficiency, a Type I right-censoring scheme with censoring rate $P_c = 0.8$ (equivalent to censoring time $c = 1.76$ h) was implemented, where each batch test terminates at 1.76 h regardless of failure occurrences.

The monitoring procedure begins with the initialization of IC process parameters, including the sample size $n$, censoring rate $P_c$, predetermined percent changed$d_P$, and the Gamma distribution's shape and scale parameters $\beta$ and $\eta$. A total of 50,000 simulation replications are defined, and the UCL is initialized with a provisional value $h$. In the data generation step, a sample of size $n$ is drawn from the Gamma distribution parameterized by $\beta$ and $\eta$. The monitoring statistic $R_i$ is then computed for the current sample. If $R_i$ remains below or equal to $h$, a new sample is generated; however, if $R_i$ exceed $h$, the sample index at which this first OOC signal is detected is recorded as the RL. This process is repeated iteratively until 50,000 run lengths are collected. The mean of these run lengths is calculated to estimate the IC $\text{ARL}_0$ corresponding to the current $h$. The UCL $h$ is adjusted iteratively until the target $\text{ARL}_0$ is achieved, at which point the final UCL is set to the calibrated value of $h$.

The monitoring process begins by defining the necessary parameters, including the sample size $n$, shape parameter $\beta$, scale parameter $\eta$, censoring rate $P_c$, and the magnitude of the shift $d_{P_j}$, followed by the determination of the corresponding control limits. A sample of size $n$ is then generated, incorporating a shift of size $d_{T_j}$, and the plotting statistic $R_t$ is computed using Equation (17). If the control chart signals an OOC condition, the RL is recorded; otherwise, the process returns to sample generation. After repeating Steps 2 and 3 for 50,000 replications, the OOC $\text{ARL}_1$ is calculated as the average of all recorded RL values.

Following Lee and Liao's experimental setup with smoothing constant $\lambda = 0.1$ and target IC $\text{ARL}_0$ of 200, we implemented both CUSUM and SR control charts for comparative analysis. The simulation-derived control limits were determined as $h_{SR} = 20.35$ for the SR chart and $h_{CUSUM} = 2.87$ for the CUSUM chart. Figure 4 presents the Phase II monitoring of all control charts for LCM data. Notably, while the CNN-based EWMA CEV chart and EWMA CEV chart triggered OOC signals at sample points 20 and 21, respectively, both our SR and CUSUM charts detected the process shift at sample point 19. This demonstrates that the detection ability of the proposed methods outperforms that of advanced CNN-enhanced methods. The proposed SR and CUSUM schemes offer two key advantages compared to CNN-based methods: simpler implementation without requiring complex deep learning architectures, and better adaptability for monitoring both shape and scale parameters in highly censored Gamma-distributed data. This makes them particularly suitable for industrial applications where computational resources are limited but reliable monitoring of multiple parameters is essential.

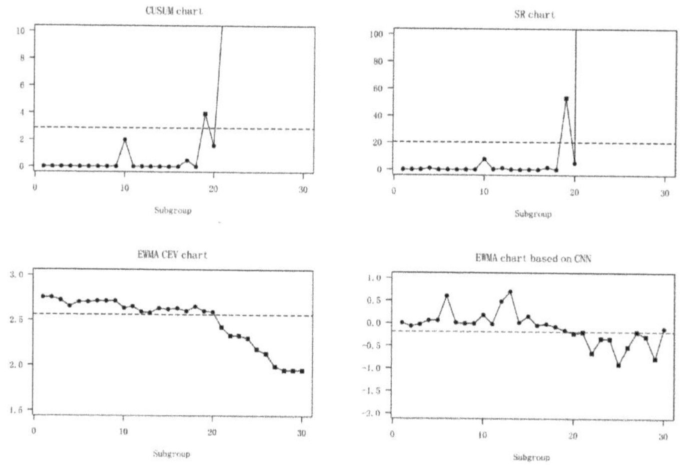


**Figure 4.** Phase II monitoring for LCM data.

## 7. Conclusions

This study has established the effectiveness of CUSUM and SR control charts for monitoring Type I right-censored Gamma-distributed lifetime data. Through comprehensive evaluation using zero-state and steady-state ARL metrics, both control charts demonstrate superior detection capability compared to deep learning-based EWMA methods across various shift magnitudes. The results reveal an important performance characteristic: while the SR chart exhibits greater sensitivity to small process deviations, the CUSUM chart proves more effective for identifying larger shifts. This complementary performance profile provides practitioners with valuable alternatives depending on their specific monitoring requirements. Notably, the proposed methods achieve this enhanced detection performance without relying on computationally intensive deep learning architectures, offering a more practical solution for industrial implementation where both statistical reliability and operational simplicity are crucial. It should be noted that the proposed method has certain limitations. It is predicated on the assumption of known parameters, and its performance is susceptible to the accuracy of parameter estimation. Furthermore, the methodology is developed specifically for the Gamma distribution, therefore, not applicable to non-parametric scenarios. The findings contribute to the growing body of research on censored data monitoring by demonstrating how traditional statistical process control methods can be effectively adapted for modern reliability engineering applications. The proposed scheme has been validated in a manufacturing context. A promising future direction would be to explore its application in new domains such as financial risk control or medical diagnosis.The existing SR and CUSUM schemes can be extended to monitor censored data from other distributions and are also applicable to Type II censoring.

**Author Contributions:** Conceptualization, H.L., P.C., R.M., and J.Z.; methodology, H.L. and P.C.; software, H.L. and P.C.; validation, H.L., P.C., R.M., and J.Z.; formal analysis, H.L.; writing—original draft preparation, H.L.; writing—review and editing, H.L. and P.C.; supervision, H.L., P.C., R.M., and J.Z.; project administration, H.L.; funding acquisition, H.L., R.M., and J.Z. All authors have read and agreed to the published version of the manuscript.

**Funding:** This research was supported by [Grant Nos. JYTMS20230768] by the Project of the Education Department of Liaoning Province, Research on Humanities and Social Sciences of the Ministry of Education [22YJC910009], National Natural Science Foundation of China [62473183], Scientific

Research Fund of Educational Department of Liaoning Province, China [JYTMS20230773], and The Education Department of Liaoning Province:[LJKQZ2021179]. Among them, the first two grants (JYTMS20230768 and 22YJC910009) are managed by Jiujun Zhang, the third and fourth grants (62473183 and JYTMS20230773)are managed by Ruicheng Ma, the last grant (LJKQZ2021179) is managed by Wei Yang.

**Data Availability Statement:** All data are available in the paper.

**Conflicts of Interest:** The authors declare that there are no conflicts of interest regarding the publication of this paper.

## References

1. Shewhart, W.A. *Economic Control of Quality of Manufactured Product*; Macmillan and Co., Ltd.: New York, USA, 1931.
2. Page, E. Continuous inspection schemes. *Biometrika* **1954**, *41*, 100–115. [CrossRef]
3. Zhang, C.W.; Xie, M.; Liu, J.Y.; Goh, T.N. A control chart for the Gamma distribution as a model of time between events. *Int. J. Prod. Res.* **2007**, *45*, 5649–5666. [CrossRef]
4. Alevizakos, V.; Koukouvinos, C. A double exponentially weighted moving average chart for time between events. *Commun. Stat.-Simul. Comput.* **2020**, *49*, 2765–2784. [CrossRef]
5. Yang, J.; Yu, H.; Cheng, Y.; Xie, M. Design of Gamma Charts Based on Average Time to Signal. *Qual. Reliab. Eng. Int.* **2016**, *32*, 1041–1058. [CrossRef]
6. Chakraborty, N.; Human, S.W.; Balakrishnan, N. A generally weighted moving average chart for time between events. *Commun. Stat.-Simul. Comput.* **2017**, *46*, 7790–7817. [CrossRef]
7. Alevizakos, V.; Koukouvinos, C.; Lappa, A. Monitoring of time between events with a double generally weighted moving average control chart. *Qual. Reliab. Eng. Int.* **2019**, *35*, 685–710. [CrossRef]
8. Shah, M.T.; Azam, M.; Aslam, M.; Sherazi, U. Time between events control charts for gamma distribution. *Qual. Reliab. Eng. Int.* **2021**, *37*, 785–803. [CrossRef]
9. Alevizakos, V.; Chatterjee, K.; Koukouvinos, C. A triple exponentially weighted moving average control chart for monitoring time between events. *Qual. Reliab. Eng. Int.* **2021**, *37*, 1059–1079. [CrossRef]
10. Lone, S.A.; Rasheed, Z.; Anwar, S.; Khan, M.; Anwar, S.M.; Shahab, S. Enhanced fault detection models with real-life applications. *AIMS Math.* **2023**, *8*, 19595–19636. [CrossRef]
11. Steiner, S.H.; Mackay, R.J. Monitoring Processes with Highly Censored Data. *J. Qual. Technol.* **2000**, *32*, 199–208. [CrossRef]
12. Dickinson, R.M.; Roberts, D.A.O.; Driscoll, A.R.; Woodall, W.H.; Vining, G.G. CUSUM Charts for Monitoring the Characteristic Life of Censored Weibull Lifetimes. *J. Qual. Technol.* **2014**, *46*, 340–358. [CrossRef]
13. Choi, M.; Lee, J. A binomial CUSUM chart for monitoring type I right-censored Weibull lifetimes. *Korean J. Appl. Stat.* **2016**, *29*, 823–833. [CrossRef]
14. Xu, S.; Jeske, D.R. Weighted EWMA charts for monitoring type I censored Weibull lifetimes. *J. Qual. Technol.* **2018**, *50*, 220–230. [CrossRef]
15. Yu, D.; Jin, L.; Li, J.; Qin, X.; Zhu, Z.; Zhang, J. Monitoring the Weibull Scale Parameter Based on Type I Censored Data Using a Modified EWMA Control Chart. *Axioms* **2023**, *12*, 487. [CrossRef]
16. Zhang, S.; Hu, X.; Zhai, C.; Wang, J.; Ma, Y. Monitoring right censored Weibull distributed lifetime with weighted adaptive CUSUM charts based on dynamic probability limits. *Expert Syst. Appl.* **2025**, *272*, 126797. [CrossRef]
17. Ali, S.; Shamim, R.; Shah, I.; Alrweili, H.; Marcon, G. Memory-type control charts for censored reliability data. *Qual. Reliab. Eng. Int.* **2023**, *39*, 2365–2384. [CrossRef]
18. Lee, P.-H.; Liao, S.-L. Monitoring gamma type-I censored data using an exponentially weighted moving average control chart based on deep learning networks. *Sci. Rep.* **2024**, *14*, 6458. [CrossRef]
19. Jiang, R.; Zhang, J.; Yu, Z. Adaptive EWMA control chart for monitoring two-parameter exponential distribution with type-II right censored data. *J. Stat. Comput. Simul.* **2024**, *94*, 787–819. [CrossRef]
20. Nadi, A.A.; Afshari, R.; Gildeh, B.S. Control charts for monitoring relative risk rate in the presence of Weibull competing risks with censored and masked data. *Qual. Technol. Quant. Manag.* **2024**, *21*, 340–362. [CrossRef]
21. Chaturvedi, A.; Joshi, N.; Bapat, S.R.; Nadarajah, S. Control Charts for the Percentiles of an Inverse Pareto Distribution Under Complete and Middle-Censored Data. *Qual. Reliab. Eng. Int.* **2025**, *41*, 1971–1984. [CrossRef]
22. Shiryaev, A.N. The problem of the most rapid detection of a disturbance in a stationary process. *Sov.-Math.-Dokl.* **1961**, *2*, 795–799.
23. Pollak, M.; Siegmund, D. Sequential Detection of a Change in a Normal Mean when the Initial Value is Unknown. *Ann. Stat.* **1991**, *19*, 394–416. [CrossRef]

24. Kenett, R.S.; Pollak, M. Data-analytic aspects of the Shiryayev-Roberts control chart: Surveillance of a non-homogeneous Poisson process. *J. Appl. Stat.* **1996**, *23*, 125–138. [CrossRef]
25. Srivastava, M.S.; Wu, Y. Comparison of EWMA, CUSUM and Shiryayev-Roberts Procedures for Detecting a Shift in the Mean. *Ann. Stat.* **1993**, *21*, 645–670. [CrossRef]
26. Zhang, J.; Zou, C.; Wang, Z. A New Chart for Detecting the Process Mean and Variability. *Commun. Stat.-Simul. Comput.* **2011**, *40*, 728–743. [CrossRef]
27. Zhang, J.; Zou, C.; Wang, Z. An adaptive Shiryaev-Roberts procedure for monitoring dispersion. *Comput. Ind. Eng.* **2011**, *61*, 1166–1172. [CrossRef]
28. Moustakides, G.V.; Polunchenko, A.S.; Tartakovsky, A.G. Numerical Comparison of CUSUM and Shiryaev–Roberts Procedures for Detecting Changes in Distributions. *Commun. Stat.-Theory Methods* **2009**, *38*, 3225–3239. [CrossRef]
29. Ottenstreuer, S. The Shiryaev–Roberts control chart for Markovian count time series. *Qual. Reliab. Eng. Int.* **2022**, *38*, 1207–1225. [CrossRef]
30. Yu, D.; Mukherjee, A.; Li, J.; Jin, L.; Wen, K.; Zhang, J. Performance of the Shiryaev-Roberts-type scheme in comparison to the CUSUM and EWMA schemes in monitoring weibull scale parameter based on Type I censored data. *Qual. Reliab. Eng. Int.* **2022**, *38*, 3379–3403. [CrossRef]
31. Meeker, W. *Statistical Methods for Reliability Data*; Wiley: New York, USA, 1998.
32. Montgomery, D.C. *Introduction to Statistical Quality Control*; Wiley: Hoboken, NJ, USA, 2020.
33. Zwetsloot, I.M.; Woodall, W.H. A Review of Some Sampling and Aggregation Strategies for Basic Statistical Process Monitoring. *J. Qual. Technol.* **2021**, *53*, 1–16. [CrossRef]

axioms

*Article*

# A Trust-Enhancing Variant of the Binary Randomized Response Technique

**Sat Gupta [1], Nikita Jayaraj [2], Mala Gupta [3] and Pidugu Trisandhya [1,4,*]**

[1] Department of Mathematics and Statistics, University of North Carolina at Greensboro, Greensboro, NC 27412, USA; sngupta@uncg.edu
[2] Department of Biomedical Sciences, Texas A & M University, College Station, TX 77843, USA; nikitajayx5@gmail.com
[3] Department of Biochemistry, University of Texas at Austin, Austin, TX 78712, USA; malagrace03@utexas.edu
[4] Department of Applied Sciences, Bharati Vidyapeeth's College of Engineering, New Delhi 110063, India
* Correspondence: trisandhya.09@gmail.com

**Abstract:** Building on recent studies on trust enhancement in quantitative Randomized Response Technique (RRT) models, this study introduces trust enhancement in a binary mixture RRT model. Our approach emphasizes building respondent trust alongside preserving anonymity. To support our theoretical findings, we conduct a simulation study. The overarching goal of our work is to shift the focus from merely protecting anonymity and accounting for lack of trust to actively fostering trust. Simulation results show that the proposed model has better quality, and succeeds in building respondent trust that results in more efficient estimates.

**Keywords:** randomized response models; respondents privacy; simulations; trust enhancement

**MSC:** 62D05

## 1. Introduction

Collecting accurate responses to sensitive survey questions continues to pose challenges due to non-response and social desirability bias. Respondents are often reluctant to disclose private or stigmatized behaviors, resulting in distorted or missing data. To address this, Warner (1965) introduced the first Randomized Response Technique (RRT) model, a survey technique that offers privacy protection through probabilistic masking, thereby encouraging truthful participation [1]. Building on this foundation, Greenberg et al. (1969) proposed the unrelated question model (UQM), which offers an alternative privacy protection scheme by including a non-sensitive question in the response mechanism [2].

Over the years, researchers have introduced numerous variants of RRT, targeting improvements in estimation accuracy, respondent cooperation, and privacy protection. Notable contributions include the Partial RRT by Mangat and Singh (1990) who introduce a truth element in the survey using a random mechanism [3], the Optional RRT by Gupta et al. (2002) who allow respondents to provide a truthful response if they do not perceive the question to be too sensitive [4], and mixture models explored by Kim and Warde (2005) [5] and Lovig et al. (2023) [6]. These mixture models perform better than the individual component models.

More recent studies have highlighted the importance of trust in RRT mechanisms. This growing awareness has led to models that explicitly account for dishonesty, such as the trust-aware mixture model proposed by Lovig et al. (2023) [6] and the trust-enhancing framework by Parker et al. (2024) [7].

Some researchers such as Jones and Sigall (1971) and Reynolds (1982) have emphasized alternative approaches like the Bogus Pipeline and Social Desirability Scales [8,9], yet RRT remains the most mathematically structured technique for anonymity in data collection. RRT models have been used extensively in real surveys. Ostapczuk et al. (2009) used a RRT model to examine the impact of higher education on attitudes towards immigrants in Germany [10]. Striegel et al. (2006) used RRT to study the prevalence of doping by athletes [11]. Kalucha et al. (2025) have used a complex RRT model to estimate the prevalence of depression among college students [12]. These studies show that RRT methodology can be used effectively in real surveys.

To evaluate the performance of RRT models, researchers have used unified measures that incorporate both estimator efficiency and respondent privacy. Contributions by Lanke (1976) [13], Fligner et al. (1977) [14], and Gupta et al. (2018) [15] have provided metrics that allow for comprehensive model comparisons. These techniques allow researchers to assess the trade-offs involved in improving estimator efficiency and protecting privacy.

The primary goal of this study is to fill a critical gap in binary RRT models where the significance of lack of trust has been acknowledged, as in Lovig et al. (2023) [6], but unlike the quantitative domain, trust enhancement has not been implemented in the binary domain. This study focuses on comparing three core RRT models. the Warner (1965) [1] indirect question model, the Greenberg et al. (1969) unrelated question model [2], and the Lovig et al. (2023) [6] mixture model. We show that the trust-enhanced models perform better than their basic counterparts with no trust enhancement. Simulation results and corresponding plots show that trust-enhanced models lead to greater estimation stability and overall model quality measured through a unified measure of model quality.

## 2. Trust Enhancement in RRT Models

The original binary Randomized Response Technique (RRT) was introduced by Warner in (1965) which offered respondents better privacy by letting them randomly choose the direct or the indirect version of the sensitive question [1]. For example, a respondent might face the direct question "did you cheat on the exam", or the indirect question "were you honest on the exam"?. Clearly, a "yes" response is incriminating for the direct question but not for the indirect question. Note that the researcher does not know which question was answered. Since then, numerous other models have been developed, including the Greenberg et al. (1969) unrelated question model [2], each adding new dimensions to the estimation of sensitive trait prevalence. More recently, trust has emerged as a critical factor in the accuracy of these models, with researchers emphasizing the importance of accounting for it (Lovig et al. (2023)) [6] and exploring trust-enhancement approaches (Parker et al. (2024)) [7]. In this study, however, the emphasis will be placed on trust enhancement in the Greenberg model and the Lovig model.

### 2.1. Previous Models

The flow diagrams below provide representations of various RRT models. We will use the notations given in (Table 1) below:

**Table 1.** Notation and definitions used in the RRT models.

| Symbol | Description |
|---|---|
| $n$ | sample size (number of respondents). |
| $p$ | probability that the respondent is in the direct question group. |
| $q$ | probability that the respondent is in the indirect question group. |
| $1-p-q$ | probability that the respondent is in the unrelated question group. |
| $\pi_x$ | prevalence of the sensitive trait in the target population. |
| $\pi_y$ | proportion of the unrelated trait in the target population (such as prevalence of April births). |
| $A$ | proportion of respondents who trust the underlying RRT model and provide a response as per the model instructions. |
| $1-A$ | proportion of the respondents who do not trust the RRT methodology to protect their privacy if the model-based response is incriminating, and switch their response from "yes" to "no", or from "no" to "yes" to avoid incrimination and maintain social desirability. |
| $P_{yw}$ | probability of the respondent entering a "yes" response for Warner's Model. |
| $P_{yg}$ | probability of the respondent entering a "yes" response for Greenberg's model. |
| $P_{yL}$ | probability of the respondent entering a "yes" response for Lovig's model. |
| $P_{yn_1}$ | probability of the respondent entering a "yes" response for the Enhanced-Trust Greenberg model. |
| $P_{yn_2}$ | probability of the respondent entering a "yes" response for the Enhanced-Trust Lovig model. |
| $p_0$ | the probability of direct questioning utilized in the Greenberg model for the assessment of Trust. |
| $\pi_{y0}$ | the probability of the unrelated trait in the Greenberg model for the assessment of Trust. |
| $\hat{\theta}$ | the estimated value of the parameter $\theta$. |

2.1.1. Warner's Model

Warner's Model is illustrated in Figure 1.

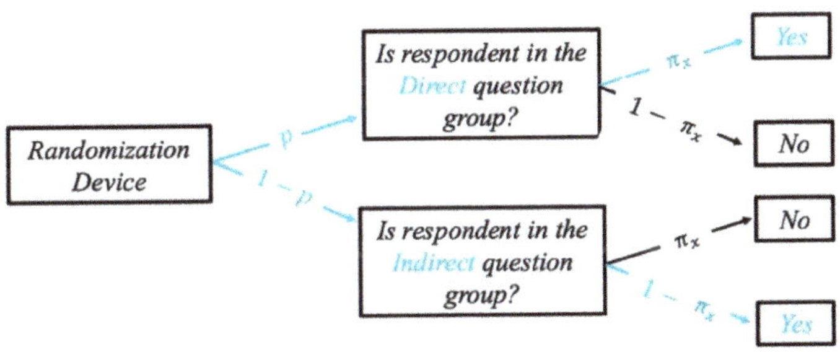


**Figure 1.** Warner's Model.

The probability of a "yes" response under this model can be expressed as follows:

$$P_{yw} = p\pi_x + (1-p)(1-\pi_x). \tag{1}$$

In Warner's model, each respondent receives either a sensitive question or an indirect form of that question, selected according to fixed probabilities using a randomization mechanism. Importantly, the interviewer remains unaware of which version of the question the respondent is answering. The diagram assumes the direct question is selected with probability $p$ and the indirect question with probability $1-p$.

From Equation (1), an unbiased estimator for $\pi_x$ is derived as follows:

$$\widehat{\pi_x} = \frac{\widehat{P_{yw}} - (1-p)}{2p-1}\ ;\ p \neq \frac{1}{2}.$$

The variance of this estimator is given by the following:

$$Var(\widehat{\pi_x}) = \frac{P_{yw}(1-P_{yw})}{n(2p-1)^2}.$$

It is recommended that an ideal choice of p for the Warner model is away from $\frac{1}{2}$, but not too close to 0 or 1.

2.1.2. Greenberg's Model

Greenberg's Model is illustrated in Figure 2.

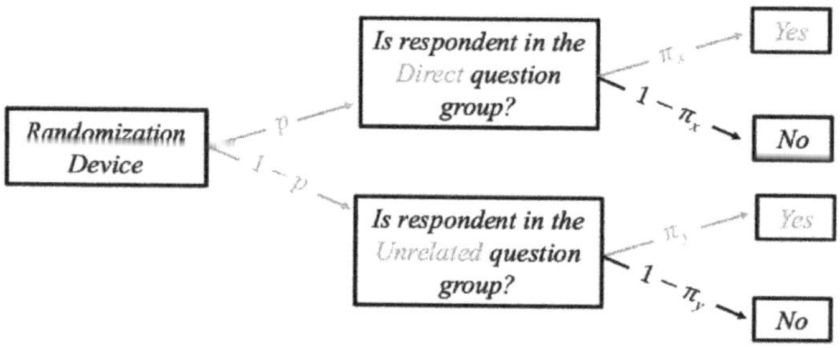


**Figure 2.** Greenberg's Model.

The probability of a "yes" response under this model can be expressed as follows:

$$P_{yg} = p\pi_x + (1-p)\pi_y. \tag{2}$$

In the Greenberg model, respondents are instructed to randomly select between answering the sensitive question or an entirely unrelated one. Because this selection is guided by a randomization device, the interviewer remains unaware of which question the respondent is addressing.

From Equation (2), an unbiased estimator for $\pi_x$ is derived as follows:

$$\widehat{\pi_x} = \frac{\widehat{P_{yg}} - (1-p)\pi_y}{p}.$$

The variance of this estimator is given by the following:

$$Var(\widehat{\pi_x}) = \frac{P_{yg}(1-P_{yg})}{np^2}.$$

An ideal choice of $p$ for the Greenberg model is one that is greater than $\frac{1}{3}$ where the model is shown to be more efficient than the Warner model. Many studies, such as Lovig et al. (2023), have used $p = 0.7$. Lovig et al. (2023) used the April birth as the unrelated trait, and accordingly used $\pi_y = 0.1$, a value close to probability of April birth [6].

2.1.3. Lovig's Mixture Model That Accounts for Untruthfulness

Lovig's Mixture model is illustrated in Figure 3.

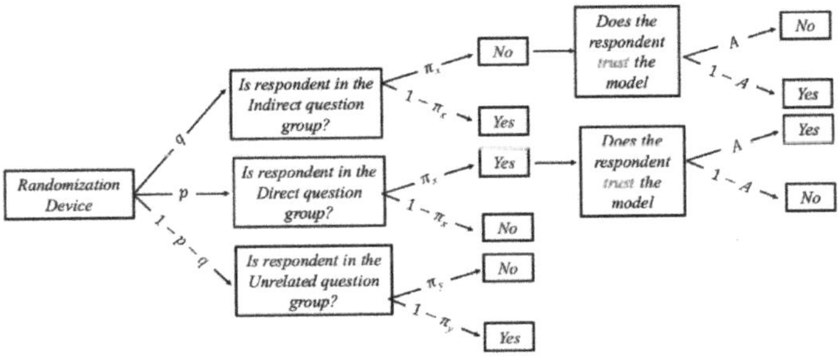


**Figure 3.** Lovig's Mixture model.

The probability of a "yes" response under this model can be expressed as follows:

$$P_{yL} = \pi_x A(p-q) + q + (1-p-q)\pi_y. \tag{3}$$

In Lovig's model, the authors built upon the framework of the Kim and Warde (2005) [5] mixture model, where respondents randomly choose between the Warner model and the Greenberg model. Lovig extended this by emphasizing the role of trust and introducing a trichotomous design. In their approach, it is assumed that if respondents do not trust the model in incriminating situations, they will flip their correct response to a non-incriminating response, which will obviously be an incorrect response.

From Equation (3), the prevalence estimator is given by

$$\widehat{\pi_x} = \frac{\widehat{P_{yL}} - q - (1-p-q)\pi_y}{\hat{A}(p-q)}\ ;\ p \neq q.$$

The variance of this estimator is given by the following:

$$Var(\widehat{\pi_x}) = \frac{P_{yL}(1-P_{yL})}{(n-1)A^2(p-q)^2}.$$

## 3. Proposed Trust-Enhanced Binary RRT Framework

In our proposed models, we aim to bridge the gap between merely acknowledging potential lack of trust and actively enhancing trust. To this end, we introduce a new variant of the binary RRT that structurally embeds respondent trust enhancement into the model. Drawing inspiration from recent trust-enhancement approaches of Parker et al. (2024) [7], we propose two binary RRT models: an Enhanced-Trust Greenberg Model and an Enhanced-Trust Lovig Model. Although the trust-enhanced Lovig et al. (2023) model will prove to be the overall best among the competing models [6], we include trust-enhanced Greenberg et al. (1969) [2] model just to include an intermediate step that shows that it can do better than the ordinary Greenberg et al. (1969) model but is not best overall.

### 3.1. Our Proposed Enhanced-Trust Greenberg Model (Model-I)

Proposed enhanced-trust Greenberg model (Model-I) is illustrated in Figure 4.

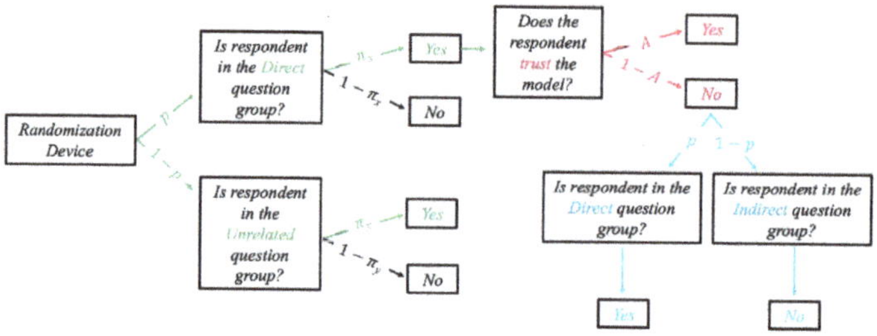


**Figure 4.** Proposed enhanced-trust Greenberg model (Model-I).

The probability of a "yes" response under this model can be expressed as follows:

$$P_{yn_1} = p\pi_x A + p^2\pi_x(1-A) + (1-p)\pi_y. \tag{4}$$

**In this model, without the trust enhancement, a proportion $p\pi_x(1-A)$ of the respondents would provide dishonest answers; however, with the enhanced-trust model, a proportion $p$ of these inaccurate responses can be corrected.**

From Equation (4), the prevalence estimator is given by

$$\widehat{\pi_x} = \frac{\widehat{P_{yn_1}} - (1-p)\pi_y}{p^2(1-\hat{A}) + p\hat{A}},$$

where $\hat{A}$ is the estimated trust parameter.

### 3.2. Our Proposed Enhanced-Trust Lovig Model (Model-II)

Proposed enhanced-trust Lovig model (Model-II) is illustrated in Figure 5.

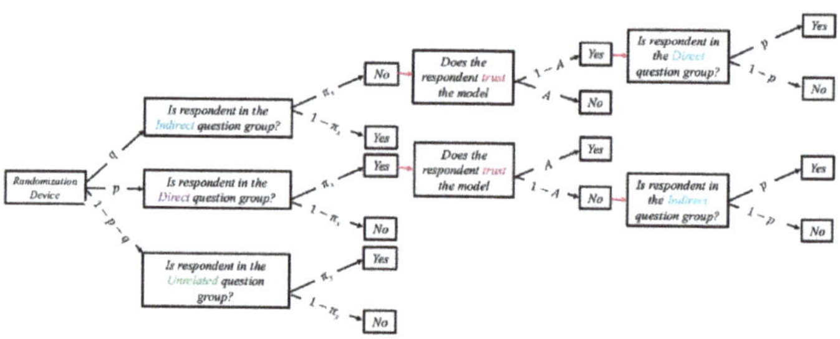


**Figure 5.** Proposed enhanced-trust Lovig model (Model-II).

The probability of a "yes" response under this model can be expressed as follows:

$$P_{yn_2} = p\pi_x A + p^2\pi_x(1-A) + q(1-\pi_x) + q\pi_x(1-A)p + (1-p-q)\pi_y. \tag{5}$$

**In this model, a proportion $p\pi_x(1-A) + q\pi_x(1-A)$ of respondents would provide dishonest answers without trust enhancement. However, with the enhanced-trust model, a proportion $p+q$ of these inaccurate responses can be corrected.**

From Equation (5), the prevalence estimator is given by

$$\widehat{\pi_x} = \frac{\widehat{P_{yn_2}} - q - (1-p-q)\pi_y}{\hat{A}p(1-p-q) + q(p-1) + p^2}.$$

It is important to point out that this prevalence estimator depends heavily on the accurate estimation of the trust parameter $A$. We will use the same approach as the one used by Lovig et al. (2023) and our simulation results confirm that $A$ is estimated fairly accurately [6].

### 3.3. *Effectiveness of the Mixture Model When Accounting for Untruthfulness*

To address untruthfulness in our model, we adopt a two-question approach used by Lovig et al. (2023) [6]. The first question is designed to estimate $A$, and this is achieved using the Greenberg model. The second question then estimates the prevalence of the sensitive trait, utilizing the proposed mixture model. We applied this approach to both of our proposed models: the enhanced-trust Greenberg model and the enhanced-trust Lovig model.

Let

$p_0$ = the probability of direct questioning utilized in the Greenberg model for the assessment of Trust,

$\pi_{y0}$ = the probability of the unrelated trait,

where $(p, q, \pi_x, \pi_y, A, n)$ are all the same as introduced in the proposed model described earlier.

**Question 1 (With Greenberg Model):** Do you trust the model?

The probability of a "yes" response and the resulting estimator are given by

$$P_{yo} = P_o(yes) = p_o A + (1 - p_o)\pi_{yo}, \text{ and}$$

$$\widehat{A} = \frac{\widehat{P_{yo}} - (1 - p_o)\pi_{yo}}{p_o}. \tag{6}$$

Since, $E(\widehat{P}_{yo}) = P_{yo}$ and $Var(\widehat{P}_{yo}) = \frac{P_{yo}(1-P_{yo})}{n}$, it follows that

$$E(\widehat{A}) = A, Var(\widehat{A}) = \frac{P_{yo}(1 - P_{yo})}{np_o^2}. \tag{7}$$

**Question 2 (Proposed Model-I):** Do you have the sensitive trait?

The probability of a "yes" response and the resulting estimator are given by

$$P_{yn_1} = p\pi_x A + p^2\pi_x(1 - A) + (1 - p)\pi_y, \text{ and}$$

$$\widehat{\pi_x} = \frac{\widehat{P_{yn_1}} - (1 - p)\pi_y}{p^2(1 - \widehat{A}) + p\widehat{A}}, \tag{8}$$

$$E(\widehat{P_{yn_1}}) = P_{yn_1},\ Var(\widehat{P_{yn_1}}) = \frac{P_{yn_1}(1 - P_{yn_1})}{n}. \tag{9}$$

To estimate the $\hat{\pi}_x$ and $V(\hat{\pi}_x)$, we use a first-order Taylor's approximation:

$$f(x, y) \approx f(a, b) + (x - a)f_x(a, b) + (y - b)f_y(a, b),$$

with $x = \widehat{P_{yn_1}}, y = \widehat{A}, a = P_{yn_1}, b = A$ in Equation (8), $\widehat{\pi_x}$ can be approximated by the following:

$$\widehat{\pi_x} \approx \frac{P_{yn_1} - (1-p)\pi_y}{p^2(1-A) + pA} + (\widehat{A} - A)\left[\frac{-[P_{yn_1} - (1-p)\pi_y][p - p^2]}{[A[p-p^2] + p^2]^2}\right] + (\widehat{P_{yn_1}} - P_{yn_1})\left[\frac{1}{A(p-p^2)+p^2}\right]. \quad (10)$$

Since $E(\widehat{A}) = A, Var(\widehat{A}) = \frac{P_{yo}(1-P_{yo})}{np_o^2}$, it is easy to see from Equation (10) that,

$$E(\widehat{\pi_x}) \approx \pi_x,$$

$$V(\widehat{\pi_x}) \approx V\left(\widehat{P_{yn_1}}\right)\left[\frac{1}{A(p-p^2)+p^2}\right]^2 + V\left(\widehat{A}\right)\left[-\frac{[P_{yn_1} - (1-p)\pi_y][p-p^2]}{[A(p-p^2)+p^2]^2}\right]^2.$$

$V(\widehat{A})$ is given in Equation (7) and $V(\widehat{P_{yn_1}})$ is given in Equation (9). The calculations for the enhanced-trust Greenberg model will follow the same way as they do for the enhanced-trust Lovig model below.

**Question 2 (Proposed Model-II):** Do you have the sensitive trait?

The probability of a "yes" response and the resulting estimator are given by

$$P_{yn_2} = p\pi_x A + p^2\pi_x(1-A) + q(1-\pi_x) + q\pi_x(1-A)p + (1-p-q)\pi_y, \text{ and}$$

$$\widehat{\pi_x} = \frac{\widehat{P_{yn_2}} - q - (1-p-q)\pi_y}{Ap(1-p-q) + q(p-1) + p^2}, \quad (11)$$

$$E(\widehat{P_{yn_2}}) = P_{yn_2},\ Var(\widehat{P_{yn_2}}) = \frac{P_{yn_2}(1-P_{yn_2})}{n}. \quad (12)$$

To estimate $\pi_x$, we use a first-order Taylor's approximation:

$$f(x,y) \approx f(a,b) + (x-a)f_x(a,b) + (y-b)f_y(a,b),$$

with $x = \widehat{P_{yn_2}},\ y = \widehat{A},\ a = P_{yn_2},\ b = A$ in Equation (11), $\widehat{\pi_x}$ can be approximated by the following:

$$\widehat{\pi_x} \approx \frac{\widehat{P_{yn_2}} - q - (1-p-q)\pi_y}{Ap(1-p-q) + q(p-1) + p^2} + (\widehat{A} - A)\left[\frac{(P_{yn_2} - r)(-p(1-p-q))}{(\alpha+\beta)^2}\right] + (\widehat{P_{yn_2}} - P_{yn_2})\left[\frac{1}{\alpha+\beta}\right], \quad (13)$$

where $\alpha = Ap(1-p-q)$, $\beta = q(p-1)+p^2$ and $r = -q-(1-p-q)\pi_y$. Since, $E(\widehat{A}) = A, Var(\widehat{A}) = \frac{P_{yo}(1-P_{yo})}{np_o^2}$, $E(\widehat{P_{yn_2}}) = P_{yn_2}$, and $Var(\widehat{P_{yn_2}}) = \frac{P_{yn_2}(1-P_{yn_2})}{n}$. It is easy to see from Equation (13) that

$$
\begin{aligned}
E(\widehat{\pi_x}) &\approx \pi_x \\
V(\widehat{\pi_x}) &\approx \frac{\widehat{P_{yn_2}} - q - (1-p-q)\pi_y}{Ap(1-p-q) + q(p-1) + p^2} + V(\widehat{A})\left[\frac{(P_{yn_2} - r)^2 (p(1-p-q))^2}{(\alpha+\beta)^4}\right] + \\
&\quad V(\widehat{P_{yn_2}})\left[\frac{1}{(\alpha+\beta)^2}\right].
\end{aligned}
$$

$V(\widehat{A})$ is given in Equation (7) and $V(\widehat{P_{yn_2}})$ is given in Equation (12).

### 3.4. Preservation of Privacy in the Proposed Models

When parameters are estimated using Randomized Response Technique (RRT) models, safeguarding the privacy of respondents is equally critical. If privacy is not adequately protected, individuals may either refuse to answer or provide dishonest responses. To address this concern, Lanke (1976) [13] proposed a metric to assess the extent of privacy loss in a model, as described below.

Let

$P(S \mid Y) =$ The probability that an individual belongs to the sensitive group, given that the response is "Yes"

$P(S \mid N) =$ The probability that an individual belongs to the sensitive group, given that the response is "No"

Privacy Loss $= \max(P(S \mid Y), P(S \mid N)) = \eta$.

Note that $\eta$ represents the maximum predictability of the sensitive trait based on the reported response. Fligner et al. (1977) call normalized $(1-\eta)$ as privacy protection [14]. It is defined as

$$
PP = \frac{1-\eta}{1-\pi_x}.
$$

Note that in a completely truthful survey, there will be complete privacy loss and hence $\eta$ will be 1, and privacy protection will be zero.

### 3.5. Proposed Unified Metric

Lovig et al. (2023) proposed a unified metric that captures both privacy and efficiency [6], and used it to define the overall model quality. It is expressed as follows:

$$
M = \frac{PP}{\text{Estimator Variance}}.
$$

### 3.6. Privacy of the Proposed Models

Following Lanke (1976) [13], privacy loss $\eta$ for the proposed enhanced-trust Lovig model is given by

$$
\begin{aligned}
\eta &= \text{Max}(\eta_1, \eta_2), \text{where} \\
\eta_1 &= Pr(S|Y) = \frac{P(Y \cap S)}{P(Y)} \\
&= \frac{q\pi_x(1-A)p + p\pi_x A + p\pi_x(1-A)p + (1-p-q)\pi_x\pi_y}{P_{yn_2}} \\
\eta_2 &= Pr(S|N) = \frac{P(N \cap S)}{P(N)} \\
&= \frac{q\pi_x(1-A)(1-p) + q\pi_x A + p\pi_x(1-A)(1-p) + (1-p-q)(1-pi_y)\pi_x}{1-P_{yn_2}}.
\end{aligned}
$$

Calculations for the proposed enhanced-trust Greenberg model will follow by putting $-q = 0$ and calculations for the Warner model will follow by putting $q = 1 - p$.

## 4. Simulation Study

A simulation study was conducted in MATLAB (https://matlab.mathworks.com/) to evaluate the performance of the proposed estimators and to compare them with existing models. For better comparison, we followed the parameter choices used by Lovig et al. (2023) [6].

Each simulation consisted of 10,000 independent repetitions, where random responses were generated under different trust levels $A = 1, 0.9$, and 0.8. For every iteration, we save the estimator $\widehat{\pi}_x$. These 10,000 values are averaged to obtain the final estimate of $\pi_x$ and the variance of these 10,000 values is used as the empirical value of $Var(\widehat{\pi}_x)$. Privacy loss $\eta$ is calculated for each iteration and is used to calculate empirical privacy protection. Empirical variance and the empirical privacy protection are used to calculate empirical unified measure $M$. The corresponding theoretical values are calculated analytically using the parameter values.

The results, summarized in Table 2, indicate that the prevalence estimator $\widehat{\pi}_x$ is very close to the true prevalence value of 0.4, confirming unbiasedness. Moreover, the empirical variances closely match the theoretical ones, supporting the accuracy of the derived expressions. As expected, the estimator efficiency ($Var(\widehat{\pi}_x)$ decreases as the trust level $A$ declines, demonstrating the trade-off between respondent trust and estimator precision.

**Table 2.** Theoretical and empirical values based on 10,000 iterations ($n = 500$, $\pi_x = 0.4$, $\pi_y = 0.1$).

| Model | p | q | 1-p-q | $A$ | $\widehat{A}$ | $\widehat{\pi}_x$ | Var($\widehat{\pi_x}$) | $\widehat{Var(\widehat{\pi_x})}$ | PP | $\widehat{PP}$ | M | $\widehat{M}$ |
|---|---|---|---|---|---|---|---|---|---|---|---|---|
| Greenberg | 0.7 | 0.3 | 0 | 1 | 1.0002 | 0.4001 | 0.0010 | 0.0010 | 0.0968 | 0.0968 | 96.4091 | 99.1116 |
| | | | | 0.9 | 0.9006 | 0.3999 | 0.0012 | 0.0011 | 0.1064 | 0.1062 | 88.3861 | 94.2058 |
| | | | | 0.8 | 0.8005 | 0.4003 | 0.0015 | 0.0013 | 0.1181 | 0.1178 | 80.9979 | 88.5820 |
| Greenberg Enhanced | 0.7 | 0.3 | 0 | 1 | 0.9998 | 0.3994 | 0.0009 | 0.0009 | 0.0968 | 0.1132 | 109.3931 | 103.9980 |
| | | | | 0.9 | 0.8998 | 0.4000 | 0.0009 | 0.0009 | 0.0995 | 0.1128 | 107.2141 | 109.1430 |
| | | | | 0.8 | 0.8002 | 0.3988 | 0.0010 | 0.0010 | 0.1023 | 0.1121 | 105.1185 | 106.8716 |
| Lovig | 0.7 | 0.15 | 0.15 | 1 | 1.0001 | 0.4002 | 0.0016 | 0.0017 | 0.4286 | 0.4291 | 252.2162 | 251.2180 |
| | | | | 0.9 | 0.8998 | 0.4006 | 0.0021 | 0.0020 | 0.4545 | 0.4551 | 219.3250 | 225.2544 |
| | | | | 0.8 | 0.7999 | 0.4006 | 0.0026 | 0.0025 | 0.4839 | 0.4842 | 188.0234 | 194.8597 |
| Lovig Enhanced | 0.7 | 0.15 | 0.15 | 1 | 1.0002 | 0.4005 | 0.0016 | 0.0015 | 0.4286 | 0.4283 | 272.9501 | 279.7032 |
| | | | | 0.9 | 0.9006 | 0.3998 | 0.0016 | 0.0017 | 0.4333 | 0.4334 | 266.5181 | 254.9553 |
| | | | | 0.8 | 0.7998 | 0.3991 | 0.0017 | 0.0017 | 0.4381 | 0.4387 | 260.1536 | 251.2456 |

### 4.1. Numerical Results

The table below summarizes results of our simulations.

We can make several observations from the numerical results in Table 2. Since the $\pi_x$ estimation depends on the estimation of the trust parameter $A$, it is important that $\widehat{A}$ is an unbiased estimator of $A$. The close match between the $A$ and $\widehat{A}$ columns confirms this. The estimate of $\pi_x$ under each model is very close to the true $\pi_x$ value of 0.4. This validates the unbiasedness of the prevalence estimator under all four models. When we look at the stability of the prevalence estimators through their variances, it is clear that the enhanced-trust Greenberg model does better than the basic Greenberg model (lower variance). Similarly, the enhanced-trust Lovig model performs better than the ordinary Lovig model. An observation that might sound misleading at first sight is that the enhanced-trust models have lower privacy protection than their ordinary counterparts. This is because the enhanced-trust models have a greater proportion of truthful responses as compared to their basic counterparts. Note that a completely truthful survey has zero privacy protection. In terms of the overall model quality measured through the unified measure $M$, the enhanced-trust Lovig model performs the best since it gives higher $M$ values at each trust level as compared to the other three models.

One can also note that if one focuses only on the privacy protection and ignores estimator efficiency, then the Lovig models perform better since they involve more scrambling. If we focus only on the efficiency (estimator variance), then the Greenberg models perform better because they involve lesser scrambling. However, if we compare the models through the unified measure, as we should, the enhanced-trust Lovig model performs the best.

Comparing the empirical estimates to their theoretical counterparts, we observe that the empirical results align well with theoretical expectations, validating the robustness of the simulation design.

### 4.2. Graphical Comparison of the Models

As further evidence of the usefulness of trust enhancement, we provide below plots comparing the trust-enhanced models with their basic counterparts (Figures 6 and 7). Plots 1 and 3 provide percent relative efficiency (*PRE*) of the trust-enhanced models using the definition.

$$PRE \text{ of Model 1 relative to Model 2} = \frac{\text{Estimator Variance under Model 1}}{\text{Estimator variance under Model 2}}.$$

Both plots show higher *PRE* value for the trust-enhanced models. Plots 2 and 4 provide a comparison of the overall model quality measured through the unified measure $M$. It is clear that the trust-enhanced models perform better than their ordinary counterparts.

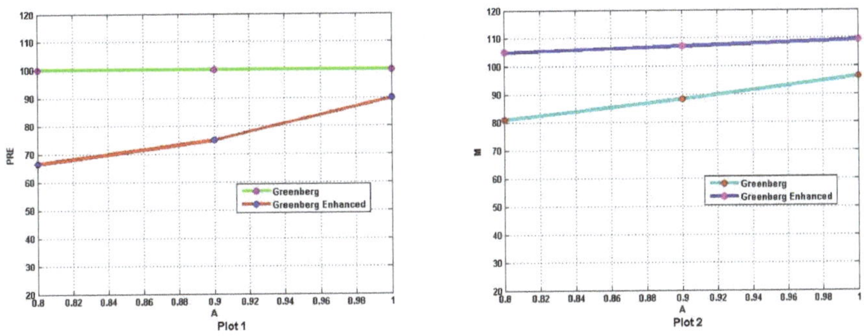


**Figure 6.** PRE and M for Greenberg and Greenberg-enhanced models for varying A.

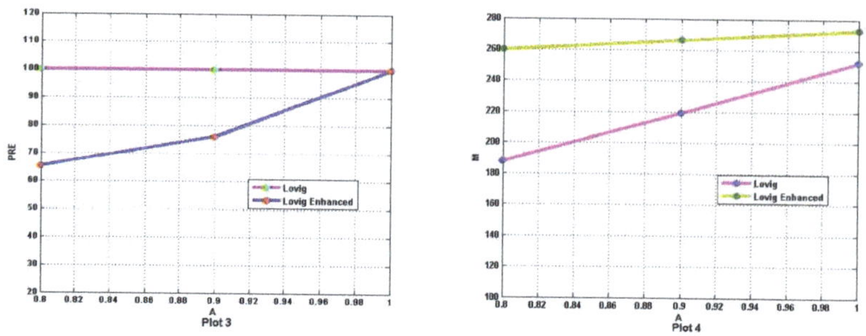


**Figure 7.** PRE and M for Lovig and Lovig-enhanced models for varying A.

### 4.3. Estimator Stability Under Different Models

The following graphs provide 95% confidence intervals for the prevalence parameter $\hat{\pi}_x$ under the four models for $A = 0.9$, using the formula

$$\hat{\pi}_x \pm 1.96\sqrt{\frac{\widehat{\text{Var}}(\hat{\pi}_x)}{500}}.$$

The four confidence intervals are as follows:

1. **Greenberg Model:**

$$0.3999 \pm 1.96\sqrt{\tfrac{0.0011}{500}} = 0.3999 \pm 0.0029$$

2. **Enhanced-Trust Greenberg Model:**

$$0.4000 \pm 1.96\sqrt{\tfrac{0.0009}{500}} = 0.4000 \pm 0.0026$$

3. **Lovig Model:**

$$0.4006 \pm 1.96\sqrt{\tfrac{0.0020}{500}} = 0.4006 \pm 0.0039$$

4. **Enhanced-Trust Lovig Model:**

$$0.3998 \pm 1.96\sqrt{\tfrac{0.0017}{500}} = 0.3998 \pm 0.0036$$

Although the efficiencies are not very different, there will be a lesser degree of respondent cooperation without enhancement of trust. That loss of cooperation is not visible in a simulation study(where responses are programmed correctly and there is no non-response) but can be very damaging in a real field survey.

## 5. Study Limitations and Future Directions

### 5.1. Limitations

The main limitation of the study is that the ultimate prevalence estimate depends critically on the estimation of the Trust parameter $A$. A poor estimate of A will in turn lead to a less accurate estimate of the prevalence. This phenomenon is noticed in a recent field study by Kalucha et al. (2025) [12]. Extra attention is needed during this step. Another limitation is that survey researchers in the RRT domain do not have a perfect method for selecting the model parameters $p$ and $q$. The only theoretical guidance is that we should have $p > \frac{1}{3}$ and that $p$ should be sufficiently away from 0.5. Keeping these two conditions in mind, we have used $p = 0.7$ and $q = 0.15$. The same choices were used in Lovig et al. (2023) [6].

### 5.2. Future Directions

The focus of the current study was to develop a theoretical trust-enhanced model and validate it through simulations. However, one could consider implementing these models in a field study on the lines of Kalucha et al. (2025) where a RRT model was used to estimate prevalence of depression among college students [12]. RRT has been used extensively in health sciences and social sciences, and one can use the proposed models in these fields.

**Author Contributions:** Conceptualization, S.G.; Methodology, S.G., N.J., M.G. and P.T.; Software, N.J., M.G. and P.T.; Validation, S.G., N.J., M.G. and P.T.; Formal analysis, S.G., N.J., M.G. and P.T.; Investigation, S.G. and P.T.; Resources, S.G.; Writing—original draft, N.J., M.G. and P.T.; Writing—review & editing, S.G. and P.T.; Visualization, S.G., N.J., M.G. and P.T.; Supervision, S.G.; Funding acquisition, S.G. All authors have read and agreed to the published version of the manuscript.

**Funding:** This research was supported by the NSF REU grant DMS-2244160.

**Data Availability Statement:** Data are contained within the article.

**Acknowledgments:** The authors appreciate the suggestions by the reviewers which helped improve the presentation significantly.

**Conflicts of Interest:** The authors declare no conflicts of interest.

## References

1. Warner, S.L. Randomized response: A survey technique for eliminating evasive answer bias. *J. Am. Stat. Assoc.* **1965**, *60*, 63–69. [CrossRef] [PubMed]
2. Greenberg, B.G.; Abul-Ela, A.-L.A.; Simmons, W.R.; Horvitz, D.G. The unrelated question randomized response model: Theoretical framework. *J. Am. Stat. Assoc.* **1969**, *64*, 520–539. [CrossRef]
3. Mangat, N.S.; Singh, R. An alternative randomized response procedure. *Biometrika* **1990**, *77*, 439–442. [CrossRef]
4. Gupta, S.; Gupta, B.; Singh, S. Estimation of the sensitivity level of personal interview survey questions. *J. Stat. Plan. Inference* **2002**, *100*, 239–247. [CrossRef]
5. Kim, J.-M.; Warde, W.D. A mixed randomized response model. *J. Stat. Plan. Inference* **2005**, *113*, 211–221 [CrossRef]
6. Lovig, M.; Khalil, S.; Rahman, S.; Sapra, P.; Gupta, S. A mixture binary RRT model with a unified measure of privacy and efficiency. *Commun. Stat. - Simul. Comput.* **2023**, *52*, 2727–2737. [CrossRef]
7. Parker, M.; Gupta, S.; Khalil, S. A Mixture Quantitative Randomized Response Model That Improves Trust in RRT Methodology. *Axioms* **2024**, *13*, 11. [CrossRef]
8. Jones, E.E.; Sigall, H. The bogus pipeline: A new paradigm for measuring affect and attitude. *Psychol. Bull.* **1971**, *76*, 349–364. [CrossRef]
9. Reynolds, W.M. Development of a reliable and valid short form of the Marlowe-Crowne SDB scale. *J. Clin. Psychol.* **1982**, *38*, 119–125. [CrossRef]
10. Ostapczuk, M.; Musch, J.; Moshagen, M. A randomized-response investigation of the education effect in attitudes towards foreigners. *Eur. J. Soc. Psychol.* **2009**, *39*, 920–931. [CrossRef]
11. Striegel, H.; Simon, P.; Hansel, J.; Niess, A.M.; Ulrich, R. Doping and drug use in elite sports: An analysis using the randomized response technique. *Med. Sci. Sport. Exerc.* **2006**, *38*, S247. [CrossRef]
12. Kalucha, G.; Khalil, S.; Gupta, M.; Gupta, S. Estimating the Prevalence of Depression Among College Students — Field Validation of a Complex Randomized Response Technique. *J. Stat. Theory Pract.* **2025**, *19*, 96. [CrossRef]
13. Lanke, J. On the degree of protection in randomized interviews. *Int. Stat. Rev. Rev. Int. Stat.* **1976**, *44*, 197–203. [CrossRef]
14. Fligner, M.A.; Policello, G.E.; Singh, J. A comparison of two randomized response survey methods with consideration for the level of respondent protection. *Commun. Stat. Theory Methods* **1977**, *6*, 1511–1524. [CrossRef]
15. Gupta, S.; Mehta, S.; Shabbir, J.; Khalil, S. A unified measure of respondent privacy and model efficiency in quantitative RRT models. *J. Stat. Theory Pract.* **2018**, *12*, 506–511. [CrossRef]

MDPI AG
Grosspeteranlage 5
4052 Basel
Switzerland
Tel.: +41 61 683 77 34

*Axioms* Editorial Office
E-mail: axioms@mdpi.com
www.mdpi.com/journal/axioms

www.ingramcontent.com/pod-product-compliance
Lightning Source LLC
Chambersburg PA
CBHW061612210926
51850CB00009B/2300